张敬鸿

Guilty of Indigence

Guilty of Indigence

THE URBAN POOR IN CHINA, 1900–1953

Janet Y. Chen

PRINCETON UNIVERSITY PRESS

PRINCETON & OXFORD

ISBN 978-0-691-15210-3

Library of Congress Cataloging-in-Publication Data

Chen, Janet Y., 1972–
    Guilty of indigence : the urban poor in China, 1900–1953 / Janet Y. Chen.
       p. cm.
    Includes bibliographical references and index.
    SBN 978-0-691-15210-3 (hbk. : alk. paper)   1. Urban poor—China—History—20th
century.   2. Poverty—China—History—20th century.   3. China—Social conditions—20th
century.   I. Title.
    HV4150.A3C44 2012
    305.5'690951091732—dc23   2011024446

British Library Cataloging-in-Publication Data is available

This book has been composed in Adobe Caslon.

Printed on acid-free paper. ∞

Printed in the United States of America

10 9 8 7 6 5 4 3 2 1

Contents

Acknowledgments

For his unwavering support and kindness over many years, and for being my teacher, my first debt of gratitude goes to Jonathan Spence. Knowing that he believed in me, even when I didn't, has made all the difference. It has been, and always will be, an honor to be his student. Along the way, I have also had the singularly good fortune of finding many other teachers and mentors. At Yale, Beatrice Bartlett, Annping Chin, Valerie Hansen, Jim Scott, and Keith Wrightson helped me become the historian that I aspired to be. At Williams College nearly twenty years ago, I walked into Gail Hershatter's class on a whim. It changed my life forever. Carol Benedict then nurtured my interest in Chinese history, and patiently tolerated my flirtation with postmodern theory.

At Princeton, the History and East Asian Studies departments have provided an intellectually stimulating environment to work. Ben Elman, Shel Garon, David Howell, and Sue Naquin have been the most generous and supportive of colleagues. Margo Canaday, Joy Kim, Michael Laffan, Bhavani Raman, and Rebecca Rix have provided friendship and encouragement. I am grateful to Kevin Kruse, Bill Jordan, Dave Leheny, Dan Rodgers, and Marni Sandweiss for taking the time to provide feedback on my manuscript as it morphed into book form. Michael Gordin deserves special thanks for his wise counsel on matters big and small, and for talking me off the ledge innumerable times.

Henrietta Harrison and David Strand both read this work at its clumsy dissertation stage, responding to an unsolicited request from an unknown person. Their perceptive and detailed comments sharpened my thinking. At the eleventh hour, Rob Culp, Eugenia Lean, and especially Keith Wailoo helped me wrestle the Introduction into shape, an act of rescue that I will never forget. Two readers for Princeton University Press read the manuscript with great care and provided nuggets of gold in their comments. Their suggestions helped me immeasurably as I made the final revisions.

This book would not have been possible without access to the rich archival materials in China. I am grateful to the staff of the First Historical Archive in Beijing, the Second Historical Archive in Nanjing, the Beijing Municipal Archive, the Shanghai Municipal Archive, and the Shanghai Library for their assistance. At Yale's East Asia Library, Sarah Elman, Ellen Hammond, and Tao Yang did more to help me finish my dissertation than they remember. At Princeton's Gest Library, Martin Heijdra and Gonul Yurkal have been my guardian angels. The kind archivists at the Salvation Army Heritage Center on three continents (in London, Alexandria, Virginia, and Melbourne) helped me navigate research from afar. In addition, Lindsey Cox graciously granted permission to publish George Walker's photographs, which appear on the cover and in chapter 4.

From inception to completion, many institutions provided the financial support that made it possible for me to do the research for this book, and to write it. The Prize Fellowship from Yale's Council on East Asian Studies, the Chiang Ching-kuo Foundation, the American Council of Learned Societies, Princeton University, and Yale University have been generous beyond what a historian studying poverty deserved. For their able research assistance at critical junctures, thanks are due to Melinda Clyne, Li Zhongyong, Mao Sheng, and Ye Minlei. Minlei also made the arrangements for a memorable tour of the Subei "countryside" in the summer of 2010, which helped me see the place in a completely different light. Finally, at Princeton University Press Clara Platter and Benjamin Holmes ably shepherded this project through the editorial and production processes. I am grateful to Joseph Dahm for his expert copyediting, and Dmitri Karetnikov for taking the extra time to rescue my illustrations.

Many friends have offered encouragement and support through the years, when this book was in the constant state of being "almost finished." Lisa Uebelacker has provided free therapy since we lived in the same dorm in 1993. Lorraine Paterson, Zadie Kenkare, and Rebecca Rix saved me from myself on countless occasions. In Beijing, Nancy Chen and Jonathan Fritz opened their home to me and fed me vegetarian dumplings by the kilo.

A small army of babysitters has helped me patch together the time to finish this book. There are far too many to name individually, but a few deserve special thanks: Faridah and Daniel Laffan, for turning babysitting into playdates; Sharon Wittlesey, for being dependable; and the Soffer in-laws, Oved, Tanya, Gad, and Katie, for being always willing to pitch in. My father, Paul Chen, did not change any diapers, but he did help me with many translations, especially with rendering idiomatic Chinese phrases into colloquial English. Above all, my mother Susie Chen logged two bitterly cold winters in Connecticut and New Jersey when both children were born, so that I could keep my head above water. For everything she has done, I can never thank her enough.

And to my family: Eli and Natalia, the delight of my life, and Benny, who has been there every step of the way—this is for you.

Princeton, New Jersey
May 2011

A Note on Conventions

I USE THE *pinyin* system of romanization, except where names are better known in an alternative (e.g., Chiang Kai-shek, rather than Jiang Jieshi).

Between 1900 and 1950, the name for Beijing (meaning "Northern Capital") changed four times, reflecting the revolving door of governments and the relocation of the capital. To minimize confusion I retain the use of Beijing throughout.

One *mu* of land is equivalent to 0.165 acres.

One *liang* of food is equivalent to 1.1 ounces.

One *sui* is the equivalent of one year in the Western calendar. In the Chinese method of calculating age, a newborn baby is one *sui* and turns two *sui* at the next lunar new year, regardless of the birth date. Thus someone identified as twelve *sui* could be ten to eleven years old by Western calculations. Since age was a factor in determining eligibility for different poorhouses, workhouses, and orphanages, I have retained the use of *sui* to correspond to the eligibility requirements.

Introduction

ON THE NIGHT of November 24, 1922, Guo Hetang was sleeping in a Beijing alleyway when a policeman from the Fourth District Precinct discovered him. As Constable Chang Quan learned from questioning him, Guo was thirteen *sui*, a native of Handan County (about three hundred miles southwest of the capital city). His mother died when he was quite young, and after his father passed away in 1921, he lived with his uncle for a while. When the uncle left town to look for work, Guo moved in with Li Kui, a neighbor who was a former soldier. In June of 1922, Li brought him to Beijing, but when they arrived he abandoned the boy at the Qianmen train station. At first Guo wandered around the city begging. A few days later he found a job carrying water for a man named Liu, who gave him a set of clothes and two meals of steamed buns each day. "But recently Liu complained that I was eating too much and kicked me out," Guo told the authorities. "The policeman found me sleeping on the street." At the conclusion of the interview, Guo signed a statement summarizing his responses with an X mark. Departing from the usually taciturn police report, Constable Chang wrote that "this young child wore thin clothing and was freezing. He shivered and his voice shook as he spoke. If nothing is done he will surely freeze to death." Five days later, the police chief inspector's office arranged for Guo to be sent to the Capital Vagrant Workhouse (Jingshi Youmin Xiyisuo), with a note explaining his history. The cover memo added that "this boy is orphaned and helpless, and deserves compassion," and also expressed the hope that he would learn a "suitable craft" at the workhouse and no longer "wander about destitute."[1]

What happened to Guo Hetang at the workhouse, and afterward? The records do not tell us. His story, described in a one-page testimony preserved in the police files at the Beijing Municipal Archive, is one ordinary example among many. However truncated and sparse, the details of this case suggest new elements in twentieth-century Chinese urban life that deserve our attention. A policeman patrolling the city streets, an orphan abandoned at the railway station, a former soldier from a provincial town passing through the capital, a young life of misery narrated to interrogators and recorded for the police file, the workhouse as a place of charitable detention—these threads underline some of the main themes of this book.

Guilty of Indigence seeks to understand what we can know of a life like Guo Hetang's in the context of urban poverty in Republican-era China. It traverses the terrain of philanthropy, punishment, social science, municipal governance, war, and revolution. But ultimately, the book focuses on the experiences of the homeless destitute, in a time of political upheaval and displacement. In considering questions such as how the notion of poverty as a social problem changed or how relief methods varied, this study places "the poor," rather than their benefactors and custodians, at the center of inquiry.

In addition to asking how the turbulence of the first half of the twentieth century affected the lives of the urban destitute, the book also traces changes in attitudes about "poverty" and the policies enacted for its alleviation. As elite opinion increasingly sounded the alarm that "poverty" was a major obstacle to the nation's aspirations for progress, officials and reformers sought solutions from different sources, including Japanese penology, Anglo-American sociology, and the foreign administration of China's treaty ports. The flow of knowledge into China from multiple contexts, intersecting with existing practices, produced new institutions that endeavored to rehabilitate the nonworking poor: by punishing their criminality, reforming their indolence, and eradicating the "parasitic" dependence of those who subsisted on charity. I argue that the emergence of these ideas and practices, embodied in the advent of the workhouse, represented a fundamental reordering of the relationship between the state, private charity, and the neediest members of society. As the concept of the "social parasite" became deeply ingrained in both the conventional wisdom and social policy, it became the rationale for the exclusion and punitive treatment of people identified as such. At the workhouse, a new regimen of detention and labor cast government officials and philanthropists in the role of wardens and caretakers of those singled out as needing punishment or deserving aid. These institutions became laboratories for the production of social citizenship, demarcating the boundaries of social belonging on the basis of labor and discipline. At the same time, the workhouse created new forms of criminality, stigmatizing those who refused to work as "vagrants" and as liabilities to the productivity of the nation.

These changes took place in the early decades of the twentieth century in China, a critical historical juncture when new possibilities emerged for imagining the relationship between government authority and the people. With the demise of the imperial regime in 1911, the floodgates opened to contestation in competing venues for political participation and civic action, the seeds of which had been planted in the late nineteenth century. Recent studies of citizenship in Republican China have analyzed its diverse forms in both ideology and practice. Historians have made clear the importance of civic rituals, sports, consumption, and education in shaping the content of political and cultural citizenship. Robert Culp, for instance, shows how secondary school students translated textbook ideals into action, as they experimented with participation in Boy Scouts and military training to constitute themselves as citizens (*guomin, gongmin*) of the Republic.[2] As various other groups, old and new, found different ways to perform citizenship, they created opportunities for political action and crafted new forms of social and cultural authority.[3]

Yet as Merle Goldman and Elizabeth Perry remind us, "citizenship implies exclusion as well as inclusion."[4] Thanks to the work of social scientists, we have a good picture of how the politics of exclusion worked in the post-1949 era. Dorothy Solinger's masterful study, for instance, explains the marginalization of rural migrants as "second-class citizens" in the urban welfare system.[5] As the socialist state established the parameters of its welfare regime, social citizenship, in T. H. Marshall's classic definition, constituted recognized claims for economic welfare and security.[6] Such parameters were not so obviously delineated in the early decades of the twentieth century. One of the goals of this study is to explore the politics of exclusion in a time when the contours of social rights and obligations were far from settled, when the practices which marked the boundaries of belonging in "society" were in the infancy of formation.[7] My research charts how starting at the turn of the century, intellectuals and officials began to define the ability and willingness of the "common people" to labor in the service of the nation-state as one of defining attributes of social membership. Even while the legacy of Confucian paternalism persisted, assumptions about productivity, discipline, and self-sufficiency became embedded in the political economy of social welfare. At a time when China confronted relentless assaults from the forces of imperialism and global capitalism, government officials and private philanthropists considered it their responsibility to confine and discipline the "recalcitrant" and the "indolent," and to harness their labor for the benefit of the nation.

Evolving over more than fifty years, this imperative to work was enacted at the workhouse and the relief home, intensifying under the ideology of Nationalist productivism and during wartime mobilization, reaching a crescendo in the post-1949 socialist state. As productive labor became a condition of social citizenship, how did those on the margins understand their exclusion, and how did they organize to defend their interests? My emphasis on the disciplinary power of the state is balanced by an equal commitment to understanding the experiences of those labeled as outcasts. I focus on Beijing and Shanghai, two cities where concerted efforts to clear the streets of vagrants, orphans, and drifters subjected the homeless to harassment, deportation, or detention. As inmates in workhouses and relief homes, those guilty of indigence became experimental subjects for bureaucrats testing a newfound belief in the transformative power of labor. My analysis illuminates how people detained under these circumstances responded to the disciplinary project of making them into "citizens," and how they coped with destitution in a period of deep social dislocation. Inmates in government custody, for instance, protested their incarceration by sending letters and petitions for release. Refugees in winter shelters resisted separation from their families as the price of receiving government assistance. Written individually or collectively, sometimes anonymously, these letters reveal both the desperation of the times and the resilience it took to survive. At the same time, sources show that punitive agencies could also function as places of refuge for those with nowhere else to turn. Petitions from desperate parents seeking asylum for their children suggest that custodial institutions served critical charitable purposes. In Shanghai, the protracted struggles of the "straw hut people" (named for the construction material of their dwellings), spanning nearly three decades, illustrate their resourcefulness in defending their homes. In a time when homelessness could be a crime, they fought tenaciously to save their huts from destruction.

These new insights into the lives of the urban destitute are documented in a wealth of materials that have survived in the archives of government agencies and private charities, but have largely been overlooked by researchers. The records of the earliest workhouses, unevenly preserved and scattered among several archives, tell primarily the story of elite motivations and offer only fleeting glimpses into the experiences of their inmates. Sources increase in scope and depth for the period after 1928, when the Nationalist (GMD) government's municipal administrations established the Social Affairs Bureau to take charge of poor relief (among many other duties). In particular, the well-preserved records of the Beijing agency provide detailed documentation of its relief institutions and include hundreds of letters that people wrote in a variety of contexts: asking for help, seeking the release of family members arrested for begging, describing starvation conditions at the government relief home.

In Shanghai, the archives of the Municipal Council, the governing authority of the British-dominated International Settlement, chronicle the efforts of shantytown residents to save their homes from demolition. In addition to police reports and administrative records, numerous letters from hut dwellers plead for the postponement or cancellation of eviction orders. Some of these petitioners wrote the letters themselves, including well-educated people who sprinkled their entreaties with allusions to the classics and semiliterate authors who wrote in the vernacular with an unsteady script. In other cases, one literate member or a professional scribe wrote on behalf of a group, and the signatories appended their name chops or cross and X marks. These first-hand accounts convey in vivid, sometimes heartbreaking detail the circumstances that reduced people to destitution, and the strategies they crafted to survive. We see how groups of shantytown residents appealed to the rhetoric of patriotism and citizenship and invoked the discourse of legal rights to claim a legitimate place in the city.

Many of these letters follow a conventional style of supplication, using the pro forma language of entreaty and stock phrases describing misery. Rendered as melodramatic narratives, sometimes with exaggerated or fabricated grievances, and mediated by the hands of scribes or literate acquaintances, these documents approximate the "voices of the poor." They do not capture their own words in a straightforward fashion—but in many cases, they come close to doing so.[8] Where possible, I have corroborated their claims against a wide range of other sources: the administrative files of workhouses and other institutions, journalistic accounts, sociological studies, and police interrogation reports, such as that of Guo Hetang described above. Taken together, these records reveal facets of people's lives that historians of China have not thought possible to study. Just as important, they provide penetrating perspectives into how the language of poverty shaped broader debates about social order and the configuration of rights and obligations. They also cast into sharp relief the central tensions between punishment and charity, illuminating the problems impoverished people confronted, as well as their hopes and their frustrations.

In tracing the interactions between concepts of poverty, social policy, and the lives of the urban poor in China, many of the issues raised in this book will resonate with historians and contemporary observers of other regions of the world. Indeed, questions that preoccupied Chinese society in the early twentieth century can be found in multiple historical contexts, from England's Poor Laws to the *favelas* of Rio de Janeiro to the American "war on dependence."[9] What constitutes a "decent provision for the poor"? "What are the limits of social obligation?"[10] While it is beyond the scope of this study to address the voluminous literature on poverty and citizenship around the world, I am attentive to specific moments of cross-cultural fertilization—the workhouse imported from the West via Japan, the role of the Salvation Army, the idea of the "social parasite" drawn from American sociology. But in the end, my goal is to show how Chinese attempts to find solutions to problems that have vexed many other societies unfolded at a particular historical juncture of imperial demise, war, and revolution. During a prolonged period of state dissolution and state formation, contestations over the meanings of poverty and the parameters of social citizenship impinged on the lives of indigents in Chinese cities in unprecedented ways. How an orphan such as Guo Hetang became part of "the urban poor," whether confinement and the imperative to work improved or harmed his life chances, how others scratched out a living on the streets, what it meant to be homeless in Beijing and Shanghai—these issues form the central concerns of this book.

. . .

Prior to the twentieth century, poverty was not yet a crime in China. Confucian elites did not view it as a "social problem" (indeed, the notion did not exist), or regard it as a barometer of moral defects and social danger. Familiar concepts from American and European history such as "the lazy poor," "the dependent poor," and "the dangerous poor" did not have Chinese equivalents. In the early imperial period, "poverty" was a morally neutral concept, reflecting fate rather than individual failure. The ideal of the "impoverished scholar" (*pinshi*) in fact lauded men who rejected worldly status and material success. By the late Ming, growing commercialization and concomitant anxieties about the distribution of wealth had eroded this ideal. Charitable institutions increasingly favored the virtuous poor, especially chaste widows and filial sons.[11] But as Philip Kuhn has concluded, even in the late imperial period, wealth and poverty remained relatively weak markers of social differentiation in Chinese society.[12]

Throughout the imperial era, "the poor" (*pinmin*) did not constitute a distinct social group. To be sure, there were people identified as such, most often in times of dearth and in the context of famine relief. Like "starving people" (*jimin*) and "refugees" (*nanmin*), "the poor" were those experiencing a temporary state of hardship.[13] A more fixed category referred to "widowers, widows, the elderly without children, and orphans" (*guangua dugu*).[14] Imperial decrees stipulated that only these solitary people, without families to rely upon, were eligible for permanent government aid, either as residents in poorhouses (*yangjiyuan* or *pujitang*, supported wholly or in part by the emperor's generosity) or as nonresident pensioners.[15] Beyond help for the most vulnerable, the emperor's obligation to provide for the economic well-being of all of his subjects constituted the bedrock of the dynasty's legitimacy. Clichés of Confucian paternalism declared that as "the father and mother of the people," the sovereign (and his officials) would ensure "the people's livelihood" (*minsheng*), while failure to "nourish the people" (*yangmin*) would fatally erode the moral-political foundation of the state.

At the same time, while being "poor" did not represent moral failure, and begging and vagrancy were not crimes, the historical record amply documents persistent distrust of transients. Such suspicions regarded drifters—particularly young male ones—as people who had lost their mooring in the community and family structure, cast adrift into a sea of crime and possibly rebellion.[16] In the Qing dynasty, the *baojia* system of household registration in theory prevented such strangers and "vagrants" from infiltrating local communities. There was often a "beggar chief" who kept watch over a roster of local mendicants.[17] As Pierre-Etienne Will has shown, preventing people from roaming the countryside or invading the cities was a chief preoccupation of Qing officials during subsistence crises. Their priority was to keep peasants at home, so that they did not "lose their place" (*shisuo*).[18]

Will's landmark study also highlights the central role the Qing government played in the distribution of famine relief during the eighteenth century. The family kinship system remained the most important safety net, and private philanthropists also played significant roles. As Will convincingly demonstrates, however, the imperial bureaucracy successfully mobilized vast resources to help famine victims through a variety of mechanisms: allotting food or selling subsidized grain from public granaries, doling out cash payments, and organizing public works projects under the rubric of "substituting work for relief" (*yigong daizhen*). Work relief in the Qing dynasty meant voluntary participation, on a noncustodial basis, in infrastructure projects such as dredging rivers and canals, repairing city walls, building irrigation reservoirs—undertakings that could employ large numbers of laborers without major capital outlays. But although officials considered *yigong daizhen* a useful method, it was a supplement to, rather than the primary focus of, traditional famine administration.[19]

The strong administrative capacity of the High Qing provides a striking contrast to the post-Taiping era, when a weakened central government largely ceded authority to local elites, a shift that has been the subject of numerous studies. Much of this research has centered on the balance of power between local elites and the state, and the implications for civil society. William Rowe's pioneering studies of Hankou and Mary Rankin's analysis of Zhejiang, for instance, demonstrate that local leaders used philanthropy as a strategy for increasing their autonomy and influence vis-à-vis the Qing state.[20] The devolution of power and the fragmentation of imperial authority were crucial factors in the eventual fall of the Qing dynasty in 1911.

The demise of the imperial system and the new Republic's rapid descent into chaos under a revolving door of warlord regimes further fueled the forces of local autonomy. As many historians have shown, local elites embarked on ambitious projects to create modern cities through reforms intent on "civilizing" the urban population. New civic groups (chambers of commerce, professional associations) and transnational voluntary organizations (the YMCA, the Red Cross) blossomed; traditional charities and associations based on native place ties reinvented themselves.[21] All of these studies have enriched our understanding of the state–society dynamic in the late Qing and the Republican period, but for the most part, the focus on urban reform and philanthropy has largely disregarded the experiences and the perspectives of the *recipients* of charity. In these works, "poor people" make only cameo appearances, as the objects of suspicion, loathing, or compassion.

Guilty of Indigence argues that "the poor" were front and center in the drama of China's tumultuous history in the early twentieth century. Although they had been there all along, in plain sight, "the poor" of the cities became visible and troubling in new ways. Beginning as an amorphous category constructed from elite anxieties about the future of the nation, over time "the urban poor" became "real," a process that Ian Hacking has called "making up people." As a concept, "poverty" was indeed a "moving target" in early-twentieth-century China.[22] This was true in Hacking's sense of dynamic interactions between the classification and the people so-classified, but also in the sense of a conceptual elasticity that stretched the term to encompass diverse forms of destitution, ranging from temporary unemployment to old-age poverty. But in contrast to the expansiveness of the idea, the interventions by and large targeted a specific manifestation of "urban poverty": the condition of homelessness. This study focuses on the changing relationship between the discursively protean category of "poverty," concerted attempts to intervene in the lives of the homeless, and "urban poverty" as lived experience.

By exploring the process by which "poor people" became a constituent feature of urban life, and the material reality of their experiences, my research takes the study of Chinese cities in a new direction. Over the past two decades, the trajectory of English-language scholarship has shifted away from the vigorous debate over civil society and its possibility or failure in China, to histories exploring different facets of urban cultural life. In the main, these studies have concentrated on the elite and middle classes.[23] Meanwhile, in Chinese-language scholarship, a subgenre loosely branded "cultural studies of the underclass" has proliferated. These histories of beggars and vagrants typically span the millennia of Chinese history, ranging freely from tales of the founding emperor of the Ming dynasty (a former beggar) to the contemporary "floating population" of migrants.[24] Hanchao Lu's recent book, *Street Criers: A Cultural History of Chinese Beggars*, is an important addition and the only English-language work on the topic. Relying on rich collections of folklore, legends, and oral traditions, Lu describes the beggar kings and the organization of their guilds. By painting a vividly panoramic view of cultural practices from the early nineteenth century to the present, moving fluidly from Inner Mongolia to Shanghai to Canton to Suzhou, *Street Criers* emphasizes an unchanging culture of mendicancy largely impervious to political upheaval and social change.[25]

In contrast, *Guilty of Indigence* draws from a different and variegated source base to locate the experiences of the "urban poor" in explicitly local and historical contexts. By paying attention to finely tuned social conditions and shifting political circumstances, this book deepens our understanding of Chinese urban poverty as both lived experience and "social problem." I have chosen to write in detail about two different cities, with the goal of highlighting the specific conditions that shaped experiences of destitution. It is illuminating, for instance, to contrast life in Beijing under a lengthy period of Japanese occupation during World War II to the divided jurisdiction of treaty port Shanghai. Furthermore, following institutions and ideas as they changed over fifty years makes it possible to underscore historical continuities and disjunctures in both discourse and practice. Whereas the workhouse has typically been relegated to a footnote in histories of the modern prison or in short-lived urban reform efforts, the longer view considers how these institutions both changed and persisted as appealing solutions to Qing reformers, Chinese sociologists, foreign missionaries, treaty port residents, Nationalist officials, and Communist (CCP) leaders. Finally, bringing the history of punishment and charity into dialogue suggests that the impulses to punish "the poor" and to help them were often born of the same motives.

In presenting a narrative of both significant historical change and surprising continuities, I also depart from the scholarship of the previous two decades that has reassessed more positively the Nationalist Party's years in power. Rejecting an earlier preoccupation with explaining the GMD's disintegration, leading to the Communist victory in 1949, recent studies have detected signs of strength and even vitality in the GMD's state-building efforts.[26] This is particularly true of the numerous works focusing on the Sino-Japanese War years (1937–45). Rather than sowing the "seeds of destruction," as the title of Lloyd Eastman's 1984 book memorably put it, historians now emphasize how the GMD's wartime policies laid the foundation for the successor Communist regime.[27] While I trace continuity across the 1949 divide, my approach generally eschews the state failure–success question as an organizing framework. Instead I ask how local agents of government power (the constable on the beat, the municipal official, the workhouse warden) attempted to police, punish, or help the "urban poor," and especially what effects these interventions had on the target populations. We see that even as institutions of labor discipline became microcosms of government collapse, they still commanded enormous powers of detention vis-à-vis the homeless, exercised in the name of charity and punishment. From the perspective of the people on the streets, this dynamic had the effect of both underscoring the power of the state and exposing its impotence.

. . .

The chapters of this book interweave social, intellectual, and institutional histories, moving between elite perspectives, government policies, and lived experience, and navigating both national concerns and local realities. Chapter 1, "Between Charity and Punishment," examines how "poverty" (*pin*) emerged as a resonant concept for reforming elites in the early twentieth century. Deeply anxious about China's precarious future, officials and intellectuals began to view "poverty" as an issue imbued with national significance. Drawing from Japanese penology and a burgeoning industrial training movement, reformers experimented with various types of workhouses, endeavoring to revive the nation on the foundation of labor. These first workhouses initially incarcerated misdemeanor convicts, and then extended detention to the nonworking poor, especially targeting "vagrants" and "beggars"—the male, mobile, and most unproductive members of society. The creation of these institutions marked a striking departure from traditional practices, anointing the combination of detention and labor as the most promising method of creating productive citizens.

In the first decade of the Republic, the advent of sociology as a new field of knowledge in China attempted to study "poverty" on a scientific basis. Chapter 2, "'Parasites upon Society,'" explores how the metaphor equating the nonworking poor with "parasites" became ingrained in sociological thinking. As left-wing intellectuals valorized labor and foreign missionaries promoted "scientific charity" based on work relief, these ideas converged with workhouses and poorhouses that provided custodial detention in the guise of both punishment and charity. In addition, this chapter begins the story of Shanghai's straw hut shantytowns, and the protracted battles between their residents and the International Settlement's Municipal Council.

During the Nanjing decade, the subject of chapter 3, ideas that had evolved since the turn of the century played instrumental roles in the formation of the Nationalist government's social policy. In *Useless to the State*, Zwia Lipkin suggested that the GMD's social engineering ambitions focused on creating a model capital in Nanjing by expunging "social deviants." But whereas Lipkin attributes the origins of the Nationalist reform effort generally to "Western ideas and policies,"[28] I argue that the GMD's extractive notion of social citizenship and assumptions about poor relief continued the trajectory of Qing reformers and drew from the discourse of productivism that emerged in the previous decade.

The outbreak of World War II in China in July 1937 launched a refugee crisis that profoundly changed perceptions of "poverty" and its realities. Chapter 4, "Beggars or Refugees?" follows the fortunes of occupied Beijing and the "solitary island" of Shanghai, against the backdrop of a broader national crisis. In Beijing, I show that while the collaborationist government largely preserved the existing structure of poor relief, aggressive policing tactics resulted in the large-scale incarceration of people who aroused suspicion simply because they were homeless. In a wartime climate, the provision of relief, frequently entangled with concerns about social order, now focused sharply on security. In contrast, treaty port Shanghai, which remained free of Japanese occupation until the Pearl Harbor attack, became a temporary haven for more than 1.5 million refugees. The initial outpouring of sympathy for war victims, many of them destitute and homeless, transformed the face of urban poverty. But when the crisis did not abate, the refugee issue hardened into "the beggar problem," reconfiguring old debates about both poverty and responsibility for poor relief.

As the civil war between the Nationalists and the Communists intensified between 1945 and 1949, chapter 5 shows how the GMD regime proved incapable of coping with increasing urban disorder in both Shanghai and Beijing. With refugees from battleground areas in the countryside continuously fleeing to the cities, the municipal governments tried to use relief agencies to serve both charitable and punitive purposes. In Beijing, desperate refugees starved in winter shelters and workhouses. In Shanghai, conditions in government institutions were equally deplorable, and many of the destitute preferred the squalor of their own straw huts to relief based on the deprivation of freedom. Thousands of refugees also forced their way into the coffin repositories of native place associations, choosing to "keep company with ghosts" rather than submit to government custody. By 1949, these grim examples of suffering fatally exposed the Nationalist government's inability to fulfill its own commitments.

It was on the ruins of such lives that the Communists could ride to victory. Yet as soon as the new regime conquered the cities, the CCP found itself confronting problems with homeless transients and refugees, just as its predecessors had throughout the Republican era. The Epilogue tells the story of the encounter between agrarian revolutionaries and the urban poor and shows how the methods the CCP adopted drew on institutions and ideas that had developed and changed over a half century. Although the perspective of government authority dominates the source base after 1949, some recently declassified archival materials make it possible to look behind the curtain of propaganda. We see how, fused to socialist ideology, the marriage of detention and compulsory labor became a potent combination aimed at harnessing the productivity of "social parasites" for the benefit of New China. And as old Nationalist winter shelters became new Communist detention centers, the urban poor found that in the People's Republic, as before, there would be no place for those who were guilty of indigence.

CHAPTER 1

Between Charity and Punishment

WHEN GUO HETANG, the orphan described in the Introduction, found himself in Beijing in 1922, the majestic but fading splendor of the former imperial capital stood as the backdrop to the misery of the approaching winter. In the aftermath of a major famine in north China, and in the midst of warlord battles for control of the city, homeless youngsters like Guo were a tragically common sight on the streets. When he first arrived at the train station and was separated from Li, the neighbor soldier, Guo might have walked into the lively market areas to the south, in the Outer City. Or he might have followed the crowd in the opposite direction and entered the Inner City, through the imposing Qianmen tower. Alone in a city of nearly one million people, the boy likely felt overwhelmed by the throngs of rickshaws and horse-drawn carts, awed by the vast expanse of Tian'anmen Square, or lost in the maze of unfamiliar alleyways (called *hutongs*). Eventually, Guo made his way to the East City, where he found work carrying water for Liu, his new employer. This was largely a residential area lined with stately courtyard houses, formerly the home of the Qing White Banners. When Guo Hetang worked for Liu in this neighborhood in 1922, the courtyard homes were crumbling, and many of the former bannermen had become deeply impoverished.[1]

The constable found Guo Hetang sleeping in the doorway of one such dilapidated house on Alley Number 9 at the end of November.[2] The weather was turning cold, but the city's winter shelters and soup kitchens had not yet opened for the season. Had Guo remained on the streets for a few more days, until the first of December, he could have joined the crowds at the nearby soup kitchen, located at the Guandi Temple outside Dongzhimen. There, each supplicant received a bowl of watery porridge on winter mornings—hardly enough for subsistence, but one of the few forms of aid available to itinerants.[3] Since this was Guo's first winter in Beijing, he was unlikely to know about the temporary shelters run by private charities such as the Salvation Army, or which temples could offer refuge from the elements, or where to find a "chicken feather inn" to spend the night if he had a few coppers.[4]

Instead, Guo Hetang found himself taken first to the local police precinct, and from there, transferred to the Vagrant Workhouse on the opposite side of the city. His journey from homeless orphan to workhouse inmate was the result of significant changes in attitudes and policies toward "the poor" (*pinmin*) beginning in the early twentieth century. To understand why police officials identified Guo as "helpless" and "in need of compassion," yet sent him to a punitive institution for "vagrants," we need to step back in time, to the final decade of the Qing dynasty, when "poverty" emerged as the subject of a national discourse about the uncertain future of China.

. . .

Just after the turn of the twentieth century, the aftermath of crushing defeats in the Sino-Japanese and Boxer Wars prompted fears that China would soon be partitioned, "carved up like a melon." In the context of intense pressures from foreign powers, especially mounting national debts owed to foreign creditors, worries about the impoverishment of the people centered on the urgent issue of China's precarious existence, transcending the realm of individual welfare. As an editorial in the influential journal *Eastern Miscellany* lamented in 1904, "In China today there are two great perils. The first is poverty (*pin*), and the second is ignorance (*yu*). One of these alone is enough to destroy the nation and exterminate the race, and yet today we have both. . . . The present situation has reached the upper limit of extreme poverty and extreme ignorance. Beyond this point we will no longer be a nation."[5] To many observers, nothing embodied national decay more viscerally than the ubiquitous presence of homeless mendicants and starving orphans in cities around the country.

In this context, proposed solutions to the problem broadly identified as "poverty" aimed to revive the nation on the foundation of labor. The final years of the Qing dynasty witnessed the beginning of a major shift in approaches to poor relief. Reformers started to view work as a panacea, seeking to transform the people into a productive force for the sake of national salvation. The movement for industrial training coincided with penal reforms that initiated prison labor and established workhouses for convicts guilty of misdemeanor offenses. Soon incarceration extended to the noncriminal poor, especially targeting vagrants and beggars—considered the most unproductive elements in society. The penal roots of the Chinese workhouse crucially shaped the assumptions that informed its operations. But from its advent, the workhouse also incorporated charitable motives. Most notably, some of the earliest institutions allowed "the poor" (*pinmin*) to apply for entry on a voluntary basis. This association of "the poor" with convicts in a system of custodial detention linked the condition of economic hardship to criminality. As "workhouses for vagrants" and "workhouses for the poor" emerged out of movements to build new industrial training centers and modern prisons, they began to change the concept and language of poverty. The transformation in thinking about "poverty" and the birth of institutions that put the ideas into practice are the focus of this chapter.

In Search of Wealth and Power

Before there were workhouses, and well before the Boxer Uprising, reform-minded officials had already been pondering the question of how to fortify the Qing state against new challenges. In the years after the defeat in the Opium Wars and the dynasty's near collapse during the Taiping Rebellion, reformers launched a program of "self-strengthening" to defend the country against foreign encroachment and restore its domestic stability. With myriad ideas and projects—ranging from sending young men to study abroad to building arsenals and railways—they hoped to discover the secret to the "wealth and power" (*fuqiang*) of the West and emulate its success. The question that Feng Guifen posed in 1861 was one that his contemporaries also repeatedly asked: "Why are the Western nations small but strong? Why are we large yet weak?"[6]

In the search for the answer to these vexing questions, Feng Guifen and his fellow reformers emphasized the economic prosperity and military prowess of Western nations, using "wealth and power" as twin benchmarks. But although China's "poverty" might have presented the logical contrast to the apparent "wealth" of the West, it did not emerge as a distinct concept in the discourse of self-strengthening. Instead, reformers focused on the country's "weakness" (*ruo*) as the negative parallel to Western "power" (*qiang*). Even Zheng Guanying, who wrote prolifically on issues centering on political economy, did not reference "poverty" as a salient concept. In his influential book *Warnings for a Prosperous Age*, Zheng argued that China needed to learn to wage "commercial warfare," pursue industrial development, as well as adopt major institutional changes in politics and education. "If China is content to remain inferior and weak (*beiruo*), indifferent to national wealth and power (*fuqiang*)," he declared, "then it can never become a great nation in the world."[7]

Like Zheng Guanying, journalist Wang Tao believed that creating wealth through industrial development was a prerequisite for national strength.[8] But apart from modernizing transportation, banking, and communications, Wang also reiterated a Confucian ideal: "The foundation of enriching the country and empowering the military depends only on the people." He improvised on a familiar theme: "If we get rid of all vagrants (*youmin*), useless people (*feimin*), lazy people (*duomin*), and wicked people (*youmin*), and return them all to agriculture, then there will be no uncultivated lands under heaven, and all will be prosperous!"[9] Here Wang took an ancient adage about "vagrants" (from the *Book of Documents*) and added the "useless," the "lazy," and the "wicked" (to him, self-evident categories that required no explanation). Thus while Wang considered industrial development to be crucial, it was no less important to return people to the land, where they belonged, as the basis for the country's prosperity.

In their writings, Wang Tao and other reformers sometimes invoked the term *pin* to describe the condition of individuals experiencing economic hardship. They rarely used it, however, to characterize the state of the nation. Then, in the waning years of the nineteenth century, the Qing dynasty's unexpected defeat in the Sino-Japanese War prompted a sharp shift in the tenor of the reform agenda. As is well known, Japan's victory sharpened the sense of national peril and galvanized political dissent.[10] For reformist elites in this period, the nation's woes also began to coalesce explicitly around the notion of "poverty." For instance, in his seminal essay "On Strength," Yan Fu introduced the ideas of Charles Darwin and Herbert Spencer, casting China's struggles in a social Darwinian framework. In the first version of the essay, published in 1895, Yan referred to China's "longstanding poverty and weakness."[11] A revised and expanded version of the essay (published five years later), elaborated, "Whether a nation is weak or strong, poor or wealthy, in turmoil or well-ordered, can be judged by three points of evidence: the energy, knowledge, and morality of its people. . . . If the people are poor the nation will not be wealthy; if the people are weak the nation will not be strong; if the people are confused, the nation will not be well-ordered."[12]

After the traumatic events of 1900, when the Boxer rampage and Allied vengeance left the fate of both the Qing ruling house and the nation in doubt, those searching for ways to save China from dismemberment began to reference "poverty" as one of its most debilitating characteristics. In 1902, Yan Fu wrote, "Among our country's greatest perils, are they not ignorance (*yu*), poverty (*pin*), and weakness (*ruo*)?"[13] The same year, when Governor Zhao Erxun outlined a ten-part reform program for Shanxi province, he declared that "throughout the entire nation, ignorant people (*yumin*), wicked people (*youmin*), vagrants (*youmin*), and poor people (*pinmin*) comprise more than half of the population." Therefore,

> We must awaken the ignorant, compel the wicked to become good, settle the vagrant and lazy ones in place, and provide for the poor. . . . If they are not brought under control, even if our troops are well-trained and equipped with sharp weapons, looking dazzling from the outside, the nation will be decayed within and infested with worms (*chong*). . . . If throughout the nine realms there are no ignorant, wicked, vagrant or poor people, then even if we encounter external difficulties, our roots will not be shaken.

Using a generic term for "worms" (*chong*), Zhao identified "the poor" as one among several types of vermin corroding the country, threatening to destroy its foundation. But through appropriate interventions, the governor expressed his optimism that the peril could be neutralized. The situation called for urgent action, Zhao concluded. The ruling houses of the Han, Tang, Song, and Ming dynasties had met their ignoble ends because they failed to "hold on to the teachings of the classics," especially the injunction to "nourish and teach the people."[14]

Writing from exile in Japan, Liang Qichao drew on different intellectual traditions to analyze the situation. During this formative period of his life (1898–1902), Liang immersed himself in Western political theory (Mill, Smith, Rousseau, Hobbes, Bentham) and read Japanese authors widely (Fukuzawa Yukichi, Katō Hiroyuki, Tokutomi Sohō, Nakamura Masanao).[15] At the time, Japanese newspapers featured regular stories about "social problems" (*shakai mondai*); journalists visited the "nests of the poor" and penned long articles depicting the misery of urban slums. Liang Qichao himself established three different journals in Yokohama and Tokyo, and through his prolific writings he became an influential voice for reform both in China and abroad.[16]

Among Liang's notable works from his exile years is "Discourse on the New Citizen," published serially in *New Citizen Journal* from 1902 to 1904. The most celebrated of these essays set forth his ideas about nationalism, citizenship, and education in a systematic fashion. Less known, but pertinent to the subject at hand, is part 14 of the series, titled "On Production and Consumption."[17] Taking political economy and social utility as the central concerns, Liang begins by asking, "Is China a poor nation (*pin guo*)? Is China a wealthy nation (*fu guo*)? ...Although this is debatable, we cannot conceal our country's poverty." In his analysis, Liang divides the population into "producers" and "consumers." The producers are the farmers, workers, and some merchants and officials. The consumers, on the other hand, include those who do not work at all (beggars, thieves, drifters, most women), as well as "nonproductive laborers" (slaves, servants, prostitutes, "men of learning"). Citing both the Confucian classic *Great Learning* and Adam Smith (specifically, Yan Fu's translation of *The Wealth of Nations*), Liang explains that national wealth depends on the accumulation of capital, which in turn rests on a favorable ratio of productive citizens to nonproductive ones.[18] Within his painstaking descriptions of different kinds of productivity, Liang also singles out particular groups for especially severe criticism. He compares "beggars" to "insects" that survive on the sympathy of others. He describes the profligate sons of wealthy families as "vermin upon the nation." As for the "men of learning," Liang calls the majority of them "parasites" (*jisheng chong*), preying like "moths (*du*) on the people and vermin (*mao*) on the nation." Finally, to conclude, he estimates that among China's 400 million people, 210 million are "consumers," meaning more than half of the population subsists on the labor of others.[19]

In his disparagement of prodigal sons, beggars, and men of learning, Liang Qichao followed Yan Fu's translation of *The Wealth of Nations*; indeed, Adam Smith himself had identified these groups as economically unproductive. But here, invoking biological parallels, Liang's critique far exceeded the original (and the translation) in its derision. To an existing vocabulary of vermin (*mao*, *du*) commonly used to vilify people (especially rapacious bureaucrats), he added the notion of unproductive people as "parasites," echoing the words of prominent Meiji intellectual Fukuzawa Yukichi.[20] At the same time, Liang's reference to vermin resonated with Zhao Erxun's "worms"; the calculation that more than half of the country's population did not contribute to the nation's overall productivity also accorded with the Qing governor's conclusions. These convergences, between the spokesman of the new liberal intelligentsia and the Qing reformer, suggest that emerging ideas about political economy shared common ground in the premise of labor productivity. And as we shall see in the chapters to follow, ideas about the importance of work and the pestilential nature of nonproducers would resonate throughout the first half of the twentieth century.

At the time, circa the turn of the twentieth century, Liang Qichao was better known for his treatises on citizenship and education than his writings on political economy. The causes that he supported during this period of exile, particularly constitutional monarchy, also earned him the enmity of Chinese revolutionaries concurrently living in Japan, who favored more radical solutions. In Tokyo, Sun Yat-sen called for a nationalist revolution to overthrow the Manchu dynasty, a political revolution to restore the people's sovereignty, and a social revolution to equalize wealth. Sun called these three aims—nationalism, democracy, and the people's livelihood (*minsheng*)—the Three Principles of the People. As Margherita Zanasi has shown, in imperial rhetoric the government's duty to provide for "the people's livelihood" and to "nourish the people" linked the legitimacy of the empire to the material prosperity of the populace. While invoking this imperial precedent, Sun also imagined *minsheng* as a distinctly Chinese path toward achieving national wealth and power.[21] In the inaugural issue of *People's Journal*, the Tokyo-based publication of his Revolutionary Alliance, Sun explained,

> Recently, patriots have exhausted their breath seeking ways to make China as strong as Europe and America. But although they are strong, in reality their people live in dire hardship. The ailments of European and American society were latent for decades. They have surfaced today and cannot be quickly eradicated. Our country will be the first to develop the Principle of the People's Livelihood. We can stop the evils prevalent in the West before they germinate, and actually accomplish a political and a social revolution at once. Then we can glance back to see Europe and America looking to us.[22]

In short, Sun believed that by promoting the welfare of the people, *minsheng* would prevent the kind of social turmoil plaguing the West and allow China to leapfrog these nations in development.

Other would-be revolutionaries in Japan echoed Sun's call to action. Writing under a pseudonym in *People's Journal*, Huang Kan (later a renowned philologist), condemned the government as "a nest of robbers," and those who enjoyed wealth at the expense of the impoverished as "thieves in disguise." Poor relief was a farce: the rich gave out watery gruel and bragged about their generosity, but in reality this was merely the redistribution of what had been stolen from the people in the first place. Proclaiming his willingness to die for "equality," Huang exclaimed, "Alas! Let the poor (*pinmin*) rise up!"[23]

But who were "the poor" and what, precisely, was "poverty"? Even as revolutionaries, liberal intellectuals, and Qing officials invoked these familiar terms with increasing frequency, they did not define them—leaving ambiguous, for instance, whether *pin* was a symptom or a cause of the nation's woes. Although rendered without explicit explanation, "poverty" was contextually correlated to scenarios of possible national extinction, and inflected with a new valence of national deficiency.[24] In the parlance of political economy, China was a debtor nation, whose "annual produce of land and labor" was insufficient to support the people. Cast in social Darwinian terms, China was also a hopeless failure in the competition of nations. Yan Fu's translation of *The Wealth of Nations* into elegant classical Chinese could hardly take the sting out of Adam Smith's words, initially penned in 1776 but sharply resonant when they appeared in Chinese more than a century later. Since the time of Marco Polo, "China has long been one of the richest, that is, one of the most fertile, best cultivated, most industrious, and most populous countries in the world," Smith wrote. But today, "the poverty of the lower ranks of people in China far surpasses that of the most beggarly nations in Europe."[25]

Given this woeful state of affairs, what should be done? Taking the long view, liberal intellectuals such as Yan Fu and Liang Qichao advocated education, constitutional reforms, and new modes of political participation, recognizing that such changes would not be swift or easy. At the same time, as these ideas about "poverty" circulated in intellectual circles, officials and reformers were crafting specific solutions with the potential to deliver speedy results. Experimenting with different relief and penal methods, they drew on the notion of "poverty" as a contributing factor to the possible disintegration of the Qing dynasty, requiring new kinds of intervention. We turn now to the industrial training and workhouse movements that began to flourish in the first decade of the twentieth century.

INDUSTRIAL TRAINING AND NEW POLICIES

In the aftermath of the Boxer War, the onslaught of foreign industry and growing debts prompted Qing officials to intensify the search for concrete ways to shore up the empire's precarious economic foundation. As part of a burgeoning vocational education movement launched during the New Policies reforms, hundreds of handicraft and industrial training centers (*gongyiju*) were established.[26] These institutions varied widely in longevity, sponsorship, and scope, but they shared the common goal of creating a more productive workforce by teaching indigents and the unemployed skills to make a living.

Although enthusiasm for industrial training peaked after the turn of the century, such projects had earlier precedents. Some nineteenth-century institutions, such as orphanages (Chinese as well as Catholic) and the venerable Hall of Universal Relief in Tianjin, had taught their residents to do simple handicrafts. Many proposals for self-strengthening had also included various forms of vocational training.[27] The Boxer catastrophe, however, created a sense of crisis and intensified these nascent efforts. In 1901, with foreign armies occupying the Forbidden City and the Qing court in exile, metropolitan official Huang Zhonghui memorialized the throne with the idea of creating the Beijing Industrial Training Bureau (Beijing Gongyiju). In the aftermath of the uprising, Huang wrote, people flocked to the capital seeking protection. But with commerce at a standstill, local residents and new arrivals all struggled to make ends meet: "[T]he strong and able-bodied wander about as robbers and thieves; the elderly and weak have ended up in the ditches." According to Huang, the majority of Beijing's residents had always been obedient subjects "content with their lot" (*anfen*). Since the foreign occupation, however, they "sit idly and cannot help but drift into the world of crime," and the number of indigents overwhelmed soup kitchens, shelters, and other channels of relief. In this dire situation, an industrial training bureau could "receive and train vagrants (*youmin*), expand the people's knowledge, redeem their economic power, and change existing customs." With the encroachment of foreign armies paralleling the invasion of foreign products, Huang believed that expanding the nation's productive base could strengthen native industries.[28]

Established in 1901 with the approval of the Qing court, the Beijing Industrial Training Bureau gave priority to homeless people from "respectable families," followed by those who used to have jobs but now "wander about destitute and homeless." "Habitually lazy" opium addicts and those who "willingly dwell among the lowlife" were the last to be admitted. Apart from such "vagrants," orphans or children from impoverished families seeking job training could also register. In all cases, the regulations required a background check and guarantors to vouch for the applicant's conduct.[29]

The Beijing Bureau was an early example of hundreds of similar institutions (variously called *gongyiju*, *chang*, or *yuan*) that proliferated in the first decade of the twentieth century, in nearly every province. Some were government-sponsored projects; others were private workshops; while still others were cooperative ventures funded with government capital, but managed by local gentry and merchants, who might also contribute money for operational expenses. A few centers offered technical crafts (metalwork, chemicals, heavy machinery), but the majority focused on simple handicrafts requiring little capital investment (embroidery, sewing, weaving).[30] While the meaning of the term *gongyi* expanded from "handicrafts" to encompass "industrial training," reflecting aspirations for modernizing industry, traditional handicrafts remained the mainstay of these projects.

For the most part, *gongyi* workshops provided rudimentary job training, recruiting apprentice workers on a voluntary basis. Some, however, also functioned as penal reformatories. For example, Jiangxi's Gongyiyuan detained the "unfilial sons" of "respectable families" at the request of the elders, in order to "restrain their wild hearts and admonish their indolent conduct." Only those who repented and "turned over a new leaf" were allowed to depart to seek their own living.[31] In Chengdu, the Sichuan Provincial Bureau for Promoting Industrial Training combined several different functions in one facility: the "industrial crafts factory" focused on technical and skilled labor, an affiliated workshop for "vagrants" offered instruction in "easily learned" trades, and a reformatory taught rudimentary skills to convicts to "transform their character."[32]

In Shanxi, Zhao Erxun likewise underscored the penal component of industrial training. According to Zhao, the *gongyichang* compelled local "vagrants" and "beggars" to work, in order to prevent them from becoming "bandits." At the same time, the governor considered industrial training centers less punitive than the criminal reformatories (*zixinsuo, qianshansuo*) that he and other officials had championed. Therefore, he recommended that convicts who performed well in reformatories be transferred to the *gongyichang* as reward for good behavior; in turn, those who excelled there could be promoted to become instructors in the reformatories. "By this kind of rotation," Zhao wrote, "those who have not committed crimes will not mistakenly break the law, and convicts may have the chance of gradually becoming obedient."[33]

As Frank Dikötter has noted, the mixture of the noncriminal poor and convicts in industrial training settings blurred the boundaries between vocational and penal institutions.[34] Indeed, Zhao Erxun's enthusiasm for "industrial training" overlapped with his support for prison labor, the subject of a memorial he sent to the throne in 1902. A year earlier, Governors-General Liu Kunyi and Zhang Zhidong had first broached the topic in a series of three memorials that set the agenda for the New Policies.[35] Zhao's proposal further specified replacing banishment and exile sentences with compulsory labor in a "criminal workhouse" (*zuifan xiyisuo*).

In his memorial, Zhao described the existing penal system's myriad problems. Many of the convicts were "in reality deeply impoverished (*pinqiong*) and also do not have any skills," he wrote. Banished or exiled to places far from home, they received one year of food rations, after which they had to support themselves. Since most could not make a living, they tried to escape. In the past such fugitives had nowhere to hide; but "since today one can travel to the four corners of the earth," escaped convicts could easily conceal themselves among the "vagrants and impoverished beggars found everywhere." In sum, "there is no place where they can be kept under supervision, and they have no wages or food. Therefore there are many fugitives, and fewer than two or three out of ten are captured." In contrast, the workhouse offered many advantages, including close supervision, deterrence ("a warning to the masses"), and self-sufficiency ("they will be able to support themselves through the skills acquired"). Moreover, custodial detention meant that convicts would not be further "polluted by bad habits," "goodness will be born out of labor," and laziness and diligence could be rewarded or punished accordingly. With fewer runaways, good commoners would not be contaminated by fugitives, and "evil and wickedness will not proliferate."[36]

Zhao Erxun's proposal received immediate attention in the capital. Five days after its submission, the local daily *Shuntian Times* praised the proposal as "good fortune for the people of Shanxi, as well as a blessing for all under heaven." The editorialist opined, "Today the number of poor people in our nation can be said to have reached an extreme," with unemployed vagrants, widows, widowers, orphans, and cripples found everywhere. "When foreigners see this, how they must collapse in laughter!" Workhouses, therefore, could partially salvage China's battered international reputation by alleviating "the nation's poverty" (*guojia zhi pin*).[37]

Zhao's memorial also introduced a new institution into the lexicon of penology: the workhouse (*xiyisuo*). In 1895, as the Judicial Commissioner of Anhui, Zhao had earlier coined the term when he proposed a reformatory called a "renewal workhouse" (*zixin xiyisuo*), but this had attracted little attention.[38] In 1902, his proposal to the imperial court was quickly broadcast to a wider audience through government gazettes, journals, and newspapers. By merging penal functions with industrial training, Zhao intended his "*xiyisuo*" to serve disparate purposes simultaneously.[39] But lest anyone misconstrue his proposal as too much of a radical departure, Zhao described it as an "imitation" of the Han dynasty practice of "hard labor."[40]

In response to Zhao's memorial, the Qing court instructed the Board of Punishment to evaluate the idea. Several months later, in April 1903, the Board recommended that Zhao's proposal be adopted: with the exception of bandits, violent criminals, and repeat offenders, all banishment and exile sentences would be commuted to six months to twenty years of compulsory labor in a workhouse.[41] Inmates who "created disturbances" or "refused to work obediently" could receive an additional three to ten years, while "those who are steeped in evil and refuse to repent" could be imprisoned indefinitely or executed. The Board expressed some reservations about potential problems with custodial detention, but it endorsed the plan as compatible with the principles of imperial law.[42]

JAPAN FEVER

Although the Qing court signaled its approval of Zhao Erxun's proposal, the imperial bureaucracy moved slowly. Zhao himself was transferred soon thereafter to assume the governorship of Hunan, and there he made plans to establish industrial training programs and a "criminal workhouse" in the provincial capital.[43] Meanwhile, in Zhili province, Governor-General Yuan Shikai (the future first President of the Republic) also began to experiment with the promise of rehabilitation through labor.[44] In April 1903, Yuan sent a large delegation on a study tour of Japan to investigate its legal, educational, policing, and penal systems. In particular, he instructed Tianjin Prefect Ling Fupeng to focus on techniques and methods of punishment. Within the next year, Ling returned to Japan twice more, specifically to inspect workhouses and industrial training programs.[45] Upon his return from the final trip, he described the fruits of his investigation in a detailed account.

Japanese prisons, Ling reported to Yuan Shikai, functioned according to the principle of differentiation. Four types of prisons housed distinct inmate populations: suspects awaiting trial, convicted criminals serving long-term sentences, debtors and defendants in civil cases, and "lazy vagrants and scoundrels" (youduo wulai) who stir up trouble. Within each prison, inmates were assigned to different workshops based on the severity of their infractions. Petty offenders were given easy tasks such as sewing and working in the print shop, while more serious offenders carved stone or cleaned chamber pots. The classification extended to food rations, where nine grades determined the precise amount each inmate received. (Troublemakers had their rations reduced by 10 percent for every offense—by the ninth level, only "one small bite" remained.) The exactitude, devotion to detail, and orderliness of Japanese prisons were qualities that Ling most admired. And in an echo of Bentham's Panopticon, he noted that while the architecture of different prisons varied (with buildings in the shape of stars, fans, and crosses), all were designed to maximize surveillance and control.[46]

In sum, Ling Fupeng praised penal administration in Japan as "leniency within an organized structure, and severity without cruelty," noting that the emphasis on labor training was especially worthy of emulation. Turning to the Chinese context, he observed that while the people of Zhili were generally honest, there were many "indolent drifters" who relied on relief every year, and so grew accustomed to handouts. These people have "degenerated into beggars and do not heed warnings or punishment." Revising the criminal law was imperative: a new system emphasizing rehabilitation through labor would transform society's liabilities into productive forces. In short, "in the villages and towns there will be fewer bandits, in the workshops there will be more hands to work, and in the cities there will be fewer lazy people."[47]

From his three tours of Japanese prisons, Ling Fupeng brought back translations of regulations, administrative procedures, even copies of the forms used to record statistics. At around the same time, other Chinese visitors and students were flocking to Japan, eager to learn the secrets of its successful modernization. Official delegations (such as the one Yuan Shikai dispatched from Zhili) and private travelers scrutinized Japan's government structure, legal system, schools, and industrial development. Many, like Ling Fupeng, focused on prisons as one of the crucial elements of Japan's new order. They learned that on the eve of the Meiji Restoration, advocates of penal reform found inspiration in Dutch, English, and American prisons, particularly the emphasis on education and labor. In 1871, Ohara Shigechika (later known as the "father" of Japanese prisons) spent six months in Hong Kong and Singapore studying their criminal justice systems. In the two British colonies, Ohara was introduced to the work of Jeremy Bentham and the concept of rehabilitation through labor. Upon his return to Japan, Ohara compiled his notes into a set of "Prison Rules," which became the basis for national law in 1872. Its provisions included replacing flogging with imprisonment and hard labor, as well as establishing reformatories (*chōjikan*) for "poor, unregistered persons who are not easily returned to their place of origin," and juveniles without proper guardianship ("idle, begging, or under the influence of evil persons").[48]

Chinese fervor for Japanese institutional models swelled in the first decade of the twentieth century, with "Japan travel fever" peaking between 1903 and 1908.[49] Visitors nearly always included prison tours as part of their itinerary; like Prefect Ling Fupeng, they recorded favorable impressions of the penal system. They noted, for example, that convicts at Tokyo's Sugamo Prison worked in twenty-seven types of industrial crafts, and all of the inmates appeared to be obedient and diligent. One traveler remarked that Sugamo resembled a "first-rate factory"; others described the facilities and amenities as superior to schools in China. Chinese visitors were also impressed by the emphasis on moral education. With lectures based on Buddhist teachings, a curriculum stressing "self-cultivation," and uplifting messages posted everywhere, an aura of positive transformation prevailed. The prison also boasted a library of five thousand books, and each inmate was permitted to keep two in his cell. Finally, Chinese travelers admired the scientific approach to penology. In order to discover the causes of criminality, Japanese administrators compiled statistics on inmates' background, behavior, and progress, in order to find remedies for "society's shortcomings." The data also enabled them to classify the inmate population and devise rehabilitation programs accordingly.[50]

In the nineteenth century, Chinese officials and visitors had expressed similar admiration for European and American penitentiaries, particularly London's Pentonville Prison. As Frank Dikötter has shown, knowledge of foreign penal practices and pressures stemming from extraterritoriality stimulated the reform of the Qing legal system in the early twentieth century. Informed by European concepts of crime and punishment, and inflected through Japanese interpretations thereof, Qing officials adopted the custodial sentence and rehabilitation as new penal principles. These ideas were implemented in China with the assistance of Japanese experts, who helped to draft new civil and criminal codes and took leading roles in legal education and prison administration. In the process, the modern prison was born in China. The historical significance of the prison has magnified the importance of the few institutions actually built in the first decade of the twentieth century: only five modern prisons were in operation before the 1911 Revolution.[51] By contrast, dozens of workhouses (*xiyisuo*) and poorhouses (*jiaoyangyuan* or *ju*) proliferated in the shadow of the penal system. Directly influenced by Japanese penology at their inception, they evolved to occupy a tenuous place at the intersection of punishment and charity.

The Birth of the Workhouse

Back in Zhili, after receiving Ling Fupeng's report, Yuan Shikai ordered him and Police Chief Zhao Bingju to set up a prison workhouse in Tianjin, to be based on Japan's "established laws and methods."[52] In addition to the burgeoning network of industrial training centers, Tianjin already had a small poorhouse, where the police sent local beggars to learn handicrafts.[53] According to Chief Zhao, however, the city teemed with thieves, hoodlums, "evil people" (*youmin*), and "evil beggars" (*e'gai*). Since foreigners and Chinese mixed freely in treaty port Tianjin, establishing a workhouse would ameliorate the chaos.[54] Yuan Shikai's decision to create a workhouse was also influenced by his dealings with the Tianjin Provisional Government, an international coalition that had controlled the city in the immediate aftermath of the Boxer Uprising (1900–1902). The Provisional Government had banned begging and rounded up indigents to work as sanitation "coolies." After the withdrawal of the Allied forces, Yuan Shikai continued to use beggars as work crews for street sweeping and garbage collection.[55]

In June 1904, the Tianjin Criminal Workhouse (Tianjin Zuifan Xiyisuo) opened, for the detention of those serving prison terms and commuted sentences, in accordance with the instructions issued by the Board of Punishment in 1903 (discussed above).[56] In addition, the workhouse was designated as a place of "punishment and warning" for repeat offenders, as well as "all local hoodlums, evil beggars, unemployed vagrants, and young men who do not obey their elders' teachings." Local officials and the police were authorized to round up this assortment of suspicious characters and transfer them to the workhouse. Funding for the first year's operations was cobbled together from a variety of sources (money formerly allocated to the now defunct poorhouse; contributions from the provincial relief bureau, four prefectural authorities, and seven local jurisdictions).[57] The architectural layout resembled the Sugamo Prison's fan-shaped structure, but in Tianjin the guards did not occupy a central, elevated tower. Extant sources do not indicate whether the sentries at the

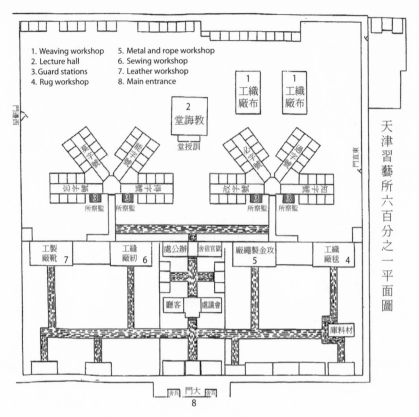

1. Weaving workshop   5. Metal and rope workshop
2. Lecture hall   6. Sewing workshop
3. Guard stations   7. Leather workshop
4. Rug workshop   8. Main entrance

Figure 1.1. The Tianjin Criminal Workhouse ca. 1905

Tianjin Workhouse were purposefully stationed in two rooms off to the side, or whether the administrators misunderstood the intended function of the Panopticon.[58]

As part of the penal system, the Tianjin Workhouse punished convicted criminals, but in a significant departure from its Japanese model, *potential* troublemakers were also incarcerated there. A strict regimen of labor and moral edification (including weekly lectures based on the Sacred Edict and "the adages of ancients and contemporaries") endeavored to "arouse their penitence."[59] The regulations also called for separate workshops for convicts and nonconvicts, as well as the segregation of juvenile offenders. In the daily routine of workhouse life, however, all were called "convicts" (*qiufan*), subject to the same regimen of punishment and training. After a three-month probation period, all inmates received 40 percent of the profits from their labor as wages, to be disbursed upon release. In terms of work hours, food rations, uniforms, and punishment for misbehavior, all received the same treatment.[60] Thus, although "evil beggars," "unemployed vagrants," and "disobedient sons" were not convicted of specific legal violations, their incarceration in a "criminal workhouse" effectively criminalized their behavior.

A few months after opening its doors, Yuan Shikai memorialized the throne to report that "positive results can already be observed" at the Tianjin Criminal Workhouse.[61] The following year, Yuan ordered that a separate Vagrant Workhouse (Youmin Xiyisuo) be established nearby, based on the same principles and methods. Its purpose, however, was "to enable the people to have permanent occupations." As Yuan noted, citing what had become the conventional wisdom, "If a nation does not have vagrants, it will be wealthy and strong."[62]

The new Vagrant Workhouse exclusively targeted noncriminal transients for detention, for an initial term of three years. The regulations provided no specific criteria for "vagrant," assuming that it was a self-explanatory category. Those who could not work (the elderly, infirm, and disabled) were barred, as were "people who wander about destitute because they are seeking relatives for support, or who are dressed in rags and mistaken as unemployed by the police." Beyond this, local officials received no other instructions. At the workhouse, the staff questioned new inmates and observed them for three days before assigning each to a dormitory and workshop, based on assessments of their character and intelligence (e.g., manual labor or the simplest handicrafts for the "extremely dull-witted"). After completing the three-year sentence, each inmate took a comprehensive test of work ability and moral character. A passing grade meant "graduation" and repatriation to his native place, where local officials were notified—ostensibly to help with job placement, but also to monitor recidivism. Graduates who wished to do so could remain at the workhouse to work for real wages. But those who failed the exam were kept in custody indefinitely.[63]

In all matters, the Vagrant Workhouse emulated the methods of its predecessor, the Criminal Workhouse. But several months after its inauguration, administrators reported that to their surprise, "vagrants" were actually more difficult to train than convicts. About half of the convicts previously held jobs and brought some skills—however rudimentary—with them. In contrast, the "poor people" (*pinmin*) sent to the workhouse were unemployed or "indolent in character." Starting from scratch, teaching them to work proved far more challenging than anticipated. Concerned that the expense involved would push the institution into deficit, the administrators contracted with private merchants to supply materials and equipment in exchange for the use of inmate labor. Following the example of Japanese reformatories, such an arrangement eased the financial burden and reduced the capital outlay required.[64]

Tianjin's two workhouses provided the inspiration for Beijing's Capital Workhouse (Jingshi Xiyisuo), established in 1906, the precursor to the institution orphan Guo Hetang entered in 1922. In Beijing, officials of the Metropolitan District introduced the innovation of allowing "poor people" to enter on a voluntary basis. As a result, the Capital Workhouse housed a mixed population of convicted criminals, voluntary recruits (who could apply by furnishing a bonded guarantee), and involuntary detainees ("those who are begging for food along the streets, harming social customs" and "those idling about, resembling bandit types"). The stated goal was to compel criminals to learn job skills, so that they would "turn over a new leaf and make use of the fruits of labor to effect goodness." Simultaneously, the workhouse would "take in the poor and teach them skills to earn a living, so that transgressions do not appear."[65] By mixing convicts with volunteers, the Capital Workhouse explicitly combined punishment for offenses already committed, with deterrence against potential crimes.

The inclusion of volunteers in the Capital Workhouse resulted in substantially differentiated treatment of convicts and nonconvicts. All inmates worked the same number of hours each day (six in autumn and winter, seven in spring and summer) at the same types of tasks (weaving, making belts, braiding rope, metal work) and attended similar classes (reading, writing, arithmetic, and "self-cultivation"). The nonconvicts, however, received more days of rest, higher wages, and less harsh punishments.[66] Most importantly, convicts who finished serving their sentences but were considered insufficiently skilled could be placed with the "poor" inmates to continue their "training." Such a provision opened the door to indefinite detention based on the judgment of the workhouse supervisors, with no recourse for appeal.[67]

In its first years of operation, the Capital Workhouse held an average of two hundred people in custody, with twice as many convicts as nonconvicts. Most convicts were petty thieves caught stealing things like clothes and food (or in one case, a street lamp), who received four-month sentences as the standard punishment. More serious crimes merited longer terms—for example, six months for pilfering a horse whip, and one year for fraud. Despite ambitions for applying the redemptive power of labor, many inmates did not actually work. As Director Shichang reported, among the convicts many were locked up for disobedience or misbehavior; the infirmary was sometimes more full than the workshops. A Manchu of the White Banner, Shichang had spent nearly three years at a police academy in Tokyo. Most of his top lieutenants received similar training, and together they supervised fifty sentries, an impressive guard-to-inmate ratio of one to four. Underscoring this disciplinary focus, qualifications for a job at the workhouse stipulated that applicants from the police academy demonstrate "a deep understanding of penology."[68]

Shortly after the establishment of the Capital Vagrant Workhouse, the Police Ministry circulated its guiding principles and procedures to provincial governors, instructing them to emulate its operations.[69] But one of the distinctive features of the Workhouse—the joint incarceration of convicts with noncriminal inmates—was soon rejected as a flawed method. In 1908, the Justice Ministry mandated the creation of separate institutions for the two groups:

> As for institutions for the unemployed poor (*wuye pinmin*), akin to the reformatories in the West or the "forced labor camps" in Japan, their nature differs widely from that of prisons. . . . The institutions for the incarceration of convicted criminals will be called "criminal workhouses," under the jurisdiction of the Justice Ministry. The institutions for the incarceration of dissolute drifters and impoverished people will be called "people's workhouses" under the jurisdiction of the Civil Administration Ministry.

Each would have a distinctive name appropriate to its function: criminal workhouses attached to prisons would "punish [crimes] that have already been done," while people's workhouses would "transform [misdeeds] that have not yet been committed."[70]

This decree, issued shortly before the collapse of the Qing dynasty, did not accomplish the goal of separating "criminals" from "the poor." But the intent to divide these two groups underlined an important difference between the modern prison and the noncriminal workhouse. The two institutions shared a common genealogy and a similar faith in the rehabilitative power of labor. The confirmed guilt of the convict, however, linked him to enduring cultural associations of disgrace and humiliation, bequeathed to the twentieth century by traditional imperial law. In the Qing dynasty, a harsh system of justice subjected criminals to corporal punishments intended to reinforce public shame and family dishonor, through "carefully orchestrated public spectacles of physical suffering."[71] Imperial law was predicated on the principle of neutralizing the convict's threat to the moral order, including—for the most severe offenders—extermination of the entire family line. As Michael Dutton has observed, the long-standing cultural vilification of criminals also evoked connotations of bestiality and enslavement. Indeed, the traditional terms for convict (*qiufan*) and jail (*laoyu*) suggest corralling, with *lao* literally meaning "animal pen."[72]

In the early twentieth century, despite the aspirations of the emerging science of penology to transform such attitudes toward punishment, old practices were slow to change. For every new model prison built, dozens of old-style gaols still confined convicts in wooden cages and iron shackles. The abolition of corporal punishment and public executions in 1905 could not wipe out images of prisoners being flogged, wearing the cangue, or dying by "a thousand cuts," all of which still lingered in the popular imagination.[73] For "the poor," to be linked with criminals in institutions of custodial detention tainted them with the guilt of convicts. As we shall see in the chapters to follow, some would challenge this cultural logic by asking, "Why is it a crime to be poor?"

In the years leading up to the Republican revolution, workhouses for criminals, "vagrants," and/or "the poor" proliferated, in varying configurations. In all, more than one hundred institutions were established across the country between 1904 and 1911.[74] Some were explicitly based on the Capital Workhouse model, while others followed the example of the Tianjin institutions. In Hunan, the governor reported that the Changsha Workhouse was such a phenomenal success that many parents asked to place their sons there to learn a trade. Within a year, thirty-seven counties in the province had established their own branches.[75] Officials from one prefecture in Zhili wrote that their workhouse aimed to stop a pattern of increasing criminality among the poor. Those who became thieves due to hunger or "drifting indolence," if unpunished, gradually grew bolder in their misdeeds. Thus, the workhouse could prevent the proliferation of more serious crimes by detaining petty offenders.[76]

FROM SOUP KITCHENS TO POORHOUSES

The growing enthusiasm for workhouses in the early twentieth century paralleled simultaneous attempts to reform traditional relief institutions in favor of more productive practices. In March 1904, Xia Dunfu, an official in the imperial Censorate, had memorialized the throne with a proposal to expand the number of industrial training workshops in Beijing. Foreign factories had invaded China and replaced human labor with machines, Xia wrote. As a result, the people were deeply impoverished—especially in the capital, where numerous "indolent drifters" and "unemployed vagrants" on the verge of starvation crowded the streets. Without jobs, they had "no way of keeping body and soul together." Repeating the stock phrase describing both their helplessness and social danger, Xia lamented, "[T]he bodies of the weak are filling the ditches, and the strong ones are falling in with bandits and criminals." Although Beijing already had several *gongyichang*, he noted that they could hire only a small number of workers. Thus, Xia proposed that the expansion of industrial training workshops could "sufficiently provide for the people and the nation" and "change shiftless indolence into diligence."[77]

Although Xia Dunfu focused on industrial training as a solution to unemployment, the metropolitan authorities found his description of social disarray alarming. Rather than providing job training on an apprenticeship basis, Shuntian Prefecture created the Five Districts Poorhouse (Wucheng Jiaoyangju), with the mission of "transforming and guiding unruly people"—specifically, first-time and petty offenders not subject to criminal prosecution. The innocuous connotation of the name Jiaoyangju (literally, a place to teach and nurture) belied its penal qualities, as the "residents" were essentially locked up and compelled to work, for terms ranging from three months to life. Through detention and labor, officials hoped to "transform evil into good" and help former miscreants "stand up in society."[78]

A year later, officials attributed the decline in the number of thefts in the capital region to the success of the Five Districts Poorhouse—certainly an exaggeration. Nonetheless, citing this accomplishment, imperial censor Wang Zhensheng proposed abolishing two of Beijing's most venerable relief institutions in favor of more punitive ones. The Hall of Universal Relief (Pujitang) and the Shelter of Mercy (Gongdelin) had provided shelter and dispensed food and clothing to the needy for nearly two hundred years, receiving substantial imperial subsidies. Their original purpose, Wang wrote, was to succor the elderly and the weak, not to feed "indolent drifters." During a recent visit, he discovered that each facility fed two to three hundred people daily, with a peak of about five hundred. Yet among these hordes of supplicants "there were not many who could be called elderly, weak, disabled, or infirm. The majority were young and healthy indolent drifters who receive two full meals a day and then roam about, or gather together and have a good time." In light of such wasteful expenditures, Wang proposed that the authorities convert the two soup kitchen–shelters into institutions like the Five Districts Poorhouse.[79]

The new Gongdelin Poorhouse opened on July 30, 1905. The poorhouse section held "indolent drifters" (sixteen to forty *sui*) while the workhouse section detained petty criminals not subject to prosecution, with sentences ranging from forty days to five years. Gongdelin continued to receive the imperial subsidies granted to the former soup kitchen. In addition, the Board of Revenue allocated ten thousand *taels* to set up the workshops, build dormitories, and extend the operations year-round.[80] The following year, the Pujitang became the Number Two Shuntian Poorhouse and began to take in impoverished people for job training. A half-day school provided education to "the poor," but opium addicts and other convicts actually outnumbered them by more than ten to one.[81]

Other prefectures and cities soon followed, converting existing soup kitchens into indoor institutions that required labor in exchange for relief. In the capital region, under directives from the Civil Affairs Ministry and the Metropolitan Police, six privately operated soup kitchens that received imperial support opened up workshops for "beggars and poor people," or appended experimental "workhouses" to their winter shelters.[82] Meanwhile, in Chengdu, Prefect Zhou Shanpei reallocated government subsidies for winter soup kitchens to two beggar factories (*qigai gongchang*) for 1,500 inmates, earning the praise of his Governor-General, Xiliang. Xiliang explained that "soup kitchens can only provide relief in the moment, and provide support without imparting education." The money would be better spent on the beggar factories, so that homeless mendicants could earn wages and learn to "subsist on their own labor."[83]

In her study of famine in north China, Lillian Li notes that after the mid-nineteenth century, soup kitchens grew in number and importance, becoming a key channel for both regular and disaster relief. By the Guangxu period (1875–1908), the majority were privately operated, though many continued to receive official support.[84] In the post-Taiping era, the soup kitchen was emblematic of "officially supervised, privately managed" (*guandu shangban*) charity. Other historians have documented the growing dominance of philanthropy in this period, a pattern that extended into the early Republican era of civil war. Corporate entities such as benevolent halls and native place associations increasingly took on the task of providing for the poor, as well as other aspects of urban administration.[85] But against this backdrop of expansive private charity, after the turn of the twentieth century, the Qing state (and its successors) also directed resources to new institutions that combined relief with punishment. Government officials did not abdicate their traditional duty to provide for "the people's livelihood." Rather, they sought to redefine that responsibility on different terms, with an updated version of "exchanging work for relief" (*yigong daizhen*). Whereas traditional work relief had been voluntary, twentieth-century workhouses and poorhouses subjected some transients—ambiguously identified as "vagrants" and "evil beggars"—to compulsory labor in incarceratory settings. Furthermore, relief was only one component of these new institutions, which simultaneously sought to contain the dangerous mobility of urban transients, increase individual self-sufficiency, and expand the productive base of the nation. Drawing on a keen sense of economic peril, these attempts to revive the nation on the foundation of labor concurred with Liang Qichao's prescription for increasing the number of "producers" while decreasing the number of "consumers."

A new cohort of institutions, established in the final years of the Qing dynasty, experimented with these new assumptions about the provision of relief. In the capital region, the metropolitan authorities established more than a dozen workhouses and poorhouses, ranging in function from incarceration to charity. At the most punitive end of the spectrum, the previously mentioned Five Districts Poorhouse operated primarily as a reformatory for convicts. Later it became a detention center for "insufficiently penitent" inmates who had completed their sentences in other institutions. Under different names, the Poorhouse continued to function in these capacities through the early Republic and the Japanese occupation.[86] The Capital Vagrant Workhouse, also discussed earlier, detained a mixed population of convicts, noncriminal transients, and volunteers. In 1909, the Workhouse cleared a profit of 1,357 *taels* from the sale of inmate products. In the early Republic, however, it slid into insolvency for a time; later it was reincarnated as a division of the Nationalist government's municipal Relief Home (see chapters 2 and 3). For those who were too old, sick, or young to work, there were at least six new year-round "poorhouses." The Outer City Poorhouse (Waicheng Pinmin Yangjiyuan) opened in 1906, designated for "those unable to work." Run by the local gentry under the supervision of the capital police, this was one of the first institutions to invoke the notion of "poor people" in its name.[87]

At the same time, other ostensibly charitable institutions included a compulsory component. For instance, the Inner City Poorhouse (Neicheng Pinmin Jiaoyangyuan, established 1908) took in "poor people" (*pinmin*) on a voluntary basis, but the police could also "use force to compel those who do not want to enter, so that the city will no longer have beggars and exposed corpses."[88] This coercive element distinguished the Poorhouse and other similar institutions from existing shelters for transients (called *qiliusuo* or *yangjiyuan*), some of which continued to operate on a seasonal basis. In addition, long-standing charities such as foundling homes, benevolent halls, and winter soup kitchens also provided relief; many of them continued to receive government subsidies. As officials from Shuntian Prefecture noted, the number of supplicants far exceeded the limited capacity at the new workhouses and poorhouses, and there were especially numerous people unable to work due to old age, illness, or disability. Therefore, "we have not been able to close all of the soup kitchens and winter shelters."[89]

Thus, in concert with these existing channels of relief, a panoply of new institutions, charitable and punitive, began to alter the urban landscape for Beijing's homeless in the final decade of the Qing dynasty. For some, they offered potentially new sanctuaries and new sources of relief, on a more permanent basis than seasonal shelters and soup kitchens. For others, however, these same institutions could be places of incarceration, jeopardizing their ability to eke out a living on the streets. In particular, workhouses and poorhouses now singled out "poor people" and "vagrants" as segments of the urban population—amorphously defined, but subject to different forms of state intervention. With the advent of "homes for the poor" and "vagrant workhouses," the notions of "poverty" and "vagrancy" became institutionalized as new realities.

Policing "Vagrancy"

The increasing detention of urban transients in newly established workhouses and poorhouses depended in large part on the modern police forces created in the early twentieth century, one of the key reforms of the New Policies period.[90] Policing itself was not new to imperial cities, especially Beijing. As Alison Dray-Novey has described, the intensive surveillance of the capital was based on unusually large and intentionally redundant forces, with the highest ratio of gendarmerie to population in the world of nineteenth-century cities. In addition, even as the *baojia* system of mutual responsibility fell into neglect elsewhere, careful census registration in Beijing kept close tabs on the population, and especially tracked "persons of unclear background" and "idlers."[91] By the late nineteenth century, the capital's annual "winter defense" (*dongfang*) campaign was well-established: a network of soup kitchens distributed food, while the gendarmerie tightened surveillance in order to ferret out the criminals assumed to be hiding among the drifters and seasonal refugees. As its name suggests, the goal of "winter defense" was to protect the city against the onslaught of indigents seeking relief and/or employment. Through the phased closure of soup kitchens in the spring and the distribution of small sums of travel money, the metropolitan authorities had a set protocol for clearing out transients from the capital.[92]

These policing mechanisms began to change in the aftermath of the Boxer Uprising. In 1901 the Qing court retained Kawashima Naniwa, the commander of the Japanese district during the Allied occupation, to take charge of police reform. As the superintendent of the Beijing Police Academy, Kawashima trained a new force for the capital, and advised Yuan Shikai to do the same in Zhili. As is well known, Yuan's pioneering police reforms were lauded as a model for emulation. In 1905, the court established a central Police Ministry to institutionalize these changes, drawing on Japanese administrative techniques to augment a traditionally expansive definition of keeping order. Crucially, professionally trained and uniformed policemen replaced the legion of "runners" and "watchmen," long despised by urban residents for their venality. Furthermore, the new police of the twentieth century gained the authority to impose punishments for minor infractions (flogging, beating, up to three months in the cangue, unspecified terms of hard labor), infringing on the prerogative of local magistrates.[93]

Japanese experts also advised the Qing court on the promulgation of the 1907 Police Ordinances, which codified these penal powers and allowed the police to intervene in the conduct of daily life in unprecedented ways. In addition to prohibitions against activities ranging from littering and public nudity to spreading rumors and urinating on the streets, the ordinances established China's first antivagrancy law. Article 7.31 authorized the detention of "vagrants and loafers without proper employment" and "evil clergy and vagabond beggars" who ask for alms in a "threatening way," with a maximum penalty of fifteen days detention and a fine of Ch. $15. Those unable to pay the fine served additional time: one day for every *yuan* owed. Furthermore, the police could subject repeat offenders or those caught committing multiple misdemeanors to additional punishments. They could release youths under fifteen *sui* to their parents or guardians; those without responsible adults to take charge of them were to be sent to the poorhouse (*jiaoyangju*).[94] This antivagrancy provision amounted to a penalty of administrative detention under police custody, and in practice did not interfere with the much longer sentences—several months to life—already routinely imposed on workhouse inmates. But by giving the police legal and broadly discretionary authority to deal with transients they deemed "suspicious," for whatever reason, the law empowered officials to punish "vagrants," "loafers," and others for their potential to disrupt social order.

Working in concert with new institutions of punishment and relief, the police could assess the level of social danger presented by homeless beggars, "suspicious persons with uneasy countenances," or "insubordinate vagrants"—and inflict punishment or impart compassion at their discretion.[95]

The Police Ordinances in general, and the vagrancy law in particular, took inspiration from Japan, and also from the foreign administration of treaty ports in China. The Treaty of Nanjing (1842) and the Treaty of Tianjin (1858) had ceded extraterritorial rights in fifteen cities and opened them to foreign residence and trade. Of these, Shanghai became a boomtown, attracting missionaries, silk merchants, and opium traders alike. In 1854, the Municipal Council, representing British and American interests, became the legal authority of the International Settlement. In 1862, the French Municipal Council began to manage the affairs of the French Concession. Meanwhile, the Chinese walled city (an area slightly over one mile in diameter) and the surrounding suburbs remained under the authority of the county magistrate. Despite these boundaries demarcating areas of extraterritorial privilege, the residents of the concession areas were overwhelmingly Chinese, outnumbering foreigners by a margin of more than fifty to one.[96]

The treaty port grew quickly, drawing fortune seekers from around the world. By the turn of the twentieth century, visitors could hear a cacophony of languages on the streets: dialects from every region of China, "guttural German alternating with Cockney slang," New York accents mingling with those of London and Glasgow. Russians, Japanese, and Indians vied for profit with Chinese compradors and entrepreneurs, all seeking a share of the lucrative trade flowing through Shanghai. Against this geography of wealth and foreign privilege, a local guidebook described the bustling lanes of the "native city" as "a wild jostle of coolies, silk-arrayed gentlemen, sedan-chairs, hobbling women, melancholy dogs, and all the flotsam and jetsam of a Chinese crowd." Indeed, the imposing neoclassical buildings along the Bund were a short distance but a world away from the Chinese enclaves.[97] As Lord William Gascoyne-Cecil observed, after two visits to the treaty port, "Shanghai is a most delightful town, although it seems commonplace to those who live there, but to a stranger it is a place full of contradictions and eccentricities."[98]

Shanghai's multinational and porous boundaries also made the city a magnet for drifters and transients, as well as for criminals trying to elude the reach of the law. In the aftermath of the Small Sword Uprising (1853) and the Taiping Rebellion (1851–64), Chinese refugees swelled the population of the concessions, and the foreign authorities began persistent but mostly futile campaigns to expel beggars and other "undesirables" from their jurisdictions—once deported, many simply waited for the police to move on to other matters and made their way back. Periodically, the Municipal Council also instructed its police to drive out the "professionals" but refer the "refugees" to Chinese charities, or to arrest all beggars "but not to interfere with pedlars or street hawkers, so long as they did not obstruct the thoroughfare." The constables, however, found such distinctions impossible to enforce. The presence of the transient population also created administrative headaches, such as the disposal of anonymous corpses and the removal of "beggar boats and huts."[99] As we shall see in the chapters to follow, these issues would grow in magnitude as Shanghai's population increased exponentially throughout the first half of the twentieth century.

To impose order on an ever more complex population, foreign concession authorities pressed the Qing government for legal authority to punish Chinese living within their jurisdictions. In 1864, the International Mixed Court was established, with a Chinese magistrate and a foreign assessor to adjudicate "mixed cases": Chinese defendants accused of crimes against foreigners, or involved in disputes with foreign interests.[100] In 1881, a revision of the original Land Regulations defining extraterritorial rights empowered the Municipal Council and its agents to detain "transient offenders," specified as "any person who has committed an offense against any provision of the by-laws, whose name and residence is unknown." Later, police ordinances authorized the arrest and deportation of beggars from both the International Settlement and the French Concession.[101]

As their reports indicate, the foreign authorities expended significant resources to enforce these laws. In the late nineteenth century, the Shanghai Municipal Police arrested nearly twenty thousand "beggars, hawkers, and ragpickers" annually, treating the majority of them as "public nuisances" and expelling them. Only a few were prosecuted in the Mixed Court, receiving punishments ranging from deportation to a fine and up to 100 blows, one month in the cangue, or six months' imprisonment in the Municipal Gaol.[102] The number of vagrancy arrests began to swell in the first years of the twentieth century. According to K. J. McEuen, the acting police chief, 1906 produced a "particularly bad record for serious crime." With "hordes of starving people" swarming into the city, from areas to the north afflicted by severe flooding, the number of "transients" arrested grew to 31,376. But McEuen also believed that the recent discontinuation of the cangue and the bamboo exacerbated the situation, by depriving the authorities of the "form of punishment most dreaded by the habitual criminal."[103] The police chief did not register the irony of his complaint: foreign claims for extraterritoriality had rested on the "barbaric nature" of the Chinese criminal justice system, and it was pressures from foreign governments that had prompted the Qing court to abolish these punishments.

The immediate cause of the "crime wave" in 1906, however, was the massive floods that devastated the northern part of Jiangsu province, called Subei (or Jiangbei). Since the mid-nineteenth century, the region had been a major exporter of migrants to Shanghai, especially impoverished people seeking winter

Table 1.1. Shanghai International Settlement

	"Beggars, Hawkers, Ragpickers" Arrested	"Vagrants" Prosecuted
1899	18,164	85
1900	17,890	49
1901	19,682	92
1902	31,768	72
1903	26,608	73
1904	32,482	71
1905	19,557	93
1906	31,376	162

Source: Annual Report of the Shanghai Municipal Council, 1899–1906.

relief or fleeing natural disasters and famine. Subei had acquired the unfortunate reputation of being the heartland of China's flood and famine corridor, a place of perpetual disasters: "for every ten years, nine calamities." The region's decline began when sea transport displaced the Grand Canal as the main method for shipping tribute grain from the south. Compounding the economic downturn, the capricious Yellow River shifted course in 1853, triggering cycles of flooding and famine.[104] In 1906, two months of torrential summer rains aggravated the destruction initially unleashed by overflow from lakes that emptied into the Huai River. Missionaries organizing relief efforts reported traveling in the region for three consecutive days without seeing dry land.[105] By the winter, when Governor-General Duanfang assumed his new post, he was engulfed by the magnitude of the crisis. Duanfang invoked familiar stock phrases to describe the situation: "The disaster victims do not have even one bite to eat. They have sold off all of their possessions and have scattered in all directions to seek food, even to the point of selling their children. Every day, people reported seeing starved corpses on the roads." Other details of the disaster, as Duanfang recorded, were locally specific. Salt ponds in towns along the southern bank of the Huai River (in the central, usually the more prosperous part of the region) had been inundated, leaving in some cases only 20 percent of the normal yield. Further north, refugees from the most afflicted prefectures congregated in Qingjiang (present-day Huaiyin), where eighty emergency shelters tried to accommodate more than five hundred thousand "starving people."[106] By the spring of the following year, the cycle of dearth threatened to continue when few were able to return home to plant their spring crops.[107]

With hundreds of thousands of desperate people on the move, and "rumors flying everywhere," Duanfang also called out military reinforcements for the province. Although only a fraction of these refugees made it to Shanghai (more than 150 miles away), the county magistrate added five hundred constables to the local police force.[108] To the foreign authorities, the (unspecified) numbers likewise seemed sufficiently alarming to warrant more intensive policing. With "a growing number of vagrants and beggars in the streets," the Municipal Council pressed the consular authorities again for the "only apparent remedy": reintroducing beating and the cangue as punishments at the Mixed Court.[109] In the short term, however, unable to enforce corporal punishment as they wished, the Council insisted that a Chinese soup kitchen on Yunnan Road move out of the Settlement, citing as the reason that "the place is a centre of attraction for hundreds of undesirables." Then, as a final resort, the Municipal Council announced that it would hire a squad of men to set up "a complete cordon" to seal off the International Settlement's boundaries, in order to prevent the influx of "beggars" during the upcoming winter (1908).[110] But the chief issue was not policing, according to the *North-China Herald*. Rather, it was the excessive generosity of treaty port residents, whose money "flows readily for any pitiful tale," giving Shanghai the reputation of a city "paved with gold. . . . [C]harity of such a kind is the falsest economy. . . . Unless we turn a deaf ear to the beggar's whine, a hundred plain-clothes constables will not be sufficient altogether to prevent the influx of undesirables."[111]

With all of these indigents converging on its doorstep, the Municipal Council did in fact disavow responsibility for "poor relief" of any kind, reiterating that this was not within the scope of its charter, declaring that "any measures of organised relief would give rise to a further influx of these undesirables."[112] In refusing to provide aid, the Municipal Council primarily had in mind "hordes" of Chinese refugees and beggars—but there were Europeans as well. Although numerically insignificant compared to native indigents, treaty port officials and residents considered "poor whites" detrimental to their own prestige. Their presence reinforced the racial element in perceptions of poverty in Shanghai, quite distinct from concurrent discussions in Beijing.[113] As we shall see, the number of White Russian refugees in the treaty port would grow after the Bolshevik Revolution. But even in the first decade of the twentieth century, there were enough sailors and other transients loitering about to worry the foreign community. In particular, U.S. consular officials forcefully prosecuted American "vagrants" who straggled in—adventurers and "beachcombers" whose behavior gave the United States a "bad name," as well as disreputable types from the Philippines, Guam, and Puerto Rico (who could claim extraterritorial protection due to American sovereignty over those territories).[114]

Within the International Settlement, there were periodic calls to build a "casual ward," in the manner of English workhouses, "where foreigners in exchange for work done would obtain supper, bed, and breakfast, so that the old plea of being unable to get work would . . . be untrue." The Municipal Council, however, rejected these proposals, insisting that for the scheme to accrue any value, it "must be preceded by the provision of the necessary legal powers to compel casuals to work in return for board and lodging. The class of casual from whom Shanghai is at present suffering is in most cases not the kind of man who will work so long as he can subsist by begging or living on the charity of others."[115]

Chinese Shanghai

Without the power to compel "casuals" to work, the Municipal Council could only appeal to other consular authorities to help defray the cost of supporting "foreign paupers," or to arrange for their departure from Shanghai whenever possible.[116] As for the Chinese, when the foreign concession police arrested "vagrants," they usually dumped them off in the adjacent territories under Qing jurisdiction. Chinese Shanghai was a subprefecture in the provincial hierarchy, and its magistrate reported to the Circuit Intendant in the bureaucratic chain of command. As such, the Chinese city did not have an independent municipal administration until 1905, when the General Works Board (GWB) was established. Although formally subordinate to the county magistrate, the GWB was empowered to manage roads, regulate commerce, and collect special taxes.[117] Under the control of local elites, the GWB also established a police academy, which put its first class through a three-month crash course, in order to have officers on the beat by the onset of winter in 1905. Local laws, following the 1907 national ordinances described above, instructed the police to watch out for "beggars and itinerant performers" and "people wearing strange costumes," as well as "solitary men and women" and "people whose origins are unknown."[118]

Shanghai was a relative latecomer to the industrial training and workhouse movements blossoming elsewhere in China. It was a city of sojourners dominated, on the one hand, by foreign interests and, on the other, by powerful native place associations, whose merchant leaders formed overlapping networks of business and charity that extended to their hometowns and beyond. While workhouses and poorhouses were proliferating elsewhere with the backing of provincial leaders, in Shanghai one proposed experimental workhouse and early prison reforms faltered as plans were repeatedly drawn up and revised.[119] In 1906, worried that "it is not a sound policy to provide support without imparting education," several gentry leaders proposed establishing craft workshops at the city's old shelter for transients (*qiliusuo*). The same year, in response to an appeal from another group of local elites, Intendant Yuan Shuxun donated five thousand *taels* and nine *mu* of land to establish a "Hall of Diligence" (Qinshengyuan), to "teach and train poor people." But several years of wrangling and bickering ensued, over proposed locations and funding problems. In 1910, the project was renamed the "Workhouse for the Poor" (Pinmin Xiyisuo), but it did not open until after the Republican revolution.[120]

Although the workhouse movement developed slowly in Shanghai, a similar premise of labor productivity began to infuse the work of private charities, particularly institutions for children. In the winter of 1906, the devastation of the floods in northern Jiangsu (which had prompted the Shanghai Municipal Police to crack down on transients) compelled a group of Chinese philanthropists to establish a new orphanage. Several of these men had long cherished aspirations for charitable work, and the specter of pitiful children "ending up in the ditches" or "falling in with bandits and criminals" stirred them to action. Shen Maozhao, a banker and merchant, obtained the use of a small compound from the American Presbyterian Mission to establish the Shanghai Gu'eryuan, which opened its doors to fifty-three boys. The church had promised use of the compound rent free for ten years. But the orphanage's Board of Directors, including prominent philanthropist Wang Yiting, decided to purchase a tract of land in Longhua (a town just outside city limits) and added separate quarters for girls.[121]

Although not affiliated with any denomination, the orphanage sought to cultivate a Christian environment. With daily prayers and Sunday designated as a day for rest and Bible study, the disclaimer that children who did not wish to participate in such activities would "suffer no discrimination" belied the institution's spiritual foundation. Equally important was the goal of cultivating diligence and self-sufficiency through labor. (Underscoring this priority, the orphanage rendered its name in English as the "Shanghai Industrial Orphanage.") In addition to receiving a standard primary school education, all children older than ten *sui* participated in "extracurricular training": gardening, tending the fruit orchard, cleaning, making rattan products, or working in the print shop. In its 1908 annual report, the administrators boasted that thirteen children were thriving in the rattan workshop, and their products, priced at 10 percent below market value, were selling briskly. Later, six children who had "more or less" mastered skills in the print shop were apprenticed to the Commercial Press.[122]

The emphasis on labor distinguished the Industrial Orphanage from a longstanding tradition of caring for orphans and abandoned children, as the notion of laboring children was imbued with new significance in the twentieth century.[123] Echoing the advocates of workhouses and industrial training, the founders of the Industrial Orphanage declared, "In the competitive era of the twentieth century, every nation must emphasize commerce; the quality of commerce depends on labor. . . . It is the key to breakthrough and triumph in commercial warfare." At the same time labor also serves three important purposes for the children's individual futures: physical development, "stimulating their sense of frugality," and "nurturing the foundation of self-sufficiency." In fact, work would check "the bad quality of dependency" commonly observed in young recipients of charity.[124]

Consciously modeled on Japanese and European institutions, the rules governing life at the Industrial Orphanage were strict. The children were not allowed to leave the premises for any reason, and could receive only two visits per year from family members. To be sure, discipline could be harshly enforced. But for at least some of the children, the orphanage was a welcome refuge from the misery of their childhood years, as painfully recounted in the institution's publications. While clearly written to elicit maximum sympathy and donations, these biographies provide us with glimpses of the period's profound social dislocations and their devastating impact. Many of the children, with absent or deceased fathers, had been raised by mothers struggling to make ends meet. A mother's untimely death could precipitate a crisis, leaving a child without any family support. On their deathbeds, several mothers implored doctors or neighbors to take their children to the orphanage. Other youngsters relied on extended family, neighbors, and even strangers. The compassion of relatives and strangers could be unpredictable, however, and many suffered terribly—kidnapped and sold, or mistreated by adoptive parents. Jia was one such orphan boy apprenticed to an ironsmith, whose master repeatedly struck him with hot pokers until his entire body was covered with scars. Zhang, an orphan abducted from northern Jiangsu and sold to a temple, ran away because the monks beat him constantly. He tended sheep and worked in a cigarette factory before finding an adoptive family—only to be kicked when he fell ill and soiled the bed sheets, "wearing out his welcome."[125] One motherless boy had an addict father "who kept company with Miss Opium all day long, lying in a stupor, as if he had ascended to paradise." The father brought the young boy to the orphanage, hoping to get rid of him. When he learned that only orphans were accepted, he pretended to be the boy's uncle.[126]

Another orphanage, the Shanghai Poor Children's Home (Shanghai Pin'er yuan), shared similar hopes for the transformative power of education and labor. The Home was established in 1909 by Zeng Zhimin, to fulfill the deathbed wish of his father, Zeng Zhu. The elder Zeng's former business associates contributed generously, including industrialist Sheng Xuanhuai, who donated a large tract of land (more than thirty *mu*). Their efforts earned the praise of Governor-General Duanfang, who described the proposed institution as the amalgamation of a foundling home and charity school. In addition, an attached "reformatory" (*ganhuasuo*) would "discipline and admonish homeless beggar children," before they would be permitted to join the enrolled students. "When an individual acquires one more skill, then society will have one fewer good-for-nothing. . . . Poor orphaned boys and girls will be able to make a living and not lose their place (*shisuo*) and sink to the level of useless people (*feimin*)." This, according to Duanfang, would greatly benefit constitutional reforms.[127]

In the first six months of 1909, the Poor Children's Home accepted applications from families who wished to enroll their sons or daughters, with a target of one hundred boys and girls, seven to twelve *sui*. After investigation of each applicant's background, many were rejected (because they were "not poor," were not Shanghai natives, had disabilities or illness, or were not within the specified age range). On the other hand, some parents declined to matriculate their children when they learned about the Home's stringent rules. As a result, the first class had only seventy-three children (fifty-three boys and twenty girls). Once enrolled, the Home removed the children completely from their former lives, permitting only one family visit per year. The separation was important, according to Zeng Zhimin, to ameliorate the effects of "poverty." "Children do not cause their own poverty," he wrote. As fetuses they had the misfortune of entering the wombs of "poor mothers" (*pinmu*); or they were born into families that became impoverished due to heavenly ordained disasters and human misfortunes. With neither the parents nor "society" able to assume responsibility of educating them, Zeng concluded, "In matters of poor relief the most pitiful and also most urgent issue is that of poor children. Uneducated children are to be feared, and poor children are also to be feared. But children who are both uneducated and poor should be feared most of all."[128]

With the determined efforts of Zeng Zhimin and the financial support of his father's friends, the Home accrued a generous endowment. The children benefited from a bountiful diet, including meat, beans, and even the occasional luxury of fresh fruits. A 1909 report observed that some of the children ate without restraint when they first arrived. A few would wolf down five or six bowls of rice at every meal, as if compensating for earlier deprivations, to the point of falling ill. To prevent such binging, the staff began to restrict the amount of food for the children, based on their age and size.[129]

Like at the Industrial Orphanage, these children attended primary school for two years and then took up vocational training, a combination that sought to elevate them beyond the ranks of manual laborers. After all, the founders proclaimed, illiterate children were destined to become "idiot craftsmen"—if they did not know how to read, how could they perform more complex tasks such as typesetting or engraving? Emphasizing diligence, frugality, cleanliness, and honesty as the primary virtues, the Home encouraged the children to strive upward. One song urged them to emulate Yan Hui, Confucius's favorite disciple and the exemplar of moral excellence: "Since antiquity our heroes have not come from rich families. The good-for-nothing sons of the wealthy are the most shameful.... Haven't you seen the great sage Yan Hui, who found happiness in living simply—the first worthy impoverished scholar!"[130]

Conclusion

At his Home for Poor Children, Zeng Zhimin constantly invoked the principle that "[e]ducation should not be differentiated by wealth and poverty." Zeng devoted his life to this cause, as did Li Tinghan, another advocate of education for the poor. In 1910, Li observed that "[p]oor children are the wicked people of the future." Without learning, skills, or family resources, they were compelled to take up a life of crime in order to survive. The future of the nation therefore depended on educating "poor children"—the "weeds" that can destroy the harvest.[131]

Thus, in the first decade of the twentieth century, a panoply of new institutions endeavored to ameliorate the problem of poverty. Through orphanages, industrial training centers, poorhouses, and workhouses, late Qing reformers hoped to strengthen the nation by putting previously idle people to work. The various institutions employed different levels of coercion, combining education and moral edification with punishment for past crimes, deterrence to prevent future misconduct, rehabilitation through labor, and job training for self-sufficiency. As we have seen, the boundaries between penal institutions, relief agencies, and vocational training centers were quite flexible. Some recruited the poor and unemployed for job training on a voluntary basis; others sought to punish and rehabilitate petty criminals and indolent indigents by compelling them to work. Nonetheless, what these institutions shared in common was the belief in labor as the solution to the problem at hand, whether the problem was labeled poverty, unemployment, indolence, or, more broadly, national weakness.

The idea of work relief, of course, was not entirely new. As discussed in the Introduction, "substituting work for relief" (*yigong daizhen*) had long precedents in imperial history; some nineteenth-century institutions had expected their residents to learn handicrafts. What was new in the twentieth-century context was the workhouse as a place of compulsory detention, and the deliberate focus on labor as the raison d'être of its mission. The names are instructive on this point. Whereas traditional charities that provided shelter to the poor highlighted the motivations of the benefactors (e.g., *Guangren tang*—Hall for Spreading Benevolence—and *Pushan tang*—Hall of Universal Goodness), the new *xiyisuo*, *jiaoyangju*, and *gongyiju* targeted indigents as the objects of reform. This marked an important shift, for with the advent of these institutions, and throughout the Republican era to follow, the combination of labor and incarceration would become the central tenet of poor relief in both government and private realms.

In fact, the terms *xiyi* (training), *gongyi* (industrial or handicrafts), *jiaoyang* (to nurture, provide for), and the verb most commonly used, *shouliu* (to take in), were often euphemisms for the indiscriminate and open-ended detention of the poor. The imprecision of the new rhetoric targeting "extremely lazy" people and suspected criminals with "uneasy countenances" resulted in the arbitrary confinement of potential, not proven, troublemakers. This new model also denoted a striking departure from traditional practices. The old poorhouses, winter shelters, and other charities (both private and public) had provided food and shelter to the poor on a voluntary basis. Although residents could not depart freely from these indoor-relief institutions, all had entered of their own (or their families') accord.[132] In the twentieth century, for the first time concerted efforts to round up vagrants, beggars, and drifters subjected the poor, guilty of indigence and suspected of criminality, to a new regimen of incarceration, discipline, and labor.

It is worth noting that the rhetoric binding "poverty" to national extinction and the new technologies it spawned were not triggered by a sudden decline in material circumstances. The first decade of the twentieth century produced no disasters, natural or human, on the scale of the Taiping Rebellion or the "extraordinary famine" of 1876–79.[133] (Although the Boxer Uprising had wreaked havoc in Beijing and parts of north China, recovery was relatively rapid.) Instead, the new discourse and methods reflected a different consciousness about the fate of the nation and new calibrations of China's weakness. The intrusion of Westerners merged with the rise of Japan as a military and cultural power to underscore China's impotence and the implications of "poverty" for the nation's uncertain future. A new world of information, available via political journals and newspapers, also meant that reports of innovations in one region and lessons learned from trips abroad rapidly spread to other areas. In short, the criminalization of various forms of "vagrancy," as intolerable manifestations of impoverishment, must be considered in the context of these seismic shifts in elite perceptions of national strength and weakness.

It is also worth underscoring features of Chinese workhouses that distinguished them from their Japanese and Western cousins. At the turn of the century in China, the workhouse was an innovation newly imported from the West via Japan. In practice, Japanese workhouses were part of the prison system. Thus, by combining convicts with noncriminals, the Chinese workhouse extended the function of its Japanese predecessor. In contrast, workhouses and casual wards in Europe and the United States, although punitive, were not penal institutions. (Their administrators tried to make them as "prison-like" as possible, but individuals, except for children and the insane, could not be detained against their will on a long-term basis.) The Chinese workhouse, operating on the principle of prolonged detention and labor, resulted in a significantly more punitive form of poor relief than their Western counterparts embodied.

Finally, this first cohort of workhouses and poorhouses for the most part targeted disobedient sons, not daughters, for detention. Some industrial training centers did establish separate facilities for women, but in the main officials and reformers viewed the itinerant mobility, suspected criminality, and perceived indolence of "the poor" as an exclusively male domain. The workhouse's origins in the penal system reinforced the link between poverty and criminality and tapped into long-standing suspicions of male transients and drifters. As one observer opined in 1904, "In the past it was said that to administer a nation is like herding sheep—you have to whip the ones who lag behind. Today we should try this on the lower classes of people."[134] Indeed, the waning years of the Qing dynasty witnessed the beginning of increasingly punitive treatment of those who "lagged behind." And as we will see in the next chapter, the first decade of the new Republic would continue this trend, with contributions from sociologists, Protestant missionaries, and a new cohort of institutions aimed at curbing the presumed indolence, mobility, and insubordination of the urban poor.

CHAPTER 2

"Parasites upon Society"

"We are starving, nothing to eat for two days."

"My poor husband, exhausted from pulling a rickshaw, started spitting up blood and died. Now my son is out there pulling in the wind and snow. Poor boy, he's only 12, he has to stop to catch his breath after every step!"

"My 71 *sui* father came home yesterday from scavenging for coal ... and dropped dead. In this hot June weather, what are we going to do without a coffin to bury the body?"

"At home it was just my mother and me, with nothing to eat. I was sold to a brothel, but I couldn't stand being beaten every day. . . ."

"THESE ARE THE laments of Beijing's poor people," wrote Chen Duxiu in 1919. "These 100,000+ suffering people frequently cry out in distress, but do the residents of the city . . . hear them?" At the time, Chen was one of the iconoclastic leaders of the New Culture movement, soon to become a cofounder of the Chinese Communist Party. In this short essay published in the magazine *Weekly Review*, Chen asked why these nameless "poor people" (*pinmin*), numbering roughly one-tenth of Beijing's population, lived in such misery. He contrasted their struggle to survive with the decadent indifference of the country's officials, who "eat birds' nests every day, play cards, stroll in gardens and ride in cars. . . . They happily fondle their ill-gotten money, planning for a lifetime of enjoyment" for themselves and their descendents. "They cannot even hear the laments of the poor! Even if they heard the pitiful cries, they only laugh and say, that's their fate! . . . But sooner or later, I think they will be forced to see, pay attention to, and feel the pain of these pitiful cries, and will ultimately be forced to utter the same sounds of woe!"[1]

Chen Duxiu's predictions for such retribution through "social revolution" (*shehui geming*) were just wishful thinking in 1919. But in his descriptions of Beijing's "poor people," stylized to evoke their speech and reflect their distress, Chen touched on questions that also preoccupied his contemporaries in elite intellectual circles. How many "poor people" were there in China, and how "poor" were they? What were the root causes of their impoverishment, and how could these be ameliorated? What was the relationship between "poverty" and the distribution of wealth? How could a nation that aspires to greatness tolerate the specter of people starving to death, pulling rickshaws like draft animals, or sold into sexual servitude for survival?

But whereas Chen Duxiu imagined a future moment of reckoning, when rapacious bureaucrats would receive their comeuppance, in early Republican China the idea of a social revolution was not yet widespread. Instead, intellectuals and reformers embraced new academic fields of inquiry to answer these questions on a scientific basis. As students of sociology, eugenics, and evolutionary biology learned to diagnose "poverty" as an acute "social problem," a proliferation of data collected on living conditions and wages reinforced the belief that China's impoverishment undermined its aspirations for progress. At the same time, as "poverty" became an expansive metaphor for national weakness, the term took on a conceptual elasticity that challenged efforts to define and quantify it. With the magnitude of the issue defying comprehensive solutions, proposed remedies for "poverty" typically targeted attributes that officials and reformers perceived to be its most destructive symptoms: homelessness, latent criminality, indolence, and "parasitic" dependence on charity.

This chapter begins by tracing the evolution of ideas about "poverty" in the early Republic. As May Fourth intellectuals and sociologists pondered its causes and consequences for the nation's future, they used the idea of the parasite to describe the nonworking poor. Juxtaposed against an emerging left-wing discourse sanctifying labor, the notion of the "social parasite" delineated the boundaries of social citizenship based on an individual's productive contribution. Those who did not "produce" were not merely useless—they "consumed" and depleted resources, sucking the very life out of society. Concurrently, reforming elites also advocated new "scientific" methods of charity, criticizing traditional practices for "pauperizing" the poor and allowing them to subsist on the labor of others. These ideas in turn buttressed previous efforts, described in chapter 1, to rehabilitate urban transients through compulsory labor. After a brief hiatus due to the 1911 Revolution, some workhouses and poorhouses established in the final years of the Qing dynasty resumed their operations. In Beijing, the government relied on a variety of institutions to provide custodial supervision of the numerous beggars, vagrants, and orphans found on the streets. As adjuncts to the formal penal system, these poorhouses and workhouses functioned in the space between charity and punishment. By the early 1920s, political chaos and administrative neglect meant that many of these institutions became virtual prisons of starvation and disease. Meanwhile, in Shanghai, treaty port officials found themselves embroiled in debates over responsibility for poor relief and engulfed in a battle over shantytowns in a time of rising nationalism. Cumulatively, the fifteen years between the fall of the Qing dynasty and the Nationalist Party's rise under Chiang Kai-shek marked a formative period in demarcating the parameters of social belonging, and in redefining the relationship between government power, private charity, and the neediest members of society. The precept that the nonworking poor should learn self-sufficiency through compulsory labor would have a lasting legacy into the Nationalist era and beyond.

DEFINING POVERTY

In the early Republic, the advent of "sociology" (*shehuixue*) as a field of academic inquiry introduced new concepts and practices to the realm of poor relief. To a new generation of Chinese students, sociology embodied the promise of "empirical" and "scientific" solutions to address the nation's problems. The earliest intellectual foundations of the field in China were established in 1903, when the works of Franklin Giddings and Herbert Spencer appeared in translation. Two years later, St. John's University in Shanghai began offering courses in the subject.[2] In Beijing, YMCA chapter secretary John Burgess helped the Peking Students' Social Service Club conduct the first "social survey" (*shehui diaocha*) in the country.[3] Five investigators (four Chinese and one American) stationed themselves inside a house and sent the gatekeeper to summon a rickshaw puller, who was invited in for tea and showered with questions: How much did he earn in a day? How many people were in his family? Could he read? What was his religion? As Burgess later remarked, "The coolie was utterly astonished at these questions." For their part, the interviewers were equally surprised—at the "startling revelations of poverty and degradation," but also at the discovery that almost half of their subjects were literate—"some of them had read the classics through, and showed it in their conversation."[4]

By 1915, the Social Service Club had grown to six hundred students, and later developed into a network of Community Service Groups focused on neighborhood improvement projects and spreading the message of Christian uplift.[5] The initial survey of rickshaw men expanded into a broader study of 302 pullers. Tao Menghe, the chairman of the sociology department at Beijing National University (Beida), tabulated and published the results.[6] Tao had studied with Sidney Webb at the London School of Economics; he returned to China in 1914 to become one of the most influential sociologists of his generation. For his part, John Burgess chaired the largest sociology department in the country at Yanjing University. Other YMCA affiliates such as Sidney Gamble (one of the heirs to the Proctor & Gamble fortune) also played instrumental roles in fostering the development of sociology.[7] Beyond academic sociology, this new field also attracted enthusiasts in wider circles of intellectuals. In a speech to the Peking Students' Social Service Club in 1920, for instance, Hu Shi described sociology as the attempt to understand the universal principles of human life and to find solutions for "social problems." Hu also stressed the importance of social investigation, comparing it to a physician's diagnosis and treatment of illness.[8] At the same time, others lamented the glacial development of a field still in its infancy. At Shanghai University in 1924, Qu Qiubai (head of the sociology department and a member of the CCP Central Committee) complained that every sociologist had a different interpretation of the definition of "sociology." As a result, the discipline was like a "treasure box stuffed recklessly" with all kinds of random and unrelated questions.[9]

By the 1920s, many Chinese sociologists and intellectuals clearly identified "poverty" (*pin*) as one of the nation's most pressing problems, echoing reformers from the final years of the Qing dynasty. In the Republican context, however, its classification as a distinctly *social* problem was new.[10] Professor Tang Yueliang of Qinghua University, for example, wrote in 1922, "Of all social problems in Peking, and for that matter in the whole country, none appears so important and glaring as that of poverty." In his 1924 textbook for middle school students, Tao Menghe concurred. Although poverty did not cause "all crimes and evil," it was responsible for a majority of them. If poverty is not eradicated, he wrote, "ugly and repulsive social phenomena such as begging, illness, filth, and gambling . . . will forever remain in society."[11]

Despite consensus about its significance, however, there was no corresponding agreement about the definition of "poverty." Tao Menghe explained that from one perspective, it was a relative concept, subject to individual perceptions. On the other hand, since "poverty" was now a "social problem" transcending individual circumstances, "an objective and universal standard" was needed: the minimum level of subsistence, or the cost of food, clothing, and shelter required to sustain a person's life.[12] The idea of pinpointing a quantitative baseline for poverty was a new concept in China, informed by belief in the power of social-scientific empiricism. At the same time, it recalls the Qing government's classification of famine victims. According to Pierre-Etienne Will, Qing officials typically divided the needy into categories like "very poor" (*jipin*) and "less poor" (*cipin*). The demarcating criteria varied widely, depending on appraisals of a family's appearance, attire, food reserves, productive ability, and property.[13] In the early Republic, attempts to define the poverty line continued to rely on similar terms. The Beijing police, responsible for household registration, used "very poor" and "less poor" to conduct an annual census; private charities then used the information as the basis for distributing aid to families identified as needy.[14] (Later, throughout the 1930s, the Social Affairs Bureau under the Nationalist government would use the same categories to tally "poor" households.)[15]

Between 1914 and 1924, various studies estimated that for a family of five in north China, the "poverty line" was roughly Ch. $100–$150 per year. Each analysis, however, relied on a different definition of what constituted "poverty." One study from 1914 used the wages of Beijing's rickshaw pullers as the approximate poverty line (about Ch. $120). In 1918, an analysis of household budgets in a Beijing suburb concluded that Ch. $100 could provide a "comfortable life"— defined as the ability to enjoy meat occasionally and tea almost every week. In rural Shandong, Anhui, and Jiangsu, villagers in 1922 needed about Ch. $150 for minimal subsistence: with this income, they were "systematically underfed" but did not starve to death. These inconsistent standards meant that estimates for the number of people who lived below the "poverty line" ranged wildly, from one-third to one-half to "the great majority" of the people.[16]

For Beijing in 1917, for instance, Sidney Gamble reported that 12 percent of the city's population was "poor" or "very poor."[17] By 1926, relying on a police census, Tao Menghe surmised that nearly three-quarters (73.3 percent) of Beijing's residents lived at or below the poverty line.[18] In addition to these disparities, another major difficulty was the lack of comprehensive data on income and wages. Most of the studies focused on north China, reflecting Yanjing University's early dominance in training graduate students and sponsoring field work. (In Shanghai, during a time of heightened labor conflicts, research tended to focus on factory workers, rather than on "poverty" more broadly.) After reviewing the inconclusive data, Tao Menghe could propose only that if the hallmark of a "progressive society" was that it sought to raise the "poverty line" beyond minimal subsistence, to the point where people could enjoy "comfortable lives," then "the great majority of people in China probably live below the poverty line." Writing in the journal *New Society*, Qu Shiying commented that it was impossible to gauge the number of poor people without an accurate census. "But I can venture this," Qu added. "There are more poor people in China than in foreign countries."[19]

Unable to establish empirical measures, analysts like Tao Menghe turned to the condition of dependency as a barometer: a person who could not "stand alone" (*zili*) or "live independently" (*duli shengcun*) was "poor" (*pin*). Dependency was not always a reliable indicator—some "poor people" refused relief because they considered it below their dignity, while others who were not indigent eagerly accepted aid because it did not require any effort on their part.[20] Nonetheless, people unable to subsist on their own labor, requiring assistance from others to survive, could be identified as "poor."[21] In short, by making self-sufficiency the line of demarcation, sociologists identified dependency as a fundamental attribute of poverty.

The concept of establishing the "poverty line" as an objective standard genuinely appealed to researchers committed to empirical investigation and solutions. At the same time, the dual perception of "poverty" as the absolute measure of minimal subsistence and a relative measure of resource distribution complicated easy definition. As an absolute measure, it raised the moral question of society's responsibility for ensuring the survival of its neediest members. As a relative measure, poverty was closely related to the thorny issue of "inequality" (*bu pingdeng*), a term increasingly linked to socialism and Marxism, new ideas concurrently entering the intellectual milieu. Yanjing sociologist Yu Ende, for example, considered the gap between the rich and the poor one of the chief culprits undermining social morality: "Although the poor labor daily, they do not get much. Although the rich loaf about every day, their wealth increases." Tao Menghe concurred: "The unequal distribution of wealth is one of the main causes of poverty. Its danger can be seen in ancient societies such as Greece and Rome and in western nations today.... No society can forever exist on economic inequality and not topple."[22]

POPULATION, EUGENICS, AND NATIONAL EFFICIENCY

While some intellectuals explored the implications of inequality, others turned to evolutionary biology, identifying overpopulation as the chief cause of the nation's impoverishment. Debates about the population problem led to a surge of interest in Neo-Malthusianism.[23] For instance, every essay in *New Youth* magazine's March 1920 special issue on population took Malthus as the point of departure. Extolling Malthusian ideas as "unshakable" truths, economist Gu Mengyu's lead article observed, "Regardless of whether one supports or opposes him, any discussion of the population problem can never get away from the ancestor of population studies, Thomas Robert Malthus."[24] At the other end of the spectrum, Chen Duxiu excoriated those who believed in the "eternal truth" of Malthusian theories. Blasting Malthus's class prejudice, Chen bristled, "Even if overpopulation were the sole reason creating poverty ... there is no reason to restrict the reproductive rights of poor people of the lower class exclusively. Where does the prerogative of the upper wealthy class to reproduce come from? How can Malthus endorse the view that the poor do not have the right to live?"[25] Taking a more moderate stance, Tao Menghe acknowledged Malthus's pioneering vision, but insisted that in "civilized societies," poverty resulted from "unequal distribution" (*fenpei bujun*) rather than overpopulation. As for China, no one knew what caused the countless numbers of "beggars and hooligans."[26]

Neo-Malthusianism was closely associated with the movement for birth control, and the names Mr. Ma and Mrs. Sang—for Malthus and Sanger—often appeared in tandem. In 1922, Margaret Sanger visited China as part of an international lecture tour.[27] During Sanger's stay in Beijing, Hu Shi invited her to speak at Beida and served as her interpreter (an "unheard of honor," Sanger was told). Students in the audience transcribed her speech for publication and distributed five thousand copies of her notorious pamphlet *Family Limitations* (in Chinese).[28] On Sanger's visit to Shanghai, Zhou Jianren (the youngest brother of Lu Xun and a leading advocate of eugenics) gave her a tour of the city. Shortly after Sanger's departure, several major publications distributed special issues devoted to birth control. The *Ladies' Journal*, for instance, lauded her visit as a mission to rescue "the enslaved and fettered women" of China.[29] At the same time, the theories of "Ma and Sang" inspired vehement opposition. Sun Yat-sen attacked Neo-Malthusianism as "poison" infecting China's young intellectuals. Citing the specter of racial extinction, Sun deplored the nation's demographic decline against the rise of America and Europe. He darkly predicted, "A hundred years from now, if our population does not increase and theirs does, they will use their numerical strength to overpower our fewer numbers, and China will be swallowed up."[30]

In 1926, heated exchanges in the influential political weekly *Contemporary Review* debated Sun Yat-sen's stance on population. One correspondent charged that indiscriminate population growth would weaken the nation, for the proliferation of "bad seeds" would exceed the "good" ones. On the other hand, Sun's defenders protested that he did not encourage people to reproduce indiscriminately. Blindly following Malthusian ideas and Sanger's methods would create detrimental consequences for the nation, for the wealthy inevitably "tried the hardest," while those who ought to practice birth control—the lower classes—rarely did. As a result, "the poor" and robbers increased "day by day."[31] Meanwhile, Chen Xiying, an editor who wrote a popular column, also entered the fray. Describing Beijing's ubiquitous beggars, Chen wrote that he occasionally gave a few coppers to the elderly ones, but always refused the entreaties of women with infants: "I cannot bear to give anything to them! These children do not understand anything of human affairs. If they die now, it is actually their greatest blessing." Fated to become beggars, thieves, or at best rickshaw pullers, for these babies survival meant only suffering. The solution, in Chen's view, was to limit the reproduction of the poor, which would benefit them individually and society at large: "Chinese people are already so poor and so useless, for their own good they should absolutely not increase the population any further."[32]

As this debate illustrates, many commentators quickly made the leap from Malthus to eugenics, using Sanger as a stepping stone. Frank Dikötter has traced the eugenics movement in China to late-nineteenth-century reformers such as Liang Qichao and Kang Youwei, who promoted it as a strategy for "race improvement." By the 1920s, ideas about eugenics, social evolution, and survival had become pervasive and attracted the attention of those thinking about the connections between poverty and overpopulation.[33] Chen Duxiu, for instance, advocated eugenic ideas even as he vilified Malthusian population theory: "The bad elements should be forcibly limited, while the superior ones should be encouraged to reproduce."[34] To the question "Why are poor people poor?" Gu Mengyu answered, "In an overpopulated society, the foul air oppresses people heavily; like frost it kills all the sprouts striving upward." In the long term, the result would be the destruction of "good breeds" and the stagnation of social progress.[35]

The eugenic discourse of evolutionary progress was closely linked to "national efficiency," envisioned as a set of strategies for maximizing the nation's labor productivity and fostering its economic development. Born of Taylorist principles of industrial management, the craze for efficiency intensified after the Great War. From Progressive-era America and Britain to Japan, "national efficiency" extended management techniques from the factory floor to every aspect of life.[36] In China, Protestant missionaries were instrumental in spreading the gospel of efficiency. The Shanghai YMCA, for instance, organized student "efficiency clubs" devoted to the purpose. Its bilingual journal *Progress* extolled the virtues of efficiency, asking, "[H]ave you given much careful, continuous, scientific, conclusive thinking to how to make your life more efficient?" By doing so, "by the application of scientific management to yourself you may be somebody . . . more useful than the man you put your clothes on this morning."[37] In 1917, Clarence Bertrand Thompson, a professor of management at Harvard and Frederick Taylor's former apprentice, delivered a series of lectures promoting scientific management at Qinghua University. His visit stirred interest in broad applications of efficiency principles. Writing in the university gazette, one professor commented enthusiastically that increasing efficiency would unify "man and machine, capital and labor, as arms to a body . . . so that each could make full use of its ability, so that nothing—neither material nor manpower—would be wasted."[38]

Tao Menghe, the disciple of Sidney and Beatrice Webb, evinced a similar faith. The Webbs were leading advocates of the "efficiency school" in Britain; the years Tao spent in London coincided with their efforts to promote reform of the Poor Laws. Following his teachers, Tao believed that efficiency promised a solution to the Malthusian dilemma: "If every person in the population of China were an efficient producer, with an equitable economic system to support their livelihood, then there is no danger of over-population. . . . Under the current political, economic, and social situation, no matter how few people there are, poverty is unavoidable."[39]

"Paupers" and "Parasites"

This emerging discourse, combining Taylorist efficiency and Malthusian alarmism, centered on escalating anxieties about China's national weakness. As Zhou Jianren explained in 1925, "For the sake of the future of the Chinese race the ideal is to improve the quality of the people, not to increase the numbers blindly." Invoking a biological parallel, Zhou observed that all species of parasites faced gradual extinction due to their "uselessness." The parasite's fate was an allegory for China, underscoring the lethal consequences of dependency: "If the Chinese people cannot create civilization ourselves, once the Western powers invade us, the majority of people will naturally become parasites, and after a long time will gradually become extinct."[40]

Zhou Jianren's eugenic prescriptions cast one of the core principles of social Darwinism in particularly strong language, but his invocation of "parasites" was quite commonplace in the intellectual milieu. In the 1920s, journals and sociology textbooks routinely referred to the nonworking poor as "paupers" (*jisheng zhe*) or "social parasites" (*shehui jisheng chong*).[41] How did these notions gain currency in China? In Europe and the United States, "pauperism" had been a crucial component of the discourse on poverty since at least the eighteenth century. A *pauper*—distinct from someone who was simply *poor*—was dependent on the charity of others (and in Britain, specifically someone who received relief under the provisions of the Poor Laws). Prior to the twentieth century, there had been neither an equivalent concept nor a comparable term in Chinese.[42] As for *parasites*, the notion of invisible "wasting worms" (*laochong*) that invade the body was well known in traditional Chinese medicine, and *jisheng* appeared in classical texts as a description of various relationships of dependency (describing an aristocrat's retainers, for instance). But until the introduction of germ theory to China in the twentieth century, as a biological organism the parasite did not exist in the medical or scientific lexicon.[43]

As noted in chapter 1, in 1902 Liang Qichao had used *jisheng chong* to denigrate the "men of learning" who contribute nothing productive to society, comparing them to "insect"-like beggars and "vermin"-like profligates. Embedded in Liang's celebrated writings on nationalism and citizenship, this particular point did not attract special attention. Likewise, American sociologist Franklin Giddings invoked an early correlation between "paupers" and "parasites." His book *The Principles of Sociology* (1896) had identified "paupers" as a "pseudo-social class" who "pose as victims of misfortune" and "desire only to live as parasites." Using a Japanese edition, Wu Jianchang published a Chinese version in 1903, but it did not find a wide readership. (Yan Fu's acclaimed translation of Herbert Spencer's *The Study of Sociology*, which appeared the same year, received all of the attention.)[44]

In the following decade, as knowledge of biological parasites spread,[45] its social corollary likewise gained currency in intellectual circles. For instance, several Chinese translations of "Communal Life and Parasitism" by Kawakami Hajime appeared in major journals. In the essay, originally given as a lecture in Tokyo, the prominent Japanese economist explained the idea of "parasitism" by using lice as an example. The Chinese translations emphasized Kawakami's view that while "social parasites" were not new to the modern age, they were now manifestations of an acute ailment. One version referred to the proliferation of parasites as a form of "anemia"—*pinxue zheng*, literally the disease of being impoverished in blood. In this analogy, beggars and robbers were bloodsuckers feeding on society, weakening its circulatory system. And although there were many reasons for a society's descent into poverty, "the primary reason is that there are all sorts of parasites. . . . We should not fear lice or worms living off our bodies. What we should fear most of all are human parasites."[46]

For American sociologist Charles Ellwood, a professor at the University of Missouri, the metaphorical mattered less than applications in social policy. Ellwood's explanation of "social problems," drawing explicit connections between *poverty*, *paupers*, and *parasites*, became highly influential in China. Shortly after the initial publication of his *Sociology and Modern Social Problems* in 1910, the textbook appeared in Shanghai in an English edition. The 1920 Chinese translation, widely adopted for classroom use, became the definitive text on social pathology, appealing to those interested in applied rather than theoretical approaches.[47] Reviews in prominent journals heralded the book as the best introduction to the field, and praised its analysis of American social problems as a "penetrating mirror" for China's own condition.[48]

According to Ellwood's explanation, "Poverty is a relative term, difficult to define, but as generally employed in sociological writings at the present it means that economic and social state in which persons have not sufficient income to maintain health and physical efficiency." Specifically, "poverty is an economic expression of biological or psychological defects of the individual on the one hand, and of a faulty social and industrial organization on the other hand." Closely related is *pauperism*: "the state of legal dependence in which a person who is unable or unwilling to support himself receives relief from public sources." In popular usage, a pauper is "a person unwilling to support himself and who becomes a social parasite," living in "a degraded state of willing dependence." Given the complexity of these issues, Ellwood criticized existing theories for seeking "some single simple explanation of ... economic distress or poverty." He disparaged Malthusianism and Marxism as reductive, and rejected the tendency to judge the moral worthiness of the poor as unscientific—"for no one can say who is the worthy and who is the unworthy in a moral sense." Instead, the "science of philanthropy" should inform charitable practices, whether public or private, religious or secular.[49]

The work of French economist Charles Gide provided yet another perspective. A professor at the Sorbonne and a champion of the European cooperative movement, Gide was widely admired in China, and his books on political economy became standard university texts in the 1920s.[50] Like his Japanese counterpart Kawakami Hajime, Gide explained the phenomenon of "society's parasites" from the perspective of evolutionary biology. But his main concern centered on the impact on the system of economic exchange. One translation pronounced that in the past, the "parasites" were the upper classes, especially aristocrats and the clergy. Today, "the most despicable parasites are those who subsist on the fruit of other people's labor"—the beggars, fortune tellers, and prostitutes whose lives constitute a form of "plunder."[51] Another translation added this coda: "Parasitism is like wild grass, once set fire, it spreads with the wind." Endemic to all forms of social organization, even Gide's own vision of a cooperative society could not eradicate parasitism completely, and may even produce "new forms of parasites."[52]

Taken together, these ideas about "social parasites" found a receptive audience among Chinese intellectuals and reformers in the 1920s. Yanjing sociologist Yu Ende urged every member of society to be productive, warning that people living as "parasites upon society" impeded social progress and development. "This is the current situation in China," Yu lamented, where there were innumerable "parasites unable to sustain themselves."[53] Furthermore, the emerging discourse of parasitism converged with longstanding assumptions about habitual indolence as a moral flaw. In the eighteenth century, the Yongzheng emperor had praised diligence and disparaged "laziness" in his elaborations on his father's Sacred Edict; imperial officials frequently characterized "vagrants" as "idlers." In the early Republic, as "indolence" transcended the individual to become a national affliction, it became the number one reason "why Chinese society does not progress," according to Qu Shiying. Qu went on to explain, "A person who loves to eat but too lazy to work just drifts about. When there is work he does not do it; when he has anything he wastes it. After a while this becomes an incurable habit. How can he not become impoverished?" Quoting O. S. Marden, the American founder of *Success* magazine, *New Youth* proclaimed, "A lazy man is of no more use than a dead man, and he takes up more room."[54] To other observers, the fate of "the Manchus" perfectly illustrated the consequences of indolence and dependency.[55] In the final years of the Qing dynasty, revolutionaries had excoriated the bannermen for "not working and not farming," blasting the imperial privileges that had allowed them to "eat off the Han people." After the demise of the Qing dynasty ended their stipends, they grew increasingly impoverished. According to Tang Yueliang, "On account of their past habits of comfort and inactivity they, as a class, loathe to work"—some would actually rather starve than exert themselves in labor.[56]

The Sanctity of Labor

If "Manchus" and "paupers" were guilty of indolence and social parasitism, then conversely the working poor were to be commended for their labor contributions to society. As Ming K. Chan and Arif Dirlik have described, Chinese anarchists in Paris, Tokyo, and Canton in the early 1900s embraced the idea of "labor" as central to their vision of a utopian society. They drew inspiration from the writings of Bakunin and Kropotkin, extolling "labor" (*laodong*) as the "greatest obligation of human life" and the "source of civilization."[57] A Meiji-era neologism, *laodong* (*rôdô* in Japanese), connoted physical exertion beyond *gong*, the generic term for "work" that alluded to craftsmen and artisans.[58] During the May Fourth era, the idea of labor as "sacred" gained wide currency among intellectuals and incipient Communists, reversing the traditional stigma against manual work. The concept originated from a speech given by Beida Chancellor Cai Yuanpei, as part of a ceremony celebrating the Allied victory in World War I. Proclaiming the dawn of a new age, Cai declared, "In the future, the world belongs to laborers! ... We must all recognize the value of labor. Labor is sacred (*laogong shensheng*)!" Li Dazhao's similarly inspired speech on the same day reiterated, "The world, from today forth, will become the world of laborers. . . . Those who do not work but eat are all robbers. Of all the Chinese people whose greed and indolence have become second nature, they are either robbers or beggars." Within the sanctified realm of labor, those who work possessed a higher morality, far superior to the "blood-sucking gentry, sages, and politicians who do not work."[59] (This rising chorus of "laborism" anticipated its importance in future CCP ideology, to be discussed in chapter 5.)

On the same occasion, celebrating the Allied victory, economist Ma Yinchu echoed his Beida colleagues' enthusiasm, saying in his speech that "China's hope rests upon laborers."[60] But interjecting a note of dissonance, Ma added that the country's chief economic problem was the lack of capital. (To demonstrate its importance, he digressed into a long explanation of the correlation between capital investment and labor productivity.)[61] Later, Ma consistently articulated a macroeconomic view and criticized his colleagues for their misguided focus on labor. "China's economic problems are rooted in the problem of insufficient capital," he wrote in 1921. "After the Great War, scholars in our country have been vigorously trumpeting 'the thousand evils of capital and the sanctity of labor,' with one singing and a hundred harmonizing." According to Ma, this constituted a deep misunderstanding of the fundamental principles of economics. In fact, human labor and capital were complementary rather than oppositional: "if labor is sacred, then capital is also sacred."[62] As the economist parted company with his left-leaning colleagues, he also assessed the emerging labor movement critically. In 1925, at the height of labor agitations sweeping across the country, Ma described such activities as tantamount to committing economic suicide. "When production stops," he noted, "you are simply waiting for death. Production is to the nation as circulation is to the body. If circulation stops, the body cannot move." Furthermore, work stoppages caused prices to skyrocket, adversely affecting the ability of ordinary people to make ends meet.[63]

Ma Yinchu was not unsympathetic to the plight of the workers, but his refusal to elevate them above all else put him at odds with an emerging left-wing discourse that sanctified labor. Union organizers and would-be revolutionaries looked to the working poor as promising sources for insurgency; researchers scrutinized their wages and diets; social reformers sought to improve their working and living conditions. In particular, the rickshaw puller symbolized both China's backwardness and the brutality of the struggle for survival. As one anonymous contributor wrote in *Weekly Review*, in a society of cut-throat competition, two rickshaw pullers quarreling over a passenger—a common occurrence—were like "two people fighting over a mouthful of rice." Meanwhile, politicians, gamblers, drunks, and the dissolute sons of wealthy families did nothing productive. If every single person in the world worked just two hours a day, there would be enough food and clothing for everyone—"So why persist in today's mode, with you eating my flesh and my sucking your blood?"[64]

As we know from David Strand's study of Republican Beijing, rickshaw pulling provided an avenue for upward mobility, as well as an "occupational life raft" for the downwardly mobile. The subject of countless editorials and studies, and as depicted in the writings of Lu Xun, Hu Shi, Lao She, and many others, rickshaw pullers represented a rebuke to the inhumanity of modern society.[65] Beyond literary and social symbol, the reality of scrapping out a living on the streets struck sociologist Li Jinghan as a completely hopeless situation. Li wrote that since the first year of the Republic (1912), due to natural disasters and continuous wars "the pressures on people's live increase day by day . . . the political situation worsens, and the number of poor people grows." All of the options available to the poor were equally dreadful: become a beggar, enlist in the army, or turn to crime and become "parasites upon society." Those "unwilling to beg or steal" could pull rickshaws and live like animals, fighting for scraps in order to survive.[66]

But for an elderly man identified only as "Ah Su's father," who appeared in a feature article in the journal *Life*, this kind of sympathy and talk about "equality" (*pingdeng*) for the poor actually made their lives worse. Ah Su's father had rented a rickshaw for a day, hoping to make a few coppers to buy something to eat. From morning to night he searched for passengers, but no one would hire him, saying they could not treat him like a draft animal. "The more civilized society becomes," he lamented, "the more difficult it is for poor people to live. . . . I heard people hollering 'universal harmony,' and 'human equality' . . . but I didn't pay any attention. I only called out, who needs a ride? . . . Ai, these dignified words of civilized people are actually telling the poor to commit suicide—if there's nothing to eat, what's equality?"[67]

Early leaders of the Chinese Communist Party were among those who most enthusiastically trumpeted the cause of "equality." For Li Dazhao, Chen Duxiu, and Qu Qiubai, the ideas they had been pondering about the relationship between labor and social progress resonated with one of Marxism's core tenets: the proletariat as the vanguard of the revolution. This convergence reinforced the perceived gulf between "sacred laborers" and the "social parasitism" of the nonworking poor. As the budding Marxists learned to apply the concept of "class analysis" (*jieji fenxi*) to Chinese society, and to imagine a socialist future for the country, they embraced the idea that exploitation of workers would inevitably lead to class struggle (*jieji douzheng*), culminating in the overthrow of capitalism. As one early Communist Party member explained, capitalists "plunder the surplus value of production" that comes from the "blood and sweat of laborers." "As the rich grow richer and the poor get poorer, eventually society divides into two big classes: capitalist and proletariat." With the triumph of socialism, "everyone will work, and all will have food to eat and clothes to wear. Even capitalists will become laborers, and everyone will enjoy freedom (*ziyou*) and obtain equality (*pingdeng*)."[68]

Initially, the nascent CCP concentrated on organizing industrial workers from its base in Shanghai. But by the late 1920s, as the center of revolutionary activity shifted to the countryside, the role of the peasantry became the subject of a heated debate. As is well known, Mao Zedong was one of the most ardent champions of the agrarian strategy. In his "Report from Hunan," Mao identified "poor peasants" (*pinnong*) as the "the vanguard in the overthrow of the forces of feudalism, and the heroes who have performed the great revolutionary task which was left unaccomplished for many years." "Leadership by the poor peasants is absolutely necessary," he declared. "Without the poor peasants there would be no revolution." Mao estimated that "poor peasants" constituted 70 percent of the rural population. Of these, 20 percent were "utterly destitute" (*chipin*): the "completely dispossessed," forced to leave home to become "mercenary soldiers, hired laborers, or wandering beggars."[69] Some of these people, however, belonged to the ranks of the "lumpenproletariat" (*youmin wuchan jieji*, literally, the vagrant propertyless class), who lead "the most precarious existence among human beings." This included peasants who have lost their land, unemployed craftsman, or victims of natural disasters forced to become bandits, beggars, or prostitutes. Numbering more than twenty million people, this group was capable of "fighting bravely," if given the proper guidance. Mao feared, however, that their destructive potential exceeded their revolutionary promise. Such transients were not fixed in the class structure of Chinese society, which rendered them possibly dangerous to the revolutionary cause. In organizing the masses, Mao cautioned, we should take care not to drive the "lumpenproletariat" to the enemy, to become "a force for counter-revolution."[70]

Early Chinese Marxists thus introduced a distinctive vocabulary to describe the problems confronting the nation, of which "poverty" did not register as an independent concept. Instead, in the language of class struggle, "poor" was a measure of the extent of economic inequality, a descriptor attached to a class status. To be sure, the degree of immiseration was important, especially to Mao. In his writings on class, Mao divided the petty bourgeoisie and the semiproletariat into subgroups based on their level of wealth, emphasizing the ability to make ends meet, rather than the standard Marxist evaluation of a group's relationship to the means of production.[71] But ultimately, the "poverty" of "poor peasants" was not a social problem. Rather, it was the product of capitalist exploitation, thus the animating force of a revolutionary storm promising to sweep away past injustices and create a new world of equality.[72]

To Nationalist Party leader Sun Yat-sen, those advocating a Marxist revolution overlooked a fundamental issue in their obsession with the redistribution of wealth. "There is no especially wealthy class, there is only general poverty," Sun declared in 1924. "The 'inequalities between rich and poor' which the people speak of are only differences in the degree of poverty." Although well-intentioned, the "young patriots" who pin their faith on Marxism "fail to realize that China is suffering from poverty, not from the unequal distribution of wealth." To Sun, the bedrock of a state's legitimacy and its most important obligation was to provide for "the people's livelihood" (*minsheng*). Quoting from the ancient classics, he reiterated, "The nation looks upon the people as its foundation; the people look upon food as their heaven." At the same time, Sun emphasized the people's reciprocal responsibility to engage in productive labor: farmers must cultivate food; industrial workers must manufacture tools; "everyone must fulfill their duty." Those who failed to meet these obligations "disqualify themselves as citizens." Elaborating on the conventional wisdom that a country without "vagrants" would be wealthy and strong, he concluded,

> Lazy vagabonds are the vermin (*maozei*) of the nation and the people. The government should force them by law to work to transform them into sacred laborers (*shensheng de laogong*), worthy to share the rights and privileges of citizens. When such vagabonds are eliminated and all people have a share in production, then there will be enough food to eat and clothes to wear for everyone, homes will be comfortable, and the problem of livelihood will be solved.[73]

By invoking the term *maozei* (literally, vermin–thieves) to describe "lazy vagabonds," here Sun draws on two different metaphors. In the first, *mao* are pests that kill plants by eating the roots of seedlings. The "lazy vagabonds," then, are akin to biological organisms destroying the foundation of a young nation—a characterization that naturalizes their pathology and implies extermination as the solution. In the second metaphor, the vagabonds are also *zei*, stealing from the productivity and prosperity of the nation. This depiction criminalizes their behavior, but suggests that they can be reformed or cured through punishment. Through the punitive power of the state ("the government should force them by law to work"), Sun draws these two etiologies together, culminating in a vision of citizenship based on the extraction of labor in the service of the state.

THE BEGGAR PROBLEM

Among the "lazy vagabonds" and "lumpenproletariat," the archetype of the "social parasite" was the street beggar, embodying physical and spiritual disease, literally infested with lice or other vermin. As the most visible manifestation of China's impoverishment, inviting the ridicule of foreigners, "the beggar" became a symbol of national failure and the target of elite anxieties about the nation's deficiency. As Tao Menghe opined, "In our society, or in any city, if there is one more beggar then there is one less person doing something useful.... A beggar is not only a good-for-nothing (*feiwu*) but also a parasitic animal (*jisheng de dongwu*)."[74] Even more vexing was the suspicion that some/many/most beggars were not actually victims of misfortune, but rather "indolent loafers" preying on the public's sympathy. The worst of the lot were the "professionals." According to the *North-China Herald*, "The habitual beggar is a workman.... Most of these old hands make a pretty good living and pity, as well as coppers, is wasted on them."[75] At the same time, however, as a symbol of social displacement, the beggar also invoked feelings of guilt. The same editorial, for instance, went on to say, "We experience a wish that our police force would sweep them off the streets, but where are they to go? They are a nuisance to us because the sight of their misery reproaches us for being well fed and warmly clad."[76] In his 1924 narrative poem "Beggars," Lu Xun conveys a similar ambivalence. Describing a street urchin wandering about begging, the narrator complains, "I despise his voice and attitude. I detest that he does not appear sad, as if this were a child's game. I hate that he chases after me with pitiful cries.... I do not give alms, I do not have a charitable heart. I am above the alms giver, dispensing irritation, suspicion, and loathing." By the end of the poem, however, the reader realizes that the narrator is also a beggar, abjectly poor himself, a metaphor for a nation of beggars. Both despicable and pitiful, beggars inspired a conflicting mixture of emotional responses.[77]

These kinds of reactions deeply troubled sociologists and social commentators. On the one hand, they viewed the public's loathing as indicative of calloused indifference to the suffering of the less fortunate. Tao Menghe, for instance, witnessed passengers tossing out handfuls of coppers just as the train departed the station—for the hilarity of watching mobs of beggars rush for the money, at the peril of getting run over. The spectacle reminded Tao of Dante's *Inferno* and starving ghosts in the Buddhist underworld—a vision of hell on earth. Another writer lamented, "Even as beggars starve, freeze, or die next to them, lots of people stand around, talking and joking as if nothing has happened.... In Europe and America the law protects even animals ... how can we sit idly by and watch our own species sink into such tragic circumstances?"[78]

On the other hand, from the opposite end of the spectrum, overly compassionate responses could lead to *excessive* charity. By one count, more than three hundred different organizations provided services to Beijing's poor in the 1920s, a significant increase from the late Qing.[79] Tang Yueliang described these soup kitchens, orphanages, and foundling homes as well meaning but "antiquated and unscientific," with "a very low standard of efficiency." Tao Menghe explained that while "relief" could temporarily ameliorate the suffering of the poor, it could not eradicate the root causes of their impoverishment. Consequently, in practice charity rewarded dependency, fostered "pauperism," and actually increased the incidence of poverty.[80] Similarly, John Burgess observed that charity "has created a beggar class, has sapped independence of spirit and has fastened on society an increasing load of incompetents and dependents." He noted that whereas an informal study counted fifteen thousand beggars in Beijing in 1921, three years later the number had grown due to the expansion of relief services: "[T]he whole system of doles is apparently pauperizing the people of the city." On this particular point, Burgess frequently cited

Franklin Giddings, his professor at Columbia, who wrote in *The Principles of Sociology*, "All modern experience of poor relief is an overwhelming demonstration that any community can have all the pauperism and criminality that it cares to pay for."[81]

ON THE STREETS OF BEIJING

Were there, in fact, ever more beggars in Beijing? Did the provision of relief actually increase, rather than decrease, the number of mendicants? What effects did these perceptions have on relief efforts and the policing of urban transients? In the first instance, the civil wars and serial natural disasters of the early Republic brought refugees and transients to Beijing in large numbers. The prospect of finding relief or employment drew them there, just as seasonal migrants and famine victims had sought aid and refuge in the capital during the imperial era.[82] But in the early Republic, the rural poor congregating in and around Beijing became more of a permanent presence than ever before. Instead of dispersing and returning home at the end of winter or when famine conditions eased, more of them stayed. In the second instance, it was one thing to say that the needy went to the city to seek aid, and another to suggest that the very provision of aid increased the incidence of mendicancy. This "pauperization" argument was a constantly asserted but never proven refrain. Finally, as the following discussion will illustrate, the perceptions—of increasing tides of urban transients, dangerously mobile, presumably indolent, creating social disorder—were not confined to May Fourth journals and sociology classrooms. On the streets of Beijing, where policing and relief practices intertwined, these anxieties at times translated into punitive actions.

To deal with the problem of transients, in 1916, the Beiyang central government renewed the Qing dynasty's 1907 antivagrancy law (discussed in chapter 1), duplicating the entire provision verbatim.[83] The law provided for a maximum detention of fifteen days for "vagrants," loiterers, and other suspicious people. Other regulations, however, in effect made it possible to incarcerate them for a much longer period of time. For example, the Vagrant Workhouse Regulations, also promulgated in 1916, stipulated that juvenile vagrants and delinquents who were "poor, suffering, and without support" or "have bad character and conduct" would be "taken in" to serve a term of three to four years.[84] These criteria reflected a mixture of charity and coercion, meting out equal punishment to those who had apparently committed no offense, as well as people of "bad character" who violated an implicit code of behavior.

The enforcement of the antivagrancy law depended largely on local police to identify and capture violators, and on sufficient institutional capacity to hold them in detention. As foreign affairs adviser Wu Zongliang observed in a proposal to President Yuan Shikai, Beijing's police had successfully cleared beggars from the main thoroughfares and put them to work as water carriers. In the alleyways and backstreets, however, many "poor women" (*pinfu*) and their children still loitered about, asking for alms. "When I visited Britain, France, and Germany, I saw no beggars on the streets," Wu wrote. Citing the European example, he proposed that "workhouses for women and children" be established. Although they deserved pity and compassion, Wu believed that "children who grow up begging with their mothers ... will undoubtedly become bandits"; settling them in workhouses would enable them to become "good citizens."[85] Another commentator, writing in the journal *People's Rights*, complained of able-bodied young men and women wandering the streets, singing for their supper. To ameliorate the problem, he proposed a national system of "vagrant workhouses," in order to "convert unemployment into employment, and transform consumers into producers."[86]

No such national network of workhouses was created, but in early Republican Beijing an ad hoc assortment of institutions functioned as an adjunct to the penal system, in the shadow of the courts and the prisons. Initially, the Metropolitan Police took over a number of poorhouses and workhouses that had been established in the final years of the Qing dynasty. The Interior Ministry later assumed responsibility for some; others remained under private management, relying to varying degrees on government sources for funding. Although ostensibly governed by law, both the policing and incarceration of urban transients depended on the discretionary authority of the police and local officials.[87] As the following discussion will underscore, a person picked up on the streets could be sent to any number of poorhouses, workhouses, or orphanages. Regulations varied widely between these different institutions and over time; incarceration criteria were inconsistently enforced; disciplinary institutions sometimes served charitable purposes, and vice versa. Whether inmates received enough food, adequate medical care, education, and/or job training reflected the fluctuating fortunes of Beijing's revolving door of governments and officials. In their operations, many of these institutions relied on the police and other government agencies: to supplement private sources of funding, investigate claims of hardship, deal with recalcitrant inmates, or track down runaways. In turn, the police depended on them to provide shelter for and custodial supervision of homeless transients.

In particular, the Metropolitan Police often deposited boys picked up from the streets at the Longquan Orphanage. Established in 1906 and affiliated with a Buddhist temple of the same name, Longquan accepted only boys between six and twelve *sui*, who attended primary school and worked part-time learning a variety of trades. The orphanage, a private charity supervised by the temple's monks, had strong ties to the Beiyang government. In the early Republic, it received monthly subsidies from the police, the Education Bureau, and the

Ministry of Revenue, and cooperated closely with the metropolitan authorities.[88] When the police picked up lost or abandoned children on the streets, they often sent the boys to Longquan if no one claimed them.

One such example was Ji Shuanzi, seven *sui*, a Manchu of the former Blue Banner. On June 26, 1915, Constable Ma found the boy wandering around the East City (near Dong Sipailou), wearing only a pair of tattered blue trousers. Ji told the policeman that he had lost sight of his mother while they were out begging, and so Ma escorted him around, asking if anyone had seen his mother or recognized him. When no leads turned up, the police sent him to Longquan Orphanage and advertised his photo in the newspaper, in the hope that someone would come forward to claim him. On the other hand, Wang Daoyu (nine *sui*) had run away from his home in Tangshan after his mother committed suicide. His father soon left to look for work; when the boy returned there was no one to look after him. After begging for some time, he met a monk who brought him to Longquan Orphanage. One night, in September 1915, the police found Wang crying on the street. When the authorities tried to return him to the orphanage, the boy refused, saying that he had been mistreated. The monks, however, denied the allegation and maintained that Wang had run away more than ten times in the past year. Wang Daoyu and Ji Shuanzi were two among countless children found adrift in Beijing during the early Republic. They turn up in the police archives and press reports with startling frequency, underscoring the desperation of broken families. In its first twenty years of operation, the Longquan Orphanage provided refuge to over three thousand such boys.[89]

For girls in similar circumstances, there were some coeducational orphanages and single-sex industrial schools. Many of them entered the custody of the state or a private charity as a result of abduction. Dong Xiaogai and Ma Xiaoshun, for instance, were two girls rescued from their kidnapper, Mrs. Zhao née Li. After Mrs. Zhao's arrest in June 1914, the authorities could not track down the girls' parents. Saying that they were from "good families" and should not be sent to the home for prostitutes, the police instead arranged for them to enter the Ganshiqiao Home for Poor Children (Ganshiqiao Pin'eryuan).[90] In other cases, when adopted daughters or child servants ran away and refused to return, claiming abuse, the police also arranged for them to enter one of these institutions.[91]

AT THE POORHOUSE

Alternatively, the Inner City Poorhouse was another possible asylum, for children and adults, homeless or otherwise. Originally established in 1908 for the elderly, young, and disabled, over time it evolved into a multipurpose institution. There was a division for the "psychologically insane" and a home for former prostitutes, called the Jiliangsuo (modeled on Shanghai's well-known Protestant Door of Hope mission).[92] In accordance with its initial charter, the Poorhouse provided shelter to those who voluntarily entered; Beijing police also used it to serve disciplinary purposes. The extant records are fragmentary, drawing primarily from police files with a strong bias toward the punitive. As a result, we know little about the volunteers and much more about those who interacted with the authorities in the context of punishment. For instance, an incomplete roster, taken from police records in the mid-1910s, featured ex-convicts considered insufficiently penitent and remanded for further detention; numerous petty thieves; kidnapping victims as well as perpetrators; and an assortment of people regarded as "crazy." These mentally ill inmates, including some so disoriented that they did not know their own names, frequently posed problems for the authorities: causing disturbances in the middle of the night; running away; and in a few instances, attempting suicide.[93]

Troubling as they were, these incidents paled in comparison to a scandal that unfolded in the winter of 1914. On the night of November 27, during a drunken brawl, four clerks inadvertently shouted out that other staff members were involved in instances of improper conduct. The next morning, a supervisor (who had witnessed the commotion) questioned the four men, to find out whether there was any truth to their intoxicated allegations.[94] The investigation that ensued turned up a missing girl: Liu Dajuzi, seventeen *sui*, who had been living at the Poorhouse with her mother and younger sister for several years. Her father was a rickshaw puller with a gambling habit; unable to support the family, he had sent his wife and two daughters to the Poorhouse. When Dajuzi vanished, she had been visiting her maternal grandfather and aunt, who lived nearby. When she did not return as expected, a quarrel erupted between her mother and another resident, Mrs. Ying née Chang. The fight between the two women centered on Dajuzi's disappearance. Mrs. Liu claimed that Mrs. Ying had conspired (with unnamed persons) to abduct and sell her daughter into prostitution. For her part, Mrs. Ying said that Mrs. Liu was trying to frame her, as revenge for an earlier refusal to lend her money.

As it turns out, Mrs. Liu needed the money to buy pills to induce an abortion, for she was four months pregnant. The putative father was Ding Xiang, a guard who had been sneaking at night into her room, which she shared with her daughters and several others. Upon questioning, one of these roommates revealed that Ding Xiang had also seduced Dajuzi, taking advantage of her mother's absence. When Mrs. Liu discovered her lover's treachery, a confrontation followed, with hysterical recriminations. Several days later, Dajuzi left the Poorhouse to visit her relatives and never returned, apparently taking her aunt's jewelry with her.

During the investigation, no one would admit to any foul play involving the missing girl. Ding Xiang confessed to the affairs with both mother and daughter, but denied any knowledge of Dajuzi's disappearance. For his offense, he was fired and sentenced to six months in the Outer City Reformatory.[95] The police procurator probed the accusation against Mrs. Ying, but she steadfastly maintained her innocence. After spending about ten days in police custody, she fell ill. Unable to obtain proof or a confession, the authorities dismissed the charges and sent Mrs. Ying back to the Poorhouse for medical treatment. They expelled Mrs. Liu and her younger daughter from the Poorhouse. Dajuzi was never heard from again.

But had someone—her mother, lover, or Mrs. Ying (and other coconspirators)—sold Dajuzi out of jealousy or for profit? Or did she run away, absconding with her aunt's jewelry? The authorities contemplated all of these possibilities, but they found insufficient evidence to prosecute anyone. The case was perplexing for its uncertain outcome, but revealing for its disclosure of institutional disarray: staff members drinking and brawling on the job; sexual improprieties; a pregnancy; a missing girl. Two years later, with these and other problems with "crazy" women apparently escalating, the Interior Ministry decided to reorganize the Poorhouse, creating a "factory workshop," a separate mental asylum, and a division for former prostitutes. Later, a "women's reformatory," for those warranting harsher punishment, was also added.[96]

Who Are the "Vagrants"?

As the case of Dajuzi's disappearance indicates, women living in institutions presented numerous problems for Beijing's municipal authorities. There were lurid scandals over fraudulent marriages and controversies over custody of young girls, with the shadowy market for women in the backdrop.[97] But out on the streets, it was men—specifically, mobile men identified as "vagrants" (*youmin*)—who posed the most menacing threat. As discussed in chapter 1, the emerging discourse of "poverty" in the first decade of the twentieth century often featured "vagrants" as one category of people contributing to the problem. In the early Republic, we find "vagrancy" increasingly invoked as an expansive metaphor for the ills afflicting China. Journalist Huang Yuansheng, for instance, lamented that, infected by the "poison" of several thousand years of dynastic rule, China had become "a nation of vagrants."[98] In his analysis of the problem, educator Song Mingzhi charted the process by which "the unemployed" (*shiyezhe*) become "poor people" (*pinmin*): within a year of losing his job, "the laborer becomes a vagrant." Song was sympathetic to the jobless and actually reserved his harshest censure for "the rich who roam about"—they were the "true vagrants," the "vermin upon the nation," and the "parasites" requiring extermination.[99] From a different perspective, CCP leader Chen Duxiu identified "unemployed vagrants" as one of the chief forces sustaining warlordism: they become mercenaries in order to survive, committing "evil acts" on behalf of their paymasters. Chen worried that the proliferation of "unemployed vagrants" would augment the power of regional militarists by providing them with "unlimited capital."[100]

The notion of "vagrancy" was thus imbued with multiple meanings of political and social chaos. As a matter of local policing, it was an amorphously defined, selectively enforced, and harshly punished offense in Beijing. Scattered arrest records in the police files from the early Republic indicate that the municipal authorities considered "vagrancy" to be primarily a masculine crime of mobility and insubordination.[101] The most common offenders were suspected thieves or other petty troublemakers who refused to confess, unemployed and/or homeless men who loitered about in a group (the proverbial "gang of three to five"), and discharged soldiers who refused to return home as instructed. Many were recent arrivals in the capital, lacking the crucial community ties that could mitigate the charge of vagrancy. Locals, however, were not exempt. Secondarily, there were those (mostly, though not exclusively, men) whose behavior marked them as perched on the verge of criminality. That is, they had *not yet* committed a criminal act—but the authorities believed that without intervention, they would "surely" or "inevitably" fall off the precipice into a sea of vice.[102] In early Republican Beijing, the combination of homelessness, suspected criminality, and perceived masculine social danger typified "the vagrant."

In one case from 1914, for instance, shopkeepers from Dong'anmen and Dengshikou (in the eastern part of the city) registered complaints about "vagrants" harassing and stealing from them. The police sent to investigate swept the area and arrested eighteen homeless men, ranging in age from fourteen to seventy *sui*: one recent arrival from Manchuria, four former Bannermen registered in Beijing, the rest from nearby counties in Zhili province. Although there was no proof that these men had committed any crimes, the police suspected that they were mixed up with a notorious gang operating in the neighborhood. Of the "vagrants" apprehended, local precinct captain Sun Bingzhang identified seventeen of them as "beggars." He sent them to the Inner City Poorhouse, ostensibly for "shelter," but clearly as a preventive measure to avert future criminal acts. The last person, Xing Lian (a Manchu from the former Red Banner, twenty-seven *sui*), was remanded for further investigation. The captain noted that Xing "does not have proper employment and resembles a beggar, but his lifestyle seems better than ordinary beggars." Despite the lack of concrete evidence, Sun considered it highly probable that Xing had committed some crime.[103] The following year, in July 1915, the Interior Ministry announced that "vagrants and discharged soldiers" were to be repatriated back to their native place, or detained under the provisions of the Police Ordinances. In the aftermath of successive warlord campaigns, increasingly alarming reports alluded to countless ex-soldiers wandering around the country. The directive instructed localities that have "workhouses" or "factories for the poor" to "settle them there," noting that "when vagrants stay a long time in a strange place, impoverished and homeless, they inevitably degenerate into bandits and robbers."[104]

Occasionally, other kinds of "vagrants" surfaced in police records: squatters who "forcibly" occupied property and refused to vacate when ordered to do so; the "dissolute sons" of formerly well-off families; pettifoggers loitering in the teahouses near the Supreme Court. In the case of the pettifoggers, the police described them as fomenting trouble by "roping people into lawsuits." They disguised their identities, in violation of rules governing lawsuits. In short, "these are unemployed vagrants who are neither professional lawyers nor legitimate representatives of the plaintiffs."[105]

As we have seen, whereas "beggars" could inspire compassion or loathing, charitable or punitive treatment, a "vagrant" was considered unequivocally wicked and criminally inclined. But from an institutional perspective, these semantic differences and the sliding scales of charity and punishment proved difficult to enforce. At the Outer City Reformatory, for instance, there were large numbers of drug addicts, unrepentant "vagrants," and offenders such as Ding Xiang, the promiscuous guard from the Inner City Poorhouse. They lived with people like Duan Jinxiang (thirty-five *sui*, a "beggar") and Wang Fumao (twenty-eight *sui*, a "poor person"), both serving "unlimited sentences."[106] Ironically, inmates accused of specific crimes—such as Ding Xiang—were given fixed and relatively short terms of punishment, typically six months. In contrast, a "beggar" or a "poor person" could be detained indefinitely in the same institution, in the guise of compassionate custody.

Likewise, Beijing's Vagrant Workhouse was not reserved for "vagrants." There was an assortment of suspected thieves and "disobedient sons," but there was also Guo Hetang, the orphan first described in the Introduction, picked up by a constable from an alleyway in the winter of 1922. The police could not track down Guo's only remaining relative (his uncle last seen leaving his hometown to look for work); at thirteen *sui* he exceeded the age limit (twelve *sui*) for entering most orphanages. The police therefore sent Guo to the Vagrant Workhouse to learn a "suitable craft," so that he would no longer "wander about destitute." The paper trail ends there, and the boy's later fate is unknown to us. We do know, however, that the Vagrant Workhouse was a revival of the former Capital Workhouse established in 1905 (discussed in chapter 1). In general, the Workhouse made no special provisions for sympathetic, as opposed to punitive, treatment of orphaned children. Unless his uncle came forward to claim him, Guo Hetang probably stayed for four years, the standard term of detention.[107] In that time, he would have spent eighteen hours a week learning to read and do simple sums, and the remaining time working in one of fifteen different workshops, perhaps sewing, making soap, or operating the printing presses. In 1912, the Workhouse reported a small profit from its sale of inmate products, and even paid nominal wages to exemplary workers.[108]

Figure 2.1. Capital Vagrant Workhouse ca. 1927

But by the time Guo Hetang entered a decade later in 1922, the institution was sliding into financial insolvency. There were about five hundred people in custody, and responsibility for the institution had passed back and forth between the Interior Ministry and the Metropolitan Police several times. In 1920, the director was arrested on charges of embezzling money and food rations intended for the inmates. While the procurator's office investigated, a process that took several months, conditions at the Workhouse deteriorated.[109] In the meantime, a brief but intensely fought war between regional militarists in the summer of 1920 brought down the reigning warlord government in Beijing, followed by a major banking crisis.[110] By the time a permanent replacement was appointed to the Workhouse, the institution was in disarray. New director Qi Yaolai found that allocations of food and money from the government soon trickled to a stop. To make ends meet, Qi mortgaged the workshop equipment, but even so the Workhouse owed over Ch. $30,000 to its creditors. From February to November 1922, he sold off old clothing and blankets in order to feed the inmates. In 1923, Qi wrote in a memo to his superiors at the Interior Ministry, "The debt collectors come one after another to the door ... if we do not raise money quickly there is really no solution for this matter of great urgency [literally, as pressing as fire searing one's eyebrows]." A year later, the government explored the possibility of converting the Workhouse into an "officially supervised and merchant operated" enterprise (*guandu shangban*), but could not find anyone interested in the project. The debts were mounting, the inmates were hungry, and orders for products could not be filled because they had no supplies. "To speak of teaching and training the vagrants," Qi wrote, "the name remains but the reality is dead."[111]

"MORE THAN THEORIZE"

The Vagrant Workhouse was not the only institution in Beijing to disintegrate into insolvency. Other poorhouses, orphanages, and foundling homes also found themselves in similar predicaments, caught in the administrative vacuum of regime changes precipitated by struggles among warlords for control of the capital. Some privately run institutions saw their benefactors sacked, and either scaled back their operations or closed their doors. Even the well-connected Longquan Orphanage was mired in funding problems, and plagued by allegations of misconduct ranging from financial improprieties to child trafficking.[112] At the same time, natural disasters and escalating military conflicts displaced innumerable people from their homes in the countryside, bringing more needy supplicants to the capital.

To meet the growing demand, new charities were established, including several of Beijing's most well known. Former premier Xiong Xiling founded Xiangshan Children's Home on the site of an imperial hunting park. Xiangshan quickly achieved fame, in part due to its founder's prominence, as an exemplary institution combining academic education and vocational training. While some children left the Home when they completed primary school and learned a basic craft, others went on to middle and high school. In the mid-1920s Xiangshan began to support their graduates who were admitted to university; some of the brightest students attended Beida, Qinghua, and Yanjing.[113] Another notable charity was the World Red Swastika Society, affiliated with Daoyuan, a religious sect that blended Buddhist, Daoist, and Christian practices. Through an extensive membership network reaching many cities, the Red Swastika Society raised money for relief work.[114]

In this time of political disarray and deepening social instability, foreign missionaries found fertile terrain for their charitable work. The Salvation Army, newly arrived in China in 1916, quickly built a significant presence in cities throughout the north. Commissioner Francis Pearce won the crucial patronage of Zhao Erxun (the former Qing official and early workhouse advocate, discussed in chapter 1), who helped the group establish its credibility and a network of donors.[115] By the early 1920s, the Army had become one of the largest providers of winter aid in the capital, blending its distinctive proselytizing style (military bands, parades, open-air meetings) with traditional relief methods. Furthermore, the Salvationists introduced an important new concept to the practice of charity in China: the compulsory "beggar colony."

The beggar colony was an adaptation of founder William Booth's vision of forming "self-helping and self-sustaining communities" for the unemployed. In his book *In Darkest England* (1890), General Booth had outlined a scheme for a network of labor colonies—in the city, the provinces, and overseas—"drawing into its embrace the depraved and destitute of all classes . . . on the simple conditions of their being willing to work and to conform to discipline."[116] As the General's foot soldiers brought the message of salvation to countries around the world, the tripartite organization of the labor colonies was truncated into a single "beggar colony" or "beggar home," with the goal of "ridding a nation of its drones, making workable material out of the flotsam and jetsam." And in some cases, compulsory detention and labor replaced the voluntary premise of Booth's original plan.[117]

In the early twentieth century, Colombo became the Salvation Army's crowning achievement in this realm. In the nineteenth century, the British colonial authorities in Ceylon had repeatedly introduced antivagrancy ordinances, but to no avail. In 1907, a new amendment banned all forms of begging, and subjected offenders to deportation (to India) or compulsory segregation and labor in "houses of detention." In 1912, the colonial government asked the Salvation Army to take charge of Colombo's detention center located on the site of a former prison, renamed the "Home for Vagrants." According to Commissioner Frederick Booth Tucker, the combination of vigorous law enforcement to control the "beggar population" and sufficient institutional capacity for custodial detention was crucial—without one or the other, the law was "practically a dead letter."[118]

In China, when Salvationist Commissioner Francis Pearce suggested the "Colombo" arrangement for Beijing, he emphasized that its efficacy depended on the marriage of comprehensive enforcement and compulsory detention. As we have seen, the capital had many poorhouses and workhouses, and the police could exercise arbitrary powers of detention. But the law had not proscribed all forms of begging, and there were not enough institutions to detain all of the people on the streets. Pearce's proposal to the Interior Ministry gained no support from a government in turmoil. But the Salvation Army's touted success in Colombo attracted the attention of social reformers in Beijing, who hoped to emulate the organization's direct influence on policy. Thus "Colombo" became a short-hand referent for an ideal approach to poor relief—according to John Burgess, "the example of what can be done by an efficient municipal government." Although he had never been to Ceylon, Burgess asserted with confidence that due to the cooperation between the Salvation Army and the government, the colony, "[p]reviously crowded with beggars, now not one is to be seen."[119] To sociologist Tang Yueliang, the Colombo model was "worthy of a trial." Underscoring the importance of conferring legal power to remove mendicants from the streets by force, Tang noted that "[n]o matter how many industrial or Beggar homes are established, so long as begging is not made illegal, the professionals will continue to beg."[120] As we shall see, the "Colombo" approach would become an important model for the provision of poor relief and the policing of homelessness in the years to come.

In the meantime, in a chaotic political landscape, Beijing's government relied on private and/or religious organizations to provide poor relief. In 1922, the Interior Ministry turned over the distribution of winter aid to the Peking Dependents' Relief Society, run by Liu Xilian of the YMCA, whom John Burgess considered his "right hand man."[121] Rather than open soup kitchens and food depots, Liu opted to establish two poorhouses, limiting eligibility to boys under fourteen, men over fifty-five, and women and girls of all ages. Several hundred notices posted at major thoroughfares exhorted "the extremely poor of Beijing, the elderly, feeble and disabled, to come quickly to register." At twenty-two designated locations (schools, churches, YMCA offices), supplicants could apply for aid with the endorsement of their local police precinct and by furnishing the name of a guarantor. According to Burgess, who served on the Society's board, this effort marked "a small beginning . . . in the direction of more scientific relief of the poor." In contradistinction to existing poorhouses, which Burgess characterized as no better than prisons, the Society's shelters promised to provide both physical nourishment and spiritual uplift. To select the "really poor" and prevent fraudulent claims, investigators verified the information provided by the applicants. This process of voluntary recruitment, however, proved more difficult than the administrators anticipated. Against a projection of 5,000, they could only find 2,084 people for the two poorhouses.[122]

The following winter, the Peking Dependents' Relief Society disbanded in favor of the Metropolitan Welfare Association, a consortium of private charities, with Liu Xilian again serving as executive secretary. The Association had been originally established in anticipation of intensified hostilities between warring factions for control of the capital. When warlord Wu Peifu's decisive victory in the summer of 1922 obviated the immediate need, the Association decided to reorganize as an agency for local poor relief.[123] As with the Peking Dependents' Relief Society, Liu Xilian and other like-minded participants saw an opportunity to introduce a more "scientific" mode of charity, in this instance through the casework method of interviewing relief applicants to verify need. But some association members, favoring traditional soup kitchens, refused to participate. When Liu persuaded Manchurian warlord Zhang Zuolin to send two hundred tons of relief grain to the capital, he gained leverage in the debate, by allotting supplies only to groups "willing to use the newer methods of relief."[124] Liu's approach entailed conducting household interviews by going door-to-door, a much more labor-intensive process than operating soup kitchens or using existing police censuses. To do the work, Liu tapped the YMCA's community service groups, staffed by eager students he had earlier trained in sociological principles and methods.[125]

Both the Peking Dependents' Relief Society and the Metropolitan Welfare Association garnered the endorsement of government officials and drew the (sometimes reluctant) participation of Beijing's most prominent Chinese charities. Through these patronage networks and consortiums, missionaries and sociologists formed close working relationships with local philanthropists and officials. In addition to leading Yanjing University's sociology department, John Burgess served on the board of several Chinese-run orphanages and poorhouses. Liu Xilian convinced warlords to contribute generously to his relief projects; the YMCA's community service groups forged cooperative relationships with local police.[126] As a result of this nexus of connections among local officials, militarists, sociologists, charities, and churches, assumptions about the "pauperizing" effects of indiscriminate relief and the need for more "scientific" methods filtered into relief practices. As John Burgess told supporters back in Princeton, "Following a comprehensive plan of Community Service for the whole city, we are doing more than theorize. Based on scientific data . . . we are giving a practical workable demonstration of the principles of a Christian social order."[127]

The devastating famine that afflicted north China in the early 1920s provided an unexpected opportunity to demonstrate the efficacy of these principles and implement them on a large scale. To alleviate the suffering of an estimated twenty million people in five provinces, Chinese and foreign organizations formed a coordinating group that eventually became the China International Famine Relief Commission (CIFRC).[128] Liu Xilian became the executive secretary of the Beijing chapter, and other Yanjing-YMCA affiliates also took prominent leadership positions. For the next twenty years, CIFRC became one of the most important relief agencies in China, and through its extensive operations put into practice the principles of self-help and self-sufficiency. For instance, Walter Mallory, the group's chief administrator in the mid-1920s, felt that the Chinese custom of giving handouts to famine victims supported them "in idleness," with the effect of lowering their morale and forcing "self-respecting country folk into the pauper class." Work relief, on the other hand, functioned as an "automatic check": by intentionally keeping wages below the normal scale (or at the level of a subsistence ration), only the truly needy would apply for relief, and the "professional mendicants" would stay away. Meanwhile, J. E. Baker of the American Red Cross (a founding member of CIFRC) urged that "those receiving aid should earn it in some fashion. The number of permanent paupers growing out of refugee camps is a constant reminder of the necessity of maintaining the self respect and self reliance of calamity victims."[129]

Mallory, Baker, and their associates were fully confident that by dictating the terms on which relief was distributed, they could vastly improve traditional charitable practices, for the benefit of aid recipients: "Quite apart from the usefulness of this work in itself, its greatest benefit is the lesson taught."[130] An estimated 7.7 million people "learned" this lesson in 1920–21, and many more in the ensuing two decades as the CIFRC continued its work. The principle of work relief that the organization advocated was, of course, not new to China. As discussed in the Introduction, "substituting work for relief" had long precedents in imperial history. But in the 1920s, aid administrators' assumptions about "pauperism" were cast in the language of social science, invoking the twin gospels of self-help and efficiency. And over the next decade, as sociology evolved from drawing a handful of students to a mandatory course for university students, and as Yanjing faculty and graduates rose to positions of influence in the Nationalist government, sociological thinking about "poverty" would permeate relief institutions and practices, and become increasingly intertwined with punishment and compulsory labor.

In the Treaty Port

If the above discussion of Beijing has emphasized the role of sociologists and missionaries in forging new assumptions about and methods of poor relief, to the south it was Shanghai's treaty port status that most forcefully shaped the discursive and physical landscape of life for its most impoverished residents. As we saw in chapter 1, the foreign concession authorities tried to police vagrancy by keeping "undesirables" out of their jurisdictions, deporting them to the Chinese district whenever possible. After the fall of the Qing dynasty, Shanghai and the nearby arsenal became coveted prizes in the battle between warlords seeking control of the strategic lower Yangzi valley. In the aftermath of the "Second Revolution" of 1913, President Yuan Shikai dismissed the national parliament and abolished local self-government, forcing the Chinese City Council to disband. For the next decade, Shanghai's Chinese districts remained under military rule, with municipal functions divided among local boards and the military police.[131] In the shadow of warring factions, traditional charities like native place associations (*huiguan, gongsuo*) and their modern cousins (*tongxianghui*) took on increasing responsibilities for a broad range of social, economic, and even judicial functions.[132] A new Charity Federation (Cishantuan), originally established by the City Council, sought to "unify" and improve charitable practices, bringing under its supervision the city's oldest and most prominent benevolent halls.[133] In particular, Federation leaders concluded that the Hall for Preserving Chastity (Qingjietang) was outdated, its aims "no longer essential to charitable work." Instead, the institution could benefit society much more as a "women's workshop."[134]

Meanwhile, in a period of political fragmentation, the population of Shanghai doubled, from an estimated 1.3 million in 1910 to 2.6 million in 1927.[135] The expansion of commerce and development of light industry drew streams of migrants who contributed to a vibrant urban culture, while cyclical influxes of disaster victims and war refugees added to a growing sense of social disorder. Gang-related violence and criminal syndicates accounted for much of the city's reputation for crime, but local news reports also frequently portrayed impoverished transients as threats to law and order, as well as indicators of widespread social disintegration: "rascal vagrants" harassing shopkeepers; "poor people" using famine as the pretext to "extort alms by force"; unemployed workers loitering about; beggars stalking passersby for handouts.[136] One commentator noted that "vagrancy" manifested itself in many forms: "[T]hese seeds of decay have spread throughout society, as numerous and as quickly as skin ulcers." If disregarded as inconsequential, like common skin ailments, vagrants can rapidly sap society's "vitality" and attack the "center," becoming an incurable disease.[137] According to an editorial in *Shenbao*, ragged street urchins and filthy beggars could be found everywhere in China, from large metropolises and famous scenic spots to small towns: "This is detrimental to the nation's civilization, the city's order and public hygiene, as well as the dignity of the Chinese race." The editorialist opined that those unable to work should be placed in charitable organizations, while "able-bodied unemployed vagrants who beg for a living" should be compelled to labor in workhouses. The expenses, while significant, would be offset by the reduction of "unproductive elements," the "countless number of people who sit idly and eat."[138]

As in Beijing, efforts to promote labor productivity in Shanghai relied on the marriage of philanthropic and government resources. In 1912, local leaders persuaded the provincial government to fund the construction of the Poor People's Workhouse (Pinmin Xiyisuo), Shanghai's first such institution. The completed structure, a fan-shaped, quasi-Panopticon layout with accommodations for five hundred people, finally brought to fruition plans initially drafted in 1906 for a Hall of Diligence (discussed in chapter 1). But soon the City Council found that it lacked the resources to fund the operations. After an unsuccessful petition to the provincial government for additional money, the Council decided to appropriate the proceeds from the "beggar tax" for the workhouse. Essentially a ransom shopkeepers paid to local beggar chiefs to keep mendicants away from their establishments, this form of extortion had long been a feature of the culture of begging.[139] In one of its final acts before disbanding by Yuan Shikai's fiat, the City Council abolished the beggar tax, calling it "an old and ugly practice." Instead, the shopkeepers would now pay an equivalent sum to the Charity Federation as a "charity tax," with the money allocated to the Poor People's Workhouse for operational expenses.[140]

The Charity Federation also helped to build a multipurpose relief institution called the New Hall for Universal Cultivation (Xin Puyutang). The original Puyutang had been built in 1867, as part of a wave of philanthropic activity during the post-Taiping reconstruction period. When the Republican revolution terminated the flow of donations from imperial officials, its primary source of funding, the hall fell into disrepair. The revamped institution, located on a large plot of land formerly used as indigent burial grounds, expanded the size and scope of its predecessor, becoming one of the largest indoor relief institutions in Shanghai. There were accommodations for 1,500 people, with a staff of twelve Catholic nuns in charge of new facilities for drug addicts, critically ill patients, and psychologically troubled residents. The county magistrate also instructed the police to bring "disabled beggars" they encountered on the streets to the New Hall, to rid the city of the unsightly spectacle of disfigured mendicants, and to search the "the old haunts" of those known to maim children in order to elicit sympathy and alms.[141]

Indigents, Native and Foreign

In the International Settlement, the plight of children became one exception to the Municipal Council's longstanding refusal to sponsor charity. The alarming number of young beggars—variously described as victims of begging rackets or willing participants in criminal pursuits—compelled officials to ask the Door of Hope mission to extend its work to taking in homeless children. The missionaries did so reluctantly, wary about altering their focus on rescuing prostitutes. But in exchange for continued support of the rescue work and a separate generous grant, in 1912 they agreed to open a "Home for Waifs and

Strays," for the (mostly Chinese) children picked up by the Settlement Police. A few years later, when two other institutions volunteered to take on the task under similar financial arrangements, the Door of Hope gladly relinquished this responsibility.[142]

The administrators of the International Settlement were willing to subsidize the care of "stray children," but they persistently rebuffed calls from both foreign and Chinese residents to contribute more broadly to poor relief. The Municipal Council did provide "grants-in-aid" to hospitals, schools, and organizations like the Door of Hope, but insisted that these served the Settlement's educational and public health needs, and could not be considered "casual relief." In 1912, the Council approved the creation of a small "casual ward" for foreign men, which provided food and lodging on a voluntary basis, to "beachcombers and the like," in exchange for work performed (chopping wood and breaking stones). But the experiment was deemed a failure, for although there was room to accommodate twelve people, there were rarely more than four or five men at any given time in the work shelter. Worst of all, officials found that instead of searching for gainful employment during the day, "these men carry on their begging," often returning at night in a state of intoxication.[143]

Then, in a departure from existing policy, in 1914 the ratepayers approved a grant of 3,600 *taels* to create a Charity Organisation Committee (COC), charged with coordinating relief work, and also to aid Eurasian families without recourse to nationally based charities. The money was earmarked for administrative expenses, with the understanding that actual relief funds would be collected from other sources.[144] Two years later, the COC's request for a fourfold increase in funding (to 15,000 *taels*) ignited a controversy. The significantly larger sum was needed to help growing numbers of indigent foreigners in Shanghai, attributed to the effects of the war in Europe. At the annual ratepayers meeting, where the measure was put forward for a vote, Reverend A. J. Walker spoke in support, saying, "I entirely fail to understand why . . . we can take care of a Eurasian boy of eight years and when he gets to eighty and is wandering about the streets it is impossible to help him." In rebuttal, Dr. H. C. Patrick made a lengthy speech denouncing poor relief as an "unscientific method." "There is a considerable difference between poverty which the Bible says we have always with us," he proclaimed, "and the pauperism which is created by the Poor Law. . . . [N]o matter what the restrictions are—no matter what institutions you erect, you will never put a stop to the growth and development of this fungus of modern life—pauperism." Most problematic of all, Dr. Patrick worried that once "you start a Poor Law for the foreigner you will be compelled to start it for the Chinese."[145]

Indeed, to those concerned about creating such a precedent, the Charity Organisation's work increasingly resembled that of the English Poor Law guardians—a disparaging comparison. By seeking to expand the COC's mandate and budget, its supporters inadvertently invited scrutiny of taxpayer-funded poor relief. To resolve the issue once and for all, the Council convened a special committee to render a judgment, one that the ratepayers agreed would become the governing standard. But the outcome was hardly a surprise, as the Council Chairman stacked the group with those hostile to the proposal.

After six weeks of deliberations, the Municipal Charity Committee concluded that "as a matter of principle" the COC's request ought to be denied. Specifically, the Land Regulations did not authorize the collection of taxes to pay for poor relief, and the Municipal Council had "no legal responsibility to maintain or assist paupers." By the logic of extraterritoriality, emigrants to Shanghai enjoy the benefits of the laws of their own countries, and should appeal to their own consular representatives for aid if in need. Whereas a state could compel its citizens to work in exchange for relief, the committee report declared, "a municipality in a treaty port" could not do so. Under the circumstances, providing relief without demanding labor in return could only have a "deteriorating effect on the character of the recipient." Finally, as a practical matter, in a city with multiple jurisdictions, to "provide maintenance for paupers" in one area while other areas declined to do so would result in all of them flocking to the International Settlement. The Committee granted that the number of foreign paupers was small; that the proposed the sum of fifteen thousand *taels* represented a trivial tax burden (less than half of 1 percent of the Council's annual expenditures); and that the majority of supplicants were ill or elderly, thus "quite incapable of work of any description." Nonetheless, citing England's unhappy experience with its Poor Laws as a cautionary tale, the Committee decided that a program of tax-funded poor relief would "aggravate rather than alleviate pauperism here."[146] A brief dissenting opinion, from one member affiliated with the Charity Organisation, contested the assumptions and conclusions of the majority report, but to no avail. The decision effectively tabled the issue, and in the years to come, the Municipal Council would repeatedly cite this verdict as justification for refusing requests to sponsor poor relief.

Bitter feelings lingered in the aftermath, and the leaders of the Charity Organisation decided to disband, saying that they could not continue to work under such conditions. The King's Daughters Society, an interdenominational Christian group of long standing, agreed to fill the void left by the COC. For the next decade, the Society's caseload reflected Shanghai's shifting demographic composition, with increasing numbers of White Russians appearing on the relief rolls.[147] Whereas "poor whites" of British and American nationality could claim the aid of consular officials and compatriots anxious to preserve their mantle of racial superiority, Russians had less recourse to similar assistance.[148] This was particularly true after 1921, when Russians émigrés became stateless as the new Soviet government stripped them of citizenship rights. The visible presence of foreign indigents, especially the proliferating numbers of Russian women working as cabaret hostesses and prostitutes, became the source of anxious commentary for "respectable" denizens of the treaty port.[149] Their discomfort and embarrassment turned to genuine alarm in the winter of 1922, when a flotilla of Russian boats docked off the coast. The estimated two thousand passengers were remnants of White Russian forces and civilian refugees who had fled from Vladivostok. Although the Chinese authorities refused to allow most of them to disembark, citing security concerns about armed soldiers, more than half gradually trickled ashore, "living for months by begging, on charity, and some few by roguery." As an editorial in the *North-China Herald* noted, "The demand for foreign casual labour here or anywhere else in China is *nil*." With "cold, hungry, and misery-tortured outcasts" and "unshaven, wild-looking" soldiers wandering the city, the editorialist cautioned against "misdirected charity" and declared that "they cannot stay here and become a permanent charge on Shanghai."[150]

Although the Municipal Council's earlier affirmation of a "no-relief" policy averted the financial burden of supporting these indigents, it hardly provided a solution to the pressing problem of policing the streets and defending the International Settlement against transients, of all nationalities. As the Municipal Charity Committee had noted, the Council had no legal obligation to provide for the homeless and the poor—but neither did its administrators possess the penal authority to impart punishment in a manner that would serve as an effective "deterrent," especially for the large numbers of Chinese mendicants.[151] Therefore, the Municipal Council began to explore other options, including the possibility of depositing them in Chinese institutions outside the concession boundaries.

They found an amenable place at the Jiangwan Model Factory and its affiliated Vagrant Factory, which had been established as a cooperative venture between local philanthropists and the Chinese regional military authorities. Situated on ten hectares in the northeastern suburbs, Jiangwan boasted over two thousand workers, twelve separate workshops, and a showroom displaying products such as carpets, bicycle tires, and toys. The Vagrant Factory accepted convicts and "unemployed vagrants" sent by any police authorities, the Shanghai Garrison, and the Mixed Court.[152] In 1922, new regulations clarified that targeted "vagrants" included unemployed drifters arrested three times within three months, discharged soldiers who disturb the peace, homeless or abandoned children who degenerate into theft and refuse to repent despite repeated warnings, and juvenile delinquents whose parents request their detention. The term of confinement ranged from six months to three years, depending on the severity of the infraction; in addition, "volunteer vagrants" could also be admitted for job training. Built for the purpose of "reforming vagrants" and as a "charitable enterprise," Jiangwan aimed to eradicate the "hidden peril" of vagrancy.[153]

To complement the efforts of the Jiangwan Factory, another group of local leaders used the premises of a defunct asylum to build the Songhu Poorhouse

(Songhu Jiaoyangyuan), intended also for beggars, vagrants, and disobedient sons. As the organizers explained, with the cost of living on the rise, increasingly aggressive beggars and vagrants constantly harassed shopkeepers and demanded alms at weddings and funerals, like swarms of "social vermin." At the same time there was also the "unbearably tragic" spectacle of children, the elderly, and the disabled crying and wailing on the streets. Accustomed to "both the hateful and the pitiful," Shanghai's residents simply ignored them all. With no limit on the length of detention, Songhu promised to "begin with charity" and "end with local order." One contributor to *Shenbao* applauded this approach, observing that while existing workhouses aimed to teach "vagrants" job skills, without "transforming their hearts the roots of their loafing character cannot be exterminated"; a few years after release "they sprout again" to become "society's vermin."[154] The project garnered the support of philanthropists, the Chinese military authorities, and notorious gangsters like Green Gang leader Du Yuesheng and Subei boss Gu Zhukan, who used good deeds to gain respectability. Songhu's administrators also invited the police of all three jurisdictions to send mendicants and disorderly transients there, adding, "If you should encounter our staff collecting disabled beggars and vagrants who resist, please offer your assistance." But when the director applied to the Municipal Council for a subsidy, to defray the cost of housing and "training" the 432 inmates brought by the International Settlement Police in the first months, he received a firm refusal, on the grounds that poor relief was not part of the Council's charter.[155]

When the International Settlement authorities insisted that poor relief was not their responsibility, they reiterated that the duty belonged to the Chinese government, foreign consuls (for their own nationals), and private charity. But when one such philanthropist, Silas Hardoon, began distributing alms at Christmas and the Spring Festival, he drew complaints from his neighbors about the crowds of "vermin and germ laden beggars" gathered around his residence. Hardoon had made his fortune in the opium trade and then augmented his wealth through property speculation. After his estate became a magnet for hundreds of Chinese mendicants in successive years, the police chief paid him a personal visit and persuaded him to discontinue.[156]

In sum, although the authorities did their best to police Shanghai's borders, transients were a constant presence in the treaty port. The attitudes and assumptions that Western treaty port officials and residents evinced about "the poor" overlapped to a large degree with the rhetoric of "parasites" and "vermin" discussed earlier in this chapter. Many complained that it was impossible to differentiate among authentic refugees, harmless mendicants, and unruly vagrants. There was a chronic shortage of affordable housing, and thousands of people lived in squalor in shantytowns around the periphery of the city, another constant source of concern and irritation. As the following discussion will highlight, in a time when government authorities targeted the homeless for punitive treatment, those who had homes fought to save them from the attempts to eradicate shantytowns.

STRAW HUT SHANTYTOWNS

Shantytowns first appeared in Shanghai in the late nineteenth century, when rural migrants flocked to work in the treaty port's new factories. After World War I, an industrial boom brought new influxes of workers, many from Subei, the region north of the Yangzi River. Some of the new arrivals lived on the boats they came in, moored along the city's many waterways. Others built makeshift huts using straw and mud, earning the name "straw hut dwellers" or "hut people" (*cao penghu* or *penghu ren*). As Hanchao Lu has described in marvelous detail, a typical hut was just a room built with a bamboo frame, plastered with mud and straw; even so this was considered a step up from living in boats.[157] The majority of straw hut settlements were built in Chinese territory, but they congregated at the borders of the foreign concessions, often directly on the boundaries.

For the most part, the Chinese authorities tolerated these shantytowns. To be sure, the local and military police could be quite ruthless in policing the streets: conducting periodic roundups; sending transients to workhouses for long periods of time. But preoccupied by factional struggles and military battles, the reigning warlords did not aggressively target straw huts for removal.[158] In contrast, to the foreign administrators of the two concessions, particularly the International Settlement, the shantytowns were a complete outrage. No matter how strictly they policed their own jurisdictions, the filth and disease were always nearby, sometimes literally just across the street. In 1921, the chief of the Shanghai Municipal Police reported that huts occupied by mill workers along Robison Road were a growing menace. Although technically in Chinese territory in the Western District, the police chief wrote, "They are practically all occupied by the families of the worst class of mill coolie, who formerly lived on boats and in Chapei [Zhabei]. The effect . . . of a close congregation of coolies of this class is not good, and will tend, in times of unrest, towards lawlessness, which is bound to effect the Settlement."[159]

In response, the Municipal Council instructed the police to remove these "squatters," noting that "the existence of these beggars is a nuisance, both to the owners and the public." If in the course of removing them "it were found that any particular squatter were authorised, the owners could easily be placated, but it seems highly improbable that there would be many exceptions." Seven hundred households were soon ordered to tear down their huts and move, an action that drew an immediate response from the Chinese government. Xu Yuan, Commissioner of Foreign Affairs for Jiangsu, lodged a formal complaint with the British Consul: "The district in question is in Chinese territory and the competent authorities are the Chinese Police. The Municipal police, therefore, should not over-step their own jurisdiction and intervene in the matter."[160]

Xu Yuan's defense of Chinese rights reflected heightened sensitivities about national sovereignty in the years after World War I. The Versailles Treaty had transferred Germany's rights in China to Japan, sparking the May Fourth Movement in 1919. A foreign concession government's attempt to eradicate a shantytown in Chinese territory provided only further fuel for protests. The Council suspended the demolitions, but behind the scenes tried to pressure the Chinese to take action. The military authorities apparently assured the Police Commissioner that they would do everything possible to have the huts removed, but five months later, nothing had been done. In December 1921, the Council finally built fences along some of the most "objectionable roads," to fortify the Settlement from the disturbing proximity of "beggar villages" and "beggar huts."[161] This episode in 1921 highlights some of the issues that would arise again in the years to come, including nationalism and sovereignty, and especially the identity and status of the hut dwellers. Were they factory workers or beggars? Were they squatters, or were they in fact renters? Later many hut dwellers would claim to be refugees, and these questions of definition and identity would become crucial in the battle over whether they were entitled to legal protection and possessed property rights.

Without Chinese cooperation, the concession authorities could do little about huts outside their borders, but they were not constrained by the same considerations inside the International Settlement.[162] In the autumn of 1925, the Municipal Council started a demolition campaign, but soon found that huts torn down one day would be rebuilt that night, in the same location, with the same materials. In November and December, two fires destroyed more than one thousand huts in Yangshupu, the largest shantytown in the International Settlement. Fires in straw hut villages were tragically common—one unattended cooking fire and a sudden gust of wind could send the entire neighborhood up in flames.[163] At the time, these two fires attracted little attention. Several months later, in the spring of 1926, the Municipal Council announced that all huts in the Settlement would be demolished by April 1. In the context of this eradication order, allegations of arson for the 1925 fires in Yangshupu appeared. Shanghai's General Labor Union (GLU) accused the Municipal Council of intentionally setting the fires in November and December and locking the hydrants nearby. An article in a GLU magazine called for the end of extraterritoriality: "On the basis of the unequal treaties, the imperialists have appropriated Chinese land to create their own concession, and now they have burned the homes of our people. How wicked! Abolish all unequal treaties!"[164] The Municipal Council strongly denied the arson charges, and in turn blamed "agitators" of trying to stir up trouble.[165]

The agitators were members of the Chinese Communist Party, which had assumed a leadership position in Shanghai's labor movement, galvanized by the May 30th Incident of 1925. On that day, the foreign police in the International Settlement had fired on unarmed demonstrators, who had assembled to protest the death of a Chinese worker two weeks earlier, at a Japanese-owned textile mill during a strike. On May 30th, when eleven more people were killed and many more wounded, demonstrations erupted in many cities. The CCP launched the General Labor Union in Shanghai to lead the workers' strike, which lasted three months.

In the spring of 1926, as the April 1 demolition deadline approached, the hut dwellers formed an organization called the Straw Hut Owners of Yangshupu. They asked civic groups and charities to intervene on their behalf, and in response to their appeal, the Chinese government promised to raise money to build housing for them. For its part, the Council agreed to postpone the demolitions for three months, to give the Chinese authorities time to make these arrangements. But by August, no housing funds had materialized, and Council administrators worried that if they did not take action soon, the cold weather would again be used as an excuse for further delays. Nothing would be done for another year, as no one wanted to be responsible for throwing people out of their homes in the middle of winter.

As the foreign authorities debated how to proceed, they received a petition from the "Committee for the Problem of Straw Huts in Eastern Shanghai." The letter explained that the Committee represented several thousand people who had come to the city as famine refugees. Although the Chinese government had in fact made arrangements for them to relocate—to an area about three miles away—the hut dwellers did not want to move. They worked in factories and at the docks in Yangshupu, and moving so far away would make it impossible for them to get to work. To persuade the Municipal Council to allow them to stay, the Committee promised to keep order in the neighborhood, build latrines, and ensure that the inhabitants did not dump trash, keep pigs, or burn spirit paper (offerings to deceased ancestors and a frequent cause of fires). The residents also organized themselves into clusters of ten households (imitating the imperial system of household registration), with a leader in each group to watch out for troublemakers, and they pledged that no new huts would be built. These promises addressed all of the reasons given for eviction. But the hut dwellers went one step further, offering to collect monthly dues and turn the money over to the concession authorities, which would, in effect turn them into ratepayers and legitimize their residence. The Council ignored this initial petition, as well as subsequent letters that grew increasingly threatening in tone, for example, "The people are ignorant, and if you leave them no choice they may take a dangerous path."[166] Another group, calling itself the "Jiangbei Association," likewise sent appeals to the foreign administrators, proposing a similar arrangement. "We have been waiting for more than three months for a response," the hut dwellers wrote. "Would you kindly tell us whether it would be best to collect taxes on a quarterly or monthly basis, . . . and how much?"[167]

Meanwhile, behind the scenes officials were debating what to do, against the backdrop of a city engulfed in waves of labor agitation, led in part by the General Labor Union. (Although the Chinese authorities repeatedly shut down the union, it continued to work underground and managed to maintain a public presence.) As rice prices spiraled upward in the summer of 1926, work stoppages and conflicts peaked. In this context, the Secretary of the Municipal Council admitted that "it is obviously impossible . . . to insist upon the removal of these huts unless alternative accommodation is provided on account of the many thousands who would be rendered homeless." Public Works Commissioner Charles Harpur concurred and noted that since the majority of occupants were mill workers and laborers, to describe the shanties as "beggar huts" was a "misnomer." Harpur also suggested that the Council cooperate with factory owners to provide adequate housing. In response, one member dryly observed that at the moment employers might not consider such calls for their cooperation with much sympathy. Furthermore, the police chief advised the Municipal Council that drastic action in this matter would be an invitation for further trouble: "Any . . . incident such as the death or injury of a beggar would fall on the heads of the Police and would make splendid capital for the present day agitator. Obviously something must be done sooner or later but . . . the present time is most inopportune to move in this matter."[168]

Conclusion

On that note, the issue of shantytowns temporarily receded into the background. The straw hut dwellers, however, would return to vex Shanghai's authorities for the next two decades—through the Nationalist Party's years in power, the Japanese occupation, and the civil war. In China's largest treaty port, the twin problems of vagrancy and shantytowns, as well as the debate over poor relief, illustrated how its foreign administrators defined eligibility for compassion and marked out behaviors requiring punitive intervention. Their concerted efforts to expunge "undesirables" (deporting Chinese "vagrants"; dismantling shack homes) underscored in literal terms that such misfits had no place in the treaty port.

At the same time that Shanghai's spatial configuration produced its own local geography of poverty, we find sociological precepts gaining currency in Beijing also resonating in the southern city. The labeling of nonproductive dependency as a form of "pauperism," the mantra of "scientific" charity, the injunction to "work for your keep" all emphasized social belonging as predicated on one's willingness and ability to work. As for those abhorring labor and dwelling willfully in a state of dependency, the emerging discourse of "social parasites" further justified their exclusion from society, by dehumanizing them as vermin.

Despite the oceans of ink spilt debating the issue, sociologists and intellectuals never accomplished their goal of defining poverty. But through their efforts, the idea of "poverty" as a social problem became firmly embedded in the conventional wisdom. In tandem, to be called "poor" started to take on clearly pejorative connotations, consistently linked to crime, prostitution, and illiteracy as a package of vices undermining the nation's progress. For instance, when the Beijing police established free schools, calling them "Half-day Schools for Poor Boys" (Pin'er Banri Xuexiao), some parents refused to send their sons there because they considered "poor" a derogatory term. The police superintendent reported that a name change, dropping "poor" from the moniker, boosted enrollment in the schools.[169]

Together, these social changes and intellectual currents intersected with new institutions and policing practices to reinforce the belief that involuntary detention and labor could transform the nation's nonworking poor into productive contributors. To those who advocated such a "scientific" approach, poor relief was a necessary evil: giving alms to the poor temporarily alleviated their suffering, but had the paradoxical effect of facilitating dependency. Therefore, relief should always be constructive, not palliative, and charities should refrain from dispensing aid "promiscuously"—that is, without differentiating between the different types of poor people.[170] As the chorus of elite opinions reiterated, "poverty" was an age-old problem that took on different significance in a new age.

And so by the beginning of the Nanjing decade, a new ideology under the loose rubric of "social relief" (shehui jiuji) emerged, combining faith in Taylorist principles of labor productivity and efficiency with the belief that compulsory labor could rehabilitate the indolent and criminally inclined poor. As we shall see in the next chapter, as the GMD consolidated its power and established its authority across the country, many of these same impulses would inform its social policy. The tensions between charity and punishment, compassion and loathing, self-help and pauperization would remain central to the dilemma of how to help the neediest members of society. Through its local bureaucracies and police forces, the Nationalist government would intervene deeply in the lives of the urban poor—for the benefit of some, but to the detriment of others.

CHAPTER 3

"Living Ghosts" during the Nanjing Decade

IN 1928, JULEAN Arnold wrote *Some Bigger Issues in China's Problems* and published it in Shanghai. At the time, Arnold was the U.S. Legation's Commercial Attaché in Beijing. His book depicted, in a series of fold-out graphs and charts, America's prosperity in contrast to China's impoverishment, as gauged by coal output, cotton and wheat production, and the number of telephones and miles of railways in service. Dr. Hu Shi, a leading New Culture intellectual, contributed this foreword:

> What is needed to-day, it seems to me, is a deep conviction which should amount almost to a religious repentance that *we Chinese are backward in everything and that every other modern nation in the world is much better off than we are.* We must know ourselves. We must confess that we are terribly poor and that our people are suffering miseries which justly horrify civilized peoples.... And for all this, we only have ourselves to blame.... Let us no longer deceive ourselves with self-complacent talks about imperialistic powers hampering our national progress and prosperity! Let us read the recent history of Japan and bury our conceit and self-deception once and for all in shame and repentance.[1]

Hu Shi was not the only one to evaluate China's international standing so harshly. YMCA social worker Luo Chunhua wrote in the same vein in 1930, "To many people in China to-day, life is but a continuous tale of want and misery. One cannot help but feel astounded at the immense magnitude and degree of poverty all over the country." Reviewing the state of the nation in statistics, Luo described a bleak situation. An estimated seventy million—the size of Japan's entire population—lived on the verge of starvation. Growing unemployment and chronic food shortages only intensified the people's suffering. Poverty, he concluded, was not "merely a local or transient evil, but a deep-rooted and nation-wide curse."[2]

Indeed, by almost any measure, China lagged behind the rest of the world. Data amassed from the previous decade's sociological research meant that the nation's poverty could now be quantified in new and specific ways. For example, studies showed that it ranked last in national wealth per capita, and next to last in mortality rate.[3] Given this wretched state of affairs, Luo Chunhua remarked, "Is it any wonder that hundreds of laborers and students are turning to Communism for comfort and relief? Is it any wonder that 'dangerous thoughts' are spreading amongst the unpropertied class as rapidly as prairie-fire?" In Luo's view, the remedies proposed for the alleviation of poverty—industrial development, migration, birth control, currency reforms, agricultural modernization—all failed to address one essential prerequisite: peace. That is, "the road to prosperity is rarely one of war; it must always be paved with peace. Peace and peace only will make China rich and free."[4]

Peace and national unification were in fact the GMD's primary objectives when Chiang Kai-shek launched the Northern Expedition from Canton in 1926. By the time Nationalist forces entered Beijing, they had driven the Communists to remote rural bases, and regional warlords had pledged their allegiance to Chiang's regime—in word, if not always in reality. The hope of peace and prosperity dawned on the Nanjing decade, the height of GMD power. During the ten years of relative political stability that followed, the Nationalist government attempted to rebuild the nation and transform its citizens. In the arena of charity and punishment, newly constituted local governments interjected their resources, policing mechanisms, and disciplinary powers into the lives of the urban poor in new ways. At the same time, worries about "parasitic" dependency prevailed, and extracting productive labor from the nonworking poor became one of the organizing principles of relief.

This chapter underscores how Nationalist assumptions about poor relief drew on the intellectual discourses that had developed in the previous decades. I begin with an overview of the intersections between academic sociology and the GMD government's relief agenda, before turning to the specific contours of changes in Beijing and Shanghai. In 1928, when Beijing lost its status as the national capital, the city fell into a deep economic depression.[5] The records of the municipal Relief Home provide us with a unique view of the lives of those who ended up in the state's custody, including beggars, drug addicts, soldiers, and people who attempted suicide out of desperation. We can see that for some, the workhouse was a place of punishment, while for others it was a refuge of last resort. In Shanghai, on the other hand, the city's divided jurisdiction provides the opportunity to contrast foreign and Chinese views of the problem of poverty. I describe how private charities functioned as an extension of government power in the treaty port, before returning to the fate of the straw hut dwellers, picking up the narrative where we left it in chapter 2. As we shall see, efforts to reform poor relief tried to classify and organize the recipients of aid into discrete categories, but often failed to recognize poverty as a continuum of misery, difficult to compartmentalize. For the urban poor of Beijing and Shanghai, the GMD's decade in power would mean an uneasy combination of charity and coercion, help and punishment.

The Sociology of Poverty

By the beginning of the Nanjing decade, the notion that "poverty" constituted China's deepest malady was firmly embedded in intellectual discourse. As one editorialist writing in a Shanghai magazine put it, "China's entire society struggles under the poverty line, and the entire race moans under its cruel oppression. . . . Simply said, poverty is the great enemy of social progress."[6] Commentators agreed that the country also suffered from physical and spiritual weakness, internecine warfare, and endemic corruption. But if China hoped to embark on a new, upward trajectory, it would first have to eradicate poverty—the root cause of the nation's woes.[7]

The growth of sociology as a field, with a proliferation of research institutes, publications, and professional organizations, expanded investigation of the country's myriad social problems. By one count, more than nine thousand studies were conducted between 1927 and 1935. At Yanjing University, John Burgess's social service approach (discussed in chapter 2) gave way to a new generation of empiricists skeptical of evangelism.[8] Robert Park, recently retired from the University of Chicago, taught at Yanjing as a visiting professor in 1932. Park proved to be an inspirational teacher and an important influence on Fei Xiaotong, later China's leading anthropologist. A sociology major at the time, Fei imbibed Park's mantra of dispassionate empiricism and learned to apply the techniques of experiential observation first to urban communities, and then to conditions in the countryside.[9] Indeed, as the agrarian crisis deepened during the world depression, the immense problems of rural poverty drew the attention of social scientists. Researchers flocked to Ding Xian, the site of James Yen's model village, and Zouping, where Liang Shuming organized his reconstruction project based on Confucian revival. In the mid-1930s, when the Rockefeller Foundation expressed interest in agrarian research, Yanjing and other institutions vied to tap this source of funding.[10]

Beyond competition for the favor of international donors, political considerations also shaped research agendas, as academics became increasingly engaged with Nationalist social policy. At Yanjing, sociology majors collected data for government research projects directed by their professors; graduate students fulfilled the field work requirements by completing internships at municipal agencies and prisons.[11] Zhang Hongjun (B.A., 1925) went on to oversee the social work division of the GMD's Social Affairs Ministry. Yan Jingyao (B.A., 1927; M.A., 1929) became a prominent criminologist and the warden of the International Settlement jail in Shanghai. In 1928, department chairman Xu Shilian predicted that "the next thirty years in China will be . . . a sociological age." He urged his colleagues and students to redouble their research efforts, in order to "furnish facts which alone constitute the sound basis of practical social and political policies." When Xu took an extended leave from Yanjing in 1933 to assume positions in Nanjing (at the Ministry of Industry, the Foreign Affairs Ministry, and the National Economic Council), he relished the opportunity to "save the country" through sociology.[12]

As academic sociology and government policy intertwined, sociological precepts about "poverty" became ingrained as part of the conventional wisdom. Writing in the progressive journal *National Opinion Monthly*, Zheng Jiangnan pressed for more precise usage of terms that had grown commonplace. In the West, Zheng explained, a clear distinction existed between "the poor" (those lacking the bare necessities to sustain life) and "paupers" (those relying upon others in order to live). In Chinese, however, what might function as corresponding terms—*pinmin* for "the poor" and *qiongmin* for "paupers"—were used interchangeably. This linguistic ambiguity obscured crucial distinctions: whereas "the poor" exist because of defects in society, "paupers" develop from "psychological abnormalities" to become social liabilities and "parasitic animals." Zheng further posited that "as a general rule, 'paupers' who receive public support . . . lose part of their citizenship rights"; therefore "the poor" and "paupers" are "fundamentally not the same in nature."[13] By thus semantically marking the boundaries of social belonging, Zheng absolved "the poor" of blame, but insisted that the parasitism of "paupers" disqualified them from full membership as social citizens.

Sociologist Ke Xiangfeng, a professor at Jinling University in Nanjing, likewise regretted the practice of using "poverty" (*pinqiong*) without differentiation from "destitution" (*pinkun*), "dependency" (*yilai*), or "pauperism" (*jiyang*). As for *pinqiong* itself, "I'm afraid there are as many definitions as there are people." To clarify, he referred readers to excerpts from G. L. Gillin's *Poverty and Dependency*, H. P. Fairchild's *Applied Sociology*, and *Prevention of Destitution* by Sidney and Beatrice Webb.[14] Ke also provided a simple diagram to illustrate:

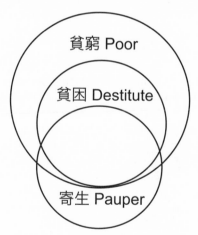

Figure 3.1. Ke Xiangfeng, *Zhongguo pinqiong wenti* (China's poverty problem), 1935

These semantic differences mattered not only in the abstract, for Ke believed that an effective system of poor relief required such precision. In his description of the British system, for instance, he faulted the Poor Laws for abetting "dependency," and increasing rather than reducing the number of "paupers." On the other hand, Ke assessed the "Elberfeld–Hamburg" method favorably, noting that compulsory work for aid recipients and the prohibition of private almsgiving constituted a model of constructive charity.[15] Overall, different practices had strengths and shortcomings, but the ideal should "combine compassion with science," upholding as the ultimate objectives "to make the nonproducers produce" and "to foster the productive ability of those who have lost it." Since "poverty begets poverty," individuals and societies find it difficult to break the cycle. For China, Ke concluded that immersing its long tradition of charity in a "scientific baptism" would liberate the nation from this trap.[16]

Herbert Lamson, Ke Xianfeng's counterpart at Shanghai University, similarly lamented poverty's "vicious circles": unemployment, disease, and crime were secondary effects that in turn increased and intensified the condition of economic impoverishment. But Lamson also pointed to the Chinese family as the progenitor of a culture of dependence. By allowing "parasitic relatives" to subsist on the labor of others, the professor explained, the extended family encouraged "a spirit of laziness" on the part of those who are "able to work and become productive members of society but do not do so. . . . In a day when China needs every citizen to be a producer of national wealth and welfare, this custom, of feeding idly upon the good fortune of some relative, does represent a problem of pauperization, even in rather well-to-do families." Of eleven major pathologies in China, Lamson declared that "the large number of paupers" ranked first, ahead of "economic insufficiency of the great masses."[17]

GMD PRODUCTIVISM AND SOCIAL RELIEF

Herbert Lamson's critique of the Chinese family cast, in sociological terms, the sentiments of New Culture intellectuals from the 1920s, who had excoriated the extended family as the bastion of Confucian values and feudalism. In the Nanjing decade, such appraisals also intersected with the Nationalist project to enhance China's productivity. Drawing on Sun Yat-sen's injunction that all must labor in the service of the state, GMD ideology espoused a productivism that forged links between work, patriotism, and citizenship. As Chiang Kai-shek declared at a service commemorating Sun in 1935, the labor contribution of individuals paved the way for national reconstruction. "As you all should know," he told students at Sichuan University, "labor and service form the two guiding principles of life. . . . A person who detests labor and indulges in leisure will become a parasite upon society. Parasites will be the downfall of the nation, resulting in our extinction."[18]

Against the Communist challenge and arguments for the redistribution of wealth, Nationalist leaders insisted that the best way to ensure the "people's livelihood" was to increase production and expand the economy.[19] Indeed, the productive impulse infused Nationalist rhetoric and policy: "work more, waste less"; "transform consumption into production"; "convert uselessness to usefulness"; "nationalize, militarize, productivize." As formulas for national salvation, these imperatives to produce incorporated notions of frugality, efficiency, and what Frederic Wakeman has termed "Confucian Fascism."[20] Furthermore, GMD productivism reproached all who failed to produce for obstructing national progress. For instance, noted educator Li Chucai characterized schools as empty "marketplaces for knowledge" that did not cultivate "productive capabilities." As a result, students learned only how to "devour" their parents' money; after they graduate they "suck up the flesh and blood" of society.[21] For his part, GMD official Wu Shangquan saw wasted potential everywhere: unemployed workers, corrupt bureaucrats, resources squandered on gambling, fashion, and entertainment. "One of the main causes of our poverty is the dissipation of our labor power," Wu wrote. He considered the extended family "a factory that manufactures vagrants": the larger the family, the more idlers; the more idlers, the more impoverished the nation. By spawning "social parasites" and promoting wasteful cultural practices (e.g., three years of mourning, extravagant funerals), the family structure perpetuated the "cycle of poverty." Rectifying the situation required "extraordinary methods," Wu claimed; only the force of law could destroy such deeply entrenched customs. For instance, in order to harness the labor power of "nonproducers" such as beggars, vagrants, prostitutes, and the rich who "idle about," the government would have to "forcibly compel these people to work and produce." As to protests that such measures constituted "an excessive expansion of government power and an infringement upon the freedom of the people," Wu retorted that since they "wantonly abuse their freedom, to the detriment of the nation and society," their actions should be considered "criminal."[22]

The rhetorical criminalization of "parasites" and misgivings about their impairment of the country's productivity drive were thus pervasive in GMD rhetoric. At the same time, however, Nationalist officials also recognized that the aspiration for state building required a coherent program of "social relief" (*shehui jiuji*). Like its imperial predecessors, the GMD considered providing aid to the helpless and needy to be one of the traditional responsibilities of government. "The people's livelihood" also incorporated the belief that public welfare, defined broadly, was crucial to a modern nation-state's legitimacy. A 1930 article in *The Chinese Nation* described a government's ability to deal with disaster relief as a "supreme test of self-reliance, the success of which cannot fail to enlist foreign confidence." In this context, China's dependence on foreign charities undermined its bid for the retrocession of extraterritorial rights.[23] Providing aid to the needy was also necessary for ensuring social stability, as people living in dire misery could be driven to desperation—and perhaps into the arms of the Communist Party. Although exiled to rural bases, the CCP retained urban underground networks, and the Nationalist government deeply feared the infiltration of agitators and spies.[24] From this perspective, poor relief was part of the strategy to counter the Communist threat. Lastly, the GMD used social policies to centralize its power. As part of the effort to exert control over associational life, the government increasingly intervened in the activities of private charities.[25] Policing the streets and monitoring public life were also important concerns, and as we shall see, these initiatives particularly targeted the urban homeless and the nonworking poor.

The suspicion that providing assistance to the poor could "pauperize" them led GMD officials to regard "social relief" as an essential component of national reconstruction—but one fraught with potential liabilities. At the national level, the Interior Ministry (created in 1929) and several relief committees assumed the primary responsibility for poor relief.[26] In addition to reforming charities and relief institutions with "scientific methods" for personnel and financial management, the Interior Ministry advocated shifting current practices from "passive relief" (*xiaoji jiuji*) to "active relief" (*jiji jiuji*). Drawing on sociological principles, officials declared that, by giving handouts to the poor as palliatives for their misery, traditional benevolent halls and soup kitchens typified the "passive" approach. "Active" methods, on the other hand, endeavored to eradicate the root causes of poverty—for example, by mandating labor in exchange for aid. In this vision, "model relief homes" would train the blind as musicians and the mute as artists, thereby resolving the livelihood problem at its source. By transforming previously unproductive people into independent wage earners, poor relief would be proactive as well as temporary.[27] As a corollary, the 1931 Civil Code reinforced the mantra of self-reliance by limiting the family's obligation to support only those incapable of earning a living on their own. As discussed earlier, many contemporaries criticized the Chinese family system for encumbering society with a large number of idle and unproductive people. By circumscribing the family's responsibility, the new law aimed to cure this weakness.[28]

Despite aspirations for a unified plan of social relief, the Interior Ministry acknowledged that local governments would have to bear the primary burden of implementation. As a national agency, the Ministry was preoccupied by larger crises, especially the exigencies of disaster relief. In 1930, the State Famine Relief Reserve Fund had set aside 1 percent of the government's annual revenues, with the goal of accumulating Ch. $50 million.[29] But before the reserves could accrue, devastating floods inundated central China in the summer of 1931, followed by severe famine conditions in seven provinces. The Interior Ministry and the National Flood Relief Commission raised money and coordinated aid to an estimated twenty-five million people affected by the disaster.[30] But officials felt that even emergency aid should be dispensed with caution. In times of crisis, rural refugees fled to cities in search of relief or employment. One Shanghai official likened these people to "crabs without legs," for whom survival depended on joining up with "vagrants" (*youmin*) and other wicked elements. They "wallowed in evil and learned the habits of drifting indolence ... becoming the so-called 'parasites' of society." Under these circumstances, "how can society be at peace? How can the nation be wealthy and strong?"[31]

The influx of newcomers also led to conflicts with local residents, and allowed local hoodlums and "depraved vagrants" to hide among them, posing as victims. Just as troubling, once in the city many refugees simply refused to leave. In one Shanghai municipal shelter, set up in 1931 to help the victims of the summer floods, three months of aid stretched into four, five, then six months. The GMD government finally delegated responsibility for dispersing these refugees to a private consortium of Chinese charities. Despite concerted efforts to repatriate them back to their hometowns, however, thousands of people decided to "forsake their ancestral homes." From the perspective of the "people's livelihood," officials concluded, "taking in" (shourong) refugees contradicted the principle of "active relief."[32]

In many cities, responsibility for both emergency aid and ordinary poor relief belonged to the local Social Affairs Bureau (Shehuiju), a newly created agency first established in 1928 in Nanjing, Shanghai, Beijing, and Tianjin. (In rural counties, there were corresponding social affairs or civil administration agencies.) The Bureau had jurisdiction over the social life of the city, from commerce and labor to the food supply and religion. In some cities the agency also took over management of the panoply of workhouses, poorhouses, and beggar shelters that had been established since the late Qing. As avid collectors of statistics, compiling information on wages, rents, and myriad "social problems," the Bureau's staff became prolific chroniclers of urban poverty.[33]

The Social Affairs Bureau also took charge of "poor people's credit centers" (pinmin jieben chu), often touted as one of the best examples of "active relief." Although GMD law prohibited usury and curbed the maximum interest rate at 20 percent, these sanctions were difficult to enforce, and the burden of debt could be crushing to those already on the brink of destitution. By disbursing small loans (typically Ch. $10–$20) as seed capital to applicants certified as needy, at little or no interest, the government hoped to break the cycle of poverty perpetuated by debt.[34] In Shanghai, the first center opened in August, 1929. The Social Affairs Bureau decided to charge a nominal interest rate, to ensure that recipients would understand that "you cannot use other people's money for free," and that "to borrow money is really not an easy matter." In 1931, the Shanghai agency approved 4,248 loans to butchers, toy makers, and fruit peddlers.[35] Another, more ambitious project was low-income housing, billed as one of the centerpieces of the GMD social program. This required capital outlays far beyond the financial resources of most local governments. As a result, many grand schemes never advanced beyond the planning stage. But in several cities, the government did build model "people's villages" that featured amenities such as running water, electricity, and medical clinics, at rents substantially below market rates.[36]

EXPLAINING POVERTY

In 1929, sociologist Li Jinghan wrote that those in the lowest strata of Beijing society were "utterly impoverished" (*qiongde yaoming*); the poorest of the poor—"half-dead and half-alive" beggars and homeless people—could barely survive. There were at least 10,000 of these "living ghosts" in the city, whose lives were hardly better than those of animals. In fact, Li lamented, "It may be preferable for them just to die."[37] Beyond the terrible specter of thousands of ghosts wandering the streets, attempts to quantify the number of "poor people" tried to gauge the extent of misery more precisely. The police census divided "poor households" into "very poor" (*jipin*) and "less poor" (*cipin*), the same categories that had been used to classify famine victims in the Qing dynasty. In 1929, the local census counted 182,386 "very poor" people in Beijing. By 1930, the number had increased to 274,318.[38] Like their imperial predecessors, however, the vague criteria used in these classifications make it impossible to determine what the figures actually measured. The data excluded refugees and transients not part of registered households, as well as the enormous numbers of unemployed residents. (One government tally, for example, cited 696,325 unemployed people in Beijing in 1933.)[39] Even discounting these factors, reliability remained questionable. In a 1931 survey of 1,200 "poor households" sponsored by the Social Affairs Bureau, sociology researchers from Yanjing University discovered that some identified as "very poor" in the census actually lived in relative comfort. Using connections or trading favors with the local police, they acquired the designation to obtain tax exemptions or coupons for free clothing and subsidized rice. Given this troubling revelation, lead investigator Niu Nai'e concluded that the 274,318 destitutes (15 percent of Beijing's population) cited by the 1930 census did not reflect the true situation.[40] But with a sample size of only 1,200 households (3 percent of the total number), the survey could not provide a more accurate measure of the city's poverty.

Despite collecting voluminous statistics, Niu Nai'e's analysis actually produced only a few facts with confidence. The household size averaged 4.03 people; the majority of the poor were locals (72 percent named Beijing as their native place); just over half of the men had jobs, mostly as coolie laborers and peddlers; slightly more than a quarter of the women were employed.[41] The survey tried to weed out ineligible ("not poor") subjects, but methodological uncertainties still cast doubt on some of the major findings. For instance, the fact that more than one-third of the respondents refused to disclose their income skewed the analysis of household income.[42] The most poignant details had little to do with statistics. Of the 151 people identified as scavengers, Niu described fierce competition among the foragers who chased freight trains to pick up stray pieces of coal. In the frenzied struggles for bits of coal, children and elderly scavengers were occasionally injured or killed by passing trains.[43]

Beyond these observations, Niu's explanations for Beijing's poverty primarily blamed the pernicious legacy of its imperial past. The impoverished Banner population, the prideful arrogance of the city's residents, and the relocation of the capital to Nanjing in 1928—these factors explained contemporary miseries with reference to the city's history. In the first instance, the survey identified one-third of the households (393 out of 1,200) as belonging to the former Banners. Of these families, 121 had no income at all; among the others, nearly 90 percent earned less than Ch. $15 per month.[44] The case of the Fus, a multigenerational saga of family disintegration, embodied the moral defects typically attributed to "Manchus." Fu Rongjun, the youngest of three brothers, lived in destitution with an older sister. Their grandfather had been a Qing official, at one point rising to the post of vice prefect of Yan'an prefecture in Shaanxi. Their father Fu Wenbing had occupied a minor ceremonial post. With additional income from the two older brothers' sinecures as well as the imperial stipend, the family had lived well, though often beyond their means. A severe but irresponsible father, Fu Wenbing introduced his sons to a life of leisure and vice. After his death and the collapse of the Qing, ending the allowance provided to Bannermen, the two older brothers still refused to change their habits. According to Fu Rongjun, they were so addicted to drugs that "they could not do without their morphine and heroin for even an instant." When the family fell deeply into debt, the oldest brother absconded, leaving a trail of creditors. The second brother married a "wanton woman." To the humiliation of the family, after pawning everything they owned the couple actually "delighted in begging."[45]

A cautionary tale of improvidence and indolence, Niu Nai'e's narrative of the Fu family saga corroborated the prevailing view that the "the Manchu problem" was one of the primary reasons for Beijing's woeful state. Indeed, in 1931 the former capital was still paying the price for the Qing conquest. Niu wrote, "Since the Qing dynasty conquered China and gave the Manchus special treatment . . . such that they reaped the fruits of other people's labor, the other races were influenced by what they saw and heard, and gradually their lives were Manchu-fied. After 200 years, such ingrained habits are difficult to change." These habits also manifested in a "special character trait" Niu considered unique to Beijing residents—pride (*mianzi*, "face"). Although some had nothing to eat, they refused to work, solely for the sake of maintaining their reputations and keeping up appearances. A product of Beijing's aristocratic past, these people, both Manchu and Han, refused to stoop to the level of common laborers. They would actually rather starve than work for a living.[46]

The burden of history was also evident in Beijing's precipitous decline after the GMD shifted its capital to Nanjing in 1928, according to Niu's narrative.[47]

Accustomed to its former glories, the city withered under the gloom of unemployment and economic depression. Some 70 to 80 percent of people who had worked for the government lost their jobs, and the press carried frequent accounts of former officials pulling rickshaws or committing suicide. Wang Youlin (forty-nine *sui*), who had been on the staff of the Foreign Ministry, was a case in point. With a monthly salary of Ch. $60, Wang had lived in relative comfort with his elderly mother, wife, and three children. When the Foreign Ministry relocated to Nanjing, he spent months searching for work, finally exhausting the family's savings. In 1931, Wang earned a meager living as a street scribe, while his wife took in laundry. With their income reduced to only $7 to $9 a month, "husband and wife face each other and weep, sighing—what could they do?" In short, the loss of the capital was one of the main reasons why Beijing society grew more desolate every day and the number of poor people increased.

Then there was the case of Fu Wenquan. Also a former Bannerman (but no relation to the Fu family described above), he worked as a newspaper deliveryman. His three brothers pulled rickshaws, while one sister-in-law worked as a domestic servant. Together, the five earned a monthly income of Ch. $24, far from enough to support a household of seventeen people. This, according to Niu Nai'e, was perhaps the "truest depiction" of poverty in Beijing. In this case, the imperial legacy and the cultural defects it bequeathed to the city did not factor in the economics of survival.[48] By using the tools of social scientific empiricism to define, count, and dissect the lives of "the poor," sociologists like Niu organized their experiences according to a framework of tabulated figures and calculated percentages. Despite annotations indicating doubtful methodologies and uncertain conclusions, scientific surveys such as this undertaking constructed the city's impoverishment as severe, but ultimately both quantifiable and surmountable.

Poor Relief in Beijing

For most of the 1,200 households who participated in the survey, there might have been a gloomy irony to the enterprise of counting the jobs they did not have and tabulating the food they could not eat. They relied on a patchwork of methods to make ends meet, on a daily and weekly basis: informal credit societies and help from family and friends; pawning a coat in summer and redeeming it in winter; begging occasionally. Many could also be found queuing up at one of the city's soup kitchens on winter mornings. Throughout the Nanjing decade, soup kitchens helped to bridge the subsistence gap for many families, just as they had during the late imperial era and the early Republic. According to sociologist Zhang Jingai's tally, nineteen kitchens in Beijing doled out over 2.8 million meals over a five month period in the winter of 1931–32.[49] Zhang's data showed that female recipients outnumbered males by more than a two to one margin. The number of supplicants peaked in January, declined slightly in February due to the Spring Festival, and rose again in March before the kitchens closed in the spring. Although crucial to the survival of the needy, soup kitchens also drew criticisms as an out-of-date and passive relief method—in Zhang's words, a wasteful stopgap measure that facilitated the spread of disease, allowed women and men to "mix indiscriminately," and "caused the poor to have dependent hearts."[50]

Continuing the tradition of "official supervision, merchant management," soup kitchens typified a "mixed economy" of public and private relief. In 1928, Beijing Mayor He Kezhi established the Poor Relief Society and served as its first president. In addition to operating eight soup kitchens (the city's leading provider), the Society also distributed food, clothing, blankets, and coal in the winter, and organized "spring relief" on a smaller scale. Although an independent agency that relied entirely on donations, the Society's government connections meant that it garnered contributions from many official sources, including the municipal treasury and the Public Security Bureau. Meanwhile, at the seven soup kitchens managed by the Salvation Army (the second largest provider of free meals in Beijing), those waiting in line had to recite the Lord's Prayer before receiving any food.[51]

For Beijing's private charities, collaborating with the government meant intensified scrutiny. In 1934, fifty-seven organizations registered with the Social Affairs Bureau, a sharp decline from the more than three hundred counted a decade earlier. The Longquan Orphanage, which had regularly cared for more than two hundred children in the early Republic, dwindled to housing just seventy-six. Meanwhile, other agencies such as the World Red Swastika Society expanded the scope of their activities. In 1935, at the Social Affairs Bureau's behest, twenty-five groups formed a Charity Federation to coordinate their operations.[52]

In addition to supervising private charities, the Social Affairs Bureau also assessed the government's own relief methods. According to official Zhang Guolin, the "people's livelihood" unquestionably formed the basis for national reconstruction. The majority of the poor, however, were "dependent in character," especially the former Banners who abhor work. In the economic downturn following the relocation of the capital, unemployment escalated to unprecedented levels, a situation exacerbated by consecutive natural disasters in neighboring provinces. As a result, beggars old and young, "pale and weak with hunger," filled the streets. Despite this grim state of affairs, Zhang declared, "We should not be discouraged, but we must at every moment strive to find a way out (*chulu*) for the poor in this time of great difficulty."[53]

As envisioned by officials, finding "a way out" required an overhaul of the municipal relief institutions. When the GMD government inherited responsibility for the existing agencies in 1927, they were in a state of disarray. More than half of the people living in the workhouses, for example, could not actually work due to illness, disability, or old age. When Li Zhengpei arrived to assume his new post as the new director of the Capital Vagrant Workhouse (where the orphan Guo Hetang had lived), he found that the staff had not been paid for months, the workshops were in disrepair, and the 340 inmates all looked "pale and sick." To make ends meet, Li launched a series of fund-raising activities (organizing a variety show; sending inmates to sell candies and cigarettes at parks). Beyond the financial shortfalls, the new overseers also detected a more fundamental problem: these institutions failed to distinguish between "relief," "education and nurture," "improving industry," and "developing skills." As a result, the inmates lapsed into indolence while in government custody; rather than cultivating self-sufficiency, the provision of aid fostered dependency—just as sociologists had feared.[54]

The first reorganization in 1928–29 divided the existing institutions into three categories. At the most rudimentary level, relief homes (*jiujiyuan*) were designated for the helpless poor—children, the elderly, and the infirm. Next, workhouses (*xiyichang*) would impart vocational training to able-bodied men, women, and youths older than thirteen *sui*. Finally, those who completed their terms at the workhouse (three years for men, two for women) could be promoted to factories for employment on a noncustodial basis. The main goal was to separate the inmate population by sex, age, and capacity for physical labor, so that "appropriate tasks" could be assigned on the basis of ability and aspirations. As part of the restructuring, the Capital Vagrant Workhouse became the Number 1 Workhouse. A former beggar shelter and a poorhouse were combined as the Number 2 Workhouse with an affiliated reformatory (*ganhuasuo*). These two institutions were designated for men and boys older than thirteen *sui*. Girls and women were transferred to the Number 1 Women's Relief Home or the Women's Workhouse, both located on the premises of the former Inner City Poorhouse (where Dajuzi, her mother, and their lover had lived fifteen years earlier).[55] In addition, the Number 2 Relief Home housed boys until they were eligible for the workhouse. The Goose Wing Tower, a building in a former imperial garden, became the site of a new beggar shelter, for homeless transients who were detained by the police, referred by the Social Affairs Bureau, or "volunteers" seeking shelter and job training.[56] Finally, an insane asylum and a home for prostitutes remained separate institutions.

Despite these attempts to differentiate the homeless, needy, and/or suspicious people taken from the streets, administrators found that their classifications rarely corresponded to reality. The number of different agencies with multiple divisions also proved difficult to manage. For example, responsibility for the reformatory passed back and forth between the Social Affairs Bureau and the police several times. Originally designated for "unrepentant" ex-convicts requiring further detention and "work training," the reformatory also periodically accommodated "poor people" (*pinmin*), "drifters" (*liumin*), and "refugees" (*nanmin*).[57] After several years of reshuffling inmates, staff, and responsibilities, in 1934 a new Social Affairs director brought the municipal institutions under the umbrella of a single Relief Home, with four divisions: one for men, a second for women, a third for children. The fourth, housed at the Goose Wing Tower, functioned as a triage center, where the staff assessed incoming inmates and evaluated their moral character and ability to work. Meanwhile, improvements such as providing running water and toothbrushes, disinfecting clothing, and adding lard to the children's diet tried to ameliorate widespread disease and malnutrition.[58] The recurring experiments in sorting and classification underscored the belief that precise arrangements of the inmate population could render intelligible the causes of their dependency, and thereby facilitate their rehabilitation. Although reality did not always validate these convictions, overall more professional management, backed by the relatively stable finances of the Nationalist government, contributed to better conditions. In June 1936, the divisions of the Relief Home held 1,118 inmates in custody. Within the previous year, 1,725 people had arrived, 1,669 had been discharged, and 231 had died.[59]

In emphasizing classification and rehabilitation through labor and education, the principles behind Beijing's Relief Home strongly correlated with the goals of the contemporaneous modern prison movement. Indeed, prison routines described by Klaus Mühlhahn bear striking resemblance to those at the Relief Home. Yet for all the similarities, a workhouse detainee was not a prison convict, whose guilt was fixed. The most severe punishment carried out at the prison was the death penalty; its counterpart at the workhouse was expulsion. Moreover, in the late 1920s and 1930s the Nationalist government became notorious for the violence and torture of its prisons. News reports and memoirs proliferated, featuring wrenching accounts of cruel treatment and starvation. According to Mühlhahn, this genre of exposés enjoyed popularity and wielded considerable public influence.[60] Although conditions in some workhouses and poorhouses could be equally dreadful, such abuses were not widely known and not aired for public consumption.

The Faces of Poverty

To the thousands of people who entered and left the Beijing Relief Home during the Nanjing Decade, the institution served multiple functions: as a place of punishment for drug addicts and "vagrants"; as a foster home for abandoned children and orphans; as a temporary shelter to those who tried to commit suicide in order to escape poverty. Whether they viewed a stay at the Relief Home as a form of incarceration or welcome refuge from the streets depended on their individual circumstances. Conversely, government authorities regarded the Home as a solution to a host of social problems.

For Beijing's transients, government attempts to impose order on the city meant intensified surveillance of their lives, with the police increasing street patrols and searching lodges and inns for suspicious persons.[61] In November 1930, the Mayor's office ordered the police to remove female beggars congregating in Tianqiao (a notorious market area) and near temples and guild lodges. Wielding dusters, these women "offered" to sweep dirt from people's path or clothing. As the directive noted, this was a tactic to harass passersby for handouts, and although the women were pitiful, their actions provoked "feelings of antipathy and disgust."[62] In a time when the social danger of urban itinerancy was considered a male phenomenon, this rebuke of female mendicants was unusual. More often, dangerous women were prostitutes or drug addicts, as the police arrest logs for November 1930 indicate. During that month, of twenty-two women remanded for temporary detention, seven were prostitutes, five were drug addicts, and three were beggars.[63]

To the municipal government, the ubiquitous presence of homeless transients, especially their corpses, also tarnished "the city's image" (*shirong*). On the night of December 27, 1930, for instance, a beggar froze to death on a major thoroughfare, but two days passed before the body was removed. Such incidents embarrassed the municipal government, which ordered the Public Security Bureau to increase its patrols. In the future, the Mayor's office instructed, corpses needed to be removed immediately. Like those in other cities, the campaign to varnish Beijing's appearance tried to conceal such unpleasant aspects of urban life, and attempted to police others (itinerant vendors, litterbugs, public urination).[64] But while most offenders received warnings or paid fines, some street mendicants were subjected to severe consequences. Worried that the hordes of beggars who descend upon tourists exposed the city to "the ridicule of outsiders," the Social Affairs Bureau asked the police to round them up. In the spring of 1936, in anticipation of a visit from an American delegation, the Mayor ordered the streets cleared of garbage and dead bodies, with all beggars arrested and brought to the Relief Home.[65]

Who were these transients wandering the streets of Beijing, and why did government officials so easily conflate them with trash and corpses? Were they, as sociologist Li Jinghan had lamented, "half-dead and half-alive" ghosts, whose lives were barely better than animals? Or were they, as others charged, "parasites" preying upon society, and professional swindlers plying a trade? These dichotomous images hinged on the observers' assumptions about individual volition—did urban transients *choose* a life of vagrancy, or did circumstances beyond their control force them to take to the streets? In a 1930 assessment of inmates at its beggar shelter, the Social Affairs Bureau concluded that of 876 people in detention, 60 percent became beggars due to "family poverty," 20 percent "external factors," 10 percent internal "degeneracy"; the rest were unknown. Of the inmates, 92 percent (811) were men; most were Beijing locals or from nearby counties in Hebei.[66] Occasionally there were unusual cases, such as that of two Chinese-speaking men, a Russian and an Estonian, who claimed to be looking for work when the police apprehended them for begging near the Forbidden City in July 1936.[67] But for the most part, urban transiency in Beijing bore the traces of local impoverishment or short-distance migration.

With young male transients targeted as the primary threat, it is not surprising to find that former soldiers or others with military ties were disproportionately represented in these cases. According to Diana Lary, by the beginning of the Nanjing decade there were some 1.5 to 2 million men enrolled in regular armies, with even higher figures for local militias and unofficial units. In addition to discharges for injury, illness, and old age, a high rate of desertion meant that large numbers of former military men floated about, with little likelihood of finding employment. A stint in the army would have attenuated ties to the connections necessary to secure jobs; ex-soldiers were also less likely to be hired, perceived as having lost the capacity to make an honest living. In fact, the Beijing police believed that demobilized soldiers committed the majority of robberies in the city, and created a special task force in 1929 to search their hideouts.[68]

Records from Beijing's Relief Home and police archives provide ample evidence of soldiers adrift in the city. In many cases, veterans were implicated in assaults, often with deadly weapons.[69] Others became homeless due to illness or combat injuries. For instance, Wang Qingzhi (thirty-five *sui*), a veteran of the eighteenth division of the army, was discharged for health reasons. When Beijing police caught him begging on the streets, they referred him to the gendarmerie stationed in the city for help. In return, the military sometimes referred disabled soldiers to the municipal government, as in the case of four young men from Manchuria injured during the Anti-Japanese Resistance in 1931. They wandered Beijing's streets by day, and at night slept on the floor of a shop whose owner took pity on them. After verifying that they were not criminals, Social Affairs officials arranged for them to enter the municipal Relief Home. Yang Tongsen (sixteen *sui*), on the other hand, had followed the Twenty-ninth Army to Shanxi and then to Beijing. Yang was one of the many boys who, too young to enlist, followed the troops doing odd jobs. In this case, Yang decided to remain when the division decamped from the city. The police arrested him for begging and sent him to the reformatory.[70] As for He Liancheng (twelve *sui*), he had been abducted to work as an errand boy in the twenty-fifth division of the army in 1934. After many months, the commander discovered the boy's presence and ordered him to leave. He intended to walk home (all the way back to Anhui), but before he could make his way out of the city the police apprehended him. While the authorities notified the local precinct in his hometown to track down his family, they sent the boy to the Relief Home.[71] The link between itinerancy and the fate of former soldiers surfaced in scores of cases. While enlistment might have provided an avenue of upward advancement for some men, the remnants of China's loosely coordinated forces often joined the ranks of the urban poor once they left the military.

The attempt to remove the homeless from city streets also intersected with the zealous prosecution of drug addicts. According to Frank Dikötter, the Nationalist drug prohibition movement primarily targeted poor young men and forced hundreds of thousands of people to undergo treatment. In Beijing, drug offenders accounted for the largest category of criminals apprehended. In 1929, for example, they constituted 37 percent of all cases prosecuted.[72] Initially, the police sent offenders caught smoking opium or injecting morphine (occasionally, using heroin) to detoxification centers and hospitals. But with a high rate of recidivism and chronic funding problems, the Office for Opium Suppression asked the Social Affairs Bureau to place some in the municipal Relief Home. Since many of the addicts were impoverished, the drug enforcers hoped that job training could be part of the solution to the narcotics problem.[73]

Other addicts were sent to "labor dormitories," with the expectation that a term of hard labor would teach them a lesson and build their physical strength.[74] But, enervated by drug use and infectious diseases, many fell gravely ill when forced to work long hours at physically demanding jobs. After shuttling the sick back and forth between hospitals, detox centers, and police precincts (which supervised the work crews), the municipal government finally decided to exclude elderly and infirm addicts from labor training. Instead, starting in May 1935, they were sent to the Relief Home, where they received special "spiritual lectures" three times a week. (That month, the Mayor himself delivered two such lectures.)[75] In the two years from 1934 to 1935, a new detoxification center in Beijing processed over ten thousand addicts.[76] Although it is unclear whether this figure reflected an actual increase in drug use or more zealous enforcement (or both), the large number of narcotics convictions brought many inmates to the Relief Home.

Lastly, in the 1920s and 1930s, the identification of suicide as a social problem drew the concerned attention of researchers and government officials. Many scholars have shown that in the late imperial period, chaste widows, rape victims, and martyrs avowing loyalty to a fallen dynasty chose suicide, which served as an expression of moral virtue or a weapon of posthumous accusation.[77] By the early Republic, however, new ideas about gender equality, virtue, and loyalty challenged the meanings ascribed to suicide. A handful of sensational cases, such as the 1918 death of former Qing official Liang Ji and the 1922 suicide of a young female secretary named Xi Shangzhen, were highly publicized and endlessly debated. In other instances, educated youths who "wearied of the world" (yanshi) killed themselves to protest the nation's bleak future.[78] But while psychological derangement, momentary lapses of reason, or passionate patriotism could explain these suicides, those who tried to kill themselves to escape poverty presented a different indictment of society. In

1930, nearly a quarter of the suicides in Beijing were attributed to destitution, while in Shanghai, "economic pressure" (22 percent) was the second leading cause behind "family problems" (43 percent).[79]

For those intent on killing themselves, jumping into wells and hanging were common methods. In addition, Beijing had several unique venues for suicides, such as the moat around the Forbidden City and lakes in the former imperial compound. Zhang Junheng, for example, had been a physician and former army captain. When he left the military, he started a hospital with a loan from an uncle. Facing bankruptcy in 1935, Zhang went to Beijing to look for work. Unable to find a job or some way to repay the loan, he went to Tian'anmen and tried to throw himself in the moat. A constable pulled him out of the water, and the Relief Home took him in while the police notified his family to claim him. Others ingested drugs or took poison. For example, Dong Gonggan (twenty-two *sui*) had served in the Northeast Army as a volunteer. In 1934 he went to Beijing hoping to enroll in the military academy and become an officer. After failing the entrance exam, Dong tried to kill himself with poison. The hotel proprietor found him unconscious and called the police, who arranged for him to go to the Relief Home. Another veteran, Yang Pin—whose given name means "poor"—also swallowed poison, but not enough to kill him. He, too, went to the Relief Home. Both Dong and Yang stayed for several months before applying for release.[80]

These acts of quiet desperation, arising from frustrated hopes and broken families, differed from the handful of sensational suicides that captured the public's imagination. For the most part, those who tried to take their own lives to escape the misery of poverty died quietly; the ones who survived warranted only a page or two in the police records. Under the GMD Criminal Code, causing another person to commit suicide could be punished by up to seven years of hard labor, a provision adopted from Qing law.[81] But when someone tried to kill himself or herself due to poverty, no one in particular—only society at large—could be blamed.

Volunteers for the Workhouse

Beggars, drug addicts, orphans, and people who attempted suicide—these were some who ended up at the Beijing Relief Home due to the intervention of government authorities, whether for punishment or charity's sake. During the 1930s, the Relief Home also received countless petitions from people who applied for permission to enter the workhouse. Many were parents or relatives who committed their children and elderly dependents to the care of the state. Others were adults who asked for admission of their own volition. To the Social Affairs Bureau, these "voluntary" (*ziyuan*) requests had to be carefully investigated, to verify the claims of hardship. Applicants were also required to provide bonded guarantors to vouch for their truthfulness—a unique feature of Chinese institutions. In general, commercial establishments provided these guarantees, with the proprietor pledging "complete responsibility" if anything went awry. The bond was usually secured with cash or by mortgaging an item of value; many pawnshops acted in this capacity. The use of bonded guarantees was not limited to workhouses. Individuals seeking employment or loans also used them, and shops with higher levels of capitalization (*ziben*) could stand surety for more complex or risky transactions.[82] In Beijing, the Relief Home required a "grade 9" bond from applicants applying for admission, the lowest level of guarantee.

While these stipulations excluded the most impoverished (unable to afford the collateral) and many new migrants (without connections in the city), extant archival sources reveal that there were large numbers of volunteers for the workhouse, reflecting the desperation of the times. This was particularly true in the immediate aftermath of Japan's attack on Mukden in September 1931, when thousands of people fled south.[83] The ensuing refugee crisis shattered many families already on the brink of destitution. Mrs. Jia Shuxian, for instance, escaped to Beijing with her two daughters after her husband, a battalion commander, died during combat. They lived with relatives for five years, but after exhausting both their generosity and resources, Mrs. Jia had nowhere else to turn. In 1936, she asked the Relief Home to take her two daughters (twelve and nine *sui*) so that she could look for work.[84] Like Mrs. Jia, many women were left to fend for themselves when their husbands died, left home to seek work, or suffered debilitating illnesses. Mrs. Min (née Song), with six daughters and an elderly mother-in-law to support, was another example. Her letter to the Social Affairs Bureau explained that her husband left home in December 1935 to look for work: "I did not expect that after he left there would be no news for eight to nine months. I did hear from someone that he was stuck because he could not find work. . . . We have sold everything in our house . . . the cries of hunger from old and young are unbearable." Mrs. Min asked the Social Affairs Bureau to take three of her daughters, so that they would not all starve to death. After an inspector verified the family's situation, the Relief Home accepted the girls in August 1936.[85] In the absence of husbands, many women left their children in the care of the Relief Home. They considered it a temporary solution, and hoped to "redeem" their children from the state's custody as soon as possible.

Occasionally, the Relief Home also accepted able-bodied men who could not make it on their own. Hu Dian'en, forty-nine *sui*, was a semiskilled carpenter from a county in Hebei province. He went to Beijing to look for work, but soon realized that there were scores of people just like him searching for employment in the city. "You have to know the right people to get a job in a factory," he explained. "If you work on the street as an itinerant laborer it is extremely difficult to make a living." After several months of scraping by, Hu had pawned everything he owned, and had nowhere to turn for help: "I call to heaven and there is no answer. I cry out to earth and there is no reply." His petition, addressed to Social Affairs Bureau Director Lei Sishang, stated, "I have thought it over and over, and I really cannot survive, especially now that it is winter and the weather turns colder each day. . . . I considered going home, but I certainly do not have the travel money." In closing, Hu beseeched the director to allow him to enter the Relief Home, appealing to his sense of "public charity" and love for the people "as if they were his own children," saying, "you cannot sit by and watch me wait for death."[86]

Based on the clear script and the rhetorical formulas of entreaty (crying to heaven and earth, elevating the bureaucrat to the position of an imperial official), we can surmise that Hu did not pen his own petition. The practice of hiring scribes to write on one's behalf has a long history in China, dating as far back as the Song dynasty. As Melissa Macauley has shown, scriveners and pettifoggers played crucial roles in the Qing legal system, writing out petitions and documents for illiterate or semiliterate plaintiffs. For the Republican era, Xiaoqun Xu has studied how petitions constituted a routine part of evolving judicial processes.[87] In this case, in the 1930s, clerks at the Beijing Social Affairs Bureau provided scribal services to those who wanted to communicate with the agency. A schedule of fees (daishu fei) appears on the back of the official petition form: ten cents for the first one hundred words, five cents for each additional fifty words, up to four hundred.[88]

Hu Dian'en's petition was almost certainly the product of such a fee-for-service arrangement. To what extent do the words, mediated through a government functionary, reflect his experiences? In many cases, clerks processed the requests in a formulaic way. There are stacks of petitions preserved in the archives that narrate, almost verbatim, the same brief account, varying only in biographical details (name, age, address). In contrast, others are poetically rendered tales of woe, full of pathos. In this instance, Hu's petition included information specific to his circumstances. After all, he was a relatively young man, without physical disabilities or dependents to support. To substantiate his application for aid, it was necessary to provide evidence that he had conscientiously sought employment, and that he was willing to work. Such details were then incorporated into a standard but dramatically narrated story of desperation.

Hu Dian'en would not have verbalized his plight in the same manner; the rhetorical flourishes belonged to the scribe. But the heart of the claim—that he was penniless and unable to make a living—came from the supplicant himself. A government inspector then corroborated his claim of impoverishment and verified the authenticity of the bonded guarantee he furnished, before officials allowed him to enter the Relief Home.[89]

Such volunteers for the workhouse were not a new phenomenon. As discussed in chapter 1, the earliest workhouses in Beijing had permitted the "ordinary poor" to apply for entry on similar terms. But there were relatively few of them, and the records have been sparsely preserved. In the 1930s, the number of applications for voluntary entry spiked. The consolidation of the Social Affairs Bureau and the Relief Home meant that the needy now had obvious destinations to seek help. Some applicants stated that they had read about the Relief Home in the newspaper or heard about the Social Affairs Bureau from neighbors, suggesting that knowledge about government agencies and institutions was in circulation.[90] In contrast to those of the earlier period, their petitions have also been preserved in large numbers, allowing us to mine them for historical details previously unavailable.

Once supplicants were admitted into government custody, petitions were also the channel for release. Leaving the Relief Home was a complicated process that required securing bonded guarantors, even if one had entered voluntarily. Concerned about fraudulent claims and adoption scams connected to human trafficking, the Social Affairs Bureau insisted on investigating all release applications by checking every detail. Some, like Ku Jingyun, simply wanted to return home. A farmer from a nearby county in Hebei, Ku arrived in Beijing in 1934 after a famine in his hometown. His twenty *mu* of "good land" was normally sufficient to support his family, but that year he did not harvest "a single grain of rice." In Beijing, his father, wife, and three children all begged for a time on the streets, until the police arranged for them to enter the Relief Home. When Ku asked for their release the following spring, he wrote, "We are originally farmers and have a home to return to. We do not want to drift about in Beiping and be beggars forever." The Social Affairs Bureau approved Ku's request in time for his family to return home for spring planting.[91] Other parents sought the release of their children from the Relief Home because they were ill or dying there. For instance, during a visit Wu Zhucun discovered that his son's feet had turned blue from the cold and were covered in lesions. He petitioned for the boy's discharge, in order to seek private medical treatment for him.[92]

In a different case, Mrs. Wu (née Deng) had been arrested for begging in 1935. When her daughter Mrs. Li petitioned for her release, she signed a sworn statement pledging to assume full responsibility if her mother were caught soliciting alms again. Like nearly all of the petitions from women, Mrs. Li signed her letter with a cross mark, signaling her illiteracy; others sometimes used a thumbprint. Instead of using the Social Affairs Bureau's services, Mrs. Li relied on Chen Guiyu, an elderly neighbor. (Her petition was one of the few that provided the name of the scribe.)[93] Wang Zhengguan encountered additional complications when he asked for the release of his mother and younger sister, who had been living at the Relief Home for more than two years. In February of 1935, Wang wrote that he recently received a raise at his job at the Telephone Bureau, and could now support his family. Social Affairs officials scrutinizing his petition found that the "grade 9" bond Wang provided from a dry goods store fell short of the "grade 7–8" guarantee required. (Whereas applicants for entry needed only a "grade 9" bond, release applications required a more substantial guarantor, presumably aimed at preventing foul play.) After a month, however, Wang notified the authorities that despite his best efforts, he had not been able to find anyone willing to furnish the required level of security. He was not a native of the city and did not have access to a social network to help him. Wang resubmitted his petition with one additional "grade 9" guarantee and asked for an exemption. After a government inspector verified the details, the director of the Social Affairs Bureau finally consented to his sister and mother's discharge. In this painstaking process, municipal officials demonstrated their fiduciary duty to the Relief Home's residents. While the conditions inside were not optimal, to officials it was preferable to releasing women and children to an uncertain fate on the outside, where traffickers were sure to pounce on them.

In summary, during the Nanjing decade many factors shaped the experiences of poverty in Beijing. As we have seen, the economic depression (which ensued after the capital moved to Nanjing in 1928 and Japan's invasion of Manchuria in 1931) triggered crises that increased the distress of an already impoverished population. In addition, Beijing continued to attract rural victims of natural disasters, migrants in search of jobs, and former soldiers looking for "a way out." For strangers to the city denied coping strategies provided by kinship networks, one solution was to turn themselves or their children in to the custody of the state. But even as some willingly entered the workhouse, they, along with others detained against their will, became experimental subjects in institutions that envisioned labor as a force for transforming social liability into productive citizenship. As laboratories for pedagogical methods informed by sociological precepts, Nationalist workhouses operated on the assumption that physical exertion in labor would eradicate the "parasitic" dependence of those who would otherwise subsist on charity, to the detriment of the nation.

To the south, Shanghai's urban poor encountered some similar circumstances—the city, too, was a magnet for rural refugees and drifters, and a victim of Japanese aggression (in January 1932). But as we shall see below, Shanghai's status as a treaty port and its more industrialized economy inextricably linked a rising tide of nationalism to the issue of urban poverty. Those who found themselves homeless or adrift could move between the divided jurisdictions of the city, in search of alms, jobs, or relief. In doing so, they also found themselves subjected to the charitable and/or punitive interventions of multiple authorities, with private charities functioning as extensions of government power.

A Beggars' Paradise?

More than any other city in China, Shanghai's juxtaposition of fabulous wealth with abject poverty inspired hyperbolic analogies. According to a typical cliché, which appeared with many variations, "on its façade Shanghai resembles prosperous heaven, yet its back side is in fact the deepest hell."[94] Unlike in Beijing, however, no one could blame "the Manchus" or the imperial legacy. Instead, even as the GMD took over control of the Chinese districts and constituted a "special municipal government" in the city, Shanghai's divided jurisdictions and the conditions of extraterritoriality were crucial factors in shaping the judgments about and the experiences of the city's impoverished residents.

From the perspective of the two foreign concession governments, the ubiquitous presence of beggars and transients undermined their ability to govern their enclaves. Multinational jurisdictions made law enforcement exceedingly complicated; upholding antivagrancy ordinances meant a constant cat-and-mouse game. The police in the International Settlement, for example, would round up beggars and dump them off in Chinese territory. But soon they would find the same people back on their doorsteps. As officials complained, in a typical roundup they could catch twenty-two beggars in the first hour; after that, the others would have gotten wind of what was happening and disappeared.[95] Despite obvious ineffectiveness, the Municipal Council persisted in conducting these periodic campaigns, for to do nothing about the problem would have been unacceptable to its ratepayers. At the same time, other interventions such as providing relief or establishing poorhouses were "out of the question," on the grounds that such measures were not part of the Council's responsibility. Reiterating arguments from a decade earlier, the Council believed that dispensing *any* kind of aid would create a "beggars' paradise" and serve as an "open invitation" to indigents from elsewhere. Specifically, unless indoor institutions wielded "penal powers" that made them "as unattractive as possible," they would become magnets for the poor—thereby exacerbating rather than solving the problem.[96] These misgivings applied to mendicants of all nationalities. Although nowhere as numerous as the Chinese, there were foreign beggars in Shanghai, mostly Russians. One report from 1931 counted 107 foreign "loafers and habitual drunkards," frequently detained on vagrancy charges, hence well-known to the police. One chronic offender had accumulated more than eighty such convictions.[97]

The reluctance to provide relief also stemmed from the suspicion that most mendicants in Shanghai (of any nationality) were not really "poor"—that they were in fact professional swindlers who earned a good living, that begging was actually a profitable trade. In 1928, the International Settlement's Health Department reported that of the beggars its inspectors examined, all appeared well nourished, and 70 percent of them could work if they were so inclined. In fact, they were not beggars "in the true sense of the term," since they performed services such as carrying banners at weddings and funerals, in exchange for sums ranging from fifty to two hundred coppers. A few years later a police report concurred, saying that those who chose to beg undoubtedly could find work: "It is a peculiarity of the Chinese to be content with the bare necessities of life and while these people can obtain enough to keep them from starving without work, they will be idle." Even more cynically, some observers alleged that those with physical disabilities inflicted the wounds on themselves (or their children), in order to solicit sympathy and alms.[98]

The skepticism that street mendicants were not really "poor"; the difficulty of differentiating between the truly needy and the "professionals"; the fear that providing relief would not solve the problem but have the opposite effect of attracting more indigents—these perceptions were not unique to Shanghai's foreign community. Many Chinese in fact shared these views. But unlike the foreigners, the GMD government felt duty bound to do *something* to alleviate poverty, for reasons already enumerated above. And in fact, the problem transcended street beggars. In a 1929 speech, Social Affairs Director Pan Gongzhan declared that these five symptoms, in order of importance, characterized the severe crisis of "poverty" in Shanghai: unemployment, crime, shantytowns, suicides, and increasingly rancorous labor disputes. If the problem of unemployment were not solved, Pan felt there would be "no hope for all of China, let alone Shanghai." Echoing his Beijing counterparts, he described the presence of soldiers and bandits everywhere, "a symptom of the severity of unemployment."[99] As a leading indicator of poverty, unemployment was the focus of many studies, with bureaucrats and sociologists alike seeking to understand the extent and the causes of the problem. But like other statistics collected at this time, uncertain methodology makes it difficult to interpret the data. How was "unemployment" defined? Most of the numbers excluded those who worked outside the formal economy, such as scavengers, itinerant peddlers, and casual laborers. In one study, only those who belonged to trade guilds were counted.[100] The terms *wuye* (jobless, having no vocation at all) and *shiye* (unemployed, losing one's employment) were often used interchangeably. But at other times, the phrase *wuye youmin* (jobless vagrant) contrasted unfavorably to *shiye gongren* (unemployed worker), implying a palpable difference.[101]

According to Pan Gongzhan, in 1929 there were approximately 500,000 unemployed people in greater Shanghai (including the concessions), out of an estimated population of 2.7 million. Of the half million figure, at least 200,000 were men. "Gentlemen! Close your eyes and think," Pan urged. "Although from all appearances Shanghai is flourishing and wealthy, how could we tolerate 200,000 jobless and propertyless vagrants ... living in destitution, dependent on handouts from others?" With so many "vagrants" wandering about, how could the rest of society sit back and do nothing?[102] In Pan's calculus, the convergence of impoverishment and unemployment produced "vagrancy" as an exclusively male threat. The 300,000 women were merely unemployed, but the 200,000 men represented a greater peril, an inflammatory combination of nonproductive idleness, mobility, and possible criminality.

To understand "why people become vagrants," in the winter of 1929 the staff of the Social Affairs Bureau interviewed 1,471 men at two temporary shelters.

The results revealed that 13 percent were drug addicts, and a few others were gamblers, alcoholics, and people who consorted with prostitutes. While there were probably some who dared not confess these habits (fearing punishment), vice played a less prominent role than bureaucrats had assumed. Indeed, officials concluded that the main causes of vagrancy were the large numbers of people without jobs (*wuye*, 21 percent) and the fact that those who lost their jobs (*shiye*) could not find new employment. The latter included unskilled laborers (16 percent), peddlers (15 percent), discharged soldiers (11 percent), a few farmers, tailors, dockworkers, carpenters, and rickshaw pullers, as well as two scribes, six teachers, and—ironically—six people who had formerly worked for a famine relief agency in the Beijing government. Among 169 veterans, only 31 had found temporary work after leaving the military.[103]

Despite these findings, the authorities continued to view unemployed drifters with suspicion, constantly referring to their "willingness to dwell in degeneracy" and propensity for "improper conduct." Social Affairs official Chen Lingseng explained that "a vagrant is certainly a member of society, and needs clothing, food, shelter, and transportation. Without the ability to make a living on his own, obviously he needs society's leftovers, becoming a social parasite." But if the leftovers fail to satisfy his needs, the vagrant develops into "the enzyme that ferments crime and evil." According to Chen, such "parasites" form "a trinity," progressing from "the vagrant" who idles about, to the more advanced and pernicious "beggars" and "hoodlums" (*biesan*).[104]

Beyond unemployment and vagrancy, Shanghai's Chinese government tried to assess the overall extent of poverty in the city. In 1929, the population census found 24,226 "extremely poor" (*jipin*) households, a total of 113,515 people, the majority of whom congregated along the peripheries of the concession areas. In 1932, a government survey identified 62,222 "poor" households, defined as both "jobless" and "propertyless." This figure, however, excluded the vast numbers of unemployed workers, rickshaw pullers, and straw hut dwellers—who were also described as "poor."[105] As these incongruous numbers suggest, poverty had different gradations, and the assessment of how many were "poor" depended upon the parameters of the definition.

POOR RELIEF IN SHANGHAI

Like its counterpart in Beijing, the Nationalist government in Shanghai viewed "social relief" as part of its responsibility and an essential component of national reconstruction. Shanghai's divided jurisdiction, however, meant that the Chinese authorities lacked complete control over matters of public welfare. New regulations in 1928 required charities operating in the Chinese districts to register with the Social Affairs Bureau and provide detailed documentation of their activities. Sixty-two organizations filed paperwork as "public charities," broadly defined to include native place associations, foundling homes, free hospitals and schools, burial societies, and seasonal relief agencies.[106]

Unlike in Beijing, where crowds gathered at soup kitchens were a common sight in winter, Shanghai's charities preferred to dole out uncooked food and avoid the logistical problems of running kitchens. In 1929, fourteen agencies distributed rice, while only two large soup kitchens served meals. The Zhabei Charity Federation fed almost eight thousand people every day, while the Tong-ren Fuyuan Benevolent Hall (one of the oldest charities in the city) fed three thousand in Nanshi. That year, private charities also distributed over 28,000 pieces of clothing, gave out more than 20,000 free coffins, and buried 38,545 bodies.[107] The numbers of needy people frequently overwhelmed the ability of these organizations to provide assistance. In 1935, for instance, the Zhabei Charity Federation reported that at dawn on January 1, the day one of its soup kitchens opened, over three thousand people showed up. When the food ran out, organizers handed out nine coppers to each person in line. The following day, twelve thousand people showed up. Although the kitchen closed at the end of February, starving people continued to wait by the entrance.[108]

In addition to outdoor relief, over four thousand people lived in eighteen year-round indoor institutions, and the Social Affairs Bureau carefully monitored their operations. For example, a survey of the five largest foundling homes in 1929 tallied an average death rate of nearly 50 percent for the preceding three years. While many of the babies were probably already ill when they arrived, to remedy the situation the Social Affairs Bureau issued new guidelines on infant care and revised procedures for dealing with abandoned or abducted children.[109] In particular, officials scrutinized the Anti-Kidnapping Society, a rescue home for prostitutes and abducted children, after receiving troubling reports of mismanagement and corruption. Inspectors found appalling conditions at the once highly lauded organization: crumbling buildings, insect infestations, and rampant disease. The Bureau ordered the administrators to make specific operational changes: quarantine the sick, install running water, build a new lavatory, shorten the maximum length of stay from three years to one, increase efforts to reunite the women and children with their families, and arrange for marriages and adoptions if they were not claimed. In addition, officials discovered that many of the boys grew up to be "lazy idlers," hardly equipped to become independent wage earners. Thereafter, if they could not find work, they would be sent off to the workhouse.[110]

Unlike their municipal counterparts in Beijing, Shanghai's workhouses and poorhouses were mostly privately funded and administered. Several plans to build government institutions (including a proposal for a centralized municipal relief home, similar to the one in Beijing) were drafted but never implemented, with ambitions surpassing budgets.[111] The financial shortfalls were further exacerbated by Japan's attack on the Shanghai region on January 28, 1932. When the hostilities ceased three months later, much of Zhabei and the surrounding suburbs lay in ruins. Japanese bombs had destroyed municipal offices, police stations, and schools, with an estimated Ch. $1.5 billion in damage. More than two hundred thousand people were displaced from their homes. The government's plans for rebuilding the war-ravaged areas, as well its blueprints for welfare projects, stalled for lack of funding.[112]

Instead, the GMD government turned to a cohort of private institutions. Officials found, however, that the Jiangwan Model Factory (discussed in chapter 2) was defunct, and its managers could not account for the disappearance of a sizeable endowment and cash reserves. The municipal government then transferred the remaining assets and facilities to Nanjing officials, who used the premises to build a new campus for National Labor University.[113] Meanwhile, the Songhu Poorhouse, which had closed in 1927 during the battle for control of Shanghai, reopened on a reduced scale. Songhu continued to collaborate with the police, serving as the repository for troublemakers (e.g., gangs operating at the docks to defraud newly arrived visitors; old-time "beggar chiefs" trying to extort money from shopkeepers).[114] In addition, Songhu conducted its own weekly roundups. On Sundays, the staff fanned out across the city in teams to "take in" street beggars. (One particularly successful day netted 232 beggars and a notice in the newspaper.)[115] But Songhu also experienced chronic financial problems. Officials of the International Settlement rebuffed its request for a subsidy, saying that of a batch of two hundred beggars they sent there, the majority were spotted back on the streets within a month. By the end of 1930, the poorhouse was insolvent, with over Ch. $5,000 owed to creditors. Officials then arranged for Green Gang boss Du Yuesheng and the Charity Federation to pay off the debts. At the government's behest, the Federation also assumed operational management, renaming it the Number 2 Vagrant Workhouse. The facility was destroyed during Japan's attack in January 1932; the inmates who were not killed ran away.[116]

The Charity Federation also shouldered the responsibility for the Shanghai Vagrant Workhouse (Youmin Xiqinsuo), established in 1927.[117] Located on a large tract of land behind the Jiangsu Number 2 Prison in the northern suburb of the city, the Workhouse held five hundred people, aged twelve to sixty *sui*. According to the founders, the goal was to give vagrants and beggars "a suitable education and skills training, so that they will turn over a new leaf. They will all learn a trade to foster the ability to make an independent living."[118] Social Affairs Director Pan Gongzhan put it more bluntly, declaring that those "who do not produce" are "bloodsucking parasites" who become the conduit for "crime and evil." Among these "vagrants," those with high aspirations end up as hooligans and thugs; the "bottom-dwellers" become beggars and tramps. The Vagrant Workhouse had limited capacity and funding, but Pan considered it an important step in the right direction.[119] Indeed, the institution garnered not only the municipal government's endorsement, but also its financial support. It

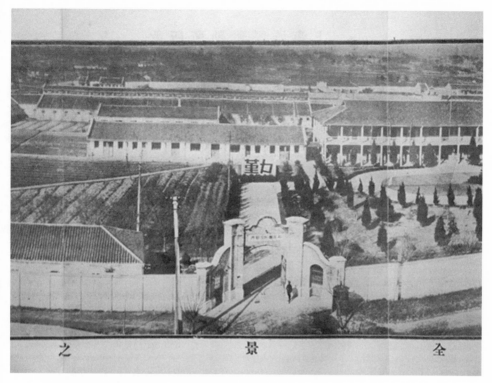

Figure 3.2. Shanghai Vagrant Workhouse, 1931
The character for "diligence" (*qin*) appears prominently in the center.

was initially privately funded, but in 1932 the Social Affairs Bureau stepped in to cover the operating expenses after the war with Japan interrupted the flow of donations.[120]

At the workhouse, upon arrival inmates were given a bath and a set of new clothes, photographed and fingerprinted, and placed in solitary confinement for "reflection." They then joined the others in one of the workshops, either making shoes or straw hats, sewing, or gluing together matchboxes. A typical week included 9.5 hours of work daily, six days a week. In the evenings, the children studied reading, writing, and mathematics, while the adults listened to lectures on topics such as diligence, frugality, and patriotism. To reinforce these messages, signs were posted everywhere urging repentance. One poster, for example, proclaimed, "Lazy, lazy, you will definitely be cold and hungry; diligent, diligent, you will certainly have food and clothing." At weekly assemblies, the inmates sang the workhouse anthem, which exhorted them to work hard and reminded them to be grateful: "I came to the workhouse suffering from cold

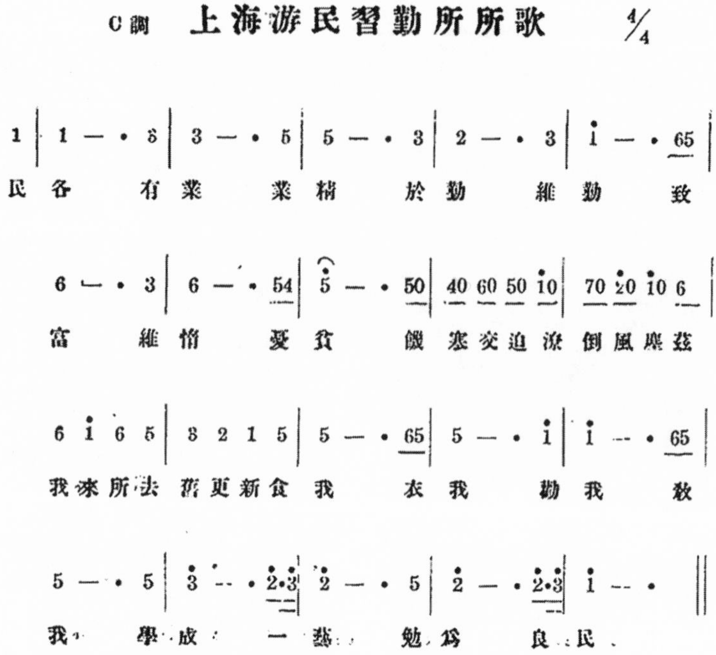

Figure 3.3. Shanghai Vagrant Workhouse official song, 1931

and hunger, down on my luck . . . I am rejuvenated, replacing new with old. I am fed, clothed, and taught, learning a trade, strive to become a good citizen."[121]

In many ways, the Shanghai Vagrant Workhouse tried to present itself as a charitable institution, invoking the idea "taking in" people from the streets, and moving them to goodness through the transformative power of physical labor and education. The reality, however, suggested something quite different. About half of the inmates were arrested by the Chinese police and sent to the workhouse as punishment; the others were referred by charities or the Social Affairs Bureau. All inmates were required to complete a one-year sentence, after which they were eligible for release—but only if they had worked diligently and promised never to beg on the streets again. The workhouse was also heavily guarded and surrounded by barbed wire, with the former warden of the adjacent prison serving as the director.

On the evening of August 30, 1929, less than three months after the workhouse opened, a group of inmates took a staff member hostage. Their demands included an eight-hour workday; a ban on torture or extreme punishments; permission to keep their doors and windows open, walk around the grounds in their free time, cook their own meals, and receive provisions from the outside. When the inmates refused to step down, the local police arrived to "pacify" them. The following day, inspectors from the Social Affairs Bureau found the offenders kneeling in the corridor as punishment. The ringleader, identified as Gong Zhikun, a native of Suzhou in his twenties, was locked up. According to Gong, the inmates had been incited when four people were flogged for a minor (unnamed) infraction. Although the inspectors found Gong's demeanor "suspicious," they took the grievances seriously. After some deliberation, the Social Affairs Bureau shortened the workday to eight hours, and allowed the inmates to walk around on the grounds in their free time. The doors and windows could stay open on a probationary basis. (The demands for cooking and outside provisions were rejected, due to concerns about sanitation, drugs, or other contraband articles.) In addition, officials reprimanded the workhouse administrators for inflicting severe physical punishments, in violation of existing regulations.[122]

After this incident, the Shanghai Vagrant Workhouse apparently operated without further problems, reporting few runaways and a relatively low death rate (about 5 percent). On the other hand, the administrators themselves admitted that they failed in their mission, for only a small number of people "truly" reformed. Once released, the majority reverted back to their old ways. In 1931, the workhouse sent inspectors to track down some former inmates, to see how things turned out. The success stories included one person who had graduated from the police academy; another was working at a publishing company (and praised for sending money home to his mother every month). Of four former opium addicts, two had quit for good—one became a teacher, another worked in a teahouse. The others, however, had relapsed. In fact, recidivism became such a significant issue that in 1934 the workhouse extended the term of detention from one to three years, and also expanded the capacity to eight hundred inmates, in part to accommodate repeat offenders. Taking cues from the GMD's New Life Movement, the directors also adopted a military protocol of marching, saluting, and standing at attention. The theory was that by nature "vagrants" liked to loaf about, and the laxity of their physical behavior mirrored their internal immorality. Enforcing a military-style discipline over their bodies would therefore help stimulate the transformation of their hearts and minds. At around the same time, the workhouse received a large donation to build a meditation hall, and began to incorporate Buddhist teachings.[123] As a result, its rehabilitation program combined a medley of different pedagogies: labor reform and moral edification with a Buddhist and militarist twist.

Of the thousands of homeless people in Shanghai, why were these few hundred singled out for punishment? As in Beijing, the majority of those incarcerated as "vagrants" were men. Initially, the workhouse featured separate women's quarters, but they were infrequently used. When the number of juvenile offenders began to rise, the administrators stopped admitting women altogether and adapted the dormitory for young men.[124] Like in Beijing, drugs were a factor, with 30 to 40 percent of the inmates identified as opium addicts. There were also a few gamblers and drunks, but the rest were simply called "lazy" or unemployed. Some people ran afoul of the law in specific ways. For example, one inmate identified as number 88 had been arrested when the police broke a counterfeiting ring. Since it was his first offense, number 88 was not prosecuted but sent to the workhouse for punishment. Among "voluntary inmates," number 165 was the only child of a prosperous family. According to his own account, he became dissolute after his father's early death, taking up with prostitutes, spending all of his time in gambling parlors and opium dens. In two years he squandered nearly Ch. $10,000 of his family's fortune. "Finally," he said, "my mother had no choice but to send me to the workhouse."[125]

From Straw Huts to People's Villages

As described earlier in this chapter, affordable housing for the poor was an issue with nationwide importance, often topping the wish list of GMD welfare initiatives. Zwia Lipkin has shown how in Nanjing, the government drafted and partially implemented plans to relocate shantytowns to designated zones. The primary motivation there was the protection of the capital city's image.[126] Although similar concerns were factors in treaty port Shanghai, the matter took on different significance in the context of extraterritoriality. In chapter 2, we saw how the issue was left largely to the International Settlement authorities in the mid-1920s, and became embroiled in controversies over national sovereignty. In 1928, the newly constituted Nationalist government found the problem intensifying. Like their counterparts in the foreign concessions as well as in other cities, Shanghai officials worried that the proliferation of hut settlements compromised sanitation and public order. In its first census, the GMD Public Security Bureau counted 113,517 people living in 25,655 huts in the Chinese district, compared to two to three thousand shanties in the International Settlement.[127] With the highly flammable dwellings frequently succumbing to fire, the problem could not be ignored.

Indeed, throughout 1928 the city's newspapers featured numerous stories of hut fires. In October, controversy erupted over back-to-back conflagrations that destroyed five hundred dwellings and rendered 1,500 people homeless. The genesis was a fire that occurred on October 5, in the vicinity of Changchun Road in Zhabei, situated at the border of the International Settlement. Although the numbers were relatively small (some one hundred huts, no deaths), the incident stirred passionate outrage. Firefighters racing to the scene unexpectedly encountered a wall, blocking access to the burning shanties at the end of the road. A crowd tried to dismantle the obstacle so that fire trucks could connect to the only hydrant in the neighborhood, but the flames quickly engulfed the combustible structures. The blame fell on a real estate company registered under a British merchant's name: the wall, on the Chinese side of the boundary, cordoned off the offensive huts and left no emergency outlet. In an editorial, *Shenbao* declared that the incident, an affront to "national sovereignty," unequivocally exposed the Nationalist government's impotence: "These foreigners regard the lives of Chinese people as worthless . . . and our government tolerates it, afraid to tear down even a wall."

In the wake of a firestorm of criticism, Mayor Zhang Xun launched an investigation. Municipal Councilor Xu Peihuang, deputized to probe the incident, reported that the victims were mostly laborers (manure collectors, sanitation workers, rickshaw pullers); many of them held leases (typically three to six years), paying about Ch. $13 annually. "For the most part they are obedient, not undisciplined vagrants without jobs," Xu informed the Mayor.[128] In a more general discussion of the issue, other officials noted that although the law prohibited straw huts, lax enforcement meant that people built them wherever they pleased. In addition to the fire hazard, the dwellings also presented multiple perils to public health: "There is manure everywhere; the smells are unbearable (especially in summer) because of the pigs; they are breeding grounds for mosquitoes." From a security standpoint, the shantytowns, where "many criminals easily mix in and conceal their weapons," were notoriously difficult to police, with a population thought to be particularly receptive to Communist propaganda.[129]

Despite these serious concerns, Shanghai officials also recognized that, given the housing shortage, an outright ban on huts would only create other, equally thorny issues. Therefore, when the authorities received requests from landowners asking to remove shanties illegally built on their property, they generally declined to intervene. For instance, the Public Security Bureau refused one request, saying "this matter is related to the problem of housing for the poor." Other officials recommended deferring action, saying that for the sake of "the livelihood of the poor we find it difficult to remove the huts immediately"; and that without a "fundamental solution," demolishing shanties en masse would only lead to more disorder on the streets.[130] Mayor Zhang Qun specifically ordered a gradual approach, noting that the International Settlement had previously tried to expel hut dwellers and push them into the Chinese district. "If we in turn drive out the hut dwellers and cause more than 100,000 poor people to lose their lifeline," the Mayor declared, "they may take the dangerous path."[131]

In 1929, Mayor Zhang established the People's Housing Committee (Pingmin Zhusuo Weiyuanhui), and appointed Councilor Xu Peihuang to be its chairman. Initial plans called for the Committee to build three thousand units in six villages, at a projected cost of Ch. $600,000 ($100,000 from government funds, the remainder financed with bank loans). Although promoted as the "fundamental solution" to the problem, the Housing Committee immediately encountered a major obstacle when the government could not muster the promised funds. A new financing plan called for 50 percent loans and 50 percent donations (to be solicited from merchants and private charities). The projections also vastly underestimated actual costs. Everything from staff salaries to planting trees and wiring electricity cost more than double the original budgets, while private donations failed to collect as much money as anticipated.[132] As a result, the Committee managed to build only one hundred units at the Number One People's Village in Zhabei in 1929. But in the same neighborhood, one single fire on the evening of January 22, 1930, destroyed more than two hundred huts, leaving 385 households homeless. Between January and September of that year, there were thirty separate hut fires in the Chinese district. In 1931, four hundred more units opened at the Number Two People's Village in Nanshi, a much heralded accomplishment. The numbers, however, were far from sufficient to meet the need.[133]

As construction of the people's villages began, the GMD government began to crack down on straw huts. A municipal order in 1930 stipulated that no new shanties would be permitted without approval. Existing dwellings were subject to immediate removal if they were situated within forty feet of other buildings, or located in commercial or "inappropriate" areas. Furthermore, standing huts were to be "cleaned up"—rearranged to create fire corridors and emergency outlets, or relocated to designated areas. An addendum specified that existing shanties would be allowed to remain, within the bounds of the regulations, until the "people's villages" were completed.[134] These regulations in turn triggered a flood of requests for the Housing Committee to provide shelter to people left homeless, either by demolition or fire. But with limited funds, in most cases the Committee could answer only that while construction was underway, there were not enough accommodations for all in need of housing, hut dwellers or otherwise. In one instance, in response to yet another request, Committee Chairman Xu Peihuang replied in exasperation, "Our city has more than 30,000 huts. If we build 1,000 housing units every year, it would take 30 years to reach the goal."[135]

Compared to the squalor of the shantytowns, the accommodations at the people's villages were luxurious. Most of the new units had separate living and sleeping quarters, a kitchen, and a bathroom, with concrete floors, windows, running water, and electricity. The villages featured amenities such as medical clinics, exercise fields, cafeterias, even barbershops and libraries.[136] Yet for many of the people assigned to live there, the people's villages lacked one crucial attribute: proximity to work. In January 1931, for instance, the Chinese municipal authorities ordered several groups of hut dwellers to move to the recently completed Number Two Village. Their huts were torn down, but of 484 households, only 168 relocated to their assigned housing. For those who worked on the docks of the Huangpu River or in Zhabei's factories, the village's location on the far southern perimeter of the city made it impossible for them to get to work. Others who had been squatting on vacant land could not afford the cost:

to move in required paying one month's rent in advance, plus another month as the security deposit. Moreover, government regulations could be onerous. The ban on pigs and chickens created hardship for those who depended on raising animals to make ends meet. When residents asked the Committee to reconsider this policy, it refused on the grounds of sanitation.[137]

With these constraints, it took the Committee six months to fill the vacancies at the Number Two Village. Soon thereafter, the residents organized to demand rent reduction. According to the manager, as several hundred people gathered on the evening of April 12, the crowd's emotions were "fanned and incited by a few troublemakers." (The date coincided with the anniversary of Chiang Kai-shek's bloody purge of Communists and labor unions in 1927, though no overt connections surfaced.) The next day, when a representative from the municipal treasury arrived with armed escorts to collect payment, the entire village refused to pay. The residents wrote to the Social Affairs Bureau and explained that this was not an act of "rent resistance" but a matter of destitution—they simply could not afford $2.50 a month, plus the 30 cent water surcharge. The authorities sent an inspector to investigate, who concluded that 45 percent of the residents had jobs, 22 percent could but did not work, and the remaining one-third were disabled, elderly, or too young to work. Of the 180 households, 79 were "extremely poor" (chipin), 92 lived in "great difficulty," and only 9 could be said to "live adequately." Despite these findings, the government refused to reduce the rent, exempting only the poorest households from paying the water surcharge.[138]

By 1935, the People's Housing Committee had disbanded, with its responsibilities reassigned to the Public Works Bureau. By then, 4,548 people lived in one thousand units at four separate sites. More than half of these residents were laborers (primarily factory workers and rickshaw pullers); the rest were small shop proprietors and peddlers, along with a few teachers, clerks, and municipal employees.[139] Although envisioned as a solution to the issue of shantytowns, the "people's villages" became housing for "ordinary people" (pingmin), out of the reach of the "poor people" (pinmin). In the meantime, the hut problem only grew, and the GMD government struggled to find a coherent strategy, oscillating between "eradication" and "improvement" schemes. After several abortive attempts at implementing different plans, in 1936 Mayor Wu Tiecheng instructed his subordinates at every municipal agency to brainstorm solutions. The proposals numbered hundreds and included forcible removal; monetary incentives to relocate; emulating the International Settlement's "no new huts" policy; putting the burden on land owners to clear out the huts; cordoning off the existing shantytowns with bamboo or wire fences. It became clear that any comprehensive resolution would require a Herculean effort, involving the overhaul of nearly every aspect of municipal governance—and money the government did not have.

After weeks of meetings and debates, the Mayor opted for a broad but simple plan, delegating "improvement" issues to the public utilities and health bureaus, and "eradication" to public security. Specific measures called for all huts to be registered (approximately forty thousand) and those situated along the railways to be relocated in three stages.[140] But although the GMD authorities did not implement any sweeping measures, conflicts periodically erupted. For instance, when one landowner in Zhabei tried to remove several hundred shanties on his property in 1936, the hut dwellers marched on government offices, accusing the owner of arson and the local police captain of colluding with him in "illegal" actions. The controversy made headlines for months, ending only after several hundred hut dwellers sued the police captain (unsuccessfully) in the local court for "abuse of official power" and "infringement of personal liberty."[141]

WHAT RIGHTS?

Meanwhile, as discussed in chapter 2, the International Settlement authorities had adopted a policy of maintaining the *status quo* on the shantytown issue after 1926. Following the May 30th Incident, as labor agitations and nationalistic protests shook the city, the foreign authorities tried to avoid publicity that would have spotlighted the sensitive issue of extraterritoriality. Therefore, the Municipal Council allowed the huts already in existence to remain, and in some cases did not acquiesce when landlords demanded the removal of squatters.[142] At the same time, sporadic evictions were necessary to enforce the policy prohibiting new huts, and even these limited actions triggered strong protests. For the hut dwellers, life in the shantytown, however difficult, would have been better than the workhouse. In a time when homelessness could be a crime, subjecting the offender to deportation or detention, to lose one's home could have devastating consequences.

In response to the Municipal Council's attempts to clear out illegal settlements, the hut dwellers organized to save their homes, appealing to the Chinese government and civic and charitable organizations for help. In several cases, they retained legal counsel and asked the GMD Foreign Ministry to intercede with the American and British consuls. In another instance, they petitioned the Chinese Ratepayers Association, which represented Chinese residents of the International Settlement. The Association's officers in turn wrote to the foreign administrators, linking the issue to larger concerns: "This not only means the loss of shelter for the poor, but also involves the nation's sovereignty, the people's livelihood, and the peace of society."[143]

In practice, unless the police patrolled every corner of every shantytown daily and kept detailed records, the policy of no new huts was impossible to enforce. To distinguish the new from the old, in 1931 the Public Works Department registered the existing huts in the International Settlement and issued numbered discs to each one. Furthermore, the Municipal Council decreed that each year 10 percent of the registered dwellings, chosen by lottery, would be demolished; within ten years, none would remain.[144] But just a few months later, in January 1932, the Japanese attacked the region. When the fighting ceased, the International Settlement authorities discovered that while they were preoccupied with the crisis, the number of illegal shacks in the concession had increased—by one count, more than doubled. In fact, to circumvent the registration requirement, residents simply built additions to the legal huts. One registered dwelling could easily have five or six others attached—one for a relative who recently came to the city, another for a son who just got married, and so on. The result was that the situation was getting worse, not better. In September 1932, the Municipal Council finally decided to take a hard line, announcing that all unregistered huts would be removed in thirty days. As the demolitions began, the authorities received a barrage of protests. The press reported that 2,400 hut dwellers sent a telegram to Chiang Kai-shek and implored him to intervene on their behalf. While there is no evidence that Chiang himself replied or interceded, the tactic of deluging the Council with pleas and complaints worked, and the demolitions were suspended.[145]

In the summer of 1936, another attempt to enforce the "no new huts" policy entangled T. K. Ho (He Dekui), the Municipal Council's assistant secretary, in controversy. As the highest-ranking Chinese on the administrative staff, Ho was deputized to handle the issue, particularly in dealing with the numerous entreaties people made, both in person and in writing. It was common for hut dwellers to show up at the Council office, asking to see him. A graduate of Harvard (MBA, 1921), T. K. Ho had worked for the International Settlement since 1928.[146] In June 1936, the Public Works Department issued eviction orders to huts deemed "newly erected" in Yangshupu, and withdrew the registration discs of some one hundred households, as part of the 10 percent reduction scheme. Residents of the huts targeted for removal gathered to form the Hut-Dwellers Federation, to solicit public support for their predicament. They hired a lawyer to pursue legal redress, and sent more than twenty petitions to the Municipal Council, many of them addressed directly to T. K. Ho. In one proposal, the Federation offered to take responsibility for managing the shanties if the Municipal Council would recognize its authority. The leaders pledged to ensure that no new huts would be built, to monitor the repair of existing structures (prevent additions and other methods of circumventing the rules), and to enforce hygiene standards.[147] In another petition, Federation representatives beseeched T. K. Ho and foreign officials with the rhetoric of humanitarianism:

> We hut dwellers are not animals, though we do live like animals. We are human beings, but we have been excluded from the ranks of humanity. . . . Straw huts that violate the law should be dismantled, but is it a crime to be

poor (*pin*)? . . . Cornered animals will fight for their lives. We have nowhere
to turn, no path forward or road back. Confronting life or death, we have no
choice but to fight to the bitter end.[148]

Leaders of the Hut-Dwellers Federation also used the press to present their
case to the public, furnishing reporters with copies of petitions and inviting
them to attend meetings with civic leaders. For instance, when the Federation
approached Yu Ya-ching, a prominent businessman and Council member,
to ask for his help, several newspapers soon featured detailed reports of an
agreement, purportedly brokered by Yu, stipulating the creation of a mutual-
responsibility system. According to press accounts, demolitions would cease
on all existing huts; every ten households would form a unit, elect a headman,
and be held accountable for each other's actions. Any breaches of the regulations would be punished by the demolition of all ten shanties. Yu Ya-ching
and other Chinese Council members did urge the foreign administrators to
take into account the hut dwellers' appeals for leniency, "which in our opinion,
merit sympathetic consideration." But contrary to news reports, no such
agreement existed: the policy remained unchanged, with only a concession of
postponing demolitions until "the end of the hot weather."[149]

The postponement was clearly temporary, and the Hut-Dwellers Federation
continued to organize, calling a public meeting on August 16 to announce the
"unity" of all shantytown residents. With more than five hundred representatives and reporters in attendance, the leaders vowed to continue the campaign
to save their homes. They also unveiled programs for educating hut dwellers in
practices of "self-government," "citizenship training," and literacy, to help them
become people who "benefit society and the nation."[150] To fund its activities,
the Federation collected annual dues from its constituents (twenty cents per
household, exempting the poorest). But soon a rival faction of disgruntled
shantytown residents complained to the authorities about deception and extortion. A group calling itself "7,000 Hut-Dwellers in East and West Shanghai
Opposed to the Hut-Dwellers Federation" claimed that the Federation's leaders professed to have influence over the Municipal Council, with bribes total-
ing several thousand dollars ($1,500 to T. K. Ho, expenses incurred to "enter-
tain" Yu Ya-ching). They apparently issued new registration discs, promising
that the huts of those who contributed to the bribery fund would be exempted
from future demolition. T. K. Ho dismissed the allegation of his involvement as
"absurd," and referred the matter to the police for prosecution.

In the course of these investigations (and others probing rumors of municipal employees receiving pay-offs), dossiers compiled by the police showed that
leaders of the Hut-Dwellers Federation included several school teachers and
one doctor, which accounted for their literacy and savvy tactics. "Contrary to
general opinion," one report stated, "not all hut dwellers are beggars, therefore
sympathy towards these people is misplaced. . . . Many of them are content to

reside in straw huts so as to avoid payment of rates and taxes." Disinclined to believe the claims of hardship, one official concluded, "We know that many of the hut dwellers are well able to afford other accommodation." Another reasoned, "The fact that squatters are in a position to employ legal assistance in presenting their case is significant and . . . if they are able to pay for such services they are equally well able to bear the cost of transferring their huts."[151]

Based on such sentiments, treaty port officials were determined to take strong action. But a riot in a shantytown, erupting several weeks later, attracted hostile publicity to the issue and compelled them to defer action once again. In late August, the Public Works Department served notice to Wang Baoliang that the addition he built to shanty number 448 on Chaoyang Road violated the "no new huts" rule. Wang responded that his home had been damaged during the summer rains, and he was merely making repairs, not "building." He ignored several deadlines, and on the morning of September 2, officers from the local precinct turned up to enforce the demolition order. Wang resisted, and soon a crowd numbering about five hundred gathered to protest. The Hut-Dwellers Federation mobilized its "Bucket Brigade" to fling the contents of chamber pots at the constables; men wielding bamboo poles and children throwing rocks turned out in force. When the fracas ended, more than forty people were injured (including several foreign officers), and twelve were arrested.[152]

In the aftermath of the incident, the Hut-Dwellers Federation was galvanized into action. They made forceful public appeals to demand compensation for the victims, and hired a lawyer to represent those charged with criminal assault. The public agitation only increased when Wang Baoliang, the owner whose hut construction–repairs touched off the brawl, died. The cause of death was contested: either he had been assaulted by the police during the confrontation; or injured by debris when his shanty was torn down; or, being elderly and already ill, never recovered from the "shock" of the incident.[153]

Ultimately, the riot and the subsequent public recriminations stiffened the Municipal Council's resolve to deal with the shantytown problem once and for all. In October, after debating and scrutinizing the issue, officials reaffirmed its existing policy of "no new huts" and the 10 percent annual reduction of existing structures. This time, however, they would follow through, for the occupiers of huts have come to believe that "the Council can be intimated and that its rulings lack decision." Beginning after the winter, the plan called for systematic demolition by dividing shantytowns into large blocks and clearing them one at a time. Rather than select dwellings by lottery or on the basis of sanitary conditions, officials thought this method would be perceived as more equitable. It would also give maximum notice to the occupants, so as to "avoid disturbances or undue hardship."[154]

With a new census showing 5,094 huts within the International Settlement's borders, the Commissioner of Public Works announced that 500 huts (10 percent) would be demolished in the spring of 1937. Publicized well in advance, the deadline of May 1 was intended to give the residents ample time to relocate, but had the effect of spurring the Hut-Dwellers Federation to action. Over several months, the group sent more than fifty letters to the Municipal Council, and dozens more to the GMD government and other organizations appealing for their support. To the Municipal Council, Federation representatives first wrote that the tenants had checked with their landlords, and none of the owners wished to evict them:

> Since our landlords do not want the land back, and we have not violated any laws or built any new huts, we cannot understand why our huts . . . must be demolished. Although our occupations are humble, we still deserve the protection of law. Although our lives are lowly, we have not committed any crimes. . . . The Municipal Council has long known that the Chinese easily submit to oppression, and when we give an inch they take a foot.

Meanwhile, to the Chinese Ratepayers Association, they wrote that since their huts were in Chinese territory and they were Chinese subjects, they hoped the Association would take up their cause.[155] Of course, this was a false claim—the huts were clearly in the International Settlement, not in Chinese territory. But that was precisely the point, to link their plight to the hot button issues of imperialism and extraterritoriality.

The appeals from the hut dwellers and their advocates alternated between pleading for mercy, appealing to nationalism, and making legal claims. One family wrote to T. K. Ho, saying that their home, "although an old house, is not a straw hut." They begged the assistant secretary to withdraw the demolition order, in the interest of "justice" (gongde), and in consideration of "the misery and pain we have suffered . . . beyond what words can describe." (Ho forwarded the letter to the Public Works Department for consideration, but did not intervene.) In another instance, one group of hut dwellers asserted, "The law protects the rights of private property. A house is private property, whether it is a mansion or a straw hut. The Council does not have the right to demolish mansions; neither should it have the right to tear down our houses." For its part, the Chinese Ratepayers Association denounced the proposed demolition as an act "against humanity" (fan rendao) and the principles of the Magna Carta, and therefore "thoroughly abhorred by the people of Great Britain."[156]

As the May 1 deadline approached, the rhetoric shifted from pleading to thinly veiled threats. A public meeting on April 25th drew 1,200 hut dwellers, widespread press coverage, and police surveillance. The Federation issued a manifesto, citing provisions from the Chinese Constitution and the Criminal Code on infringements against property and the freedom of abode. The manifesto concluded, "It is said that the Shanghai Municipal Council intends to destroy our buildings and damage our property. We do not think the Council will really do this, since it is formed by law, governs by law, and is an organ for the execution of law.... But if we cannot receive protection, we will have to act in self defense as provided for in Articles 23 and 24 of the Criminal Code."[157] To members of the Municipal Council, the hut dwellers hinted in a letter that they may burn the huts to sacrifice themselves, and asked, "Is there no one in China or abroad who will seek vengeance for the unjustifiable deaths of more than 1,000 hut dwellers? Who will be held responsible? The Council will be accused of cruelty," and "this could be a repeat of the May 30th tragedy."[158]

The invocation of May 30, 1925, the day when foreign police had fired on unarmed demonstrators in the International Settlement, escalated the stakes in this battle. Concession officials started to worry about the possibility of trouble. Rumors were flying in the press—that the hut dwellers were planning a big demonstration; that they would throw acid at the police and provoke them into firing at the crowd; that they were planning to burn down their own huts and blame it on the foreigners.[159] On the morning of April 26, three thousand people began to march toward the Council's office on the Bund. The Shanghai Municipal Police intercepted them, and after some wrangling, allowed twelve delegates to proceed. The crowd eventually dispersed, but only after warning that if they did not receive a satisfactory reply that afternoon, they would repeat the demonstration the next day. A secret police report on the incident noted that people agitating for abolishing extraterritoriality were encouraging the hut dwellers to clash with the police, hoping to provoke an incident similar to that of May 30th.[160]

Two days later, on April 28, the Municipal Council convened an emergency session. At the meeting, Secretary G. Godfrey Phillips (the Council's chief administrator) said that he felt "uneasy" about the situation, and feared that once the police started to use force, they would "need to carry it through to the end, no matter at what cost." With over six thousand armed "squatters," Phillips worried that "forcible Police action might involve loss of life which might result in a repetition along similar lines of the incident of May 30, 1925." Given the circumstances, the Secretary recommended a payoff, to offer Ch. $10 dollars per hut for people to move, and negotiate up to a maximum of $15. Chinese members of the Council argued for higher payments, saying that they should not risk people's lives over such small sums of money. They were, however, overruled by the foreign members, who formed the majority and felt that any compensation would be treated as a precedent: whatever is offered "they would ask for more." But most importantly, all agreed that the payment should be identified as a "compassion grant"—not "compensation"—for these were illegal squatters, *not* entitled to compensation.[161] After some negotiation with T. K. Ho, the hut dwellers agreed to the terms for $14 dollars per hut, a sizeable sum of money (sufficient to pay several months' rent, for instance, for a room in the GMD's "people's village"). Aside from the money, the settlement also meant that the hut dwellers avoided demolition of their homes. Being able to tear down their own huts was crucial, so that they could preserve the materials to rebuild elsewhere.

The agreement appeared to be satisfactory to all of the parties involved, and the hut dwellers began to dismantle their homes in exchange for the promised payments. Despite the resolution, however, bitterness lingered. "Where are the hut dwellers to go?" asked one commentator, writing in a Shanghai magazine. The city's prosperity had been built on the backs of these rickshaw pullers, peddlers, and laborers; "now that Shanghai is flourishing, there is no longer a place for them."[162] The GMD party paper in Shanghai explained the issue in this way:

> From a sociological point of view, this is a very serious matter! . . . These hut dwellers belong to the most miserable class in society. Although they labor with blood and sweat all day long, they still cannot maintain a minimum livelihood. If this continues long term and society does not devise a suitable method to help them survive, serious disturbances will certainly occur in the future.

Even the tabloids weighed in, decrying the treatment of hut dwellers as "the dregs of humanity" (renzha), akin to "the dregs from bean curd or sugar cane. . . . They toil away, but once their blood and sweat are sucked dry, the capitalists cast them on the streets," just like garbage.[163]

CONCLUSION

The protracted battles between the hut dwellers and Shanghai's Municipal Council highlight two crucial points about the experiences of the urban poor. First, to observers, both Chinese and foreign, straw hut villages were filthy slums, the breeding ground for disease and crime. From the perspective of their residents, however, the dwellings provided shelter and a place of belonging, giving some stability and structure to lives that were on the edge of fracturing. Moreover, in a time when the urban homeless were targeted for deportation or punishment, the possession of a home—however humble—attested to some status of residence in the city. Whereas Hanchao Lu has described the occupants of straw huts as "a Chinese version of the homeless,"[164] here we see hut dwellers clearly staking claims for their homes on the basis of property rights. Far from seeing themselves as "homeless," shantytown residents insisted that their homes differentiated them from the vagrants and beggars who disrupted social order.

Some of the rhetoric and strategies that the hut dwellers used in the struggle to save their homes—appealing to the notion of rights, invoking the law, hiring lawyers—indicate detailed knowledge of these institutions and norms. Ultimately, their assertions depended on persuading anyone who would listen that they were not squatters or interlopers, but rather law-abiding, gainfully employed residents who paid rent. Therefore, despite their impoverishment, they were entitled to the same rights as those who lived in mansions. By challenging the foreign authorities on their own discursive terrain of rights and law—the moral high ground that justified extraterritoriality—the hut dwellers tried to shame them into canceling the demolition orders.

Second, the hut dwellers' shrewdest strategy was to link their plight to nationalism. This, combined with the threat of collective violence, ultimately forced the foreign authorities to yield and compromise. Our view of Chinese nationalism in the Republican period is dominated by student demonstrations, organized boycotts, and labor strikes. We know that the urban poor sometimes joined these movements—for example, rickshaw pullers and even beggars went on strike as gestures of solidarity. The case of Shanghai's hut dwellers adds a different dimension, underscoring how people treated as "the dregs of society" used the elite language of patriotism and rights to demand their inclusion. Asserting that "we are also Chinese subjects," they protested what they viewed as oppression at the hands of foreign imperialists. And by doing so, they consciously linked their fate to the fate of the Chinese nation.

The final agreement, reached in the spring of 1937 for the relocation of the hut dwellers, was never fully enacted. Three months later, on August 13, Japan once again attacked Shanghai. The foreign concessions would remain neutral zones until the Pearl Harbor strike, but in the interim the refugee crisis completely transformed the situation. Thousands of straw huts were destroyed in the fighting by fire, rendering the shantytown issue largely obsolete. As we shall see in the next chapter, in its place an immense refugee problem emerged, drastically altering the contours of debates about urban poverty.

The opening salvos of war also ended the decade of Nationalist dominance. During ten years of political stability, through the provision of relief but with the condition of mandatory labor, the GMD government tried both to help the poor and to control the social danger they represented. The incarceration of the homeless, who were not guilty of crimes apart from loitering about, begging for alms, appearing dangerous, or looking suspicious, followed the trajectory launched by Yuan Shikai's experimental workhouses in 1905. The disparagement of the nonworking poor as social parasites targeted their productive liability to the nation, another distinctly twentieth-century notion. The impact of the World War II on these ideas and practices will be the subject of the next chapter.

CHAPTER 4

Beggars or Refugees?

ON THE NIGHT of July 7, 1937, skirmishes between Chinese and Japanese troops near Beijing's Marco Polo Bridge broke out, marking the beginning of World War II in China. The fighting quickly spread, and by month end Japanese forces had consolidated control over the region. An all-out assault on Shanghai in August, followed by the December slaughter of civilians and soldiers in Nanjing, forced the Nationalist government to flee. Chiang Kai-shek led his troops and supporters first to Wuhan, then to Sichuan, where he set up a temporary capital in Chongqing in October 1938.

For the refugees who followed the Nationalist retreat and for the people left behind in occupied China, life became a series of calamities on top of miseries. Beyond displacing millions of people from their homes and intensifying the subsistence crisis, the war also fundamentally transformed perceptions of poverty. With refugees swelling the homeless population, it became virtually impossible to distinguish legitimate war victims from the indigents who had always been there. Who were the genuine refugees deserving assistance? Who were the professional panhandlers and the "vagrants"? Suspicions abounded, of enemy agents masquerading as refugees, or affluent migrants illicitly benefiting from charity.

This chapter traces the effects of the war first in occupied Beijing, where life under Japanese rule has been recalled with great bitterness, but has received little historical attention. Drawing on the records of the collaborationist government, I show how in a wartime climate, the provision of relief, always linked to concerns about social order, now centered on security. While existing relief agencies continued to serve both charitable and penal purposes, new institutions and aggressive policing tactics resulted in the large-scale incarceration of people who had done nothing apart from arouse suspicion because they were homeless. Then I turn to Shanghai, where more than 1.5 million Chinese sought safe haven in the concessions protected by extraterritoriality, a crisis vividly chronicled in the records of the Shanghai Municipal Council. For many of the resident poor and new arrivals, the war ravaged already precarious lives. The lucky ones found places in refugee camps and other temporary accommodations, but conditions in some shelters soon degenerated into squalor. Meanwhile, the unlucky ones were incarcerated and compelled to work. Yet, as we shall see, desperation also emboldened shantytown residents to fight for their homes. By using the language of justice, pleading for compassion, and seeking redress through the law, they invoked the rhetorical power of social citizenship to protest their exclusion.

In the past decade, this period of "Anti-Japanese Resistance" has become a burgeoning subfield of research. Voluminous studies from China tend to portray the war years as a time of heroic resistance and national unity against a rapacious enemy. In English-language scholarship, historians have identified the political shifts and social changes of the period as a major turning point and as the genesis of future developments in the People's Republic. Taken together, the new scholarship views the Sino-Japanese War as a transformative moment in modern Chinese history.[1] In this chapter I show how the wartime climate, rather than a fundamental break with the past, intensified the productive impulse, the seeds of which had been planted decades earlier, and sharpened the contrast between the "parasitism" of the nonworking poor and labor as a form of patriotic resistance. The imperative to police the suspected criminality and unrestrained mobility of the urban homeless evolved from policies and attitudes that had taken root since the turn of the twentieth century. At the same time, however, the war produced new kinds of displacements, shattering existing assumptions about the causes of and solutions for "poverty."

The Refugee Crisis and GMD Social Policy

The eight long years of the war created a national crisis of unprecedented magnitude. Tens of millions of people, fleeing the advance of the Japanese army, initially streamed out of north China in the summer of 1937. After the fall of Shanghai and Nanjing later that year, they headed for central China, before evacuating to the southwest.[2] With so many needy people on the run, the war years witnessed a significant expansion of welfare programs earmarked for refugees. In particular, the GMD government played an instrumental role in mobilizing resources for relief. Through its National Relief Committee (NRC), the regime-in-exile created an extensive network of agencies, overseeing the distribution of Ch. $4.9 billion in aid to more than thirty million people.[3]

Throughout the war years, as harrowing tales of enemy atrocities and heart-wrenching stories of orphans became regular features in the press, officials and relief organizers implored the public to help. In her speeches and writings, Soong May-ling (Madame Chiang Kai-shek) frequently invoked the plight of refugees. In 1938, for instance, she called on "those with strength to contribute their strength and those with money to contribute their money," to help "our victimized compatriots who are homeless and helpless." Of the tens of thousands of children, bereft of parents and homes, Madame Chiang asked, "How can we allow them to drift about as beggars or criminals, or to become famished bodies crying in hunger?"[4]

With unprecedented numbers of child victims and previously well-off people joining the ranks of the destitute, refugee status gained a new moral legitimacy, and being "poor" could take on inflections of patriotic sacrifice. The crisis also fostered a sense of solidarity with displaced migrants. As Fan Renyu, a prominent educator, wrote in 1938, "It could be said that every son and daughter of China and every descendant of the Yellow Emperor has ... become a refugee."[5] War was indeed "a great leveler," as shared experiences of hardship attenuated former disparities of wealth and status.[6] But for those accustomed to comfort and privilege, the fall into destitution could be disorienting. In Chongqing, journalist Li Luzi observed a beggar using a refined Shanghai accent to curse passersby, who refused his solicitation: "Damn you scoundrels! You don't know what I was made of. ... I used to make and spend big money, run up tabs at the brothels ... and put on airs." Li described many others with formerly prosperous backgrounds now living on the streets, and remarked, "Who knew that life could be so cruel? And who knew that 'big shots' could become 'tramps' (biesan) so quickly?"[7]

At the same time, with innumerable "tramps" on the streets, and social structures and government institutions in collapse, sympathy for refugees collided with perceptions of their social danger. Concerns about enemy infiltration and sabotage in the wartime climate also heightened existing worries about people on the move. How to count refugees, control their mobility, and make them accountable soon evolved into persistent preoccupations. The Nationalist government required that all refugees apply for transit passes and "refugee certificates" to verify their status as authentic victims, as well as testify to the extent of their impoverishment. At transit stations, security measures stressed vigilance against enemy agents masquerading as refugees, with frequent injunctions for relief workers to investigate claims of hardship and ferret out imposters.[8] Given the continual influxes of people into Chongqing, security there was especially tight, with aid efforts and policing concerns closely intertwined.

From a longer-term perspective, Nationalist officials also worried about the potentially "pauperizing" effects of government relief. Aid to refugees was intended to be temporary, with shelters slated to operate for six months. Government handouts and private relief were meant to be provisional responses to an extraordinary situation. Certainly no one expected that the crisis would be so prolonged. When the refugee population increased rather than decreased over time, government policy and public discussions shifted discernibly. By 1939 and 1940, commentators and officials began to emphasize "refugee production" (nanmin shengchan) as an important component of the war effort. Finance Minister Kong Xixiang (H. H. Kung, Chiang Kai-shek's brother-in-law) noted in a speech of January 1939 that, in the past, relief methods primarily relied on handouts, which fostered dependency on the part of recipients. "An old proverb says: 'A beggar for three years disdains to become an official.'. ... How can an individual who does not subsist on his own labor resist the enemy, and how can we build the nation?"[9] Accordingly, the NRC established "refugee factories," created employment referral programs, and offered incentives to encourage migration to remote regions. The GMD propaganda bureau advertised the scheme of setting up small enterprises to engage refugees in "productive work" as "holding the promise of self-sufficiency." With several hundred thousand people making straw sandals for soldiers, "China's grave refugee problem is gradually finding a solution ... in perfect harmony with the nation's avowed policy of self-sufficiency and reconstruction."[10] By 1940, *Central Daily News* could boast that one of the main improvements in government relief policy was transforming "passive handouts" (*xiaoji shiyu*) into "active production" (*jiji shengchan*). As an example, the article cited the experience of several thousand refugees recently settled in a mountainous county near Yan'an, the Communist stronghold. Whereas previously they "sit and wait for food" (*zuo'er daishi*), with the GMD government's help they now "subsist by their own labor" (*zishi qili*).[11]

North China under Occupation

Meanwhile, in the summer of 1937, the Japanese army swiftly overran north China and consolidated control over the region. Initially, the military skirmishes of early July hardly perturbed Beijing's residents, accustomed to news of Japan's imminent invasion since 1931. Wounded soldiers and civilian refugees did trickle into the city, and a consortium of private charities mobilized emergency teams to provide medical care and send food to the countryside. Then, as the military situation grew more critical, the sound of artillery and cannon galvanized residents into action. One journalist described the city aflame with patriotic fervor, "the people as if intoxicated and crazed." But when Nationalist forces evacuated at the end of July, the city seemed to die overnight. The gates were locked, and rumors proliferated—of the Japanese army's impending takeover; of people ingesting opium to commit suicide; of "local hoodlums" gathered in the Outer City, biding their time. With the transportation network completely shut down and commerce at a standstill, food shortages ensued and prices skyrocketed. Refugees streamed in whenever the city gates opened; wafts of smoke floated above courtyard homes as people hastily burned their books and papers.[12]

To calm such fears, a self-appointed cohort of leaders formed a Peace Preservation Committee on July 30. When the Japanese entered Beijing a week later, they found the group already taking charge of municipal functions (for instance, enforcing martial law), and confirmed it as the de facto administration.[13] Despite this orderly political transition, Ida Pruitt, the head of Peking Union Medical Hospital's social work department, later recollected, "Those first days after the Japanese took the city were difficult days. No one knew what was going to happen. The Chinese stayed in their homes and their shops as much as they could and watched."[14]

What they witnessed in the summer and autumn of 1937 was a systematic effort to secure Beijing against potential agents of disorder. On behalf of the occupation authorities, the Peace Preservation Committee closed major Chinese newspapers and took control of the railways and public utilities.[15] The top priority was to hunt down Nationalist soldiers and Communist infiltrators, suspected of hiding out among refugees, unemployed workers, and other transients. The Japanese military police closely monitored train stations and the nine city gates, searching even the produce bundles of elderly vegetable peddlers. The Chinese police checked household registers and lodgers at hotels and temples, assuming that "if there is a man extra he is . . . a guerilla or a bandit; if there is one short then he is assumed to have joined the guerillas."[16] Police chief Pan Yugui called on residents to report suspicious activities, saying, "Our city's suburbs are extensive and the residents are mixed, making it easy for bandits or Communists to hide out." To his staff, Pan warned that the Communists used "crafty and deceptive words, promising equal property and wealth . . . to entice those who are impoverished and down on their luck."[17] For its part, the Japanese army announced that all "bad elements" (drifters, Communists, and anyone who resists) would be "swiftly taken care of."[18]

In this climate of fear and uncertainty, Beijing's new authorities considered the thirty thousand refugees in the city to be security risks, not legitimate recipients of aid. In the summer of 1937, private charities assumed almost the entire burden of providing relief to the destitute and the homeless. The Salvation Army, the Red Swastika Society, the Red and Blue Cross, Buddhist groups, and secular organizations established shelters, distributed food and clothing, and buried the dead. By one count, thirty-five privately organized shelters opened in temples, schools, and the cloisters of Catholic churches.[19] Apart from destitute new arrivals, the jump in prices for food and everyday necessities meant the local poor could no longer make ends meet. As police precincts conducted household checks for security purposes, the Salvation Army worked in tandem to identify needy families and distribute grain coupons. At a food depot, Salvationist officer Frank Waller observed that for the city's impoverished people, starvation—always waiting on the doorstep—had "pushed open the doors. . . . Men, women, and children, half-crazy with the heat and the fear lest there might not be enough grain to feed such a crowd, fought and struggled to get in," where they could redeem their coupons.[20]

Despite many scenes of desperation, the quick withdrawal of Nationalist forces and the battlefront's migration to the south averted a drawn-out refugee crisis in Beijing. By the early autumn, only a few thousand people remained in shelters around the city. Inevitably, the ones left behind were the most destitute, with nowhere to go. Then, as autumn became winter, life began to revert back to normalcy as Beijing residents adapted to occupation. Prospects for the immediate winter looked grim, however. The main problem, as Ida Pruitt wrote to donors in England, was "that of a city of poor made poorer," victims in the

Figure 4.1. Salvation Army officers distributing grain, Beijing, August 1937
Photo by Ida Pruitt. Courtesy of Schlesinger Library, Radcliffe Institute, Harvard
University.

calculus that "the longer the war lasts the more hope for China and therefore
for peace of the world."[21] Government aid was limited, and private charities,
facing a significant drop in donations, planned to dispense relief on a much
reduced scale.[22] Even institutions of long-standing struggled to keep operations going. The Longquan Orphanage (described in chapter 2) took in fewer
and fewer children, as donations and rental income declined.[23] At the Xiangshan Children's Home, founder Xiong Xiling had intended to evacuate the
children from Beijing, but died in Hong Kong in December 1937 before he
completed the arrangements.[24]

During the first winter, the Salvation Army's seven soup kitchens fed 4,200
people daily and provided 480 beds in eight shelters. Before disbanding in

Figure 4.2. The waiting crowd at a Salvation Army soup kitchen, Beijing, August 1937
Photo by Ida Pruitt. Courtesy of Schlesinger Library, Radcliffe Institute, Harvard University.

December, the Peace Preservation Committee also operated six kitchens and arranged to deliver fifty thousand packets of white sugar to "poor households" as special tokens of its solicitude. The report of this final act of generosity must have seemed farcical, appearing next to the headline of an impoverished man who attempted suicide, by slicing his own neck with a cleaver.[25] The successor authority, the North China Provisional Government, was established on December 14, 1937, one day after the fall of Nanjing. Besides expanding the policing apparatus in support of the campaign of against enemy insurgents and spies, the Provisional Government also established a central Relief Ministry. Appointed the Relief Minister in January 1938, Wang Yitang acknowledged the enormity of the task in familiar terms:

Figure 4.3. Scene at a Salvation Army soup kitchen, Beijing, August 1937
Photo by Ida Pruitt. Courtesy of Schlesinger Library, Radcliffe Institute, Harvard
University.

The Buddha once said, "If I don't enter hell, who will?" I approach my job
now with a similar mindset.... We can see that the nation's people are impoverished, and out of 100 more than 90 do not have enough to eat. An old
proverb says: "The people are the foundation of the state, and the people
regard food as heaven." That our government cannot feed the people is truly
a shameful matter.[26]

At the same time, Wang blamed "Communist bandits" for the people's suffering. The government had organized relief for the poor, he declared, but the
Communists sabotaged such efforts. "Whatever they could take, they took long
ago. What they could not take, they destroyed, so that no one else could have
it.... The police and our ally's army have saved you from the flood waters and
from the fire. You must do your utmost to help them.... The sooner bandit
suppression is completed, the sooner we can implement the relief program."[27]
To counter the Communists' appeal, Wang portrayed their promises of redistribution as handouts, a form of "passive relief" that cultivated habits of dependency. Work relief, on the other hand, provided food to the needy but also
channeled their labor into production. "When the majority of disaster victims
have food to eat, the slanderous words of the Guomindang and the Communists naturally cannot entice them to take the evil path."[28] By linking the im-

poverishment of the people to the potential appeal of the enemy, Wang underscored the importance of relief as a political weapon.

The Beggar Shelter and the Relief Home

But what happens when disaster victims do not have food to eat and they take the "evil path"? For the occupation authorities in the Beijing, the answer was to establish a temporary beggar shelter, "to clean up the city's appearance (*shirong*) and prevent bad elements from disguising and passing themselves off as beggars."[29] With the municipal Relief Home already at full capacity, and citing the specter of people freezing to death on the streets, at the end of November the Police Bureau sent out patrols to bring "beggars" to a temporary facility.[30] Located on the premises of the Hebei Number One Prison, making use of a block of unoccupied detention rooms and offices, the site physically manifested its penal purpose. Within two weeks, precincts around the city had apprehended over 700 people, exceeding the projected capacity of 500.[31] This rapid influx of inmates overwhelmed the staff and created chaotic conditions. At the end of December, a medical report indicated that of the 914 inmates, more than 100 were critically ill. (Another 200 also had serious but non-life-threatening skin infections.) That month, 43 people died in custody, including a sixteen-day-old baby born to a female inmate. In his postmortem reports, filed nearly daily throughout December, the director blamed the high number of deaths on drug addictions and illnesses contracted before arrival.[32] His memos also indicated that the government repeatedly declined his requests for more resources for medical care. (Even the most rudimentary supplies, such as gauze and ointment, were in short supply.) Medical visits, scheduled twice per week, gave the physician the impossible task of tending to more than 200 patients within three to four hours.[33]

Despite these problems, with 827 people in custody at the end of the first winter, Mayor Yu Jinhe (who also held the concurrent post of police chief) praised the shelter and authorized its permanent status, removing the word "temporary" from its name. The inmates, however, were not to remain indefinitely. After four to six months of detention, those with relatives in the city were released on bond. Among those without families, the weak and young were transferred to the Relief Home, and the able-bodied dispatched to different agencies as coolie laborers. This policy was intended to ensure that there would be room to accommodate new arrivals. Mayor Yu also noted that among the inmates there were many "with skills" and many with families to rely upon: "They became accustomed to begging due to their indolent natures. There's no reason to take in these kinds of people. As long as there is a guarantor to pledge that they will stay off the streets, they should be permitted to leave."[34]

The objectives of the Beggar Shelter thus differed from the operating principles of the municipal Relief Home. As discussed in the previous chapter, in 1934 the Nationalist administration had established the umbrella organization, with the vision of reforming indigents and converting their social liability into useful labor. During the summer of 1937, the Relief Home had continued to operate in the transition, though on a reduced scale and in bureaucratic limbo. In October, the Social Affairs Bureau slashed the operating budget by 30 percent, straining resources as a steady stream of new arrivals entered. By winter, the newly constituted municipal government formally revived the Relief Home, and made the budget cuts permanent.[35] A new statement of purpose declared that the Home would use "Asia Revival" to inspire the inmates to "reform their former indolent ways and cultivate good habits." Although reflecting Japanese aspirations for pan-Asian hegemony, the goal of rehabilitation through labor was virtually indistinguishable from the former administration. Adult inmates were to repent of their "degenerate conduct" through work; the children would learn self-sufficiency with education and job training. The collaborationist government also kept intact the Relief Home's organizational structure and policies: separate workhouses for men and women; a ward for children and women unable to work; and a division for the elderly and disabled. As inmates resumed their "labor training," they made towels, shoes, rattan chairs and baskets, or embroidered linens and pillows—just as they had during the Nanjing decade.[36]

As before, during the occupation years the Relief Home was inundated by petitions from people seeking help. It remained the primary municipal relief agency and continued to reflect a mixture of charity and punishment, intermingling volunteers and detainees. Among the Home's residents were Sha Cuitian (nine *sui*) and her brother Sha Zhongqi (six *sui*), committed to the state's care because their mother feared that their father would sell them to support his drug habit. In September 1938, Mrs. Sha went to the police to ask for help. According to her statement, her husband had been sent to detox centers several times; each time "he did not repent and resumed his habits." Unable to support her two children, Mrs. Sha hoped to look for a job as a domestic servant. But she worried that in her absence her husband would sell them. Given the circumstances, the police arranged for them to enter the children's ward.[37]

At the Relief Home, the two Sha children lived with about four hundred others, many similarly placed in the state's custody by their parents. Others were abandoned or lost children like Youli, found wandering the streets the previous winter. The boy could provide the police with only imprecise information: he was about eight *sui*; his father was Chinese (surnamed Zhu, formerly employed as a mailman, recently arrested); his mother was Russian; he lived in Tianjin's French concession, at a house with the number plate six. The previous day, Youli told the police, he had been playing on the street outside his home when a stranger, a Chinese man, invited him to go to Beijing. They took the train together, and after disembarking the man disappeared, leaving Youli to wander the streets. That was where the police found him. For more than a month, Youli remained in police custody while they sent word to Tianjin to look for his mother. But when the authorities there failed to find a family corresponding to the boy's description, Youli was sent to the Relief Home, where he lived for more than two years. Then, in September 1940, a teacher named Xu Chengshu adopted Youli. But just five months later, Xu returned him to the Relief Home, saying that "family education alone could not remedy the child's indolent nature." Fearing that Youli would "take the crooked path," she sent him back to "learn a proper skill and correct his nature, so that he may be prepared in the future to stand on his own" (*zili*).[38]

We have no idea what kind of misbehavior Youli actually committed to trigger the action of annulling his adoption. And as far as the archival records show, Youli was never reunited with his family and his fate is unknown to us. Other children were rather more fortunate. In July 1938, three Russian boys entered the Relief Home because their mother Dan Ning had been caught stealing and sent to prison. The court arranged for Dashi, Waxi, and Yuela to go to the Relief Home. When Dan Ning finished serving her sentence six weeks later, her application for the release of her children was granted.[39] Another family, Cheng Li Jizhen and her two young sons, entered the Relief Home together in the winter of 1941. The following spring, Mrs. Cheng petitioned to leave to look for a job, hoping to earn enough money to hire a doctor to treat one of her sons, who had fallen ill. A few weeks after leaving the Home, however, Mrs. Cheng returned. Although she had previously worked for the Tianjin police, without family or friends in Beijing she could not find anyone to provide the bonded guarantee required to secure employment. The authorities took special pity on her; when a vacancy turned up, Mrs. Cheng was given a job on the police force.[40]

From a punitive perspective, the Relief Home functioned during the occupation years also as a reformatory. In May 1938, for instance, the Outer Second District precinct received a letter accusing Sheng Zishan and his wife of kidnapping Huang Jinling, forcing her to work as a prostitute, and "depriving her of freedom." Upon investigation, however, the police concluded that Huang was actually the culprit in this case. She had worked as an unlicensed prostitute, and had asked Sheng to provide introductions and a bonded guarantee in order to land a more lucrative job in a brothel. When Huang subsequently ran away from the brothel, Sheng lost the money (Ch. $50) he had furnished as a bond. He then found her and locked her up. To retaliate, Huang asked someone to write the accusatory letter. The truth eventually emerged after the police investigation. Finding that she had repeatedly lied and confessed only under duress, the authorities sent Huang to the women's workhouse division of the Relief Home as punishment.[41]

Many of the circumstances narrated above echo accounts from the previous decade under GMD rule. But there were also new elements. For instance, petitioners for aid now included numerous war widows, and soldiers with the dubious status of having fought for the now-departed Nationalists. In the heat of military skirmishes in the summer of 1937, the Chinese Red Cross had tried to shield GMD soldiers from the wrath of the Japanese army by counting some as "slightly wounded" and sending them for treatment.[42] But soldiers later seeking discharges from the hospital had to obtain the approval of the police. The Japanese army also targeted veterans for investigation and remanded those who seemed "suspicious."[43] Under these circumstances, the Red Cross and other hospitals made concerted efforts to repatriate military men or arrange jobs for them. According to the regulations, able-bodied ex-soldiers with nowhere else to go would be conscripted into the Japanese labor corps, while the seriously disabled would be placed in the Relief Home.[44] But administrators there tried to block these transfers, saying they had limited food and supplies. Such claims were not entirely fabricated, but when they resisted accepting even two soldiers from the Red Cross Hospital, they were clearly concerned about the possible ramifications of harboring Nationalist veterans.[45]

The most contentious issue for the Relief Home turned out not to be trouble with GMD spies masquerading as wounded soldiers, but the transfer arrangement with the Beggar Shelter. To Relief Home officials, such an arrangement turned their institution into a dumping ground for the police, who sent the most problematic cases: people with severe physical or mental disabilities, and those with nowhere else to go. The periodic infusions of such inmates also strained scarce resources. Therefore, the director tried to block each transfer with protests that the Home was at full capacity or had "limited rations."[46] In October 1940, for instance, of the 205 inmates scheduled for transfer, the Relief Home accepted only 43. The rest were discharged on bond or expelled.[47]

Compared to the police's abysmal management of the Beggar Shelter, the Relief Home under the Social Affairs Bureau fared somewhat better. It did encounter its share of problems, with intermittent episodes of runaways and rebellious inmates. In one case, four women conspired to set fire to the Relief Home to escape. On at least one occasion, the government received a complaint alleging graft and abuse. (Investigators discounted the accusations after concluding that the inmate who lodged them "seemed to be crazy.") And in the summer of 1939, a dormitory collapsed, burying seven boys in the rubble. One eventually died of injuries, and five others were permanently disabled.[48] Apart from these issues, through the occupation years the Relief Home functioned much as it had under the GMD. In 1941, there were about 1,400 inmates in its four divisions (a modest increase over the previous decade), with spikes in the winter to nearly 2,000. The administrators prided themselves on running a professional institution, with a strict code of conduct and careful attention to moral education, employing methods tailored to the different "nature and character" of the residents in various divisions.[49]

In the meantime, conditions at the Beggar Shelter failed to improve significantly, with another epidemic of deaths in January 1941 drawing scrutiny. (In total, ninety-eight inmates died in the first three months of that year.) When asked to account for the high number of casualties, Director Wang Zihe blamed the lack of resources and support: "I have repeatedly applied for more funds to pay for medicines and supplies. But due to the constraints of government funding, these hopes have come to nothing. I have only been able to make do within these limits to maintain the situation."[50] Despite his efforts to displace blame, Wang's replies proved unsatisfactory to his superiors. In the summer of 1941, Mayor Yu Jinhe decided to shift responsibility for the Beggar Shelter to the Social Affairs Bureau. "Taking in beggars is only a temporary measure," Yu wrote. "If we seek a fundamental solution, this cannot be divorced from the matter of relief."[51] Relief matters logically belonged to the realm of social affairs, and as the Bureau prepared to take over, its staff critically scrutinized the shelter's operations. Investigators reported that the dormitories were relatively clean, but they also found filthy work rooms, appalling hygiene, and a mediocre staff. In general, the conditions were no better than those at the privately run and notoriously dreadful winter shelters (*nuanchang*), where there were often more dead than living. Most importantly, the inspectors noted that the food rations were "excessive." Each inmate received one *jin* and ten *liang* of cornmeal a day (equivalent to about 1.75 pounds), much more than the amount allotted at the Relief Home. The attention to rations implied that the new overseers suspected embezzlement, a common problem at many institutions. The Social Affairs Bureau could not corroborate these suspicions, but more than three months later senior administrators continued to complain that although they repeatedly issued instructions to decrease the rations, no changes had been made. Finally, criticizing the shelter's operations as "not well-developed and in need of reorganization to increase revenues," the Bureau dispatched a manager from the Relief Home's labor division to help implement changes.[52]

Despite the transfer of responsibility to the Social Affairs Bureau, the Beggar Shelter retained its primarily penal focus. As part of a series of "law and order" campaigns coordinated by the Japanese army across north China, Beijing police swept the city for transients. Among those caught in the dragnet were hundreds of petty thieves and drug addicts, sentenced to serve two months at the Beggar Shelter. Shelter managers found these "vagrants" difficult to control, and asked for twenty pairs of shackles to restrain the unruly ones. They comingled with inmates like Sun Yue, arrested on the evening of November 25, 1942. Describing the "crime" in this case, the precinct chief wrote in the arrest log: "63 *sui*, loitering on the streets late at night. Has no residency certificate, no job, no home; not a thief."[53]

Ultimately, the Social Affairs Bureau proved unable to improve conditions at the Beggar Shelter in any meaningful way. Wang Zihe remained the Director—whether he was the source of the problems we cannot know for sure. Then, in May 1945, the Mayor's office received a petition from a man identified as "Beggar Wang Fatang." The original complaint was not retained in the files, but the flurry of memos that followed enumerated Wang's accusations for investigative purposes: physical abuse, rampant corruption, starvation conditions. The most shocking allegation was that disobedient inmates were "buried alive." The inspectors dispatched to investigate found no evidence of murder; it was evidently a ploy to garner attention. But they did present a damning indictment of nearly every aspect of the Shelter's operations. Their report concluded that "apart from the specific items enumerated, the most important one is that the shelter has not fulfilled its original aim. Among those who become beggars, the majority are willing degenerates or addicts. But among them are also some who have been abused by society and have no way to make a living." Those responsible for the shelter have not been able to meet the inmates' basic needs for food, clothing, and medical care, contributing to their "dejected spirits" and many deaths. The staff has also failed to uphold the operating principle, which should be "on the one hand 'take in' (*shourong*), and on the other hand 'train and educate' (*xunyu*), in order to cultivate self-sufficiency and also benefit society." Finally, "the staff members are as severe as prison guards. Although they have remained within the bounds of pedagogical standards, they also lack wisdom and sympathy."[54]

In the wake of these revelations, officials drafted a reform plan, the provisions of which further exposed the severity of the problems. The plan called for the regulations and procedures to be revised to "accord with reality"; for the inmates to receive hot water and food rations "without deductions"; for school-age children to attend two hours of classes every day; for improved medical care and hygiene to lower the death rate. When they did occur, deaths had to be promptly reported and processed for burial: "The Shelter is not to lose the bodies due to disorderly confusion." Lastly, the staff was warned not to whip or abuse the inmates: "That the inmates have been reduced to beggary deserves pity. The staff must have compassion in their hearts. If the inmates make mistakes or act disrespectfully they can be sternly reprimanded, but they cannot be beaten or abused."[55]

Throughout the occupation years, Beijing's police and municipal institutions thus functioned in tandem to dispense punishment and provide relief. But although the Social Affairs Bureau and private charities also augmented their seasonal aid programs, every winter the press reported frequent instances of suicides due to poverty. Accounts of exposed corpses appeared next to announcements of lost or abandoned children, sometimes featuring blurry photos. To alleviate the distress of an impoverished population, *Shibao* (the city's largest newspaper) conducted an annual fund-raiser, coined the "one dollar can save one life" campaign. In one appeal for donations, the editors asked, "Why is it when Berlin conducts a Christmas fundraising drive for the poor, they are able to collect several thousand marks in one day? We have been toiling in Beijing for several months and have not even collected 10,000 *yuan*! The Germans are not necessarily richer than the Chinese, but they have more sympathetic hearts."[56]

To prompt readers to greater generosity, the paper launched a series called "Inspections of the Slums." With headlines exclaiming "A Poor Infirm Woman Says 'I'd Rather Die!'" and "A Poor Infirm Old Man on the Verge of Death!" these articles depicted the lives of the city's most destitute. One essay described the Anhui Huiguan (a lodge for sojourners from that province) as a hovel of penniless families. In fact, in this neighborhood, rickshaw pullers were considered well-off. Another article, titled "A Newborn Infant, Cold and Hungry, Awaits Death," quoted a desperate mother: "I am not afraid to die, but this poor baby, who knows what sins he committed in a previous life to be born into this family. . . . I have so little milk to give him. Every day he cries constantly. But what can I do?" As her tears flowed, her husband also wept, joined by four other children who did not understand their parents' sorrow. Overwhelmed by the tragic scene, the journalist departed in haste: "I could not bear to watch any longer. I tossed out a few clothing coupons [relief tickets], lowered my head, and left without a word."[57]

Through these entreaties, *Shibao* collected Ch. $4,350 for poor relief in the winter of 1938–39. With the money the paper distributed noodles and $1 to "extremely poor" families. Another campaign followed, urging readers to "smoke one less cigarette" and donate the money.[58] But the funds could not possibly meet the needs of the thousands who needed help. Even residents with money had to stand in lines for hours to buy "mixed flour" (*hunhe mian*), a coarse blend of corn, millet, or beans adulterated with corn husks, wheat chaff, and dirt. As time passed and the Japanese army monopolized greater shares of the food supply, the "mixed flour" grew increasingly dark in color, with additives outweighing real grains. It was difficult to digest and caused severe gastrointestinal problems, but many had no choice but to eat it.[59]

Despite these miseries, the residents of Beijing were fortunate when compared to the people living in rural north China, where the Japanese military used scorched earth tactics (take all, kill all, burn all) to pacify the countryside. Although they controlled the urban centers and railways, the Japanese continued to battle Communist insurgents, local warlords, and defeated GMD troops in the surrounding rural areas.[60] After the outbreak of the Pacific War, Japanese extractions and labor conscriptions intensified in north China. By 1943, people in the countryside could barely survive on tree bark and grass. According to the Communist paper *Xinhua ribao*, all the farmers in the region had become beggars: "To become a beggar is nothing to be ashamed of, but since no one has anything to eat, who are you to beg from?"[61]

A SOLITARY ISLAND

The accommodations that Beijing's relief and security agencies forged with the Japanese occupation authorities thus crucially shaped the experience of the war, especially for the homeless and destitute. To the south, in treaty port Shanghai, Japan's attack on August 13, 1937, ignited an acute refugee crisis, one that would transform both the perceptions and realities of poverty. As densely populated Chinese districts in the suburbs endured intensive bombing throughout August, tidal waves of people sought refuge in the foreign concessions exempt from the terror. Meanwhile, residents with the resources to do so fled, creating a two-way traffic jam of confusion and panic. Incoming trains and boats packed with refugees were filled just as quickly with passengers eager to escape. Some 300,000 people departed the city between August 12 and 24. But as the Japanese army tightened its grip on the region, the number of people seeking refuge in Shanghai dwarfed the exodus. By mid-September, the population in the concessions had more than doubled, from 1.5 million to over 3 million. Most of the new arrivals and many of the residents who remained were destitute, with an estimated 100,000 homeless people living precariously in the "solitary island" (*gudao*).[62]

Meanwhile, in Nanshi, the Chinese district in the southern part of the city, thousands of refugees were trapped between the locked gates leading to the French Concession and the Japanese army. Father Jacquinot de Besange, a Jesuit priest, negotiated with the Japanese to establish a safety zone that sheltered an estimated 250,000 people, in an area of slightly more than one-fourth of a square mile. Elsewhere, private charity consortiums, native place associations, and religious and civic groups mobilized to provide relief. By November, when the Nationalists evacuated from Shanghai, 310 refugee camps across the city housed nearly 400,000 people. Despite this significant mobilization of resources, the situation remained desperate, with thousands wandering the streets, seeking refuge in alleyways, abandoned buildings, or wherever they could find shelter.[63]

The withdrawal of the Nationalists left responsibility for refugees primarily to private charities, for the foreign concession authorities continued to insist that poor relief, even on an emergency basis, was not their responsibility. But as the situation threatened to spiral out of control, the Municipal Council began to subsidize refugee camps indirectly, either by paying the rent and utilities or allocating land to private charities. In December 1937, the magnitude of the crisis finally led the French Municipal Council to introduce an "entertainment tax" of five cents per dollar on theater tickets. A month later, the International Settlement adopted the same tax, dubbed the Voluntary Entertainment Levy, with proceeds directed to the relief effort.[64]

The majority of refugee camps were initially housed in schools, temples, and vacant buildings. Some were hastily set up with scant attention to sanitation; others were orderly and closely supervised. Health inspectors, for instance, found as many as three hundred people crammed into one house, and in one case, five thousand people in a temple compound with room for two thousand. They also warned that with poor ventilation and no water or lavatory facilities, some of these camps would quickly become prime breeding ground for disease.[65] In contrast, the Great World, Shanghai's premier entertainment hall, accommodated four thousand refugees in an orderly fashion. The new residents converted the theaters, where pleasure seekers used to enjoy opera performances and magic shows, into dormitories covered with straw mats and hay. Although they were impossibly crowded, with people inhabiting every inch of space (even the stair landings), a Boy Scout troop and two hundred volunteers maintained some semblance of order. Some reports described refugee camps as almost idyllic places. One journalist portrayed one such shelter as a tranquil rural village, with children playing "marbles" and a piece of meat for each person every three days.[66]

But other camps were more like prisons, with inmates locked up. With typical food rations limited to two daily meals of rice (or rice porridge) and a sprinkling of salted vegetables, malnutrition soon became a serious problem. The lack of essential vitamins in the diet caused scurvy, beriberi, and chronic skin infections. Dysentery was also widespread, the result of poor sanitary conditions. In the autumn of the 1937, an outbreak of cholera struck the camps, with the first reported case coming from the Great World. From there the epidemic raged through the city for six weeks, with over 1,600 confirmed cases and 484 deaths, most of them in the camps.[67]

As the military crisis continued with no sign of abating, existing shelters soon exceeded their maximum capacities. With the onset of colder weather and thousands still waiting for help, relief organizations built straw huts on vacant land along the perimeter inside the concessions—the same type of structures that the Municipal Council had previously condemned. Although the foreign authorities continued to harbor concerns about the hazards of such dwellings, they could not object to their use as refugee shelters without offering alternatives. As the least expensive form of accommodation, straw huts soon sprang up wherever there was vacant land, even in cemeteries. In addition to providing shelter and food to war victims, relief organizations also made arrangements for the departure of as many people as possible.[68] With so many refugees in the city, worries that they would become a long-term burden surfaced. The *North-China Herald* heartily endorsed the efforts to remove people, remarking that "there is a practical reason for swift benevolence for . . . the evacuation of the refugees is a direct insurance against future trouble. Quietness and patience have their limits."[69]

From their underground cells, members of the CCP hoped to provoke this quietness and patience into action. In 1927, the GMD's bloody purge had driven the Communists from Shanghai. A decade later, only about one hundred cadres remained. Within the first year of the war they infiltrated thirty refugee camps to recruit, including two of the largest shelters run by the International Refugee Committee (IRC).[70] On the first anniversary of the Marco Polo Bridge Incident, administrators at one of the IRC camps found a duplicating machine and hundreds of anti-Japanese pamphlets and articles.[71] At another shelter located in a cemetery, the Shanghai Municipal Police discovered that a refugee named Gu Zhen had paid a group of children to parade down Nanjing Road and shout anti-Japanese slogans. Gu gathered twenty-one boys and gave them twenty cents each for breakfast, a list of slogans, and instructions to throw stones at any Japanese they passed. Before the boys left the camp, their furtive behavior attracted a guard's notice, and they were prevented from carrying out the demonstration. By then, Gu had disappeared.[72] While the authorities could not prove that the Communists had instigated these incidents, they took extra precautions to block overt displays of anti-Japanese sentiment, which could invite reprisals from the army that surrounded the "solitary island."

Winter Corpses and Spring Coffins

The first winter after the outbreak of the war was bleak. With the onset of cold weather, what had been an acute crisis hardened into a grim tale of death statistics. During one cold spell, burial societies reported collecting more than four hundred corpses on the streets. Many of the dead were found naked, stripped of their clothing and possessions.[73] In the IRC's six camps, the death rate skyrocketed more than tenfold. One journalist lamented that while in the past corpses were occasionally found on the streets, now "they are everywhere in this 'solitary island.' You find bodies not only in small alleyways and doorsteps, even on crowded streets there are many stiff corpses. . . . This 'solitary island' has become an island of death."[74]

The litany of press reports depicting the plight of refugees stirred the compassion of Shanghai's residents, as no other accounts of destitution had before. A letter to the *North-China Daily News*, for example, declared,

> Those who have been able to peg out a claim on a stone doorway are regarded as fortunates. The Winter will bring a very heavy toll amongst these pitiful beings, many of whom are likely to accept even death as a welcome relief. . . . Many are families of honest and hardworking labourers, but what

lies before them, if charitable funds run out and they find themselves without anywhere to turn to keep body and soul together?[75]

Indeed, in the early months and throughout the first winter, sympathy for war
refugees ran high. Shanghai's residents, Chinese and foreign, opened their
pocketbooks generously, with the vast majority of relief funds coming from
private donations.

The coming of spring in 1938 ameliorated the winter's heavy death toll but
revealed a related problem: an enormous backlog of unburied corpses. In the
Chinese tradition, funerary rituals required that the dead be returned to their
ancestral homes for burial, so that later generations could make appropriate
sacrifices to their spirits. In large migrant communities such as Shanghai, native place associations helped arrange coffin shipments, temporary burials, or
storage in special repositories (*binshe*) for members who died away from home.
Over time, coffin repositories sprang up as commercial establishments.[76] As
existing facilities filled to capacity during the war, native place associations
rented vacant lots to store the overflow, with mountains of coffins only loosely
monitored. Others made consignment arrangements with shipping companies,
but as the weeks ticked by and traffic remained closed, coffins piled up along
Shanghai's waterways. The number of corpses collected from the streets com-
pounded the problem. Trucks from the Public Benevolent Cemetery became a
familiar sight as they made early morning rounds to gather bodies that had
expired overnight.[77]

With the coming warm weather, rotting corpses emerged as a festering public health problem. In early March, the authorities ordered managers at one site
in the French Concession to remove the ten thousand coffins stored on its
premises immediately. Boats moored along the waterways were given a week to
clear out. Although the repositories tried to notify families to claim the bodies,
it was impossible to make arrangements on such short notice. In cooperation
with the foreign health departments, six charities organized a cremation program and disposed of thirty thousand corpses.[78] Cremation violated the sacrosanct practice of burying the dead intact, but under the circumstances it was the
only solution. Despite these measures, complaints continued. One foreign resident objected to a large repository in his neighborhood, saying, "This means
that Tunsin Road ... is to be made a 'dump' for Chinese, both living and
dead. ... A summer, virtually as prisoners in Shanghai, is a cheerless enough
prospect, without having coffins and refugees on our doorstep."[79] By the end of
the year in 1938, the Health Department reported that it had cleared out one
hundred thousand corpses in six months.[80] The public outcry over abandoned
corpses highlights one stark feature of the lives of the poor during the war. In
life, they had suffered extreme deprivations and misery; in death they could not
find the solace of a decent burial and a final resting place, so important to the
Chinese. In 1938, 68 percent of Chinese deaths in the Settlement were exposed

corpses left on the streets, mostly beggars and babies. Subsequent winters brought further misery, with mounting death tolls.[81]

Production and National Salvation

As death dominated news headlines throughout 1938, calls for work relief followed, once again trumpeted as the panacea for poverty. Efforts to put refugees to work began in that winter. At some camps they earned ten cents a day to work as cooks and coolies. At others, women learned embroidery or were placed in jobs as servants, while men performed manual labor. One IRC camp opened a co-op to sell snacks such as *dabing, youtiao,* and fried peanuts. A report in March 1939 estimated that thirteen thousand people were participating in some form of production, about 10 percent of the number of refugees.[82]

As for the rest, an article in *Shenbao* described the general perception that they were free loaders: "The camps do not take in refugees (*nanmin*), but instead shelter a bunch of lazy people (*lanmin*)." One observer griped that most of these "so-called refugees" were "comparatively rich" people busy amusing themselves in Shanghai's theaters and nightclubs.[83] Others grumbled that many had found work but refused to leave the comfort of the camps, where they enjoyed free shelter and food. The *North-China Herald* suggested that such "affluent" refugees could be induced to leave by eliminating rice from the rations, for if the camps provided "only corn meal mush, its free clients would quickly decide to pay for their own meals at some other place." Abolishing the policy of allowing refugees to leave the premises to work would also force those with jobs to depart. As for people who decry these measures as "inhumane," they "must be invited to furnish the funds necessary. . . . Those who are unable to do so have no right to insist that other people assume the burden for them. It is a case of put up or shut up."[84] In short, sympathy for refugees plummeted as the crisis continued, with their dependence on charity increasingly viewed with suspicion and impatience.

In order to cut costs and promote self-sufficiency, in October 1938 the Federation of Charities converted two of its camps into "refugee self-provision shelters" (*nanmin zijisuo*), which eliminated food rations. By January 1939, five other sites had opened along the same principles. A Chinese correspondent, writing in *Shenbao*, opined that these shelters "reduce the burden of public expenses and can also increase production. . . . Isn't this killing two birds with one stone?" Likewise, the Refugee Relief Committee started a "Production Education Fund" and advocated separating truly helpless refugees from the young and able-bodied: "If we do not differentiate between them . . . this will not only cultivate habits of dependency, but also create countless idlers and unemployed vagrants." In the long term, "[b]y teaching them the path of production . . . the nation will be able to add to its productive elements. When peace returns ... refugees can use these skills to eke out a living and will not have to rely on others. Throughout the country the hidden problem of poverty will end."[85] In May 1939, the Committee sponsored an exhibition showcasing refugee-made products (e.g., toys, back-scratchers, and rugs), declaring that "to implement production is to stabilize social order ... to implement production is to protect the central national policy!" The chairman proclaimed that for refugees to "sit idly and eat for a long period of time ... only cultivates their laziness. Over time they become society's parasites and deplete the nation's strength."[86]

By 1939, the move toward replacing charity with work was well underway. In February, *Shenbao* reported that the Nationalist government in exile had enacted a policy of compulsory labor in refugee camps, exempting only the elderly, the very young, the disabled, and the infirm. Those who refused to work were punished (reduced rations, detention, military conscription, or expulsion). Although the directive did not apply to Shanghai's concessions, the IRC quickly followed, adopting "compulsory work" (*qiangpuo gongzuo*) in its camps.[87] In sum, through labor, both private institutions and government authorities hoped to promote self-sufficiency and reduce the number of dependent people. Since charity exacerbated indolent habits, work would prevent the proliferation of "social parasites." At the same time, "refugee production" became a rallying cry for the cause of national salvation, linking the labor of war victims to the cause of Anti-Japanese Resistance.

THE BATTLE OVER STRAW HUTS

As discussed in chapter 3, the Municipal Council had fought protracted battles against the proliferation of shantytowns throughout the 1930s. To the consternation of its officers, the 10 percent annual reduction plan (adopted in 1931) had done little to contain the metastatic growth of illegal settlements. During the war, the refugee crisis introduced new complexities into this issue. In addition to previous questions of legality and property rights, the presence of homeless war victims forced humanitarian considerations directly into the debate. Moreover, it became difficult, if not impossible, to distinguish the formerly despised "hut dwellers" from refugees occupying abandoned buildings and vacant lots.

At the outset, however, to the authorities it appeared that the war had one fortuitous side effect: the destruction of many straw hut settlements. In late November 1937, the deputy police chief reported that fires had incinerated approximately 80 percent of the huts in Zhabei and Hongkou; "reliable sources" also informed him that "the Japanese would offer no objection to the remaining 20% being demolished and in fact would welcome it." Publicly, of course, officials could not collaborate with the Japanese to destroy Chinese homes, but they certainly did not regret the elimination of straw huts during the hostilities.[88]

Yet the refugee crisis created a shantytown problem of a different dimension. In abandoned schools, along creeks and waterways, and on vacant land, refugees unable to find shelter in official camps built their own makeshift accommodations. Initially, the Municipal Council suspended its 10 percent annual reduction campaign, removing squatters only if their huts obstructed traffic or if owners complained.[89] There were simply too many refugees with nowhere to go, and insistence on a tough eviction policy would mean assuming the burden of providing food and shelter for those left homeless. When pressed by landowners, however, the authorities felt compelled to act. Throughout 1938 and 1939, a stream of requests for intervention poured in. Property values in the concessions were rising and owners were eager to profit by selling or building on vacant land. Meanwhile, desperate refugees increasingly encroached on available spaces.[90]

For their part, when faced with eviction, hut dwellers organized to defend their homes in myriad ways. In scores of cases, they directly appealed to the Municipal Council with written petitions, and often sent representatives to make their case in person. Shantytown residents also tried to enlist the help of civic organizations that had come to their aid in the past.[91] As the war dragged on, some became more aggressive, resulting in escalating conflicts. In March 1938, for example, the police served notice to a group living on Amoy Road to move within three days, on the grounds that their huts were unsafe for occupation. When inspectors arrived on the eve of the deadline to survey the situation, the residents verbally abused them and pelted them with manure. After the authorities denied their request to relocate to a nearby lot, five hundred people stormed into a refugee camp under construction and moved in. T. K. Ho, the Council's assistant secretary, tried to mediate a resolution to the standoff. It took several days for him to secure permission for this group to move their huts to another area.[92]

Although many of their attempts to avert eviction were ultimately unsuccessful, hut dwellers negotiated for extensions and maneuvered for better terms with a variety of tactics. In a case from 1938, one group tried to bargain by invoking the Council's previous "compassionate grant" of Ch. $14. In November, the Silk Goods Dealers' Association had asked for the eviction of 170 households from its property on Cunningham Road, and offered to pay each Ch. $10 if they vacated immediately. The Council informed the group that if they did not comply, they would forfeit the "relief fee" and their huts would be demolished. Faced with the imminent destruction of their homes, the residents sprang into action. They sent a series of appeals to the Chinese Ratepayers Association and the District Citizens' Federation, including the following:

> We hut dwellers on Cunningham Road comprise 576 households and some 10,000 people. We are mostly refugees from Hongkou and Zhabei. At first we lived on the streets; later, charitable organizations placed us temporarily in refugee camps, where we received food, clothing, and shelter. We did not think it was good to rely on others indefinitely, so with the approval of the International Relief Committee we built these straw huts ... where we expected to live peacefully through the winter.

The landlord's order for 170 of the households to move came as "a bolt out of the blue," leaving the remaining 400 families anxious about their fate:

> This unjustifiable action will render us homeless, and in this winter weather may cause many to die of cold and hunger. Are we refugees more insignificant than insects, which are small but still strive to live? No matter what, we shall struggle to survive. Ten *yuan* cannot purchase the appeasement of our hearts. In offering us compensation the landlord is following the example of the Municipal Council, which in the past offered fourteen *yuan* per family to the hut dwellers on Yanshan Road.... Although we are poor and ignorant, we know how to distinguish between what is beneficial to us and what is not.

The attempt to negotiate for more money was only partially successful. Although the owners refused to increase the compensation, they did give the stipend to 33 more households. At the end of November, 203 families each received Ch. $10, and they moved without incident.[93]

Another group of refugees tried for three years to collect the Ch. $14 payment from the Municipal Council. The "Longjiang Road Hut Dwellers" had been promised compensation for the demolition of their homes, scheduled for October 1937. The outbreak of war in August, however, forced them to flee. They elected representatives to petition the Municipal Council, specifically asking for the promised payment. Their first letter described a desperate situation: "Although there are many refugee camps, they are all filled to capacity, and there is no place for the late-comers.... Separated from their families, the elderly and the children are wailing and weeping. Although the lot of all refugees is miserable, the most miserable of all are those who have come from the Longjiang Road huts."[94]

When the Council did not respond to this initial plea, the group adopted an aggressive tone: "This morning we saw Foreign Constable no. 53 and Sergeant no. 1566 with three Chinese constables set fire to sheds put up by refugees from the Chinese territory. This is most inhumane. This indicates that the Council also burned the straw huts in the Eastern District.... If our request is not granted, people will accuse the Council of burning our huts." When their representatives visited the Council office to present their certificates, assistant secretary T. K. Ho informed them that the war had voided the previous promise of compensation.[95] Three years later, the same group of refugees, now living in an alleyway, again petitioned the Council. In a letter dated May 6, 1940, they wrote,

> The price of rice has reached unprecedented heights. We 45 refugee families living the alleyway consist of more than 200 persons, old and young. We have neither food nor shelter, and we sleep on broken bricks. Both wealthy and poor are all human beings. Even birds have nests and beasts have dens. Why has the Council no compassion for us? . . . The Council has broken its promise and is evading payment in disregard of our difficulties. . . . We poor people do not value our lives dearly, because if we die, it means the end of our troubles. But justice is justice. It is definitely stated in [*sic*] the form that each family will be granted an allowance of $14.00.[96]

Four days later, the refugees sent a second letter stating that six of them were gravely ill, and reduced their demand to Ch. $10 per family. They also threatened to make trouble:

> If our request is not granted, then we cannot be blamed if all of us . . . all come to the Council office and defecate all over the place. We do not care if we are arrested and punished, since we will die anyway. Please understand that we have nowhere else to turn. . . . Any incidents that may result will be unpleasant. We will not leave until we are satisfied. . . . Although this is a small matter, human lives are not to be treated lightly.[97]

In contrast, on the same day the group sent a separate letter addressed personally to T. K. Ho, evincing a completely different attitude:

> We poor refugees living in the alleyway have no shelter. . . . We are starving and freezing, and the end is near. We have submitted our pitiful entreaties a hundred times, but the Council has turned a deaf ear. If we refugees give up all hope and die, it will be too late for the Council to regret its indifference. . . . May Your Excellency's descendants be ever prosperous. Will the Secretary kindly ask the foreign officials to find a way to save our insect lives? The families now living in the alleyway truly have no other choice. We are people, not animals. . . . Please help us in the same spirit as you once did when you performed the wonderful act of asking the Council to defer the demolition of our huts.[98]

After receiving this letter, Ho agreed to see representatives of this group. In reply, the refugees wrote that when his invitation arrived by messenger, "all of us kneeled to receive your letter; it was like receiving a stay of execution."[99] By addressing him as Your Excellency (*daren*) and mimicking the language and posture of subservience, these refugees tried to alter the terms of their relationship to Ho, shifting him from a municipal bureaucrat to an imperial official. By hearkening to the ideal of a bygone era, when officials had moral responsibility for the welfare of the people, they hoped to move him to action on their behalf. Furthermore, by pointing to Ho's previous attempts to help the poor, they sought to identify him as a sympathetic advocate, distinct from the "foreign officials" who callously ignored their pleas. (Ho did meet with two representatives, but only to inform them again that the outbreak of war voided their certificates and the promise of relief payments.)

A different case from 1938 also illustrates the hut dwellers' persistence in defending their homes. In the fall of 1937, five hundred refugees from Zhabei paid Ch. $100 to lease a plot of land off Singapore Road. The following summer, rumors circulated that the landlord was about to evict them, and the residents paid several go-betweens to negotiate on their behalf. In July, the Japanese Military Police informed them that they had ten days to move. Faced with the imminent loss of their homes, the hut dwellers appealed to various charities and the Municipal Council for help.[100] Meanwhile, several newspapers carried accounts of the story as yet another example of conflicts between squatters and landowners. On July 21, *The Standard* followed up its initial report with a letter from the hut dwellers themselves: "The report published by your paper on July 18 regarding hut dwellers on Singapore Road is not correct in some points." In this letter, the refugees refuted the assertion that they were illegal squatters, and demanded that the paper publish a retraction. A subsequent investigation revealed that the entire incident was a fraud. The owner did not wish to evict them; it was a "local bully" named Zhu Hongjun who extorted "negotiation money" from them and then bribed the police to expel them. When the hut dwellers realized that they had been cheated, they were incensed. By their own admission, "not considering the consequences, the men, women, elderly, and young all gathered around, gave Zhu a sound thrashing, and covered him with feces."[101]

Other hut dwellers turned to the legal system for redress. In 1938 Yang Caiqing, the owner of a large plot on Chibang Road, decided to terminate his lease with his tenant Zhang Guisheng. When Yang visited the property, he realized that Zhang had sublet the land to two hundred hut dwellers, who were living in eleven large sheds. He tried to evict them but discovered that six of the huts held municipal permits issued during the 1931 registration drive. The Council ordered the residents of the five unauthorized structures to relocate at once. Officials also ruled that those with permits could remain, leaving it up to Yang to negotiate for their removal. Using his connections, the owner reached an "understanding" with the Council's deputy treasurer: he would agree to a tax assessment of Ch. $600, in exchange for help evicting the squatters. Yang also prevailed upon an officer of the Standard-Vacuum Oil Company (his employer) to write to the Council on his behalf.[102] Nonetheless, the authorities concluded that the six sheds with permits could not be demolished and advised Yang to seek redress in court.

Six months later, in April 1939, Yang obtained a court judgment giving the "trespassers" three months to vacate the property. The hut dwellers went to see T. K. Ho and showed him the verdict. According to Ho's memo, "After reading it, I told them that they had no case" for an appeal.[103] With the deadline to file an appeal approaching, Yang predicted that the legal costs would "scare them away." In the meantime, he refused to pay the land tax:

> If the Council will, on the grounds of my nonpayment of land tax, barricade my land . . . a peaceful and voluntary evacuation will be the result. No squatters will be foolish enough to leave their goods inside a strong barrier waiting for the court to dispose of in my favour. This land belongs to me and the squatters have no right to stay. . . . The Council has a right to bring pressure on my land for payment of land tax now over due.

On August 1, the Public Works Department enclosed the property with a barbed wire fence, leaving only an opening large enough for the passage of one person. Although it was not uncommon for the Council to barricade shantytowns along the concession boundaries (considered necessary under the "unsettled conditions . . . as a means of dealing with certain doubtful characters"), the acquiescence to such a cruelly ingenious ploy was highly unusual.[104]

Three days later, the hut dwellers sent the following letter to the Council, reiterating that they were legal tenants, not trespassers:

> Now our landlord Yang Caiqing has conceived another trick. He is purposefully delaying payment of the land tax. As a result on August 1 the Council barricaded the property, and we are locked up like beasts deprived of freedom of movement. The Council has also deputized some armed constables to patrol the place and to prohibit us from leaving. Not only are we now unable to work, but our lives are also endangered.[105]

They begged the Council to allow them to pay a deposit as guarantee for the tax, so that the fence could be removed. When they received no reply to this initial entreaty, they sent a second letter written in English. A third letter arrived several days later: "The Council should institute legal proceedings against the landlord for nonpayment of the land tax. But it is unfair to interfere with the livelihood and freedom of third party individuals. According to the Land Regulations, there is no such provision authorizing the Council to take such drastic action."[106]

Against Yang's expectations, the hut dwellers did file an appeal, suing him for "offense against personal liberty." In turn, the landlord countersued them for trespassing. At the end of August, the district court issued its verdict, finding that since the Municipal Council, not the landlord, had erected the barricade, Yang did not violate the hut dwellers' personal liberty. At the same time, since the residents presented their lease and receipts for rents paid, they were not guilty of trespassing. After the judgment, the hut dwellers again wrote to T. K. Ho asking him to remove the fence. Attaching a copy of the verdict, they asked, "As we are not unlawfully occupying the land . . . to whom does the responsibility for the barricades actually belong?"[107]

Still the Municipal Council refused to remove the fence, and in the meantime the legal proceedings continued. By October 1939, three suits were pending, with the hut dwellers bringing both civil and criminal complaints against Yang in the Jiangsu High Court, and the landlord suing them for damages in the Shanghai jurisdiction. In March 1940, the final verdict ordered all of the hut dwellers to vacate the property by April 3. Two weeks after the deadline, Yang asked the municipal demolition squad to enforce the eviction at his expense. Finally, on May 2, under the watchful eye of the police, the occupants pulled down the huts themselves and left the premises without incident. As a final coda, the Council sent Yang a bill for the fence, the demolition services, and the outstanding taxes.[108]

The Paradox of Squatters' Rights

Unfortunately, the paper trail ends there, and the fate of this group of tenacious and resourceful hut dwellers remains unknown. What we can glean from their story suggests that despite their impoverishment, they possessed a sophisticated understanding of the law. And although they ultimately lost the battle, by doggedly fighting a much more powerful landlord in court and working through customary channels, they gained a year and a half of reprieve from eviction. Indeed, in all of the above cases we see that people did not accept the loss of their homes without putting up a fight. They repeatedly petitioned the Municipal Council and various organizations for help, often directly soliciting the aid of T. K. Ho, the Chinese official. They engaged in a variety of stalling tactics, sometimes blatantly defying eviction orders, daring the authorities to remove them by force. Many of them came from Zhabei and had battled the authorities over their huts before the war. They knew that fearing unrest, the Council did not undertake the large-scale removal of people lightly. Occasionally, the hut dwellers threatened to make trouble, and directly retaliated against those who exploited them. At the same time, in order to dispel the prevailing view that they were illegitimate interlopers, they emphatically rejected the label "squatters" and insisted on the status of authentic war refugees or legal tenants. Most importantly, they attempted to shift the terms of the discussion from property to human rights. By comparing themselves to insects and animals and asserting, for example, that "[b]oth wealthy and poor are all human beings," they called attention to their desperate struggles for survival. Such claims argued for the fundamental right of all people to a minimum standard of living, an implicit rebuke to a society that devalued their lives.

These drawn-out battles between refugee–squatters and property owners prompted angry responses from the community. Many complained that the shanties were filled not with refugees, but "a bunch of loafers and human para-sites of the lowest and worst type," or that these encampments were a continu-ation of prewar trends, exacerbated by the government's leniency. But the mag-nitude of the refugee crisis made it difficult to distinguish illegal shantytowns from legitimate shelters for war victims. While "squatter villages" were un-doubtedly a "menace to public health," the *North-China Herald* acknowledged that "it would be inhuman to deny these unfortunates the attenuated safety" of the concessions. At the same time, appalling conditions called for urgent rem-edies. In a full-page photo spread showing one such "squatter village," open coffins littered the grounds, a sight described as "deplorably too common around Shanghai at the moment."[109]

In May 1938, the onset of hot weather and the fear of summer epidemics created a sense of urgency to address the problem. A census showed over seven thousand huts (with some forty-five thousand occupants) located along the western perimeter, and reportedly growing daily.[110] Although these shanties were not in the concession, they posed a grave threat. As Dr. J. H. Jordan, the Commissioner of Public Health, noted, "The danger from outside will soon nullify all our efforts within." But the issue was complicated:

> It is not possible to abolish the huts without running the risk of rendering a large number of people homeless. It is not possible for them to move on for reasons which are obvious to all, hence it is to be regretted that until circum-stances change, squatter huts and villages are an unfortunate necessity, though one which might quite easily involve the town in an epidemic of terrifying magnitude.

After reviewing the conditions at the worst sites, Dr. Jordan proposed a sanita-tion plan, with water drainage, latrines, waste removal, and a reliable water supply as minimum standards.[111]

As the Municipal Council considered Dr. Jordan's proposal, some officials expressed the concern that doing anything for the "squatters" would amount to de facto recognition. When one official suggested that refugee camps and squatter huts were part and parcel of the same problem, others sounded the alarm that treating "squatters" as "refugees" could result in the obligation to feed them. After much debate, the Council approved part of Dr. Jordan's proposal, authorizing the Public Works Department to hire one hundred workers to re-move waste and build drainage systems at the worst sites.[112] But even this mod-est plan drew the ire of some foreign residents. As one enraged correspondent wrote to the *North-China Daily News*,

> Truly an amazing situation; that the Council should contemplate providing sanitary amenities for improving the welfare of a body of persons who have entered into wrongful possession of someone else's land. Is it then the Council's policy to grant certain recognition of squatters' rights, if so, not a

vacant piece of land within the defence perimeter will be safe from this form of aggression.[113]

The paradox of "squatters' rights" stirred debates in other contexts as well. In September 1938, lawyers representing Atkinson & Dallas (a prominent architectural firm) complained that although the owners had hired a watchman to guard a large parcel of land on Avenue Haig, two thousand people had broken in and built 250 huts on the property. But an inspector sent to investigate found that in fact the "squatters" paid rent to the watchman (Ch. $2-3 per hut per month); the site had also been incorporated into Dr. Jordan's sanitation campaign. In considering the case, the Council's Acting Secretary noted, "It appears that some of the squatters may claim rights to squatting, by virtue of rent payments to the watchman of the land." Even such a tentative conjecture provoked a sharp rejoinder from one Council member: "I would like to know 'How squatters can claim *rights*, & in what court?'"[114]

In another case the same month, one group of hut dwellers complained that after the Council installed a drainage system, their landlord ordered them to move: "Zhao Shunlin did not object to our occupying the land when it was covered with cesspools, but now he insists on resuming possession and has ordered us to tear down our huts." Their entreaty found a sympathetic audience in Dr. Jordan, who wrote that the landowner was "taking unfair advantage of the improvements wrought to his property." "While it is true that these squatters have no right whatsoever on the land," Jordan suggested intervention: "At first sight this may appear to be a somewhat foolish measure to take as it is recognising squatter encampments. On the other hand, the question might be considered from a slightly different angle, namely that of the right of a population to live." A terse reply, however, reminded Jordan that the there was hardly enough land for refugee camps, let alone for "squatters."[115] The matter was dropped, denying the appeal to "the right of a population to live."

From Refugee Crisis to Beggar Problem

During the war's second year, the Municipal Council had taken steps to assume tighter control over the refugee population. Nearly a half a million people were dispersed from the International Settlement, but some sixty-five thousand people remained in the camps.[116] As the battlefront migrated to the interior, many property owners returned to Shanghai and asked camps to vacate their land. Confronting numerous such requests, in August 1938, the Council leased three plots of land on Yenping Road to set up a consolidated camp. The Voluntary Entertainment Levy would pay the rent, with private charities assuming responsibility for other expenses.[117]

A series of construction problems delayed the scheduled opening of the consolidated camp. The selected sites were garbage ditches, filled in and covered with earth and ash. In mid-September, the Federation of Charities reported that although a thin layer of dirt concealed the trash, an offensive smell persisted. Since the ground was not firm, in time the garbage would decompose, and the huts would collapse. Despite these concerns, the Council rejected the request for money to build a more solid foundation. In early October, a health inspector added his criticisms, observing that the process of digging drainage outlets exposed the garbage underneath. In the kitchen, he commented that "I have rarely ever seen a bigger number of flies than on this food." Although the camp did have two luxuries (electricity and water) the inspector recommended postponing the opening to fix the problems, advice officials disregarded when they transferred five thousand people there just days later.[118]

In the consolidation process, the Municipal Council also classified the remnant refugees into three groups: (1) the "wholly destitute," who need food and shelter; (2) the homeless, but able to feed themselves; and (3) "those who can afford both food and shelter," who should be eliminated from the camps. The Yenping Road sites were designated as category two hostels. For the "wholly destitute," the Council developed another camp on Tunsin Road, with capacity for eight thousand to twelve thousand.[119] The Tunsin Road camp provided adequate facilities, but its location outside the Settlement boundaries stirred protests. Two groups of refugees sent letters to the Shanghai Relief Society, objecting to their removal outside the safety of the concession. The Council ignored these protests, however, and in the process 30 to 40 percent of the refugees refused to move and "voluntarily disappeared."[120]

Some of these refugees moved across town to the French Concession, but there they also encountered inhospitable conditions. Since the outbreak of war, the Salvation Army had been running a shelter on Rue de Sieyes on behalf of the International Relief Committee. When Brigadier Bert Morris approached the French Council for additional financial support, officials agreed—but on the condition of imposing a more punitive regimen. In the spring of 1939, the Salvation Army converted part of the refugee shelter into a "beggar camp," with a bamboo fence enclosing two large straw huts. Morris touted the effort as "trying to make decent citizens out of beggars," and invoked as an example the Salvation Army's success in Colombo. For the next year, the French Police processed more than eight thousand beggars through the camp. It closed in 1940 when the landlord declined to renew the lease; the remaining inmates were dispersed.[121]

Over in the International Settlement, the liquidation of refugee camps began in earnest just as the Salvation Army's experiment in the French Concession drew to a close. The Municipal Council asked relief organizations to repatriate the remaining residents and prepare to shutter all of the sites. Those leftover would be classified as "beggars." The goal was to terminate assistance to all able-bodied people and substitute "the care of beggars for the care of refugees."[122] At Tunsin Road, where fifteen thousand people lived, the Shanghai Relief Society began to clear its rolls with offers of travel money (and a bonus for early departure). The Federation of Charities embarked on a similar program for the nine thousand refugees in its two camps. By June 1940, only fifteen shelters remained in the International Settlement. But the people left, with nowhere to go, proved to be the most difficult to disperse. More than a year later, some thirteen thousand lingered, despite increasing offers of repatriation money.[123]

The closure of the camps and the designation of the remaining population as "beggars" marked the end of unrestricted assistance for refugees. The Municipal Council was no longer willing to shoulder the indirect burden of providing for all comers without discrimination. As relief organizations closed their doors, "the refugee crisis" gradually became the "beggar problem" in Shanghai. Within three years, the status of refugees had eroded to the extent that Cai Renbao, the director of the Refugee Assistance Committee, found it necessary to remind his staff: "You must not forget that refugees are not slaves, and certainly not convicts. Refugees are citizens who are victims from war zones during this period of national calamity. . . . They are compatriots who stand in the same place as the rest of us."[124]

As "refugees" became "beggars," the liquidation of the camps also brought to the surface an issue that had been simmering for some time. Although the war led to an enormous increase in the number of homeless people in the concessions, the outpouring of sympathy for refugees muted the disparagement of beggars for several years. But as the crisis dragged on with no end in sight, the problem emerged once again as a leading public complaint, with demands for the authorities to "do something" resounding in the foreign press. The following letter from "Disgusted" and its complaint about a beggar loitering near a bus stop captures the sense of antipathy and repulsion:

> It would appear that he is suffering from an infected leg; is surrounded by several tins in which he keeps his food and which he probably uses to hold his urine, etc. . . . He is covered in vermin and during the day is busy catching lice. . . . I really cannot understand why such a pest should be allowed to park on this spot under the noses of the Chinese police who are on duty near this spot. Perhaps they have no sense of smell? Here's hoping that this bird will be removed to the hospital without further delay.[125]

Gangs of street beggars presented an even more ominous threat. The *North-China Herald* complained of a "large army at loose on The Bund . . . preying on the lorries unloading rice, wheat, cotton, etc." Under the "pretence of starvation," these hordes freely pilfered "in a manner only slightly removed from theft," and profited handsomely for their efforts. Far from pitiful, they were in fact professionals plying a trade. The scheme of using children as "bait" to solicit alms also stirred censure: "There are large numbers of waifs and strays who appear on the streets and get into the hands of the Fagin type colloquially called 'wild uncles,' who exploit them and keep them in permanent bondage through cruelty, and live on their earnings."[126]

The concession authorities took these complaints seriously.[127] Throughout the first years of the war, the police periodically attempted to clear the streets. By rounding up beggars and sending them to refugee camps, the authorities in effect repudiated any distinction between the two groups.[128] And as in the past, beggars left in another jurisdiction would soon be back. The International Settlement police accused their counterparts in the French Concession of dumping large numbers of "diseased Chinese," and posted guards at the borders to chase them back. For their part, French officials claimed that they were merely "returning" these beggars, since they had come from the International Settlement in the first place.[129]

The closure of the refugee camps only exacerbated the problem. The "voluntary disappearance" of those who refused relocation reduced the number of people dependent on charity. But many of them simply reappeared on the streets as beggars, adding to the "ghastly tale of daily deaths."[130] The pressure on the Municipal Council to "do something" intensified in 1940, heightened by an epidemic of typhoid fever in May. In order to alleviate public alarm about "lousy persons of the beggar class" spreading the infection, Dr. Jordan proposed that the police bring them in for disinfection and then return them to the streets. Although he acknowledged that refugee camps rather than "street vagrants" could be the source of infection, Jordan felt he had to do something to "allay public concern." For his part, the police chief conceded that it was impossible to distinguish beggars from "other classes." But since "such classes cannot be compulsorily detained by the Police for delousing," while beggars could be enticed with the offer of a free meal, some action was preferable to none. After a long debate, the Council approved the proposal and set a target of five thousand beggars for the delousing treatment.[131] The police chief's candid admission that it was impossible to identify "beggars" underscored the dilemma confronting the authorities. They felt compelled to take action, but ultimately did not know how to distinguish those who posed an actual danger to public health or social order, from the ones who were mere nuisances.

It was no coincidence that the issue of the "beggar menace" erupted into public debates in 1940. Since the outbreak of the war, the community had responded generously, time and again, to repeated appeals for refugee relief. With the concession authorities determined to keep poor relief out of their official realm of responsibility, private charity carried the day. But three years later, with more than ten thousand refugees still in the camps, and thousands more living on the streets, a sense of charity fatigue set in. The liquidation of the Jacquinot Zone in June 1940 added more homeless indigents to their midst; some seventeen thousand Jewish refugees had also arrived, swelling the number of destitute foreigners in the city.[132] Meanwhile, the war news from Europe grew

The Fuel for Salvation

Figure 4.4. *North-China Herald*, February 5, 1941

bleaker every day. What would become of their Shangri-La and their lives of privilege? How much more? How much longer? For some, the "hordes" of beggars "plying their trade" were the most visible signs of the city's decay, and the aggression of panhandlers only intensified the sense of loathing. It seemed as if Shanghai's concessions had become the dumping ground for the poor and desperate from all over the world. For others, the headlines of death statistics and the pitiful entreaties of child beggars served as daily reminders of their privilege and good fortune, invoking sympathy, guilt, irritation, and anger all at once.

As public pressures escalated, one International Settlement official noted, "I feel that the Council can hardly face the ratepayers again without having done something about the beggars." Likewise, the chief health inspector observed that "the spectacle of men and women lying on the pavements of the principal streets of Shanghai awaiting death is becoming too frequently horrible to escape notice, and a public scandal is looming in the near future."[133] These recurring complaints and the sense of unease about beggars—their filth, suffering, aggressive tactics, and the exploitation of children—echoed familiar refrains from an earlier era, not unique to wartime Shanghai. The refugee crisis, however, further complicated ambivalent attitudes toward poverty and charity, as it became impossible to differentiate between the truly needy and the professional beggars who had always plagued the city. It was in response to this dilemma and the mounting public outcry that the Municipal Council took the unprecedented step of creating a camp to incarcerate beggars.

The Salvation Army Beggar Camp

The idea of establishing a "police-controlled concentration camp" for beggars had been proposed and shelved several times before.[134] In January 1940, the Municipal Council again discussed the "compulsory detention" of beggars, and rejected "pauper relief" out of the conviction that "such would involve the provision of an institution of indefinite permanence, with its attendant continual drain on philanthropic resources." Instead, the proposed site would incarcerate all beggars "regardless of whether they are simply indigents or professional beggars." Unlike those in refugee camps, these inmates would not be released unless they could secure guarantors to pledge that they would not return to the streets. With compulsory detention, "the truly destitute will be given a chance of rehabilitation, and the professional beggar forced to mend his ways or remain within the camp." To mitigate the concern that this would foster a "beggars' utopia," officials suggested that "if stringent restrictions are imposed . . . these will to some extent operate to prevent the attractiveness of the camp." The *North-China Herald* concurred, commenting that "it is very probable that once this news gains currency amongst the professional begging fraternity many who at present make the International Settlement their happy hunting ground will depart for fresh woods and pastures new."[135]

In March 1940, the Council secured the Salvation Army's agreement to manage the camp and assume its operational expenses. The Council was willing to underwrite some costs, but reiterated its long-standing policy against poor relief. Instead, officials hoped that the public would contribute to the cause, as it is "a problem which so closely touches all sections of the community and which it is in the interest of everyone to solve."[136] Despite the determination to avoid financial responsibility, the Council did earmark 40 percent of the proceeds from its Voluntary Entertainment Fund to support the camp, and made a donation of Ch. $100,000 to the Salvation Army, an unprecedented sum.[137]

The plan initially called for the detention of all beggars without discrimination, but with a capacity of two thousand the camp could accommodate only a fraction of Shanghai's homeless. Which "types" should be targeted first? Brigadier Bert Morris, charged with the overall operation, suggested that "a distinction should be drawn between the merely destitute and those who are of mendicant character," and "the worst types should be tackled first including those who are physically repulsive." At the same time, the camp should focus on "the out and out destitute people" while avoiding taking in the "merely poor," since "there is no limit to the poor."[138] As for the "professional beggars," they were not the "real menace." According to Dr. Jordan, although the public objected to this type the most,

> They looked worse than they were, and it was a profession with them and they made good sums of money. . . . The beggars that really worried the health department were people who had become refugees due to the war and who had drifted into bad habits and become drug addicts and otherwise diseased; refugees who had been thrown out of refugee camps and had been given repatriation money but who had never been repatriated; they were the new beggar menace and problem, as against the old beggar problem which was purely and simply a racket and a very good one.[139]

Despite many such discussions, neither the Municipal Council nor the Salvation Army established clear criteria for the detention policy.

On January 1, 1941, Council Chairman W. J. Keswick presided over a ribbon-cutting ceremony marking the opening of the "Salvation Army Beggar Camp," located in a former primary school.[140] Twenty-four huts made of bamboo and straw served as dormitories. The school building housed the kitchen and a medical clinic; classrooms, workshops, and a Gospel House remained under construction. The plan called for fifty beggars to be processed and admitted every day (photographed, fingerprinted, "thoroughly scrubbed," and given new clothes upon arrival). At the same time, officials ominously noted that "the death rate will be very high, since many of those brought in from the streets will have fatal illnesses."[141] Since there were no clear guidelines, it was up to the police to decide which people to arrest. In the first three weeks of January, the police sent 732 beggars to the camp. Among them were 78 male and 35 female drug addicts; 195 had "chronic skin disease," 37 were blind, 22 had no legs, 2 were paralyzed, and 1 was a "dumb idiot." The rest had "no disease."[142]

In its first month, the camp functioned smoothly. Brigadier Morris predicted that there would no beggars on the streets within ten years. A visitor during the Spring Festival found 1,053 inmates (598 men, 241 women, 153 boys, and 61 girls). To celebrate the New Year, each person received four ounces of pork. The

Figure 4.5. "Cheerfully going to the Beggars Camp," 1941
Courtesy of the Salvation Army Australia Southern Territory Archives, Melbourne.

camp was "immaculately clean"; when questioned, "Many of the inmates expressed their gratitude for the shelter provided for them and appeared to be quite contented. . . . Although simply garbed, the inmates of the camp were not clothed in tatters and presented a different spectacle from the mendicants who infest the streets."[143]

Despite such optimism, problems quickly surfaced. Less than three months after its opening, Morris reported that the camp's existence was in danger, with operational costs far exceeding funds as prices continued to rise. Morris warned that if he could not feed the inmates, he would have no choice but to open the gates and permit them to leave.[144] In April, the inmates rioted and about ten escaped by jumping over the fence. When interrogated about their grievances, "they blamed the manager and threatened to burn his quarters down." But

Figure 4.6. "Morning exercises are done by all at the Beggars Camp," 1941
Courtesy of the Salvation Army Australia Southern Territory Archives, Melbourne.

mostly they wished to leave the camp.[145] By May, an inspector reported that conditions had deteriorated beyond any decent standard. The latrine drains were blocked, and despite numerous requests for repairs, nothing had been done. As a result, "the beggars are defecating on any available place." In October, merely ten months after its inauguration, only 600 inmates remained (including 250 children), less than a third of the projected capacity. Over 2,000 people had been "rehabilitated" and released, but among them were many "poor people" (*pinmin*) who had been wrongfully detained and released on bond.[146]

The beggar camp faltered so quickly for a number of reasons. The lack of financial resources was a major factor, for despite initial hopes, public subscriptions proved insufficient. The economic conditions of wartime Shanghai, with hyper-inflation and rice shortages, aggravated an already precarious situation. Then, Brigadier Morris's departure in April 1941 meant the loss of an energetic advocate with a long track record of fund-raising and service in Shanghai. (His replacement, Major George Walker, had worked for the Salvation Army in China for many years, but primarily in the north.) Although widely lauded as an innovative solution, the camp did not solve the beggar problem. Taking two thousand people off the streets was an important gesture to counter criticisms that the Council did nothing about the issue. This number, however, amounted to only a small fraction of the homeless people in the city.

Figure 4.7. "Beggar children also enjoy a Sports Day," 1941
Major George Walker is in uniform at right. Courtesy of the Salvation Army Australia
Southern Territory Archives, Melbourne.

By the autumn of 1941, less than a year after the camp opened, the authorities were already investigating other options for dealing with the beggar problem. To share the financial burden, the Municipal Council asked for the cooperation of the Chinese collaborationist government and the French authorities.
At a meeting in October, representatives from the three administrations agreed
to create a "beggar city" (*qigai shi*), in the form of "an agricultural settlement,
where destitutes would be able to work and rehabilitate themselves." Many options were discussed, including an abandoned university compound, or expanding the existing Salvation Army camp.[147] After some consideration, the committee decided to make use of a former "people's village" with three hundred
brick houses.[148] The Chinese municipality agreed to provide the use of the village at no cost and pay for the necessary repairs. Two thousand beggars from
the International Settlement and a thousand from the French Concession
would be the first inmates, and the two foreign governments would shoulder
the cost of operational expenses. An editorial in *Shenbao* expressed the hope
that given a better environment and the opportunity to make a fresh start, beggars could "turn good." A month later, however, these plans collapsed when the
Chinese mayor suddenly announced that the site was slated for "other purposes," prompting speculation that the Japanese authorities opposed the cooperative venture.[149]

The Salvation Army Beggars Camp marked a turning point in the Municipal Council's policy on poor relief. The decision to devote significant resources
to an indoor institution was a significant departure from years of rejecting pre-

cisely that commitment. By insisting on the Salvation Army's joint participation, the Council hoped that the private sector would share the burden of operating the camp. For Shanghai's indigents, the new approach also signaled the advent of a policy of incarceration. Under wartime conditions, the authorities opted to disregard previous concerns about the legality of detaining the noncriminal poor.

AFTER PEARL HARBOR

With the collapse of plans for the "beggar city" and in anticipation of a harsh winter, on December 5, 1941, the Municipal Council asked the Salvation Army to expand the existing camp to shelter ten thousand people. But Japan's attack on Pearl Harbor two days later aborted the plans. Major George Walker told reporters that the camp could not accommodate any more people, and that the proposed expansion was impossible. For the time being, he could only bicycle around town, distributing coupons for winter clothing to the needy. Meanwhile, the death toll continued to grow, with over ten thousand bodies found on the streets in two months.[150]

The outbreak of the Pacific War dramatically reconfigured Shanghai's political landscape, as the Japanese assumed control of the foreign concessions. In the International Settlement, a new Municipal Council formed, with Okazaki Katsuo as Chairman and a new majority of Japanese members.[151] Some employees, such as T. K. Ho and others from Allied countries, remained in their positions. Prior to their removal in 1942, G. G. Phillips, the Council's chief administrator, and J. H. Jordan, the Commissioner of Public Health, tried to organize a Relief Committee to distribute food to the needy. Their efforts, however, did not advance beyond a series of contentious meetings and memos.[152]

As the city's food supply ran dangerously low in the months after Pearl Harbor due to the American blockade, the new Municipal Council began a large-scale evacuation program. In March, the authorities ordered the closure of all camps and the dispersal of all refugees (more than ten thousand people). Only unclaimed children were permitted to remain in the care of private charities, with the pledge of Council support.[153] Although a decree ordering the expulsion of all street beggars was quickly dropped, due to the impossibility of enforcement, *Shenbao* declared that "the refugee problem of the past four years has come to an end." The death toll, however, belied this sanguine announcement. During one four-day cold spell, 810 bodies were found in the two concessions. The overwhelming numbers forced burial societies to place multiple bodies in coffins, stuffing five or six children, even up to twenty infants, in one box.[154]

Among the refugee children who remained, several hundred were housed at the former Salvation Army Beggar Camp, where already deplorable conditions deteriorated even further. Daily food rations consisted of two bowls of thin rice porridge. Cesspools filled the grounds; the dormitory huts were barely habitable. Worst of all, the camp faced a mortuary, now overflowing with the dead. In the summer the smell of decomposing bodies permeated the premises. In 1942 and 1943, 250 children lived in these conditions. Deaths peaked in October 1942, when 52 of them died from disease and malnutrition. During an inspection the following year, a Council member found the children "in an absolutely pitiable state"; most of them suffered from tuberculosis.[155] Finally, just before its formal dissolution, the Municipal Council agreed to transfer the camp to the YWCA, where the children in its care at least received enough to eat.[156] By this time, the authorities had given up all pedagogical efforts and merely hoped to improve the basic living conditions to meet a minimum standard of decency.

For the Chinese collaborationist government, Pearl Harbor also signified a turning point. Since the outbreak of war in 1937, the areas formerly under Nationalist control had seen a succession of ineffectual administrations. The first, called the Great Way Government, lasted less than five months. According to one historian, it was "a sorry sight of unknown politicians who were whisked in from outside."[157] Then, under Mayor Fu Xiao'an, Shanghai became a "special municipality" under the auspices of the Reformed Government established in Nanjing. Fu was best known for surviving several assassination attempts—until one fateful morning in 1940, when his cook hacked him to death with a cleaver while he slept. With an anemic revenue base, and caught in the rivalry between different Japanese military commands, Fu's administration garnered no real authority.[158] For instance, in 1939 the police chief issued orders to each district to apprehend all "unemployed vagrants and local hoodlums" and send them to workhouses. But without money to establish detention centers, the chief soon amended his instructions to deportation.[159] Meanwhile, a new Social Affairs Bureau assumed responsibility for welfare programs (the "people's villages," winter and refugee relief), and established two new relief homes: one for women, another for children, the elderly, and the disabled.

When he took over as mayor following Fu Xiao'an's gruesome death, Chen Gongbo was a high profile official in Wang Jingwei's Nanjing-based collaborationist regime.[160] After the outbreak of the Pacific War, the Allies relinquished their extraterritorial claims in China. The Japanese reunited Shanghai's divided jurisdictions under Chen's authority in 1943, as a gesture toward restoring China's "sovereignty." Chen embarked on a series of reforms, including cleaning up the city's appearance by relocating huts, licensing itinerant vendors, and clearing out coffins.[161] In addition, an overhaul of the municipal government in March 1943 created a new Social Welfare Bureau (Shehui Fuliju), tasked with oversight of private charity and winter relief. The new agency took the lead in establishing the Shanghai Indigent Training Center (Liumin Xiqinsuo), located on the site of the former Vagrant Workhouse (discussed in chapter 3). When consideration of this new beggar camp began in 1942, the tripartite division of Shanghai was still intact. The three municipalities deputized the Red Swastika Society, a religious charity with extensive operations, to manage the workhouse. The original plans called for two thousand inmates, divided among the three jurisdictions, with financial contributions allocated proportionally. Despite the ignominious experience of the Salvation Army camp, the organizers thought it was a good model for the new institution.[162]

When police brought the first batch of 1,000 inmates to the workhouse in May, nearly half were immediately disqualified (drug users, those with communicable diseases, the "feeble minded," those deemed "really not a beggar"). The 526 considered eligible signed affidavits attesting to their willingness to enter the workhouse: "Formerly we loitered on the streets, without food, without clothing. Fortunately the three authorities and the World Red Swastika Society have saved us. We should wash our hearts, use our hands, and exert our own sweat. . . . We are now indigents, in the future we shall become good people. We pledge that from today forth, we will stand upright."[163]

But as with many other institutions, these aspirations foundered. The workhouse hobbled along, with dwindling numbers of inmates reflecting diminishing government support. The Red Swastika Society, however, was able to raise some money from its own network of members and donors. Its workhouse inmates thus fared somewhat better than those living at the municipal Relief Home, where conditions were desperate, as attested by a series of appeals from its residents. In April 1943, Sun Mingqi, the new director of the Social Welfare Bureau, received the following letter from eighteen Relief Home residents:

> Our food rations have been cut. The weather has turned cold, but we have not been given blankets or clothing. The ones who fall ill seek medical care but do not get it. We don't know if this is the way we are to be treated in the future, or if there is some kind of fraud going on. We will not rest until we express our complaints, so today we will describe the treatment we have received and respectfully ask the Bureau to investigate.

The letter went on to describe the previous year's hardships. The summer months were especially miserable, when they received only thin gruel and a half a bowl of rice each day. Some tried to find family and friends for help, but few people had such contacts, and the rest "could only tighten our belts and starve. In the afternoons we were often dizzy and faint with hunger and had to lie down." In desperation some residents drank water to assuage their hunger pangs, but ended up with severe diarrhea because they did not have fuel to boil the water.[164]

Some months earlier, several people had secretly sent a letter to the government to plead for help. Unfortunately, the tactic backfired. They received no reply to their entreaty, and in retaliation the Relief Home's director ordered a lockdown. No one was permitted to leave, receive visitors, or otherwise have contact with the outside world until the culprits confessed. After several days the residents were in a panic, as occasional visits from friends and family brought extra food. One person named Shao Baoquan could not bear the hunger, and decided it was preferable to leave the shelter and beg for a living. So he took the blame for the letter and was expelled. "After this episode was over, we poor residents were all frightened and warned each other not to repeat it . . . it would be digging our own graves." They continued to suffer until the spring, when new directors took up posts at both the Relief Home and the Social Welfare Bureau. Only then did the residents dare to send another letter asking for help. In response to this description of their plight, the Bureau sent Inspector Shi Kouping to assess the situation. Shi concluded that "all the residents were emaciated and weak, showing obvious signs of malnutrition," but that conditions were better under the new management. Therefore, officials decided that "the situation has passed" and took no action.[165]

Contrary to expectations, life at the Relief Home did not improve. Two months later, a group of former soldiers, some with war injuries, went to the administrative offices to demand more food. According to Director Zhang Yichen's report, these veterans "actually dared to . . . come to the office to create disturbances because they thought they did not get enough to eat"; they even beat up Xu Kezhong, the person in charge of rations. Although Xu tried to reason with them, they forced him to sign a letter guaranteeing he would "forever satisfy their requests for food." As punishment, the culprits were to be transferred to the Red Swastika Society's workhouse.[166] When they learned of their imminent expulsion, the group wrote a letter explaining their side of the story:

> The truth is that since he arrived Xu Kezhong has been embezzling the residents' food. Every day, none of us can even have one full meal. We endured such hunger but there was nothing we could do. Under the peril of starvation we elected representatives and sent them to beg for changes to our treatment, but to no avail.

After this initial complaint, their rations were cut even further, to the point where each person received only a half a bowl of noodles at every meal. In desperation, eighteen people confronted Xu. He "refused all of our entreaties and tried to evade all responsibility," and the group became agitated: "We are all soldiers. Our knowledge is simplistic and our tempers are volatile. . . . We surrounded Xu and wanted him to answer us . . . but we did not harm a hair on his body." To conclude, the offenders asked for a reprieve on the basis of their service to the nation:

> We sacrificed ourselves for the nation and became cripples. . . . Except for passing our days at the Relief Home we have no other life line. Sending us to the workhouse would deprive us of our lives; it is also contrary to the nation's repayment for our sacrifice. . . . We have already lost our ability to make a living—how can we labor at the workhouse?

This letter triggered yet another inquiry, and in the meantime the expulsion was postponed. Six months later the culprits were finally transferred to the workhouse for punishment.[167]

By September 1943, the situation was so dreadful that the entire population of the Relief Home (350 people) jointly sent a telegram to the Director of the Social Welfare Bureau begging for his help. The letter stated that in the past, the conditions were barely tolerable:

> This year the situation has become even worse and inflation has reached a peak. But the money allocated for the residents' food has not increased by even one *fen* [cent]. . . . And in recent days the situation has reached the end of the road. . . .
>
> For more than two weeks we have been given chicken feed instead of rice. Although we are hungry, the wheat chaff is hard to swallow. It is deficient in nutrients and difficult to digest, such that many of us have suffered severe diarrhea. . . . Moreover, because the Relief Home has run out of money, soon we will not even get wheat chaff to eat, and all of us will face death together.
>
> For the widowers, widows, and crippled among us to die is no great pity. But there are also more than 180 children, and for them to die with us is an affront to heaven. The Relief Home is a municipal relief agency, and the protection of the crippled, elderly and weak is one of the nation's social policies. . . . With Your Honor's vast benevolence and pity for the people . . . you certainly cannot bear to sit by idly while we starve to death.

In conclusion, the residents implored the Director to increase their food allowance, so that their "ant lives can survive to see another day."[168]

In response to this letter, the Bureau sent yet another inspector, who verified that the situation was indeed quite desperate.[169] But conditions continued to deteriorate. In October Relief Home Director Zhang Yichen reported that six people had died in less than one week, and noted that they had not received any food or money for more than five weeks. There was only enough to give the residents one-tenth to one-half pound of "food" every day: a combination of wheat chaff and broken rice, with a bit of steamed bread and occasionally some beans. In desperation, Zhang organized a fund-raising show. This money proved crucial, as allocations from the government trickled to a stop in the winter of 1943. In the ten months from April 1943 to February 1944, seventy-one residents (about 20 percent) died from malnutrition. By the spring of 1944, the Social Welfare Bureau began the process of closing the Relief Home. The administrators notified the families of children living there to collect them; the unclaimed were given away in adoptions or sent to Nanjing.[170] When the Home closed in October, the 182 remaining residents were transferred to a recently opened Vagrant Labor Camp (Youmin Laodongying).[171]

Although it was ostensibly a charitable rather than penal institution, the conditions at the Relief Home bore grim parallels to the contemporaneous suffering and starvation of POWs in Japanese internment camps all over Asia. In Shanghai, the Japanese authorities began to detain Allied nationals in November 1942. George Walker of the Salvation Army was among the first group sent to the Haiphong Road Camp. In the spring of 1943, Allied nationals on the Municipal Council staff were interned in two different places, one called Ash Camp. Ash Camp derived its name from the two feet of ash used to fill in the swampy land, recalling similar conditions at the Council's own Yenping Road refugee camp in 1938.[172]

By the final winter of the war in 1944, life for the impoverished in Shanghai reached a new nadir. People living at the "people's villages" were starving. Bombing from the first phase of the war had reduced the Nationalists' proud housing achievement to piles of rubble; at some of the former model villages, not a single window or door remained. Nonetheless, people moved in and found shelter in the ruins. For winter relief, Chen Gongbo's administration mounted a feeble aid program. Most charities closed their doors. Only seven soup kitchens and three shelters remained open, providing the barest measure of help for the city's indigents.[173]

Conclusion

The Japanese surrender in August 1945 ended a bitter chapter in China's history. For eight long years the nation endured fierce assaults and occupation, but the country's plight had also inspired an outpouring of sympathy and contributions for refugee relief. Against the enemy's brutality, a surge of national solidarity vowed to create a New China, strong and productive, out of the crucible of suffering. Eight years later, however, an exhausted nation limped to the armistice. The tales of misery and deaths had become so widespread that recurring headlines of body counts and appeals for help no longer inspired shock or pity.

As we have seen, during the war years government relief in Beijing became more closely entwined with security concerns than ever. But the Japanese occupiers did not intervene directly in the management of the Relief Home or the Social Affairs Bureau. In particular, the Relief Home functioned in much the same way it had during the previous decade. Indirectly, however, the conditions of the occupation meant that resources were channeled to policing rather than for relief. In Shanghai, we saw how the war showcased the city's best qualities and exposed its ugliest attributes, juxtaposing generous efforts to help war victims against landowners seeking to evict refugees. As the months became years, the continued presence of so many impoverished people and the specter of their desperation strained resources and goodwill. Increasing suspicions of the homeless poor underscored the reality that the boundary between the deserving and the undeserving, always tenuous and difficult to police, could no longer be even vaguely delineated. Refugee or beggar? Tenant or squatter? Did squatters have rights? These questions had important implications for the people struggling to survive, and their attempts to claim a legitimate place in the city asserted a fundamental right to a minimum standard of living.

Finally, while the wartime climate reinforced the imperatives of productivism, the national crisis also produced new kinds of displacement, fracturing the coherence of prevailing views about homelessness and vagrancy. Some observers went further, to reconsider the correlation between labor and parasitism, or refute the link between impoverishment and crime. One *Shenbao* commentator asked, "Poverty is not a crime—so why are there so many detention centers set up for the poor?" Another presented a series of foreign proverbs to illustrate that "poverty is not a vice," contending that "many of the world's great figures have experienced poverty." And writing in an influential journal in 1944, Zhou Xianwen posed the familiar question: "What causes poverty?" But countering the view that indolence was the source, Zhou concluded that under the ravages of war, "Even if you are diligent and frugal all your life, you will still die a poor man."[174] In sum, the shattering impact of the war upended existing paradigms and categories, calling into question the certitude of the conventional wisdom about "poverty."

In the summer of 1945, as the millions of people displaced by the war returned to their homes, they faced the daunting tasks of rebuilding their lives and coping with an unprecedented level of destitution. At the same time, residents of formerly occupied areas greeted the return of the Nationalists with optimism, celebrating the reunification of the nation under one government. In both Shanghai and Beijing, the victorious homecoming was tempered by the physical wreckage, and the number of difficult issues bequeathed by their predecessors, including the chronic beggar problem and the continued proliferation of shantytowns. But for the urban poor, the autumn of 1945 dawned on a hopeful note. As life slowly returned to normal, the impoverished people of the cities looked forward to finding new jobs, the resumption of charity and welfare services, and perhaps, better days ahead.

CHAPTER 5

Keeping Company with Ghosts

ON AUGUST 6, 1946, Shanghai Mayor Wu Guozhen invited reporters and donors to visit a newly established workhouse, the Refugee and Refugee Children's Shelter (Nanmin Nantong Shourongsuo). Coinciding with the one-year anniversary of the Hiroshima bombing and Japan's subsequent surrender, the festive occasion featured a tour of the premises, performances by the in-house marching band, and a demonstration of "military-precision exercises" by the refugees. As numerous press reports explained, orphans, vagrants, drifters, and others despised as "rubbish" were "embarking on the path of new life" at the shelter. In particular, observers lauded the rescue of homeless youths reclaimed from the streets to participate in society and the nation. One correspondent described the Mayor, visibly moved to tears, watching "those innocent children, the buds of China's new life, shouting thunderously in unison: Long live Chairman Chiang [Kai-shek]! Long live the Chinese nation!" Then, addressing the children, Mayor Wu made the following speech: "Little friends, this is the single happiest day of my life since I came to Shanghai. There has been nothing but disappointment and anguish since my arrival. But seeing all of you here today makes me rejoice. . . . Although you have all suffered terribly, the government promises to help you become useful people." Another account, while applauding the transformation of refugees from "the dregs of society" to "useful material," provided this assessment:

> There are two worlds in Shanghai. How many people are whirling about, dancing in "heaven," both day and night? And how many people are living on the streets of "hell," in winter and summer? If the people of "heaven" constitute the "cream" of the nation, then those in "hell" must be the "dregs" of society![1]

The contrasts—of heaven and hell, between the Mayor's joy against his "disappointment and anguish"—were thus interspersed with aspirations for China's renewal. But in the main, observers evinced high hopes that through the efforts of the workhouse, the productive labor of refugees could be harnessed to contribute to the nation's postwar recovery and future prosperity.

Such hopes were swiftly dashed in the coming months, as the Nationalist government confronted the enormous task of reconstruction while fending off the Communist insurgency, and as the civil war intensified. By 1947, famine afflicted central and south China, with dire estimates counting 6.7 million people facing imminent starvation, and 32.8 million more seriously undernourished (out of a population of approximately 450 million). Officials in charge of famine relief at the United Nations Relief and Rehabilitation Administration (UNRRA) offered this sobering appraisal: "The enormous destruction and derangement of the war period were superimposed . . . upon an even broader, deeper and more permanent disequilibrium. As a result, the deficiencies in China's economy . . . reached staggering proportions during and immediately following the war years."[2] In Shanghai, the summer's celebration at the refugee workhouse soon gave way to grim realities, as the municipal government's mounting financial problems ended allocations of food and money. And as the general situation in the city deteriorated, one winter shelter manager commented, "The bitter winds of winter sharpen the divide between heaven and hell in Shanghai. The wealthy enjoy warmth in their high rise buildings; the streets and alleyways are filled with the piteous cries of hunger. . . . The ones abandoned by society can only wait for charities to come by and collect their corpses."[3]

This chapter begins with a brief discussion of the national challenges the GMD regime confronted, before turning to the lives of the urban poor in Beijing and Shanghai. The municipal archives in these two cities have preserved a particularly rich set of materials documenting the depth of the crisis, including detailed administrative records from government agencies such as the workhouse described above. Remarkably, the sources also include hundreds of letters from refugees seeking help, petitions from hut dwellers trying to save their homes, and reports of mistreatment in winter shelters and relief homes. In the chaos of the civil war period, the Nationalist government tried to cope with the refugee crisis and increasing urban disorder by using its welfare agencies to serve both charitable and punitive purposes. Getting people off the streets and into municipal institutions prevented starvation and death. Just as importantly, these policies also tried to curb an increasing tide of lawlessness and possible Communist infiltration. From the perspective of the urban poor, the government's insistence on criminalizing homelessness accentuated the importance of home. They fought to preserve their straw huts or sought shelter in cemeteries and coffin repositories, preferring the squalor of the shantytown or "keeping company with ghosts," rather than submitting to government custody. Their struggles to survive underscore the human dimensions of the Nationalist regime's collapse. In a time of political chaos and deep dislocations, contestations over social belonging and productive citizenship were interwoven into the battle to realize competing visions for the nation's future.

THE NATIONALIST REGIME IN CRISIS

For the GMD government in its final years in power, the intensification of the civil war undermined efforts to alleviate the deepening social crisis. By 1948, the number of refugees approached fifty million. Ten million people faced starvation; many were so desperate that they subsisted on tree bark and roots. But with military expenditures draining the treasury, the national relief plan funded aid to one million people, just 2 percent of the total in need.[4] With hopes for a quick victory shattered, officials heaped blame on the Communists, saying that they "intentionally wreak havoc . . . plotting to increase the government's troubles." At the same time, they recognized that failure to provide adequate relief to those fleeing from the "Communist bandits" undermined popular morale and contributed to social unrest. Just as they had throughout the Nanjing decade and the war years, government directives and policies stressed "constructive welfare" and labor productivity. Officials from the Social Welfare Ministry, for instance, declared, "In the short term, we must help refugees survive. But we must also focus on cultivating their self-reliance, transforming depletion into production." Even the elderly should not merely "grow old in peace"—they should "grow old with usefulness." As for the infirm and injured, "We should ask how we can ensure that those who are disabled do not become useless to society."[5] In addition, the national "Social Relief Law" ordered "compulsory labor" in workhouses for the "habitually lazy or unemployed vagrants," and "disciplinary relief" for those with "bad character and conduct, with criminal tendencies."[6]

Despite these ambitions, hyperinflation and the collapse of the economy sharply diminished the regime's ability to implement its agenda. Average prices had increased two thousand-fold during the Sino-Japanese War. The inflation index declined after the Japanese surrender in August 1945, but spiraled upward again several months later. The most severe effects were in urban areas, where restaurants doubled and tripled their prices in a single day, and a wheelbarrow of money could hardly buy a sack of flour. Even beggars refused to accept currency notes smaller than Ch. $1,000—a story the CCP advertised to ridicule the GMD regime.[7] As disillusionment with Chiang Kai-shek's government set in, rice riots erupted in major cities across the country. Protesting American intervention and the civil war, waves of student demonstrations engulfed universities and middle schools throughout 1946 and 1947, culminating in a series of "anti–civil war, anti-hunger" campaigns. As Jeffrey Wasserstrom has shown in his study of Shanghai students, they made particularly effective use of symbols of starvation as rallying cries of protest.[8]

Testimony from across the political spectrum described the venality of Nationalist officials and the disastrous consequences of government incompetence. As the Communist press described it, in Hangzhou rapacious bureaucrats returned to "suck the people's blood," and the enchanting beauty of West Lake became the venue for suicide attempts.[9] Going home to Changsha, a writer for the nonpartisan journal *The Observer* described it as a descent into hell. When he took a stroll by the bank of the Xiang River, he encountered "beggars everywhere . . . and more prostitutes than fish in the river." Soon, the writer lamented, they will join the corpses scattered among the detritus of ruin.[10] Even the Nationalists' triumphant return to its capital in Nanjing quickly crumbled. In the winter of 1946, news of refugees starving to death on the outskirts of the city jolted the writers at the GMD's own *Central Daily News*, who demanded to know, "Where did the relief funds go?" and "Who is responsible for this?"[11]

Undoubtedly, the situation would have been even worse without foreign aid. In November 1943, the United States and forty-three other nations had created the UNRRA, in anticipation of overseeing the postwar rehabilitation effort. The first Chinese field office opened in Chongqing before the end of the war, and the first aid shipment (7,000 tons of wheat) arrived in the winter of 1945. Before disbanding two years later, UNRRA delivered 2.5 million tons of supplies to China, making this the largest UN program in the world. To coordinate the complex logistics, the Nationalist government established the Chinese National Relief and Rehabilitation Administration (CNRRA) to distribute aid in two forms. Free or "almost free" relief opened soup kitchens or gave out allotments of food; work relief employed laborers to restore farmland to cultivation, repair railways and roads, or work on sanitation, drainage, and irrigation projects. Although its charter prohibited political bias, the UN agency admitted that CCP-controlled areas received only a paltry share of the supplies.[12] For their part, the Communists excoriated Chiang Kai-shek for betraying China's national interest in exchange for American aid. In the first fourteen months of the UNRRA program, they complained, supplies delivered to the "liberated areas" amounted to less than 2 percent of the total.[13]

At the conclusion of the Sino-Japanese War in the summer of 1945, the Communists had established "liberated areas" in the northwest and other scattered pockets of territory, encompassing approximately ninety million people. From Yan'an, the terminus of the Long March in 1935, the CCP had scratched its way back from the brink of annihilation to build a revolutionary holy land.[14] Like those of the GMD, Communist rhetoric and policy trumpeted "production and self-help" (*shengchan zijiu*), reiterating that the struggle against the Japanese enemy was not only "a war of military might, but a war of production. Victory or defeat will not only be decided on the battlefield, but also in the factory."[15] In the base areas, the injunction to work was encapsulated in the aphorism, "If you want to eat, you must produce" (*yao chifan, yao shengchan*). CCP notions of labor productivity, however, differed from that of its Nationalist rival in singling out labor as the defining attribute of humanity—that which accounted for evolution "from ape to human." Frederick Engels's original formulation of this concept had appeared in a Chinese translation in 1928. According to Sigrid Schmalzer, this had a decisive influence on popular understandings of human origins and evolutionary science.[16]

For our purposes, the corollary of "labor created humanity" meant the dehumanization of those who refused to work, casting the incorrigibles as no better than beasts. In the 1940s, those who repudiated labor were called *erliuzi* (meaning idler or loafer) in Communist parlance, and subjected to a sliding scale of reform methods ranging from gentle persuasion to violent struggle sessions. Cadres made particularly effective use of public shaming tactics. For instance, this song circulated in a county north of Yan'an: "*Erliuzi* Li Guangming is fond of eating and adverse to work. Consorting with prostitutes, gambling, and smoking—he does it all, caring naught for family or kin. . . . Among the *erliuzi* of the entire city he is number one." By rousing community sentiment against such "good-for-nothings," CCP officials boasted that they succeeded in re- forming some 5,500 people, from "parasites (*jisheng chong*) that do not labor but do evil" to "good citizens of the new society."[17]

After the Japanese surrender, as Communist forces raced from Yan'an to Manchuria, the battle for control of the Northeast intensified at the end of 1945. The following year, when the CCP took over the administration of cities and towns throughout the region, its strategy focused on public security and economic rehabilitation.[18] Then, as the battlefront migrated southward, under- cover agents in cities intensified efforts to organize opposition to the National- ist regime, infiltrate the GMD military and administrative agencies, and carry out sabotage operations. The urban revolution centered on forging alliances with factory workers, journalists, voluntary associations, and especially the bur- geoning antiwar student movement.[19] In Beijing, small Communist cells dot- ted the city's margins, including hideouts at Longquan Orphanage and on the campus of Yanjing University. Cadres also joined the ranks of itinerant ped- dlers and rickshaw pullers: their large numbers made it easy to blend in; their occupational mobility diminished the suspicion of moving about the city. In Shanghai, CCP agents found convenient hideaways in the shantytowns, and offered literacy classes to attract support from hut dwellers. But apart from some sporadic efforts, the "scattered elements" of the urban underclass, consid- ered difficult to mobilize, remained peripheral to the Party's revolutionary strategy.[20]

"We Are Refugees, Not Poor People"

In Beijing, the optimism accompanying the Nationalist government's return quickly evaporated. In October 1945, the police reported that they were finding many corpses on the streets, even well before the winter freeze. But at the paltry wage offered, few porters were willing to bury the bodies. That winter, twenty- two soup kitchens served over two million meals to the needy, while seven municipal winter shelters housed thirty-five thousand people. A year later the Winter Relief Committee estimated that one-third of the city's residents were "destitute" (*chipin*), and expanded the relief campaign to thirty soup kitchens and ten shelters.[21]

The escalation of the civil war in Manchuria in the winter of 1946 deepened the crisis, as thousands of desperate refugees sought safe haven in Beijing. By the spring, the fighting had spread throughout neighboring Hebei province, bringing fresh influxes of victims. With an emergency grant of Ch. $500 million from the central government, the municipal authorities set up one main shelter for 1,500 people and seven reception stations for 2,500 others.[22] As the Communist offensive advanced south from Manchuria, 20,000 refugees arrived in the spring of 1948, followed by the announcement that 300,000 people would be evacuated from the Northeast, with most of them headed for Beijing. There were so many refugees that emergency relief became simply part of the government's "ordinary work."[23]

For the newcomers, those lucky enough to find shelter in the Beijing camps discovered dire conditions and the barest modicum of aid, for the Relief Committee was chronically short of money. Many sites were merely makeshift shacks and tents, hastily erected in parks and temple courtyards. Rations typically allotted about a pound of food a day for each person, supplemented with clothing and blankets if available, but no fuel for heating or cooking. Foraging for firewood, refugees cut down trees wherever they could find them, triggering confrontations with local residents. At one shelter housed at Donghuang Temple, some resorted to dismantling altar pieces and burning historical relics and books.[24] At Nianhua Temple, crowded conditions escalated tensions between three groups sharing the premises: fourteen hundred students from Rehe, eighty students from Manchuria, and a military intelligence unit. Some of the Rehe contingent were sleeping along the outside corridors linking the temple buildings, which were covered but not enclosed. During a heavy rainstorm in July 1948, these students forced their way into a room claimed by the military officers. The brawl that ensued wrecked the premises. Sacred texts and scrolls were stolen, prompting angry complaints from the resident monks. The Social Affairs Bureau tried to mediate and find other accommodations, but the only available place was a temporary beggar shelter. Unwilling to live with the beggars, the Rehe students returned the stolen objects and agreed to share the space.[25]

At the Ditan Shelter, located in a park just north of the former imperial city, conditions were slightly better. The refugees there lived in a dormitory and had access to a reading room and a medical clinic. There was little to keep them occupied, however. The lone handicraft workshop remained mostly idle for lack of supplies. The supervisors tried to maintain a schedule of lectures, cleaning tasks, and long rest periods. In addition, they suggested closing the communal kitchen and requiring the refugees to cook for themselves, just to keep them busy. When the shelter's three-month term was about to expire in August 1947, refugee Liu Zhensheng wrote to the Mayor to ask for an extension on behalf of the group, quoting the government's own directive on aid for citizens who had escaped from Communist territory. The Mayor allowed the refugees to remain for one additional month, but terminated food rations for the young and able-bodied. To encourage them to leave, shelter administrators urged them to enlist in the GMD Youth Corps as "a promising path out of the darkness." But only three volunteered, and two were ineligible as they exceeded the age limit (twenty-eight *sui*).[26]

For the homeless and desperate looking for a way out, the government became the last resort. A farmer named Su Changhua, for instance, wrote that when the Communists arrived in his hometown (in Hebei's Changping County), they "looted, plundered, burned and killed." His family of eight fled to Beijing to escape these "unspeakable cruelties."[27] In another example, a worker named Sun Shulun explained that he had been caught in the chaos of the Japanese surrender in Yantai (a port city in Shandong province). He escaped as "Communist bandits" took control of the city and started to "settle old scores" and "equalize property." After searching for work for many months in Beijing, Sun eagerly went to apply at a factory that had advertised in the newspaper—only to be turned away because he had no guarantor. "I have fled to Beijing from the bandit areas, a stranger in a strange land," Sun lamented. "Where can I go to find this kind of guarantee?"[28]

For destitute refugees such as Sun Shulun, securing a bonded guarantor was nearly impossible. In fact, under the circumstances, the Social Affairs Bureau could hardly enforce its own requirement that such guarantees accompany aid applications. Instead, the Bureau accepted notes from native place associations and other organizations such as the YMCA, willing to vouch for a supplicant's trustworthiness. The Hebei Native Place Association provided so many references that it used a form letter printed specifically for this purpose. Other associations issued refugee certificates (*nanmin zheng*) to substantiate claims of hardship.[29] These references proved vital, as illustrated in the case of Rui Da, a Christian preacher from Hebei's Luan County. In March 1948, Rui wrote to the Social Affairs Bureau asking for a place in the refugee shelter. His landlord in Beijing had recently evicted his family of seven, and they could not return to their hometown in Communist-held territory. Officials instructed Rui to obtain a letter from his native place association or provide a reference from a trusted authority. Rui responded that he had been away from home for more than twenty years, working for the church. As a result, no one at his native place association could vouch for him. But officials refused to make an exception, rejecting his request to substitute a private letter of introduction from the foreign pastor of his church.[30]

Many of the letters that refugees wrote to Beijing's authorities followed a rhetorical formula of entreaty. They aimed to solicit maximum sympathy, often narrating tales of suffering with stock phrases, peppered with anti-Communist sentiments. One unusual letter, from a refugee named Song Weizi, breaks from this convention. In August 1947, Song lived at the Ditan Shelter, which was about to close. He wrote to the Hebei Relief Association, asking officials there to intervene on the refugees' behalf. Instead of recounting a personal biography of misery to elicit compassion, Song offered this analysis:

We are refugees (*nanmin*), not poor people (*pinmin*). Refugees and poor people are completely different. Refugees are intellectuals and the bourgeoisie who, due to the oppression of Communist bandits, were forced to abandon their homes and flee for their lives. They especially deserve compassion. Refugees occupy an important position in society and in the nation. The poor are actually just impoverished people (*qiongren*) who do not know how to be self-reliant, who are completely dependent in character. They have no place in the composition of society and the nation.

According to Song, while "refugees" received only some food and sundry provisions, Beijing's "poor people" received far more generous treatment, an inequity that elevated them above those more deserving of compassion and aid. The government should "make a clear distinction between refugees and poor people," and immediately rectify this injustice.[31] Song thus sought to bolster the status of "refugees" by arguing for the social exclusion of "the poor." Emphasizing the class difference, he rejected the common conflation of the two groups. In this logic, the willing and ingrained dependency of "the poor" justified their exclusion, while "refugees" like Song, unwilling victims of Communist oppression, embodied a circumstantial and temporary form of destitution.

Song Weizi's belief that "the poor" received preferential treatment stemmed in large part from the disparity between the temporary aid "refugees" like himself received and the long-term relief given to those living in municipal agencies such as the Relief Home. To Song, whose stay at the Ditan Shelter was about to be terminated, "the poor" seemed to have access to continuous sources of food and shelter. The common practice of pitching tents for refugees on the premises of the Relief Home's various divisions contributed to this perception, for when these temporary stations were dismantled and refugees dispersed, the Home's residents remained. But as we shall see below, in reality conditions at the municipal institution were hardly better, and the only discernible difference was the degree of coercion involved.

Become Useful Citizens

As previously discussed, Beijing's Relief Home was created as an umbrella organization in 1934 and had continued to operate during the Sino-Japanese War. When Nationalist officials resumed control in October 1945, they preserved the existing structure and appointed Xiao Zhichao, a graduate of Yanjing University, as the new director. Director Xiao declared that he would "emphasize moral education" and "work skills," so that his charges could acquire the ability to make a living on their own and "become complete and useful citizens."[32]

Initially, the mantra of usefulness permeated life at the Relief Home. The children began a program of "half-work, half-study"; the women learned embroidery as an antidote to their "unhealthy inclinations." Director Xiao also devised a plan to create a large working farm (on the vast grounds of the Temple of Heaven), in part to supplement the meager diet, but also to alter the "ostentatious and indolent habits" he felt some had learned in the city. Through agricultural work, Xiao imagined that they would learn to "work hard without complaint," imbibe the spirit of frugality, and acquire knowledge (e.g., about fertilizers and pesticides) suitable for modern village life.[33] But these aspirations soon foundered, as Xiao struggled just to feed the residents and keep the Relief Home financially solvent. The conditions were deplorable: the clothing and blankets were no better than rags; the workshops and classrooms had virtually no equipment or supplies; there was rampant insect infestation and little medical care; the dormitories were impossibly crowded; the buildings were in disrepair, with roofs so leaky that one supervisor said it was like living in the open.[34]

The situation would have been far more dismal without supplies from the CNRRA—sometimes flour and canned meat, other times milk or blankets. When the agency disbanded at the termination of the UN program in November 1947, the Relief Home lost its most crucial food source. By the winter of 1948, Director Xiao reported shortages of everything, lamenting that "the dormitories have long been full, and the problem of food grows more acute every day." He could not accommodate any more newcomers, and asked the police and the Social Affairs Bureau to send people elsewhere.[35] Despite these dreadful conditions, the Relief Home turned away hundreds of people asking for shelter, either for themselves or their family members. Many registered to wait for an opening, a palpable indication of their desperation.[36]

A partial list of Relief Home residents illustrates their varied backgrounds: "homeless," "impoverished," "elderly and without support," "injured during battle and cannot return to hometown," "lost," "discharged from the military with nowhere to go." One large contingent the police sent included many children caught stealing, loitering, or begging around markets and parks.[37] The recurrent narratives of children inadvertently separated from parents or relatives, or abandoned at the railway station, recall the plight of youngsters from earlier years of the Republican era. At the same time, we can detect more acute social displacement than in years past, in the many cases of educated people seeking shelter at the Relief Home. In addition to thousands of student refugees, like the ones from Rehe embroiled in the temple brawl, there were people like Mrs. Gao Li Jiangyan, who wrote to the Mayor for help in July 1946. Orphaned at a young age, Mrs. Gao had grown up at the Xiangshan Children's Home and graduated from middle school. She became a teacher, and later worked for the municipal orphanage in Nanjing. Misfortune struck in 1946, when her husband, an employee of the railway ministry, suffered a debilitating leg injury and lost his job. The couple and their five children, including a two-week-old baby, lived in one small room at a guesthouse. On the verge of starvation, Mrs. Gao did not have enough milk to nurse the baby. The Mayor forwarded her supplication to officials at the Social Affairs Bureau, who instructed her to register for milk powder for the baby, and allowed one of her sons to go to the Relief Home.[38]

In other cases we can detect the government's deepening anxieties about Communist infiltration. For instance, Zhang Shengquan (sixteen *sui*, from Hebei's Changping County) had just completed a sentence (for an unspecified crime) at the police reformatory. While he was in detention, Communist forces took over his hometown. The police feared that if released, Zhang would return home and be "used" by the enemy; therefore, he was remanded to the workhouse. Likewise, the police suspected that a Russian man arrested in December 1947 was a spy. "Iwaou" (a Chinese transliteration of a Russian name) could speak both Chinese and Russian. He told his interrogators that he grew up in China and now lived in Tianjin. The Beijing authorities considered him an "international hooligan" (an unusual designation) and sent him to the Relief Home. A few months later, the Tianjin police claimed him for further investigation.[39] In fact, the municipal government repeatedly warned the administrators of the Relief Home as well as the refugee shelters to watch out for signs of covert activities. According to one secret directive, "The Communists will try to entice city residents who have weak resolve," and the poor could be particularly vulnerable to their propaganda. By the end of the civil war period, a barrage of these kinds of communications to relief agencies indicated the government's increasing concerns about Communist infiltration among the urban poor.[40]

MARRIAGES AND ADOPTIONS

To ease the overcrowding at the Relief Home, the administrators arranged adoptions and marriages whenever possible. Potential adoptive parents and grooms could apply to the Social Affairs Bureau for a child or a bride, by furnishing information on their family history, employment, and income. Although the Social Affairs Bureau did not specify a minimum level of wealth, applicants were required to secure three bonded guarantors and prove their ability to support a family. Bureau inspectors scrutinized all applications carefully, interviewed employers, neighbors, and guarantors, and made inquiries in the applicants' hometowns if they were not Beijing locals. Intended to prevent fraud, abuse, and concubinage, these investigations could take more than a month to complete.

Such vigilance paid off for the authorities in one case from May 1946. An Hutian had applied to adopt a child, identifying himself as a ticket checker employed at the transportation ministry. The investigator found that at the address given, An was a household servant and not the man who applied for the adoption. In another case, Zhang Shuchun, a barbershop owner, applied for a wife in July 1946. The Social Affairs Bureau discovered a discrepancy between Zhang's actual age (twenty-eight *sui*) and what he had written on his application (twenty-four). Although a minor detail, the inconsistency prompted scrutiny, which intensified when the authorities learned that Zhang's parents were unavailable for questioning. (They lived in Changping County, their hometown.) It took over two months for Zhang's parents to send written confirmation of their consent. Officials also demanded that his neighbors furnish additional affidavits swearing that he was single. Finally, four months after he initiated the application, the Social Affairs Bureau permitted Zhang to marry Tian Xiumin.[41]

Once approved, prospective grooms and parents were shown photos of eligible women or children and allowed to select one. They paid a small donation and signed affidavits stipulating they could be subject to criminal prosecution for abuse. Arranged marriages culminated in a formal ceremony held at the Relief Home, with the Director officiating. Wedding photographs preserved in the Relief Home's files show couples in Chinese-style wedding gowns and robes; several were dressed in Western-style formal wedding attire.[42]

For arranged marriages, the Social Affairs Bureau preferred men who had never been married before; for adoptions, couples without any surviving children. The policy was probably designed to avoid complications involving extended family members, and also to prevent concubinage.[43] Occasionally, officials allowed exceptions, as in the case of Huang Jinbo, forty *sui*, a merchant with two daughters from his first marriage. After the authorities verified that Huang's wife had died from illness in April 1947, they permitted him to marry Chen Aicun (thirty-four *sui*), a former prostitute who had entered the Relief Home in 1946. Other former prostitutes who married included Gao Yushan (twenty-three *sui*) from Henan, who had run away because her madam mistreated her. Gao entered the Relief Home in August 1946; a year later, she married Dong Jihai, a barber. To prevent any misunderstanding, the Social Affairs Bureau asked Dong's mother to provide written consent to the match.[44]

Applicants for wives included merchants and barbers, and also butchers, ironsmiths, and handicraft workers. As Ruth Rogaski has suggested for the Hall for Spreading Benevolence in Tianjin, recent migrants without a network of friends and kin to help find a wife might have considered this type of institutional matchmaking a valuable service. Others possibly found it appealing to marry a solitary woman without potentially difficult relatives; the expectation of sexual virtue was also important to prospective grooms.[45] In Beijing, however, this expectation would not have applied to the women openly identified as former prostitutes in the Relief Home.

Occasionally, husbands returned their brides to the Relief Home—for disobedience, laziness, or "incompatibility." The most unusual case was that of Zhou Siyuan (eighteen *sui*), who married a man named Liu Chunfang on February 13, 1946. Due to incomplete records, we know little about this couple, except that twelve days after the wedding, Liu brought Zhou back to the Relief Home. He asked to divorce her on the grounds that she could not bear children. To prove his point, Liu provided a certificate from the hospital where doctors diagnosed his wife with genital hypoplasia (incomplete genital development), a condition deemed incurable. Under the circumstances, the Relief Home had no choice but to take her back.[46]

For the women and children married or adopted from the Relief Home, it is difficult to assess to what extent *they* had a choice in the matter. Before leaving the Relief Home with their new husbands or parents, the brides and adopted children had to sign consent forms. These form letters, however, offer no clues to indicate their personal wishes. I have found no instances where a woman or a child refused to marry or be adopted. This could be a matter of incomplete documentation; alternatively, it could mean that they were not consulted. Given the terrible conditions at the Relief Home, some might have viewed an uncertain fate in marriage or adoption as a chance to escape.

CLEANING UP THE CITY

Meanwhile, as part of a broad effort to clean up the "city's appearance" (*shirong*), Beijing Mayor Xiong Wu embarked on successive campaigns to register itinerant vendors, control traffic, and sweep garbage from the streets. A month-long *shirong* competition in 1946 pitted the twelve urban districts against each other in a contest of tidiness. The criteria specified that street peddlers should be banned from major thoroughfares, shop signs and advertisements put in order, and graffiti scrubbed from the walls.[47] The beautification campaign also included numerous injunctions against beggars. The police chief repeatedly ordered street sweeps, saying their ubiquitous presence "both contravenes humanitarian principles and also harms the city's appearance." As the cultural capital of the nation and host to a constant stream of international visitors, Beijing could not tolerate transients loitering on the streets.[48] The National Military Commission forwarded complaints from the U.S. Marines stationed in the city, citing swarms of mendicants constantly harassing the servicemen at markets and near the train station. Calling this a repulsive affront to "national prestige," the chief ordered his precincts to clear out those areas. The campaign that followed included outright arrests, but the police also used the promise of food to "entice" beggars to bring them into custody.[49] When the civil war intensified, the focus on urban transients shifted from appearances to security. With reports circulating that Communist agents were disguising themselves as beggars to enter the city, the Mayor instructed the police to exercise extra vigilance, especially when they encountered mendicants "who can read or seem to have some knowledge." But given the number of formerly well-off and educated people now eking out a living on the streets, the precautions aimed at ferreting out spies and saboteurs resulted in many people "arrested by mistake."[50]

When the police detained beggars and other transients, they sent the most "dangerous" ones to the police reformatory, and the rest to the Social Affairs Bureau for placement in the Relief Home or one of the temporary camps. At the Beggar Shelter established during the Japanese occupation, Nationalist officials found all "empty words" and no real improvement in the deplorable conditions (described in chapter 4), and decided to replace long-time Director Wang Zihe. But the transition took more than two months to complete, and in the interim (from November 1945 until the new director arrived in January), the shelter ran out of food.[51] In 1946, municipal officials changed its name to the "Commoners Workhouse," saying that the reference to "beggars" as bestowed by the collaborationist government was "inappropriate." The number of inmates dwindled to about 150, and the workhouse gradually folded. At the same time, other "commoner workhouses" were established, including one housed at the Lama Temple (Yonghe Gong, a popular tourist attraction today). By 1948, when winter shelters closed for the season in the spring, they opened as "beggar camps" the next day.[52]

As the civil war entered its final stages, the crisis of homelessness overwhelmed both efforts to help the needy and attempts to control transients. The police reformatory for petty criminals began releasing inmates when food supplies ran out. Local constables complained that they had difficulty finding institutions or hospitals willing to accept the sick beggars they found on the streets. With so many deaths, the cost of burials became a crushing burden for agencies already struggling to remain solvent.[53] In addition, since the Relief Home would no longer accept people, homeless children and the elderly could be sent to only the beggar shelters. In one case, when the police asked the Social Affairs Bureau to find a spot for an old man living on the streets, the director replied, "The Relief Home is completely full. This man's clothes are tattered and he resembles a beggar. Send him to the beggar shelter."[54]

The case of Hao Zhongqing underscores the futility of government relief in the final years of the Nationalist regime. Hao was fifty-three *sui*, a well-educated man from Hebei who had formerly worked as a government civil servant. In November 1947, Hao made his way to Beijing after apparently suffering a mental breakdown, attributed to the trauma of war and separation from his family. He registered for aid with his native place association, which then referred him to the Social Affairs Bureau. Officials there arranged from him to go to the Ditan Shelter, but in his troubled state Hao could not adapt to the austere conditions. After several incidents of violent and disruptive behavior, the authorities transferred him to the Lama Temple workhouse, considered an institution better equipped to restrain his outbursts. Hao asked to leave after just one day. According to the administrators, as someone with a "superior background," he could not cope with the restrictions placed on the rest of "the uneducated beggars." And when the workhouse director tried to persuade him to stay, Hao grew violently agitated. He remained at the Lama Temple for one month, until the staff could no longer tolerate his behavior and discharged him.

Four months later, Hao lodged a complaint with the government. In a four-page typewritten letter brimming with anger and paranoia, he poured forth his grievances. His complaint indicated an unstable psychological state (describing sinister plots to murder the inmates, inveighing against staff members who conspired against him). The investigation eventually dismissed the accusations as the wild invectives of a deranged man. Yet officials evinced more sympathy for Hao than other troublemakers, describing him as a victim whose class status set him apart from the common criminals and "tramps" they were accustomed to handling. Officials also seemed to recognize the precariousness of their own situation in this man's history. After all, Hao had been a government employee before his precipitous fall into homelessness; a twist of fate could easily reduce them to his condition. But ultimately, there was little officials could do to help him. As the civil war lurched to its conclusion, Hao Zhongqing went off to fend for himself on the streets of Beijing.[55]

Thus inundated with refugees from the battlegrounds in the Northeast, Beijing's officials struggled to get people off the streets, and to take care of them once they entered government custody. With military expenditures commanding up to 90 percent of government budgets and as foreign aid trickled to an end, relief institutions disintegrated into prisons of starvation and disease. In the Shanghai region, the battle for the strategic Yangzi River delta created a similar crisis of displacement for hundreds of thousands of people. In early 1946, the CCP controlled northern Jiangsu, but a GMD counteroffensive reclaimed the entire area by early 1947. By year-end, the battle swung decisively in the Red Army's favor. As the region oscillated between Communist and Nationalist forces, war victims streamed south to Shanghai. Of the more than one million people who fled to Shanghai in the late 1940s, those from Subei formed the largest block of refugees in the city.[56]

Between Heaven and Hell

As discussed in chapter 1, Subei had been a major source of migrants to Shanghai since the mid-nineteenth century. Between 1911 and 1949, there were seventeen major natural disasters in the region, an average of one every two years. Of these catastrophes, fifteen were floods, and in combination with periodic droughts, war, and epidemic diseases, many consecutive years of famine resulted. Even during periods of relative stability, such as the Nanjing decade, rice yields averaged less than one-third of the harvests of more fertile counties in the southern part of the province.[57] As Emily Honig has shown, in contradistinction to the rise of Jiangnan as an economic and cultural center, "Subei" became a symbol of rural backwardness. "Subei swine" was a common curse in Shanghai's local dialect, with the place name used as a term of denigration to demarcate class and status hierarchies in the city.[58]

During the Sino-Japanese War, the Communist New Fourth Army built a significant presence in the area straddling northern Jiangsu, eastern Henan, and northern Anhui. From behind enemy lines, the CCP tried to expand its control of the region without provoking open confrontation with the GMD.[59] After the Japanese surrender in August 1945, the CCP continued its expansion, establishing the Jiangsu-Anhui Border Area Government in October. Land reform campaigns followed soon thereafter. By the spring of 1946, Liu Jiping, a top cadre in the border government, reported significant progress in education and political reforms, adding that "[t]he 'Jiangbei lowlifes' and 'country bumpkins' that the Shanghainese and other city dwellers looked down upon are now synonymous with 'progress' and 'happiness.'"[60]

This optimistic assessment proved premature, however, as northern Jiangsu soon became a military and political battleground. Peace negotiations between the two parties stalled, despite the mediating efforts of American envoy George C. Marshall, and the area became one of the first targets of the renewed GMD offensive. Immediately after the second ceasefire expired on June 30, 1946, Chiang Kai-shek dispatched a force of 150,000 to drive the Communists from their stronghold, declaring that he would "take care of the Subei problem in two weeks." In fact, the fighting lasted through the winter, but eventually the Nationalists managed to retake all of the county seats and large towns. In the face of the enemy's all-out assault, CCP forces initially retreated, and then launched a comeback.[61]

The eruption of fighting in 1946 coincided with the CCP's land reform campaign and also with summer floods, a nearly annual occurrence in the region. The floods of the late 1940s, however, were some of the most devastating episodes in recent history. In 1946, flooding rendered more than one million people homeless. The year of seesaw military battles, 1947, witnessed record rainfalls in July, when a month of continuous rain inundated half of the farmland and created nine million victims. With recurring summer disasters leading to spring famine, incessant warfare and political reprisals, as well as serial epidemic outbreaks, it was no exaggeration for the people of the region to characterize their lives as "never a year of peace."[62]

As northern Jiangsu alternated between Nationalist and Communist control, the region also became a political combat zone, the front line of the contest for the "hearts and minds" of the people. For the CCP, while the people of Jiangnan dwelled in the darkness of Nationalist rule, "Subei" represented "a society of light and promise," where the Border Area Government pledged that "not even one person will starve to death." This was an audacious promise, given the prevailing sentiment that these were the worst times since the "extraordinary famine" of 1877–78, during which an estimated ten million people perished.[63]

But a mass exodus of refugees undermined these rosy portrayals, and highlighting the flight of "Subei refugees" from Communist territory became one of the GMD's favorite rhetorical weapons. It was not just political partisanship—liberal journals and independent newspapers also viewed the refugee crisis as an indictment of the CCP. One news report stated, "In view of their miserable homeless lives, Subei refugees have recently voluntarily launched a 'return home for the harvest' campaign." More than one thousand people armed themselves with weapons and reportedly clashed with Communist troops to take back their villages.[64] In the battle of public opinion, "Subei refugees" emerged as the centerpiece of a political tug of war. Who was responsible for their misery? Why did they leave their homes—was it to escape an oppressive GMD government, a ruthless CCP regime, famine, or some combination of these factors? Both sides presented themselves as champions of the wretched "Subei refugees," using their plight as political capital to disparage the enemy.

Chiang Kai-shek himself used "Subei refugees" as an impetus for military action. In his final meeting with George Marshall before the ceasefire expired, Chiang told Marshall, "Presently countless refugees have been forced to flee from the Subei region. . . . The entire world agrees that to safeguard the people is the government's responsibility. Now that several hundred thousand refugees cannot return home, how can the Nationalist government proclaim itself as such to the Chinese people?"[65] In response, the CCP accused Chiang's regime of using "Subei refugees" to manipulate public opinion: "The description of Subei as a dark hell is just part of their malicious propaganda."[66] On the contrary, it was Chiang Kai-shek who "turned a blind eye to the flooding in Subei," prolonging the civil war even if it meant sacrificing the lives of all the people of Subei.[67]

By the autumn of 1946, as the military situation swung in favor of the Nationalist army, the Shanghai newspaper *Shenbao* sent a team of correspondents to investigate the situation.[68] From towns throughout the region, dispatches described the "liberation of the liberated areas" and the "rebirth of Subei." According to their informants, under the Communist "bandit" government, tens of thousands of people died of starvation the previous winter. Then, in the midst of the summer battles, Communist forces slaughtered those who tried to flee. Refugees congregated in the large towns, even taking shelter in cemeteries, pitching their tents next to unburied coffins. "The flames of war rage everywhere; the torrential flood waters surge without end," one headline sighed. "They sit or lie on top of the coffins, separated from the dead by only a thin partition."[69] When Jiangsu Governor Wang Maogong toured the disaster area the following spring, he remarked, "The autumn crops have all been completely submerged; there is not a single grain to be harvested; and the starving people are wandering and drifting from place to place."[70]

As the dueling sides traded volleys about "Subei refugees," the starving people from northern Jiangsu did drift from place to place, in search of work and/

or relief. According to government tallies, when the civil war erupted in the region, there were 2.1 million refugees dispersed in fifty-five cities in Jiangsu. By the first half of 1948, this figure had increased to more than 10 million.[71] Private charities, such as the Subei Refugee Relief Association (Subei Nanmin Jiujihui), opened branch offices throughout the province to raise money. The provincial government established relief stations in cities and large towns, to hand out food, provide medical care, and organize work relief. Such efforts, however, could not keep pace with the tide of needy people.[72]

TROUBLED WATERS

As in the past, many of these refugees from Subei headed for Shanghai. But whereas previously they had congregated in unskilled, low-paying sectors of the economy (working as rickshaw pullers, dockworkers, or night soil and garbage collectors), during the civil war their composition shifted to include significant numbers of landlords and students.[73] To help their fellow provincials, the Shanghai branch of the Subei Refugee Relief Association organized fundraisers throughout 1946, some of them perfectly attuned to the city's entertainment culture. A "Miss Shanghai" beauty pageant, for instance, featured popular film stars and an appearance by renowned Peking opera singer Mei Lanfang. At an event hosted by the city's cabarets and nightclubs, proceeds from one evening's entertainment were pledged for Subei refugee relief. But to some observers, the advertisements for the fund-raiser, urging participants to "dance one more dance, save one more life," seemed indicative of the hedonistic and "pathological psychology" of Shanghai residents.[74] Despite these criticisms, through these high-profile events the Subei Association raised large sums for refugee relief. From June to December of 1946, 58,827 people from thirty-four counties registered with the Association. Those who could demonstrate a verifiable need were given blankets, clothing, and one bag of flour for two adults (forty-four *jin*, approximately forty-eight pounds). Such handouts were considered only a temporary solution. Reiterating what had become firmly embedded in the conventional wisdom, Subei leaders proclaimed that "active" relief methods to cultivate self-sufficiency were preferable and established a small loan program and a workshop to employ twenty-five young men.[75]

In many ways, the Subei Association was typical of Republican-era refugee relief efforts, invoking commonplace assumptions about how best to provide aid to people displaced from their homes. But the unique place of "Subei refugees" within the contours of Shanghai's local politics also cast the situation in a different light. The Association's vice chairman was Gu Zhuxuan, the gang boss known as the "Subei Emperor." (Gu was most notorious for his conviction on murder charges in 1936, followed by the verdict's reversal. The press coverage of the twists and turns of the case dominated news headlines for a year.)[76] As we

Figure 5.1. "Charity dance! Disaster relief! Dance one more dance! Save one more life!" *Zhoubao*, August 3, 1946

shall see below, the shadowy world of Shanghai's gangs played an important role in the fate of refugees in the city.

The Subei Refugee Association also tried to intercede with the government on behalf of their provincials who were straw hut dwellers and itinerant peddlers, targets of a municipal clean-up campaign. In the name of improving the "city's appearance" (*shirong*), the authorities announced that, after a short grace period, shantytowns would be torn down, peddlers banned, and rickshaws prohibited in 1946. In addition, native place associations and coffin repositories were given four months to clear out the estimated one hundred thousand corpses they were storing; after the deadline, all remaining bodies would be cremated.[77] In September, the Subei Association called a news conference to draw attention to the dire effects of the straw hut ban. Many groups joined the petition, and in the face of a strong outcry, the government postponed the demolition order.[78]

Of the different blights on the city's image identified in the campaign, the injunction against peddlers had the most immediate impact. In Shanghai, an estimated 150,000 people scratched out a living by selling goods and services on the streets and in makeshift stalls all over the city. The ban prohibited all such vendors from the central business districts (except for those selling food and cigarettes), citing traffic obstruction and the pernicious effect on the "city's appearance."[79] Before the ban took effect on November 1, 1946, the peddlers appealed to Mayor Wu Guozhen to rescind or extend the deadline. When the mayor refused, they simply defied the ban. In late November, a crackdown resulted in the arrest of more than seven hundred people. On November 30, a large crowd (between several hundred and several thousand, according to conflicting reports) gathered at the police precinct, where some of the detainees were held, to demand their release. In the riot that followed, "agitators" threw stones at the police, who in turn brought out high-pressure hoses and called in the riot squad. As the crowd continued to grow, shots were fired, and the "mob" proceeded on a "rampage of destruction" along Nanjing Road, the heart of the commercial district. The *North-China Daily News* hinted at Communist perpetrators, reporting remarks circulating through the crowd, such as "Chou En Lai was right" and "The time has come." The authorities believed that rumors of detained vendors dying from starvation or committing suicide in the police station, spread by "undesirable elements," fomented the crowd's anger.[80]

Two days of unrest followed, but by December 2 the streets were calm, and life had resumed its normal pace. The hawkers had also returned to their customary spots, selling tins of Canadian sausage and corned beef and hash stamped with the U.S. Army seal.[81] The Mayor concluded that the scale and organization of the disturbances indicated the handiwork of "conspirators," seeking to provoke bloodshed in order to spread chaos.[82] But an editorialist writing in *Shenbao* admonished the authorities to reflect on the incident: "The peddlers are only eking out a living; if they had ... any other options, why would they brave the elements to peddle their wares on the streets?" The ban was not unreasonable, but "the government must give them a way out, so that they can survive." Meanwhile, the *North-China Daily News* observed that the disturbances were symptomatic of the city's problems. Obviously there were people eager to spread discontent and ready "to fish in troubled waters." If the economic situation continued to deteriorate—an inevitability, it seemed— "those engaged in spreading discontent and eventual disorder will find their task easier than it appears to be at the moment."[83]

By the end of 1946, the waters were indeed troubled for the Nationalists. The CCP seized on the incident as indisputable evidence of the ruling regime's tyranny. Its magazine *The Masses* (*Qunzhong*) denounced the crackdown, asking, "What crime did the peddlers commit? ... Why have they been arbitrarily arrested ... and their wares confiscated? How is this conduct any different from brazen robbery?" The Nationalists had already sullied "the nation's appearance"

Figure 5.2. "Only big officials are permitted to get rich, the little people are not allowed to eat." *Qunzhong*, December 9, 1946

(*guorong*) by selling out to American interests—what is a "city's appearance" (*shirong*) under the circumstances? If the government truly cared for the city's appearance, what about the dead beggars on the streets? Accompanying the editorial, the magazine's cover depicts a fat "capitalist bureaucrat" wearing a mask labeled "city appearance." He is wielding a gun in one hand and with the other squeezes the life out of an emaciated street vendor. As for the allegations that the Communists had instigated the riots, "We do not want to claim credit for heaven's feats or engage in pointless debates. We only want to lay out the objective truth, which is that the Shanghai peddlers' uprising ... was the people's spontaneous struggle for survival and the inevitable outcome of the GMD government's reactionary rule."[84]

GOVERNMENT RELIEF IN SHANGHAI

While the Nationalist government attributed the peddlers' riot to the handiwork of agitators, the disturbances exposed the depth of popular discontent and offered a menacing preview of future troubles. Wu Kaixian, the director of Shanghai's Social Affairs Bureau, acknowledged that survival compelled many criminals to take the "dangerous path." Citing Mencius and the Buddhist exhortation for charity, Wu declared that relief should be one of the government's main priorities.[85] In 1946, the government's plan defined "social relief" as "curing social illnesses, promoting social safety, and transforming uselessness into usefulness and depletion into production." On the other hand, officials also blamed the proliferation of "vagrants" and unemployed hoodlums on the "poisonous legacy" of extraterritoriality. These criminal elements "completely subsist as parasites upon society"—"the hidden peril of the future" and an "evil force" that could be exploited by Communists.[86]

Shanghai's municipal welfare institutions incorporated all of the motives that Wu Kaixian alluded to—punitive, charitable, and productive. One of the first postwar government agencies to open was the Refugee and Refugee Children's Shelter (Nanmin Nantong Shourongsuo), described in the introduction to this chapter. Established in November 1945, the shelter was situated on the site of the defunct Red Swastika Society Indigent Training Center. Despite the innocuous name, the charter specified that inmates were to be committed to custodial detention for a minimum term of two years, so that "drifters, beggars, and lazy idlers" could learn self-sufficiency and "cease to be society's parasites."[87] The initial plan called for accommodating up to ten thousand people. But administrators struggled to find basic provisions for a fraction of that number, cobbling together government allocations, private donations, and CNRRA supplies. The conditions grew so deplorable that when the shelter admitted 182 children in the winter of 1946–47, Rae Levine, a CNRRA child welfare specialist, protested in horror. "I, as well as others in CNRRA," Levine wrote, "have seen the camp and consider it entirely unfit for human habitation, especially for children, except as a temporary reception centre." The dead and the living languished together, "without medical attention contamination and contagion will inevitably spread." Given the situation, Levine urged that the children be sent elsewhere until improvements were made.[88]

Despite these misgivings, officials soon designated this shelter for the exclusive care of children. The camp became the Children's Training Center (Ertong Jiaoyangsuo), a division of the Shanghai Municipal Relief Home. In the winter of 1946–47, the Social Affairs Bureau created the Relief Home as an umbrella organization to oversee the city's permanent institutions, including a Workhouse (Xiyisuo) for 1,500 men and a Women's Training Center (Funü Jiaoyangsuo) for 500 women. In the summer of 1947, the Children's Center added about 1,400 youngsters (98 percent of whom were boys), and a separate division for the disabled and infirm (Canji Jiaoyangsuo). Like its Beijing counterpart, Shanghai's Relief Home was both a punitive and a charitable institution, a place for beggars, drug addicts, "indolent drifters," orphans, and former prostitutes. Municipal regulations set the term of detention at one year, which the administrators could increase or decrease "as necessary."[89]

Under the auspices of the Relief Home, the Children's Center aspired to training the future generation to become the nation's "primary force for production." About 40 percent of the children attended school part-time, and 228 enrolled in occupational training classes—most learned to sew, while a few trained to become telephone operators, typists, or radio technicians. But for the most part, the children worked to sustain themselves. In the first six months of 1948 they planted and harvested more than four thousand pounds of cabbage, mended eight thousand pieces of old clothing, repaired tables and chairs, fixed windows and doors, gave each other haircuts, and buried the corpses of those who died.[90]

Meanwhile, at the Workhouse, the men sewed military uniforms, grew vegetables, and made matchboxes or washed laundry as contract laborers for local factories. Most inmates were petty criminals (pickpockets, thieves caught pilfering cotton from open-bed trucks), beggars, and homeless "vagrants."[91] On the streets, young men also came under special scrutiny as they scavenged for garbage, solicited alms, or simply drifted about without apparent purpose, particularly if they were "dressed in rags," if they got into fights, or if their "movements seemed shady."[92] Many were arrested on suspicion of belonging to local gangs, especially one Yellow Cow gang of thieves. By 1947–48, all city residents were required to carry a "citizen identification card" (gongmin zheng). If those stopped for questioning could not furnish this document or another form of verifiable identification, they could be arrested. For example, the police sent one unfortunate man to the Workhouse, after he had too much to drink at a relative's house and forgot his ID card.[93] As an emblem of citizenship, the card conferred credentials of belonging and signified that its holder was accountable to government authority.

The Women's Center focused on "fallen women" (*lunluo funü*), in particular those reduced to beggary and prostitution. Initially, the Social Affairs Bureau designated a livestock market to be the center's facility. But an artillery unit occupied the buildings and refused to leave, even after the Mayor's personal intervention. The administrators crammed the first group of women into one empty room at the Workhouse, and then moved them to the premises of the defunct Shanghai Industrial Orphanage (originally established in 1906).[94] The dilapidated facilities were bad enough, the administrators complained. Even worse, the women sent by the police were of "mixed origins." They ranged in age from three to eighty *sui*; more than half were disabled or seriously ill, some on the verge of death. There were amputees and blind inmates unable to move about; others were "crazy" and had to be physically restrained. These factors contributed to a chaotic situation, "a great impediment to making progress in education and training." From this inauspicious beginning, the Women's Center never recovered. It could not find a permanent facility, and at its peak enrolled two hundred women, fewer than half of the projected capacity. The majority were arrested by the police, with former prostitutes accounting for the largest group (20–25 percent). There were also some beggars and a few former domestic servants, now homeless and caught wandering the streets.[95]

In addition to the specific problems each division encountered, municipal administrators confronted basic difficulties. Most critical were feeding and clothing the inmates. Initially, they relied on the CNRRA, but as in Beijing, the Relief Home lost its primary source of rations when the agency disbanded. Thereafter, chronic shortages forced the administrators to borrow from the Winter Relief Committee, plead for allocations from other municipal agencies, and suspend new admissions.[96] One report acknowledged that the children received less than a cup of rice a day (half of what they were supposed to get), and one-third of them were perpetually hungry. By August 1948, food was running out, and fewer than 20 percent of the workhouse inmates were actually working. Most of them were ill, as they logged more than 1,500 visits at the infirmary that month. By October, the Relief Home could not purchase even the small amount of flour needed to make paste for gluing together matchboxes, and shut down the workshops.[97]

Given the conditions, it is not surprising to find a high incidence of runaways. With four divisions located on separate premises, the Relief Home needed a large number of guards. The Social Affairs Bureau could not always afford the cost, and the local police could be unreliable or demanded bribes. In December 1947, repeated escapes from the Workhouse prompted the director to form patrol teams with trusted inmates.[98] The guards were needed to keep the inmates in, but also to keep intruders out. On two occasions "local hoodlums" masquerading as soldiers abducted ten women at gunpoint from the

Women's Center. In the spring of 1948, one thousand soldiers billeted at the Workhouse were wreaking havoc. They commandeered the workshops, and used so much electricity and water that the Relief Home could not pay the bills. In November 1948, when one police contingent was transferred, leaving the Workhouse temporarily without guards, local residents broke in to steal food.[99]

Although rarely substantiated, allegations of corruption and abuse also beleaguered the Relief Home.[100] The most serious scandal occurred in June 1948, when Mrs. Huang née Wang died after a severe beating at the Women's Center. Huang was in her early twenties, a native of Piaoyang County, Jiangsu. Unfortunately we know nothing else about her—not her given name, nothing about her husband or family—only that the police had brought her to the Relief Home on December 10, 1947, telling the administrators that she was lost and homeless. We also know, based on the postmortem investigation, that sometime during the winter, Huang tried to run away with another woman, Zhou Yufang. Both were caught and beaten. The Director of the Women's Center, Sha Sailan, either instructed or permitted (it is unclear which) her staff to strip off Huang's clothes, tie her to a chair, and leave her overnight. Staff member Chen Nianci apparently took pity on Huang and covered her with a blanket. At dawn, Chen took away the blanket so that no one would know what he had done. Several months later, on May 11, 1948, Huang tried to run away once again, this time in the company of Feng Fengmei. That night, some neighbors heard sounds of whipping and cries for help, and summoned the police in the morning. When officers from the local precinct arrived, they found Feng injured and Huang bleeding uncontrollably. The police took them to the hospital and brought Director Sha to the precinct for questioning. More than a month later, Huang died at the hospital from complications, due to either a miscarriage or a heart condition.[101]

The Social Affairs investigation into this case began in earnest only after Huang's death. The long delay meant that conflicting accounts about what had occurred were difficult to corroborate with physical evidence. Under questioning, Dai Xiuming, a staff nurse, admitted that he had known about Huang's pregnancy for some time: "When we gave the inmates vaccination shots two or three months ago she said that she was pregnant, so she did not get a shot." Dai, however, did not record the pregnancy on the medical chart.[102] Five inmates wrote to the Social Affairs Bureau, claiming that Dai and another staff member had conspired with the neighbors to accuse Director Sha of murdering Huang: "The truth is that Huang had been ill for many months, and the Director took extra care of her."[103] Sha denied any participation in the abuse, claiming that renegade staffers carried out the beating without her knowledge. Moreover, Sha insisted that Huang died from a heart condition, and that only Feng had tried to run away that night.[104] For their part, the staffers all denied culpability, confessing at most to slapping the women a few times. Chen Nianci, who had helped Huang after her first failed runaway attempt, provided the most revealing testimony. Below is an excerpt from the transcript of his deposition as recorded in the police files:

> Q: What happened after Huang and Feng were caught?
> A: Yang told Shen to beat them with a stick. Shen brought two sticks and gave them to me, and told me to beat them.
> Q: What did you do?
> A: I said that the stick is too small, how can I use it?
> Q: Then what happened?
> A: Shen went to get a long bamboo whip.
> Q: What happened next?
> A: I did not hit them....
> Q: What happened next?
> A: The two women kneeled down and begged me, saying Mr. Chen, please save us.
> Q: What did you do?
> A: I asked them, your room was locked, how did you get out?
> Q: What was their answer?
> A: They said the door was not locked.
> Q: Then what happened?
> A: Yang asked who was on duty and performed the bed check.
> Q: How did you answer?
> A: I said I was on duty and I locked all the doors.
> Q: What did Yang say?
> A: He said they just said the door wasn't locked. I said to the two women, I locked the door, how did you get out? Then I smacked Feng once on the head with my hand, and continued to ask how they got out.
> Q: How did they reply?
> A: Feng said that they used a needle to pick open the lock.

At this point, Yang and Shen started to beat the women, and sent Chen upstairs to quiet down the other inmates who were yelling. When Chen returned, Huang and Feng were gone.[105] The investigators did not press Chen on his evasive answers or interrogate him about his motives. They did, however, question him more extensively than any of the other witnesses, suggesting that they thought he played a crucial role. The investigators also did not probe the contradictions between Director Sha's statement and the police report, or take the testimony of coconspirator Feng Fengmei seriously.[106] Thus we are left with many questions. Did Chen try to help Huang escape by leaving her room unlocked? Did he refuse to beat her out of pity or guilt? Had Huang come to the Relief Home already pregnant? If not, who was the father? The investigators did not pursue any of these questions. After reviewing the conflicting evidence, Social Affairs officials ordered an autopsy. When Huang's exhumed body proved decomposed beyond any possible assessment, the authorities dropped the matter.[107] A few months later, Director Sha, who had been accused of embezzlement and drug use in the past, was quietly replaced. The other staff members implicated in the case remained in their positions.[108]

There is much about Mrs. Huang's death that remains unknown. We know even less about the others, men, women, and children, who lived and died while in government custody. But we do know that as the Relief Home slid into financial insolvency and chaos, the administrators tried to devise new ways to discharge the inmates. In October 1948, citing "administrative difficulties," the director of the Workhouse drew up a plan for releasing inmates before they completed their sentences. The Children's Home allowed the youngsters to apply for extended home leave; many never returned.[109] Another tactic encouraged men to volunteer for military service. Offering a variety of incentives, the Shanghai Garrison and other units recruited inmates to join their ranks. This served the needs of both the Relief Home (to discharge inmates it could not feed) and the military groups (increasingly desperate for fresh recruits). In October 1948, ninety workhouse inmates enlisted to serve in Jiading County, in return for a uniform, a pair of shoes, and a stipend of Ch. $150 (in gold *yuan*, the new currency). The director indicated that the cash incentive was too low to attract more enlistees, and later offers used rice rather than the increasingly worthless money. Taicang County, for instance, signed up thirty-three men in December with an offer of new uniforms, blankets, and three piculs of rice.[110]

"Sweeping Garbage from the Streets"

Ironically, some of the workhouse inmates who enlisted in the Nationalist armies had been incarcerated because the government considered their homelessness a threat to society. Like their British and French predecessors who had previously governed the foreign concessions, the GMD authorities repeatedly rounded up transients for either deportation or detention. In December 1945, for instance, the police chief ordered local precincts to clear out the hordes of beggars who loitered on the city's many bridges. They kept watch at both ends, and as vehicles slowed down to make the crossing, they would converge to solicit alms. If the beggars considered the amount given stingy, they would curse and throw garbage at the passengers.[111] But as in the past, the police found that their patrols and periodic roundups could hardly stem the tide of homelessness. Deporting beggars only temporarily removed them from the city. One precinct reported that the process was completely futile, for the mendicants inevitably made their way back to the city. The captain asked the other stations to stop sending beggars to him, for his limited budget could not afford the gasoline required to make these frequent out-of-town trips.[112]

If deportation proved ineffective, incarceration was too costly. For its part, the Social Affairs Bureau continued to reiterate the importance of "active relief," and decreed that all homeless refugees, unemployed vagrants, and wandering children should be "taken in" (*shourong*) for job training and work relief. Yet, the police complained, when they brought transients to the Relief Home or winter shelters, they were frequently turned away. For instance, a campaign to clear Nanjing Road and other commercial thoroughfares foundered when the various agencies could not agree on who was supposed to go where. The Huangpu precinct complained that the Women's Center refused elderly women or anyone with children. The Children's Center wanted only boys. The Workhouse and the Asylum for the Disabled were the most selective, rejecting almost everyone with their many restrictions. Thus, "in reality it is difficult to exterminate the roots [of the problem] and completely stamp out vagrants and beggars."[113] The receiving institutions were equally frustrated. To these administrators, the police seemed incapable of following the regulations. They constantly arrested and brought the wrong people, creating innumerable problems when family members turned up to claim people who could prove that they were *not* beggars or vagrants.[114]

With the continual influx of refugees exacerbating the homeless problem, the municipal government expanded the winter relief campaign under the supervision of Deputy Mayor He Dekui. Known as T. K. Ho in his former life as Assistant Secretary of the International Settlement, he had played a leading role in battles with hut dwellers in the 1930s (as discussed in chapters 3 and 4).[115] The Winter Relief Committee sought contributions from private sources to supplement government funding, and operated three large winter shelters (*bihansuo*) and thirteen work relief stations (*gongzhensuo*), most housed in makeshift sheds and straw huts. Every night, staff members circled the city in trucks looking for homeless refugees, and tried to persuade them to go to the shelters. Police patrols also conducted periodic sweeps, searching areas where refugees congregated. At the shelters, the staff separated the men, women, and children, and sent the young and able-bodied (between sixteen and fifty *sui*) to one of the stations assigned to repair the Huangpu River. Workers received nominal wages, with a bonus if their output exceeded the quota of digging 1.5 cubic meters a day. Meanwhile, infirm refugees were transferred to the Relief Home's division for the elderly and disabled. Suspected thieves and gang members were sent to the Workhouse, where they could be more closely supervised.[116]

Like other Nationalist institutions, Shanghai's winter shelters aspired to transform the formerly "useless" members of society into new citizens.[117] According to Zhang Shude, the manager of the Number 1 Winter Shelter, many of these unfortunates had taken the path of degeneracy and needed "transformative education" (*ganhua jiaoyu*). At the same time, the shelters also took in large groups of refugees—"like sweeping up a large heap of garbage from the streets, which improves the city's appearance." After the first winter, Zhang concluded that "when we opened the greatest fear was that the refugees would not come; when we closed we feared that they had nowhere else to go." Combining active and passive relief methods proved more difficult than anticipated, and the fruits of "transformative education" were few. But Zhang felt certain that although forty-one inmates had died in his custody, without the shelter ten times that number would have perished.[118]

Nearly three thousand people spent the winter of 1946 under Zhang Shude's supervision. His casually derogatory remark about sweeping garbage from the streets reflected the reality of the shelter, more than the pontification on labor's transformative power. An anonymous letter from "one city resident" described the refugees' experience at the winter shelter in 1946. First, Anonymous declared, "[N]o matter if they are volunteers (*zitou*) ... or tramps, beggars and drifters arrested by the police (*jusong*), all the poor people (*pinmin*) are treated like criminals." When the refugees entered the shelters and found locked doors and sentries posted at the gates, they could not understand why: "They are not criminals. In providing temporary relief to the people, why does the government worry about runaways?"[119] As the rest of the letter attested, running away was actually the most logical course of action. At the shelter, the refugees were constantly hungry; the staff beat them at the slightest provocation; some of the women were molested or raped. Indiscriminate arrests meant that many were wrongfully detained as "beggars" when they had jobs and families. Worst of all, the policy of separating families in effect "treat the refugees like animals." Under these circumstances, Anonymous alleged, "it's no wonder that when arrested, refugees would rather jump from the police trucks and risk death than enter the winter shelter."[120] This litany of complaints evinced detailed knowledge of the winter shelter's operations, suggesting the author was likely an inmate himself.

Anonymous did not exaggerate, as other sources corroborated his descriptions. The separation of families was the most frequently voiced grievance. One group calling itself the Refugee Self-Governance Association protested that splitting up the family amounts to "cruel oppression," "cutting off reproduction and threatening the extinction of the Chinese race." For those who had just narrowly escaped with their lives, family was all they had left.[121] Asked to respond to these criticisms, manager Zhang Shude answered that the policy was intended to "reform the refugees' bad habits, and promote a life of lawful order. . . . When the refugees first arrive it's hard for them, but gradually they get used to it and get on the straight path."[122]

Police records also verify Anonymous's accusation that many taken to the winter shelters were not beggars or vagrants. Zhao Xiaoguozi, an elderly woman scavenging for grass and bits of rice, was mistaken for a refugee and dragged off. Qiu Dagen (nineteen *sui*), a house painter enjoying a day off, was arrested as an "unemployed person." Wu Xinzhen, a forty-two *sui* coolie laborer from Pudong, was detained when he went shopping one day. Pan Liangui, blind in the left eye, was arrested for obstructing traffic while selling candy downtown. These were a few of the hundreds of people whose family enlisted the aid of native place associations, trade guilds, or local officials to secure their release. The lucky ones might have been detained for only a few days; others remained locked up or were forced to join work relief teams for several months.[123]

In fact, there were so many mistaken arrests that another shelter manager, Zhou Zuwang, complained to the Social Affairs Bureau about the police department's ineptitude. Family members constantly showed up at his shelter to redeem innocent people who had been arrested as unemployed vagrants, homeless refugees, or petty thieves. Zhou's staff could hardly cope with the volume of requests, sometimes more than ten every day. The press also blamed the shelters for all of these wrongful detentions. Zhou asked the police to exercise more careful judgment, and requested that the arresting officers handle the applications for release (and face the ire of the families). In response, the Social Affairs Bureau suggested to the police chief that his department adopt a new guideline: detain only people without family, who might later come forward to ask for their release. A simple inquiry before making the arrest could prevent future problems.[124]

If their family members could not secure their release, many tried to run away. In February 1948, the manager of one work relief team reported that of 100 refugees sent to his station, 75 escaped within a few weeks. The same month, 220 people absconded from the Number 3 Winter Shelter, including 34 on one night.[125] Some officials blamed the high incidence of runaways on resistance to restrictions imposed on their freedom. They also thought that some must have been hoodlums who detested work, or drug addicts in need of a fix.[126] But as one police inspector, sent to investigate a wave of escapes, concluded, "Each time I go to the winter shelter the poor people there cry of hunger. In this condition, securing the premises is truly difficult." From the Number 7 Work Relief Station in Pudong, refugee Xu Jiafu wrote this parting note to the Winter Relief Committee: "We do not get enough to eat . . . and when we don't have the strength to work they hit us . . . we get up early to work, and go to bed hungry at night. We don't even get tea and have to drink from the river. Today I left because of their oppression. Who does winter relief actually relieve?"[127]

In addition to perpetual hunger, other conditions at the shelters were also deplorable. It was not unusual to find a hundred people jammed into one room without ventilation. At the Number 1 Winter Shelter nearly half of the refugees suffered from serious illnesses. But apart from occasional visits from the Red Cross, there was no medical care. The Jiangsu provincial authorities received so many complaints from refugees in Shanghai's shelters that they conducted their own investigation in March 1948. Staff members dispatched to inspect the situation concluded that living in such desperate conditions made refugees susceptible to the "poison" of Communism. If the Shanghai government failed to provide adequate relief, they were likely to "take the dangerous path."[128]

From its hopeful beginnings for "transformative education," the winter shelters thus deteriorated into confusion and chaos. Allegations of embezzlement and fraud were so commonplace that the government could not possibly investigate them all. As in Beijing, relations with local residents were volatile. There were numerous complaints about refugee work teams cutting down trees and stealing chickens, vegetables, firewood, and tools. Left unsupervised at the construction sites, gangs of refugees preyed on the neighbors.[129] Despite the managers' repeated requests for increased security, the government simply could not afford to pay for hundreds more armed guards. The volatile combination of hunger, frustration, and negligence eventually erupted in violence. In April 1948, refugees at the Number 8 Work Relief Station went on strike when their wages were not paid on time. According to the manager, this was an unintentional error; according to the refugees, it was evidence of corruption. When the manager summoned the police, however, the local precinct's four constables had no weapons to enforce order. A month later, another pay dispute led to a near riot. The refugees erupted when they heard rumors that the manager and engineers in charge had conspired to cheat the workers out of their bonuses, by undermeasuring the amount of work they had completed. After this incident, the manager resigned out of frustration, saying, "These refugees are fortunate to receive help. They are not only ungrateful, but deliberately make trouble. They have insulted the staff and incited the others, probably harboring evil intentions." In May 1948, the manager of the Number 12 Work Relief Station tried to transfer Li Huizhen, the leading troublemaker, to the Workhouse, in order to separate him from his followers. Li's brother-in-law soon arrived with reinforcements. After beating and tying up the manager, they stole rice, cash, and the account books.[130]

Hut Dwellers in the Age of Democracy

Given the state of relief shelters and camps, for refugees and new arrivals to Shanghai, living in their own straw huts must have seemed a better alternative. As discussed in previous chapters, neither the International Settlement nor the GMD administration had been able to resolve this thorny issue in the previous decades. Now, as the sole municipal authority in Shanghai after the Japanese surrender, the Nationalist government confronted the problem on an even greater scale. The number of shantytown huts mushroomed, reaching two hundred thousand with nearly one million residents by the end of the 1940s.[131]

In November 1945, the Public Works Bureau issued regulations prohibiting straw huts that infringed upon public roads or waterways, or presented a danger to public health or "the city's appearance." Structures that did not violate these conditions could remain, if the residents applied to the Bureau for an exemption valid for up to two years. The others would be demolished at the owners' expense with ten days' notice.[132] This announcement, coinciding with the controversy over street peddlers and citing much the same rationale, provided additional ammunition for the Communists. An article in *The Masses* condemned the action as "driving the poor to death" for the benefit of property owners. "Whenever the Shanghai authorities open their mouths," the Communists declared, "they talk about 'democracy' and 'serving the people.' With this kind of 'service,' the city's poor can clearly see which 'people' are served."[133]

Despite these allegations, the government actually did not enforce the ban strictly. Had they done so, the authorities would have further fueled the problem of homelessness, at a time when they were already struggling to keep order on the streets. Over the next three years, the Public Works Bureau and the police tried to contain the spread of shantytowns by prohibiting the construction of new huts. (The key was to tear them down before they were occupied, for once people moved in, "the difficulties compound.") As for the existing structures, thousands of hut dwellers submitted exemption applications, hoping to legitimize their homes. The licenses issued by the Public Works Bureau provided a temporary reprieve, but as a judge from the local district court noted, they conferred no legal standing. From his perspective, there was no question that property deeds trumped these documents of "temporary registration." But other officials observed that the licenses gave the hut dwellers a sense of "assurance" and "inadvertently created more trouble" when property owners sought their removal.[134]

As disputes proliferated, municipal officials received a barrage of entreaties from the hut dwellers making the case that they were entitled to preserve their homes. In December 1947, for instance, the Zhonghua Number 1 Textile Mill asked the Public Works Bureau to remove more than one hundred huts adjacent to its premises, citing the fire hazard they posed. On behalf of the group, Wang Fubao wrote to the Mayor to explain that they were refugees from Subei, and protested that the factory owners had "no regard for whether the poor live or die." "This is the age of democracy," Wang wrote. "How can they be allowed to tyrannize and cut up the little people like meat and fish?" If the huts were dismantled in the middle of winter, the residents would certainly perish. "We, old and young, might as well submit our lives to beseech the authorities to uphold humanitarianism and save the poor people's lives."[135] The police investigation concluded that the huts violated the regulations: they were built too closely together, obstructed the road, and constituted a fire hazard. In these kinds of cases the Mayor's office generally declined to intervene, and referred the matter to the Public Works Bureau to adjudicate.[136]

Public Works officials, however, found it difficult to balance the complex considerations governing the hut policy. As Director Zhao Zukang explained, on the one hand, public health, fire safety, and security concerns dictated that the shanties should be eradicated. On the other hand, the reality of the severe housing shortage and the problem of shelter for "the poor" compelled a "lenient and flexible" approach. Legal questions, intermingled with humanitarian and public welfare concerns, made arbitrating these cases exceedingly complicated. Zhao also referred to the many instances of landlords and "local bullies" exploiting the hut dwellers' vulnerability, through extortion and fraud. Yet shantytown residents were not blameless, especially the ones who assaulted Public Works personnel sent to investigate or enforce the regulations.[137]

In some cases, government priorities dictated the removal of straw huts. In April 1946, the Public Works Bureau ordered the eviction of more than four hundred homes and shops in Fahuazhen (in the Western District) to begin a major drainage project. The residents protested that their homes were not straw huts—they were actually built of brick, and many were multistory structures. "For the Public Works Bureau to call them huts—doesn't this disregard the truth?"[138] In another instance, more than four hundred people from Subei had built eighty huts on a small vacant plot of land in Yangshupu, the site of the protracted battle with the International Settlement authorities a decade earlier. In the autumn of 1948, they received an eviction notice from the Air Force, ordering them to move within ten days to make way for a "national defense" construction project.[139] When another group of Subei refugees, camped out in two hundred huts in Yangshupu, received a demolition notice from the local police precinct, they appealed to the Social Affairs Director for help. During the Sino-Japanese War, they wrote, they fled to the city "believing that Shanghai was heaven." Initially overjoyed at their narrow escape from the enemy, they quickly found that their urban relatives were equally impoverished, and the rents were sky-high. Government shelters were full, but in any case they did not want to "rely on the government's assistance and add to its burden." Among the two hundred households, about half of the residents were coolie laborers, 20 percent were beggars, and the rest were scavengers and peddlers. "We eat leftovers from the garbage, wear rags for clothes, and take shelter in these straw hut hovels, living barely human lives." Despite this entreaty, the Social Affairs Bureau referred the matter to the police.[140]

In October 1948, the Social Affairs Director also received the following letter from Chen Jingsong, the lead petitioner representing a group of refugees:

> We humble people are natives of Jiangsu, Shandong, Henan, Anhui, and Hubei. We all hated the disturbances caused by the Communist bandits; we only feared that we would be subject to their cruelty. With no choice but to leave our homes, we drifted to Shanghai [in 1947] to seek a living and food to eat. We had nowhere to go for shelter. Our relatives and friends all lived in cramped quarters themselves—we could not ask them to shelter us. This was a pitiful situation. Every night we carried the elderly and held the children by the hand, and slept on straw mats to preserve our lives. Combed by wind and washed by rain, we endured this for more than a year, swallowing hardship and suffering sorrow. Those who heard about our plight—there were none who were not sympathetic.

After more than a year of living on the streets, this group managed to build huts near a creek off Lujiazui Road in Pudong. They described their new neighborhood as "unbearably dirty and smelly," but noted that when they arrived, dozens of families had already been living in makeshift houses along the creek for more than two years. Shortly after the new arrivals settled in, the Public Works Bureau and the police brought eviction notices. Several months of harassment and negotiations followed. The letter concludes, "We are writing to inquire why there are repeated orders for the common people to tear down their homes. This creek is really not a major thoroughfare. But if we follow the orders for demolition, where will these five, six hundred people go?" The plea to spare their homes was followed by fifty-six names and their signature marks (some with thumbprints, others with name chops). The petitioners also included a careful drawing of their neighborhood, marking the geographic details of their plight.[141]

There are many more letters like this one preserved in the files of Shanghai's municipal agencies. In groups of twenty or two hundred, hut dwellers begged officials to spare their homes. Eviction would have rendered them homeless, in a time when homelessness could be a crime, and street people were targeted for detention. The deplorable state of the city's shelters and relief institutions would have meant an uncertain fate in government custody. All of these factors motivated hut dwellers to fight for their homes. Referring to themselves repeatedly as "poor people" or "common people," they tried to appeal to the officials' compassion and sense of justice, even to "democracy." By arguing that their lives mattered more than the city's appearance or traffic congestion, they claimed a fundamental right to shelter and a minimum standard of living.

Subei People and Guangdong Ghosts

As we have seen, the deplorable condition of Shanghai's winter shelters was well-known to officials and to the refugee population. As the housing shortage in the city grew more severe, thousands of displaced people decided to improvise their own solution rather than accept government aid based on the deprivation of liberty and the separation of families. In October 1947, more than one thousand refugees from Yancheng (one of the counties in Subei most devastated by summer floods) moved into the Pingjiang Gongsuo's coffin repository in Zhabei.[142] On behalf of the group, refugee Wang Buxiao wrote to Social Affairs Director Wu Kaixian, describing the "abyss of suffering" as their hometown fell to the Communists twice in the past year. They came to Shanghai only to encounter hunger and cold, with prospects for even more misery with the approaching winter. The group took shelter in the coffin rooms, "where the buildings are very spacious and we do not bother anyone." Citing a government directive on refugee relief, Wang asked the Social Affairs Bureau to designate their shelter as an official site and give them food and clothing, so that they could "weather this crisis and preserve our ant lives."[143]

By the end of November, several native place association managers had lodged complaints about Subei refugees occupying their premises. The intruders had stormed in and removed all the coffins; some even threatened to dump out or cremate the bodies. The squatters were living in the storage rooms and camping at the burial grounds. For these associations, these acts were tantamount to the highest possible crimes. Providing resting places for members unable to be buried in their hometowns was one of most important duties of any native place organization. Their coffin storage repositories and burial grounds were sacrosanct. Tampering with the dead was not only unlucky; it profoundly violated the cultural reverence for the deceased. To get the authorities' attention, one association manager protested that "these so-called refugees are of unknown origins and dubious backgrounds," infiltrated by local hoodlums, criminals, and possibly Communist spies.[144]

The "so-called refugees" responded by making their own case to the authorities. In a letter to the Social Affairs Bureau on November 29, 1947, Jiang Junqing (the leader of refugees occupying two facilities) wrote that in their hometown in northern Jiangsu, "treacherous bandits" were promoting "rent reduction," "settling accounts," and "burn all, kill all, loot all."[145] They escaped with only their lives and begged their way to Shanghai. Of more than three hundred thousand Subei refugees in the city, Jiang wrote, "most of us eat in the wind and sleep in the dew, wailing from hunger and cold." All of the reception centers and shelters were full, and his group found that the rooms at the Hudong and Datong Associations could each accommodate four people comfortably. "We are only temporarily borrowing these rooms, and we have consulted the managers, who have expressed deep sympathy [for our plight]," Jiang explained.[146] In fact, the two associations vociferously opposed the refugees' presence, but to no avail. The managers complained to the government that the squatters had removed more than one thousand coffins and strewn them around the courtyard. As a result, families could not reclaim the corpses, and the associations could not accept new ones for storage. Manager Yang Zhaoyong wrote, "The refugees are flouting the law. They are extremely evil.... They are obviously organized and bad elements are undoubtedly involved.... With this kind of wanton action the damage to the families who have stored coffins here may be small, but the injury to local order is enormous."[147]

Meanwhile, the Chao-Hui Native Place Association for sojourners from Guangdong found nearly one thousand refugees occupying the coffin repository at its cemetery (called Chao-Hui Shanzhuang, located in the old Chinese district Nanshi).[148] On December 1, managing director Zheng Ziliang sent an urgent telegram to the Mayor, complaining that the local police were powerless to remove the squatters. "Without regard for the law or for Heaven," the refugees broke the doors and windows, destroyed the furniture, and disturbed the coffins. They also conducted secret meetings in the middle of the night, undoubtedly plotting to harm "public good." Indeed, Zheng feared that Communists had already infiltrated this group. The chairman of the association added his protests, saying that the refugees have "caused a lot of damage; both the living and the dead are not at peace." Then, over the next three weeks, Zheng Ziliang sent letter after letter to the police and the Mayor's office, reiterating the complaints.[149] Zheng was a well-known figure to the authorities. He was not only a leader in the Chaozhou sojourners' community; as the boss of a Red Gang secret society, he was also a notorious figure in Shanghai's gangster world. Like Du Yuesheng, his counterpart in the Green Gang, Zheng had parlayed his mobster credentials into positions of public prominence, including appointment as an alternate representative in the National Assembly.[150]

On December 26, the group encamped at the Chao-Hui cemetery sent its own letter to the Mayor. "With nowhere to turn, we are temporarily borrowing the empty rooms at the Chao-Hui Shanzhuang, where there are no coffins," the refugees wrote. "We are keeping company with the ghosts just to survive." The previous day, officers from the local precinct had taken away three refugees and posted eviction notices, saying they intended to return with full force to arrest everyone else. Zheng Ziliang instigated this action, the refugees alleged, by conspiring with the police captain, who was a fellow provincial from Guangdong. "This is like throwing stones at someone who has fallen into a well. The tens of thousands of refugees in the city are anxious and filled with indignation. If you allow Zheng Ziliang to act as he pleases, when we give an inch he will take a foot. This will surely result in tragedy, and who will be to blame?" In closing, the refugees appended a list of eleven declarations, labeled "Our Sorrowful Pleas":

1. We ask the police to follow its own regulations and handle the matter fairly.
2. We ask the police not to listen to Zheng Ziliang's slandering words.
3. As a representative in the National Assembly, Zheng Ziliang should stand with the people and create a friendly relationship with refugees.
4. If a tragic incident occurs Zheng Ziliang will be responsible.
5. Zheng Ziliang should not be the enemy of Subei refugee-compatriots.
6. We beseech the police to take the position of mediator and protect the refugees.
7. You should protect the dead, but you should protect the living even more.
8. According to news reports the winter shelters are for vagrants and thieves. The government should not have us righteous people mix with them.
9. The winter shelters are infested with drug addictions, syphilis, and all

kinds of other infectious diseases. The government should care about our health and should not send us where we will be infected with evil and disease.

10. The winter shelters are for those without families, spouses, siblings, or children.

11. Are the lives of Subei's righteous people worth less than the damned ghosts from Guangdong?[151]

As their words attest, the refugees saw government shelters as places of punishment, and they adamantly refused to be identified with the criminals and "vagrants" detained there. Moreover, the insistence that they were "righteous people" and "compatriots" constituted a demand for social inclusion, arguing that they were deserving of at least the same respect as the dead. In fact, by cursing the corpses, the refugees were reversing the invectives often heaped on them—as interlopers, as "Subei swine," as less than human.

On December 29, municipal leaders convened a meeting to discuss the problem. Social Affairs official Cheng Zudai reported that he had personally inspected the situation at several sites. He concluded that about 80 percent of the squatters were "truly impoverished refugees"; the remaining 20 percent were peddlers and coolie laborers. At the Chao-Hui cemetery, Cheng saw signs proclaiming the refugees' refusal to join "beggars and thieves" at the municipal shelters. The meeting ended with the agreement that all of the municipal agencies would work together to resolve the problem, but with no real plan of action.[152]

A few days later, Mayor Wu Guozhen issued a directive ordering the immediate transfer all squatters to the winter shelters. There the authorities would separate the young and able-bodied from the old and infirm, and put them to work. In a personal letter, the Mayor assured the Committee for Sojourners' Affairs (a federation of native place associations and guilds) that with this plan, all refugees occupying association property would be removed. Those who refused to comply would be arrested for disorderly conduct.[153] Despite these assurances, the number of refugee squatters had grown so large that evictions would require overwhelming force. In early January 1948, a joint complaint from eleven native place associations counted nearly seven thousand refugees occupying their premises. The two largest groups were three thousand at the Pingjiang Gongsuo and two thousand at the Chao-Hui cemetery. According to the police chief, "[R]efugees forcibly occupying native place associations and cemeteries has become a social problem." At the same time, if the refugees complied with the orders to go to the winter shelters, in truth there was not enough room for all of them. For instance, the authorities repeatedly commanded Jiang Junqing's group to go to the Number 3 Winter Shelter, but this camp could actually accommodate only two or three hundred people.[154]

From the Chao-Hui cemetery, an increasingly frustrated Zheng Ziliang sent a four-page typewritten report in mid-January 1948, describing the refugees' activities in detail. He had spied on their late-night meetings, and recorded everything he observed. For December 17, Zheng's notes indicated that the refugees had organized themselves into household registration teams. Some of them could afford to hire rickshaws or owned bicycles, Zheng insisted; "there is no shortage of people who eat abundant meals and wear elegant clothes." At 10:00 a.m., doctors and nurses from the Public Health Bureau arrived to give vaccination shots. The next day, a photographer from the American magazine *Life* came to take pictures. On December 26, Zheng had watched as several hundred refugees gathered to listen to "inflammatory speeches." He quoted the instigators as saying, "The authorities have ordered us to move into the winter shelters. We vow not to go. We are not tramps and beggars, and we don't need 'relief.' If the police come to evict us, let's all rise up and resist." At a late night meeting on December 27, Zheng Ziliang copied down some of the slogans posted on the walls. "Are Subei people worth less than Guangdong ghosts?" "The police should not only listen to one side of the story and disregard us refugees." "The winter shelters are dormitories for tramps, beggars, 'diseased ghosts' and opium addicts." "We ask Zheng Ziliang to have compassion." By January, Zheng Ziliang wrote, bristling with indignation, the burial grounds resembled a small market, with vendors peddling their wares everywhere.[155]

As winter turned to spring and the stalemate remained unresolved, the native place associations warned that the conflict would erupt during the Qingming Festival ("the day of sweeping graves"), a holiday to commemorate the deceased. The Chao-Hui Association's leaders wrote that "gnashing their teeth in bitter hatred," their members vowed to punish the refugees for their despicable conduct. A clash during the annual gathering at the burial grounds would be inevitable. In fact, Zheng Ziliang told the police that one of his members who worked at a radio station had broadcasted a call to arms, and one thousand Chao-Hui natives were planning to confront the refugees. In the meantime, the refugees mobilized their own networks in the Subei gangster world to defend themselves. On the afternoon of April 5 two trucks carrying sixty armed Chao-Hui natives headed to the cemetery, intending to take back their burial grounds from the interlopers. The police intercepted them before they could enter the premises, and persuaded them (with their own show of force) to leave.[156]

The immediate crisis averted, Shanghai's authorities continued to vacillate about how to resolve the problem. Initially, they had refused one group's request to provide water, on the grounds that since the refugees had been instructed to go to the winter shelter, they lived at the coffin repository by choice. But by the spring, the Social Affairs Bureau sent a truck to dispense rice porridge to Jiang Junqing's group. Later the police distributed rice certificates to another group, which allowed them to apply for relief rations.[157] At the same time, the authorities fumed that the refugees had repeatedly defied the ultimatum to leave, ignoring deadlines, eviction notices, and threats of forcible removal. They made excuses, or simply refused to comply. The police requested instructions from the Mayor's office again and again, asking whether force should be used and, if so, to what degree.[158] But like the International Settlement's struggle with the hut dwellers in previous decades, the GMD administration did not have the will to remove thousands of people by force, and did not want to risk bloodshed in the event of strong resistance. Moreover, if they succeeded in removing all of the squatters from the coffin repositories, the authorities would be responsible for providing food and shelter to them. With two rival gangs in the background of the standoff, choosing one side could precipitate more trouble than it was worth. Given these constraints, officials limited their action to token gestures, such as tearing down forty-four huts on the premise of the Chao-Hui cemetery on one occasion.[159]

By the autumn of 1948, the numbers of refugees keeping company with ghosts had grown even larger: two thousand at the Yanxu Association, one thousand at the Xijin Association, five hundred at the Jingjiang Association, several hundred more at the Yangzhou Association—the list goes on and on.[160] While no precise figures are available, a conservative estimate would easily exceed fifteen thousand. In September, in response to the report of yet another group occupying a coffin repository, Mayor Wu Guozhen wrote in exasperation that "the refugees have been persuaded and ordered time and again to move, yet they refuse. At the same time they are not willing to participate in work relief or go to the shelters, and the Relief Committee has no way to force them to move."[161]

Conclusion

The specter of thousands of people living in coffin repositories and cemeteries vividly underscored the desperation of the times. In their struggle for survival, the Subei refugees dramatically violated a cultural taboo. Their defiance of authority and clash with the once-powerful native place associations produced the remarkable archival records that allow us to learn about their experiences, in a way that is not possible for the innumerable others in equally miserable circumstances. Contesting their exclusion from the living, the Subei refugees claimed that as *refugees*—not "tramps or beggars"—they were entitled to the right to live.

Such a simple claim dealt a shattering blow to the Nationalist government's legitimacy as it teetered on the brink of collapse. If one of the hallmarks of enlightened government was helping its neediest citizens—as the regime itself had insisted—then the GMD failed abysmally in its final years in power. The prevailing view of the civil war period suggests that, more than any other issue, mismanagement of the economy fatally undermined public confidence in the GMD. In particular, scholars have pointed to the ruinous effects of the inflationary spiral on the urban middle class, especially salaried professionals such as teachers and government employees.[162] As we have seen, the escalating urban disorder and the privations of the destitute provided even more damning indictments of the ruling regime. The deplorable state of winter shelters, corpses on the streets, refugees wreaking havoc—all provided daily, indisputable reminders of the government's indifference and incompetence. At the same time, from the perspective of the urban homeless, even as the Nationalist regime crumbled, its institutions of punishment and charity still wielded enormous powers: to confine or to help, often making the margin of difference between life and death.

During the civil war years, the GMD's ineptitude and disregard for the miseries of the people provided ample ammunition for the rival Communist Party's propaganda. Yet the CCP itself did not turn to the urban underclass to lead the revolution. With only small underground cells in both Beijing and Shanghai, the Communists focused on mobilizing students and intellectuals, regarding them as better allies. Like their Nationalist adversaries, the Communists viewed "beggars" and "vagrants" with suspicion. The lumpenproletariat, after all, was too deeply mired in poverty to play a significant role in the revolution. It was only in the very final stages of the civil war, when victory was all but assured, that the CCP began to mobilize "regiments of poor people" (*pinmin tuan*) for the coming liberation of the cities.

When the GMD government inaugurated the "gold *yuan*" currency reforms in August 1948, it was a last-ditch attempt to salvage the regime's economic disintegration. In Shanghai, Chiang Ching-kuo, the son of Chiang Kai-shek (later his successor as the President of the Republic of China on Taiwan), took charge of the implementation, which created only new levels of chaos on top of already widespread destitution.[163] In September, Chiang gave a lecture at a gathering of the GMD Youth Corps Fraternal Association. "Today, our nation has one big affliction," he began, "which is that while many people know that we are an impoverished country, they insist on putting up a rich front." In Shanghai, although some lived in prosperity, "the great majority of people still live in straw huts and garrets. There are even many thousands or tens of thousands who are homeless, wandering on the streets and in the alleys, or moaning in fields and ditches. They have virtually become a horde of beggars, who consider a pair of straw sandals a luxury beyond their reach." In the past, according to Chiang, no one would admit that China was a poor nation. "Today, we are truly a poor nation. But surely we cannot continue to descend into poverty! No—continuing the descent into poverty is certainly the way to destruction." Chiang used this stark appraisal to justify the currency reforms. The real purpose of the program, he declared, was to "eradicate the phenomenon of economic inequality in society. More specifically, it is to prevent the trend of the rich getting richer and the poor getting poorer."[164] But it was too late—it would take the Communist revolution to precipitate fundamental changes in the country's social and economic structures. Thus, the GMD's final years in power were marked by hunger, death, and destruction, the spiraling descent into poverty that Chiang feared.

Epilogue

"If you're missing a leg, don't you still have hands to work?"
—*People's Daily*, April 1949

WHEN SOLDIERS OF the People's Liberation Army (PLA) entered Shanghai on May 25, 1949, after brief clashes with retreating Nationalist forces in the suburbs, they found a hollow shell of a city. Despite Chiang Kai-shek's vow to "defend to the end," the Communists encountered little resistance. Chiang himself had sailed for Taiwan two weeks earlier, leaving his son to empty the banks and complete the transfer of gold reserves and other assets to the island. For a month before the final evacuation, martial law and a climate of fear prevailed as GMD agents rounded up suspected Communists and executed them on the streets. Then, with the PLA's arrival, the city awakened overnight, with red flags and banners appearing to proclaim, "Long live the Chinese Communist Party!" and "The sun has come out!"[1]

By the time the Communists took Shanghai, Party leaders had learned valuable lessons about how to carry out the "pacification" of cities. With experience gathered over three years, starting in Manchuria in 1946, cadres now had specific instructions and procedures for ensuring a smooth transition: disarm the enemy; unite urban workers, students, intellectuals and "all laboring people"; gain control of police and military agencies; prevent the "possibility of plundering by the urban poor." The agrarian revolutionaries regarded the task of urban governance with wariness. As the breeding ground of imperialist influence, cultural hedonism, and Nationalist power, the urban landscape presented a formidable challenge. The top priorities for "taking over" included maintaining public security, restoring financial stability, and reviving industrial production.[2] In particular, jump-starting Shanghai's commercial and industrial enterprises was crucial, an undertaking complicated by a wave of labor unrest and lingering hostilities with the departed Nationalists. From across the Taiwan Straits, Chiang Kai-shek launched a naval blockade and continued to rain bombs on the city. Rumors of Chiang's imminent return spread, with the Nationalists reportedly gloating, "We'll be having our new year's feast in Shanghai!"[3]

RETURN HOME TO TAKE UP PRODUCTION

In these crucial transition months, the CCP moved quickly to replace the existing urban household registration system with its own administrative apparatus

of districts and neighborhood committees.[4] The millions of refugees still loitering in the cities also demanded immediate attention. Within two weeks of
Tianjin's surrender in mid-January 1949, the CCP sent 20,000 people back to
their villages throughout north China and in Manchuria.[5] In Beijing, the next
major urban center to fall on January 31, the authorities also began a rapid repatriation campaign, offering free passage to those willing to leave. About
5,000 people remained in the former Nationalist refugee shelters, the most
obvious candidates for immediate removal in the effort dubbed "reducing the
parasitic population" (*jianshao jisheng renkou*). But when cadres identified an
additional 160,000 people and prepared for large-scale dispersal, protests
forced them to abandon those plans.[6] Instead, the new government concentrated its efforts on demobilized GMD soldiers lurking about the city. Public
notices announced that former enemy combatants and their dependents who
registered and turned in their weapons by the February 25 deadline would be
rewarded for their cooperation; those who failed to do so would be treated as
"illegal" belligerents.[7] As discussed in previous chapters, ex-military men had
received intense scrutiny from Republican-era authorities, perceived as the
most mobile and dangerous of urban itinerants. For the new PRC regime, confronting unknown numbers of possibly armed and hostile enemy soldiers was a
key issue on the security agenda.

At the end of the summer, the process of clearing out the capital continued,
with "dispersal committees" (*shusan weiyuanhui*) dispatched to identify additional targets for removal. This round of door-to-door interviews, following a
just-completed household census, aroused widespread suspicion. From all
around the city, problems proliferated. Residents in the Seventh District, wary
of former Nationalist policemen sent to gather information, refused to answer
questions. In the Third District, of 17,231 people identified as eligible for repatriation, only 29 said they were willing to return to their homes in the countryside.[8] Meanwhile, cadres from the Second District asked for guidance in many
individual cases, underscoring their uncertainty about who should be forced to
leave or permitted to stay. Long-time Beijing residents without "laboring ability," living in destitution—stay or go? Landlords and ex-GMD officials with
property but no jobs in Beijing—stay or go? And what about Mrs. Xiong, a
Chinese woman whose English husband recently returned to London, but sent
sufficient money to support her and her daughter—stay or go? The bewildering
diversity of circumstances confounded inexperienced cadres, who admitted
they did not know how to adjudicate the complexity.[9]

In Shanghai, the "return home to take up production" campaign likewise
focused on those willing to leave, with four hundred thousand departing within
the first months. But the respite was temporary, for many people soon headed
back to the city. A summer typhoon led to severe flooding in the countryside,
triggering a "reverse flow" (*daoliu*).[10] Moreover, beyond the first wave of volunteers, convincing people to leave proved difficult. Some simply did not want to

go—although considered "refugees," they had no desire to return to rural life after years of residence in the city. Former landlords heard rumors that the wealthy would be "buried alive" and feared retribution. Meanwhile, the penniless thought that "repatriation" was just another name for conscription; they worried that they would not receive an equitable share of the land due to their long absence; or they doubted whether the CCP would "truly take care of our needs." Finally, there were the belligerents. In response to a cadre's attempt to convince him to leave, one man retorted, "I have not eaten food from the government or worn clothes from the government. The bones and flesh on my body belong to me. If I want to go home, then I'll go home. It has nothing to do with you."[11]

To deal with multiple forms of resistance, officials from the Civil Administration Bureau instructed local cadres to use "patient persuasion," in order to expose the rumors as falsehoods and "smash such muddled thinking." To the question "If we stay in Shanghai and just get by, we will probably not starve to death—so why go back to the countryside?" they should explain that while the old society provided "passive relief," the new People's Government would develop "active production" to improve their lives. "If you try to get by in Shanghai, you are only looking for bitterness. You cannot improve your life this way and it will also have a negative effect on society. You should go home for production as soon as possible." The policy of "patient persuasion" specifically precluded coercion, and directives warned cadres against overzealousness or "hardening" the mobilization campaign into "compulsory orders."[12]

At the same time, officials also realized that the voluntary nature of the repatriation campaign engendered many problems, for without thorough "ideological change" many refugees failed to understand the meaning of "return home to take up production." They held the government responsible for resolving every difficulty, and griped when the solution was not to their liking. Easily frustrated, they gave up whenever they encountered problems and tried to return to the city. Indeed, "flowing backward" undermined the entire dispersal effort. In north China, where summer floods followed the spring drought, eight million people lost more than half of their harvest in 1949. Despite admonitions not to "flee famine blindly," many of them headed for Beijing. Meanwhile, from September to October 1949 the Shanghai authorities sent 7,210 refugees to the countryside. But in those same two months, more than 10,000 refugees entered the city, including 1,277 coming for the second time.[13]

A Lightning Strike

The continuous arrival of new refugees thus exacerbated an already considerable problem of urban homelessness. To the Communist authorities, some of the people living and begging on the streets were victims of feudalism and imperialism, unwillingly cast into the world of mendicancy. But others were "professionals," "dependent in character," who refused to work for a living. "They have become society's parasites," declared the *People's Daily*, in rhetoric reminiscent of treaty port Shanghai and Republican-era Beijing. To "convert parasites into producers," the new regime proposed "substituting work for relief" and "educational reform"; those unable to work would be given shelter and food. "But relief alone is not a good method. The elderly, weak, and infirm should also be organized to do simple productive work. If you're missing a leg, don't you still have hands to work?"[14]

Instead of building new detention centers, the new regime used existing GMD institutions as the "foundation." In Beijing, the Beggar Management Committee designated the premises of the former Relief Home as a clearing-house, to process detainees for placement in one of four divisions: the Home for the Elderly, the Commoners' Workhouse, the Women's Training Center, and the Children's Center.[15] Likewise, in Shanghai the four divisions of the new Production Training Institute were housed on the premises of the existing Relief Home, where 1,333 people remained. (Most of them were elderly or sick; those able to run had escaped long ago.) The "takeover" cadres described these institutions as emblematic of the failed regime: merely "window dressing," with the sole mission of preventing inmates from escaping. As for the "truly impoverished people—nobody cared whether they lived or died!"[16] In contrast, the People's Government promised to use "education as the primary principle and control as the supplement," in order to "enlighten their consciousness gradually, transform their parasitic mentality, and foster their labor ideology."[17] Newly appointed administrators also worked to reform the staff of "holdovers" from the GMD regime: their attitudes should conform to an outlook of "serving the people," and inmate abuse would be strictly prohibited.[18]

With Nationalist workhouses thus rearranged as Communist detention centers, the next phase of reducing "the parasitic population" began. In Beijing, the campaign targeted "beggars," as well as prostitutes and the clergy of the city's temples.[19] From May to December four separate "beggar roundups" netted 3,703 people. The first campaign focused on "those with deeply ingrained habits of hooliganism" and the leaders of beggar gangs. Also caught in the dragnet were a smattering of "unemployed poor," destitute peasants, and former soldiers, but for the most part the authorities considered these the "professionals." In July, the second round of 1,330 arrests coincided with the heavy summer rains, when large numbers of disaster victims entered the city. Cadres concluded that as the legacy of several thousand years of feudalism, the problem could not be solved overnight. Some beggars apparently misunderstood the meaning of "liberation" as freedom to do as they pleased. Others thought that with the arrival of the CCP, as the "proletariat" (*wuchan jieji*) they could act with impunity.[20]

Once arrested, the detainees were understandably fearful. They schemed to escape or begged to be released. A few even pretended to be "crazy," hoping to be let go, for in the past some Nationalist institutions had excluded the mentally ill. Their Communist custodians attributed these reactions to the inmates' experiences during the Japanese occupation and under GMD rule. Meanwhile, mistaking the "reform and education" process as a form of job training, some "unemployed workers" and "the poor of the city" went to register at the old Relief Home. They grew agitated when they arrived at the workhouse and saw "ragged and dirty beggars and thieves everywhere." With such a mixed lot ("professionals," destitute old women, petty as well as hardened criminals), the process of transformation was painstakingly slow. The pedagogical method centered on "speaking bitterness," inviting detainees to articulate their experiences of oppression under the Japanese and GMD. Who was responsible for your impoverishment? How did you become a beggar? Although they were initially reluctant to speak out, answering these questions produced cathartic effects. Cadres also explained that whereas the Nationalists cared about only the "city's appearance," the new government would seek a fundamental solution to the "beggar problem" through production. And in case anyone harbored hopes of the GMD's return, the lessons also emphasized that the imminent national victory would inaugurate a new world with zero tolerance for the "shameful lives of parasites."[21] Gradually, through the attentive care of cadres, who nursed the sick back to health, helped inmates write letters home, and spent time talking with them individually, "their emotions turned from fear to tranquility, from pain to happiness." The children attended school; the disabled pitched in to help with small tasks; 694 men and women, organized into four separate "labor brigades," headed off to repair sections of the Yellow River or settle in Inner Mongolia and Chahar. In short, the Beijing authorities considered the initial campaigns to "reform" beggars to be quite successful.[22]

In Shanghai, where the presence of even more numerous refugees was complicated by the influence of criminal syndicates, the campaign to get rid of "parasites" required different tactics. For decades, the city's legendary gangs had reinforced their power through alliances with treaty port and Nationalist officials. Chiang Kai-shek himself was a member of the Green Gang and a disciple of its notorious godfather, Huang Jinrong. Stripped of official patronage after the Nationalist departure, the gangs kept a low profile, but continued to operate for some time without harassment from the government. According to one CCP official, in the early months "we lulled them into lowering their guard."[23] Then, on December 14, under cover of night and "as sudden as a flash of lightning," Public Security and Civil Administration cadres rounded up more than 4,800 "vagrants." The product of weeks of planning, the crackdown lasted several days and cast a wide net over suspected gang members, petty criminals, and the destitute homeless. A concurrent population registration drive sent five thousand cadres fanning out across the city to check paperwork, count straw huts, and ferret out illegal residents. As a result, hoodlums and thieves, drug users and sellers, young prostitutes and elderly women, orphaned and abandoned children, the infirm and disabled were brought to police precincts for investigation.[24] Despite the detainees' varied backgrounds, the authorities considered this a campaign against "vagrants."

With several thousand people in custody at precincts around the city, family members (and possibly criminal associates) turned up one after another, demanding their release. The police decided to move all of the "vagrants" to one central location for processing, and scheduled the transfer to take place at dawn to avoid trouble. But the news spread quickly, and more than one thousand people gathered at the destination's main entrance—"the women wailing for their husbands, the children crying for their fathers, the strong young men intending to break in. . . . It was utter chaos." The crowd blocked the entrance so that the trucks ferrying the detainees could not enter. The police tried "patient persuasion," but the protestors grabbed their weapons and shouted, "The people's government is unreasonable! The Communist Party arbitrarily seizes innocent people!"[25]

As for the detainees, the disturbances and the government's policy of "no beating, no cursing" emboldened them. Taking advantage of a lull during the lunch hour, about five hundred people attempted to escape. At a prearranged signal, they rushed to the wall; forty to fifty managed to scale it before a warning shot compelled the others to stop. When the authorities finally restored order and dispersed the crowd at the gate, they began the process of sorting and classifying. Those considered "not from Shanghai" were sent home; the rest were remanded to one of the divisions of the Production Training Institute. By February 1950, there were 6,293 inmates. The youngsters at the Children's Production Institute cleared away the garbage on the premises and planted vegetables. They also learned to operate the seventy sewing machines left from the GMD days and made more than one thousand sets of winter clothing for themselves. The Women's Production Institute had only six sewing machines, but the inmates managed to stitch enough clothes for themselves and the staff. At the disabled division, amputees hobbled on their stumps to harvest cabbage and made nine hundred pairs of shoes.[26]

Meanwhile, the young, able-bodied men at the Labor Production Training Institute proved to be the most recalcitrant. They used many forms of passive resistance (feigning illness, pretending to be crazy or deaf) and direct opposition (one inmate smashed a statue of Mao Zedong "as revenge"). They reconstituted their criminal affiliations and pressured those inclined to cooperate with the authorities (e.g., ostracizing them as "stooges"; beating one person to within an inch of his life). Visitors hid contraband in the food they brought, while family members on the outside busied themselves working connections, plying cadres with gifts—anything that might buy their freedom.[27] Like in Beijing, reform methods in Shanghai's Production Institutes relied on "speak bitterness," patient "ideological work," and labor. But the more numerous "va-

grants" in Shanghai, with less malleable criminal elements, compelled a different solution. In this case, officials thought it would be best for their ideological
reform and labor training to take place far away from the city.

To Subei—and Back

The chosen destination was Subei, the region in northern Jiangsu province that
had been a perennial source of migrants and refugees to Shanghai (as discussed
in previous chapters). A tract of 200,000 *mu* of reclaimed land in Taibei County
(present-day Dafeng, near the city of Yancheng) was set aside to build a "New
People's Village" (*Xinmincun*). In mid-March 1950, two contingents of more
than 5,000 people set out from Shanghai's Production Training Institutes, leaving only the youngest children and 123 adults (who were probably too old or
sick to make the journey). About 2,500 prison convicts joined them.[28] CCP
officials envisioned the Subei resettlement project as the fulfillment of "making
people anew" through labor. To their consternation, the personnel assigned to
the state farm proved to be the first source of trouble. Many of the cadres did
not want to leave Shanghai and considered the assignment a demotion; some
expected to return to the city as soon as they escorted the detainees to Subei.
Forced to stay and work in harsh conditions, with few marriage prospects ("in
Subei you can't even find a dog to marry"), they became disgruntled, with "hundreds of defects" emerging from their "confused ideology" and "unwilling
hearts."[29]

Despite reports of these problems at the outset, Mayor Chen Yi insisted that
the Subei project was the "correct policy." The Mayor calculated that 13,300
detainees from Production Training Institutes and the prisons, plus their
10,000 dependents, could be transferred to the state farm. With the Nationalists continuing to bomb Shanghai, removing these people from the city would
ease a major security concern and also free up space at the detention centers for
new arrivals.[30] But before the plan could be implemented, more bad news arrived from Subei. In July, a cohort of about 1,000 detainees moved from a village, where they had been temporarily camping, to the site of the New People's
Village. Covering a distance of twelve miles on foot, they were caught in torrential rains en route and arrived completely soaked. What they saw further
depressed their spirits: a desolate and flooded area, infested with mosquitoes,
without any of the promised amenities. They grew "agitated and confused," and
people started to run away, about two or three every day. On July 15, detainees
assaulted four cadres, beating them to "a bloody pulp." The next day, they packed
up their belongings and said, "We're off, see you in Shanghai." In a coordinated
escape, 830 people absconded, fleeing in three different directions.[31]

The incident triggered immediate action at the highest level in Shanghai. In
addition to launching a manhunt (eventually recapturing 631 runaways), the

Party Secretary sent a team of thirteen investigators to Subei, to find out what went wrong. In the appraisal that followed, some errors were easily attributed to the misconduct of low-level cadres in need of "thought reform" themselves. While some apparently treated the detainees with excessive cruelty, others erred on the side of excessive sympathy. There was plenty of petty corruption; in addition some brazenly took advantage of the detainees' vulnerability. In one of the most egregious cases, one cadre took a watch belonging to a convict; when the owner protested, he beat him to death. In another instance, a cadre stole a large sum of money from public coffers and absconded with a detainee's wife. Apart from personnel issues, the reports also documented management problems not unlike those from the Nationalist era. The conditions in the New People's Village were abysmal. The detainees defecated everywhere, as there were no bathrooms. The only source of water was a river located almost two miles away, and they were forced to drink from a muddy pond. In contrast to the promise that "Subei will have every amenity," the investigators concluded that with shoddily built accommodations, constant flooding, and rampant insect infestations, it was hardly surprising to hear the detainees say, "We prefer Shanghai's jail to Subei's water prison." In addition, insufficient security made it easy to escape, and rumors that runaways returned to Shanghai to "live it up" only enticed others to follow.[32]

Beyond the circumstantial conditions, most of which could be ameliorated with additional resources, wrongful detention was the issue that fueled the strongest sense of discontent. Many detainees rejected the claim that they were "vagrants." Some said that they were disaster victims from Subei, who had recently fled to Shanghai to escape the famine, only to be arrested and sent back as criminals. For others, officials had promised that their families would soon join them in Subei "to settle down together." This assurance persuaded them to leave Shanghai; when the promise was broken, they felt "cheated by the government" into a form of labor conscription. Other malcontents were ex-convicts, who had already completed their sentences, or they were accused criminals awaiting trial. Unable to bear the prospect of an "indefinite labor sentence" in Subei, they felt that running away was the only option. Conflicts between nonconvicts and convicts also aggravated the sense of injustice, with the former complaining about being treated like criminals. "The vagrants and the convicts look down on each other and often curse each other." The investigators concluded that in order to stabilize the situation and ease the disgruntlement, the government needed to review all claims of wrongful detention and render clear verdicts for cases in legal limbo.[33]

As far as the archival records show, no such review was ever conducted. The only people given early discharge from Subei were those with connections like Zhang Delong, whose father worked for the postal service in Shanghai. On behalf of the elder Zhang, the postal workers union repeatedly petitioned for the release of his son. In September 1950, the Party Secretary's office sent an irate note to Subei, saying that after three months, "the matter has caused extreme disgust" among the workers. It "cannot be delayed without resolution any longer. . . . Tell them to send Zhang Delong back at once, and check into why there has been such a long delay." Although the Public Security Bureau had arrested Zhang as a "hooligan" and opposed his release, upon intervention from the top the Subei authorities sent him back immediately.[34]

Of the 7,840 "vagrants" sent to the New People's Village in 1950, a report later estimated that 20 percent had been "indiscriminately captured, randomly arrested," with many "refugees" wrongfully treated as "vagrants." Under pressure to find an outlet for the large numbers of "vagrants," and especially in the aftermath of a Nationalist bombing in February that left more than five hundred dead, Shanghai officials had rushed to send people to Subei. "We recognized that social reform is a long term process, yet the demands of security were pressing. . . . We overemphasized the security imperatives and did not consider a unified method to address the roots of the problem."[35] Indeed, in reports filed from Subei, officials alternately identified the detainees as "vagrants," "convicts," "settlers," "disaster victims," and "refugee-compatriots," underscoring the uncertainty of their status. The failure to differentiate the innocent from "vagrants" undermined the entire project, and undercut the claim that the Communist regime was different from its predecessors.

Even as Shanghai officials dispatched people to Subei, Subei people were fleeing in their direction. An estimated two hundred thousand disaster victims converged in the city in the autumn of 1950, forcing the government to suspend its repatriation campaign. That winter, forty-four winter shelters were established in temples and lodges for nine thousand people.[36] Apart from providing food and shelter, officials felt the most important task was to teach them that "blindly running from famine" cannot solve the problem, and that "production and self-help are the only ways out." Initially, the shelters provided a daily ration of five *liang* (approximately 5.5. ounces) of rice per person and permitted the refugees to go out to beg. To the cadres' dismay, they found that once turned loose on the streets, the "disaster victims" formed gangs and wreaked havoc. The government then more than doubled the allotment of food (to twelve *liang*, approximately 13.2 ounces) and prohibited begging, which alleviated the first set of problems but created another. According to one report, with such a "high standard" of provisions, "the disaster victims sprouted the ideology of long-term dependency on relief and refused to return home to take up production." They even sent word advertising the government's generosity, encouraging family members and friends to join them in Shanghai. The following month, with the rations readjusted down to eight *liang* (approximately 8.8 ounces), officials determined that this was the "appropriate" amount of food—sufficient for subsistence, but not so excessive as to induce dependency.[37]

The Urban Poor in New China

This delicate balance also governed the distribution of aid to the "urban poor," considered legitimate city residents, but who occupied a tenuous position in the hierarchy of the urban population. In January 1949, Beijing Party Secretary Peng Zhen spoke to cadres preparing to enter the city for the takeover. "How should we regard the problem of poor people (*pinmin*)?" Peng asked. "Are the urban poor (*chengshi pinmin*) a revolutionary group or a reactionary group?" This was a critical distinction, and Peng declared,

> In principle they are revolutionary.... But within this group the divisions and classes are so complex that we can not treat them indiscriminately. This group includes people from all walks of life: some are hooligans, some are thieves, some are spies, and some are reactionary running dogs. There are also landlords in exile, declining aristocrats, and true laborers who cannot make ends meet. Among these people, the laborers are our friends.[38]

According to this logic, the government would render assistance only to the "true laborers"—friends of the regime willing to work. The mantra of self-help governed relief policy, punctuated by constant proclamations that New China would be a society of "producers." Wherever and whenever possible, the "urban poor should be organized to produce and help themselves."

In the early 1950s, apart from emergency relief (*jijiu*) and benefits for military dependents, CCP policy generally limited eligibility for direct aid (in money or in kind) to those "unable to continue living" (*wufa jixu shenghuo*) or "truly unable to produce" (*queshi wufa shengchan*). Furthermore, government assistance was intended to be "supplementary" and did not absolve the recipients of the duty to work. Emphasizing the "glory of labor" and the "shame of relief," neighborhood committees investigated claims of hardship and posted relief rolls each month, as a form of community surveillance.[39] Later directives restricted eligibility for both long-term and temporary relief to those "residing in urban or suburban districts, not the peasant population." This was one component of a broader policy that privileged urban residents, and in this case, it had the effect of hardening the line between "the urban poor" and the transients who did not belong in the city.[40]

At the same time, officials repeatedly invoked the promise that "not one person will starve to death," a pledge first pronounced during the civil war years (discussed in chapter 5). By contrasting its compassionate stance to the GMD's indifference, the new regime cited the people's welfare as one of the pillars of its political legitimacy: only by solving the "livelihood problem" could the CCP establish the "material basis" for security. In 1950, for instance, Vice Interior Minister Chen Qiyuan explained that throughout China's history it was commonplace for millions of people to starve to death in times of disaster or dearth.

In 1931 alone, 3.7 million died under the GMD's watch. Although the PRC had been established for only one year, Chen said, the government has "by and large fulfilled its guarantee . . . that 'not one will starve to death.' The deaths of some people in some localities deeply aggrieve us, but it is far from the historical record's depiction of fields strewn with emaciated corpses."[41]

The calculus of government assistance thus cautioned against the pauperizing effects of excessive sympathy, but also directed local cadres to distribute adequate aid, "so that the urban poor would not degenerate into beggars."[42] Indeed, the distinction between the two groups assumed greater import than ever, as "poverty" (pin) became an explicitly politicized concept, with its most salient form manifested in the "poor peasants" (pinnong) of the countryside. The elevated status of "the poor" in New China largely dissociated the condition of impoverishment from its former status as a national affliction and social problem. This conceptual shift, reflecting radically different ideological underpinnings, cast the economic distress of the people as one of the driving forces of the revolution. But as Peng Zhen alluded to above, "the urban poor" could not be uniformly regarded as friends of the regime, requiring disparate treatment based on their productive contributions to the nation.

In Shanghai, for instance, the ubiquitous "hut dwellers" were recognized as belonging to the ranks of laborers, and thus eligible for government assistance within the same parameters as the "urban poor."[43] As discussed in previous chapters, straw huts had been the subject of government concern and popular agitation in the past decades. In the early 1950s, Shanghai's authorities did not call attention to the issue of shantytowns, where nearly one-fifth of the population lived.[44] Instead, officials took only incremental steps, such making infrastructure improvements (running water, latrines, garbage disposal) or helping those rendered homeless (by fires or typhoons) rebuild or relocate. Until the late 1950s, when brick housing compounds replaced several of the most notorious shantytowns, the huts were considered a legacy of the reactionary GMD regime that left Shanghai "riddled with a thousand scars."[45]

The most privileged constituency among "the urban poor" was the "unemployed workers" (shiye gongren). Differentiated from the far more numerous people who never held jobs (wuye), they were cousins of the working class anointed as "masters of the country," and thus beneficiaries of measures aimed at restoring industrial production.[46] After all, as Peng Zhen explained, "The Communist Party is the party of workers. . . . Some people say that the Communist Party is the party of poor people (qiongren). This is not entirely true. In Beijing there are beggars and bankrupt former officials and landlords who are also 'poor.' We are not the party of poor beggars."[47]

The unemployment problem was severe everywhere in 1949, but it was especially acute in Shanghai, where capital flight and the reorganization of staterun enterprises resulted in massive layoffs. In 1950, 115,000 people registered with the unemployment office of the Shanghai Labor Bureau, more than ten times the number in Beijing. Then, during the 1952 "Five-Anti" campaign targeting capitalists, as more shops and factories were shuttered, the number seeking unemployment assistance peaked at 414,000 (more than 20 percent of the workforce).[48] Although Beijing had only a fraction of Shanghai's unemployed workers, officials there grew frustrated by their attitude of entitlement. Many apparently considered "work relief" demeaning, or griped that the paltry wages were not enough for their cigarette money. Although national directives had instructed local officials only to "reduce" their economic difficulties, the workers demanded that the government "immediately and completely solve their problems." They failed to understand that until the national situation improved, the government could take only incremental steps to help.[49]

With partial government assistance and limited opportunities for full employment, many laid-off workers joined the legions of itinerant peddlers plying their wares and trades on the streets. As discussed in chapter 5, protests against the GMD ban on peddlers in Shanghai had erupted into a riot in 1946. At the time, as the opposition the CCP had exploited that incident as yet another indication of Nationalist indifference to the plight of ordinary people, excoriating the concern for "the city's appearance" (*shirong*) as typical of the GMD's preoccupation with façades over substantive social policy. In 1949, with more than 150,000 peddlers in Shanghai and some 50,000 in Beijing overrunning the streets, the CCP confronted the problem as the ruling regime. In dealing with an issue that affected the livelihoods of hundreds of thousands of people, Communist officials tread cautiously. They usually invoked the language of "management," not "prohibition," and situated the problem in a familiar narrative of GMD regime failure.[50] In Beijing, Party Secretary Peng Zhen and Mayor Ye Jianying held an open meeting with the city's peddlers to discuss the situation on May 23, 1949. More than one hundred people attended, and Ye began his address in this way:

> Comrades! We have invited you here tonight to discuss the situation, using the evening hour so that it would not interfere with your business.... Your lives are very bitter, and in the past you have suffered a lot of oppression and misery. The Communist Party is leading the Chinese people's revolution in order to liberate the oppressed and suffering people. We have no experience with managing peddlers. We are the students and you are the teachers. So we want to consult with you about how to handle this, gathering everyone's opinions as the basis for our action. But first I'd like to ask all of you to answer a question: In the past, did the GMD mayor or any officials ever hold a meeting with you? How did they treat you?

The meeting transcript recorded the crowd's answer: No, never. They only whipped us and sent down orders.[51]

The Mayor continued, "Comrades, they are reactionaries and they are unreasonable.... In several decades of rule, did any official in Beijing ever treat you like human beings? Only the Communist Party treats people like human be-ings." After warming up the audience with such invectives against the old re-gime, Ye praised peddling as a "legitimate business" and peddlers as "belonging to the ranks of laboring people.... You are far better than those parasites who do not work at all." According to Ye, the proposed regulations would not pro-hibit peddlers altogether, only "organize" them in order to reduce the number of traffic accidents, issue licenses (to differentiate lawful sellers from the riff-raff), ferret out GMD agents, and collect taxes (an "honorable responsibility" for national reconstruction). The Mayor also pointed out that with ever-increasing numbers of peddlers, intense competition made it impossible for anyone to earn enough money to survive. Lastly, he asked for a show of hands indicating approval for these measures, and received unanimous consent. To conclude, Ye declared, "We are not doing this just for the sake of the city's ap-pearance (*shirong*). Whenever peddlers see the two characters *shirong* they say, 'Our stomachs have no *neirong* (contents), what is there to say about *shirong*?' We are not using a command method to ban peddling; we are not like the GMD reactionary government."[52]

It was a masterful performance, aimed at dispelling resistance to regulations issued the next day. The announcement affirmed peddling as a legitimate oc-cupation, but stipulated that all must apply for licenses, pay taxes, and conduct business at "suitable" locations (one of thirteen designated markets).[53] Through-out the implementation process, cadres emphasized "management without ex-pansion and without prohibition" as the guiding principle. They underscored how the new regime's aims differed from those of its predecessor, and eschewed the language of the "city's appearance."[54] Instead, officials relied on "persuasion" to garner cooperation. A graduated fee schedule also provided incentives to relocate, giving preferential rates (two *jin* of millet per month) to those willing to set up on the city's outskirts. By contrast, those who insisted on selling in the central business districts paid up to thirty *jin* of millet.[55]

Such carefully crafted messages, however, could not overcome the conflicts that simmered and erupted on the streets. Many peddlers did register for li-censes, but they soon grew resentful of those who avoided paying the requisite fees and taxes. From the perspective of the licensed vendors, the scofflaws gained a significant advantage and could undersell their competition. Alterca-tions also broke out at the designated markets, when itinerant hawkers bra-zenly sold their goods at lower prices in front of the authorized stalls. The Commerce Bureau did not have sufficient personnel to deal with all of the itinerants, who soon outnumbered the licensed.[56] Moreover, officials found that the policy of "no expansion" provoked antagonism. As Commerce Bureau Di-rector Cheng Yongyi reported in September 1950,

There are too many poor people in our city. Every market has seen the influx of new unregistered peddlers who claim hardship ... it is exceedingly difficult to ban them all. . . . When you tell one peddler that he is not allowed to sell his wares, he says: "I haven't eaten for several days. If you don't believe me, you can go to my house and see for yourself. What would you have me do? You've got to give me a way out!"

Cheng likened the task of enforcing the ban against unregistered peddlers to riding a broken bicycle uphill. With unemployed workers, students, and disaster victims from neighboring counties constantly asking for permission to make their living on the streets, "insisting on the policy of no expansion incites the dissatisfaction of the masses." Growing enforcement problems also "undermined the government's authority," and local cadres themselves were beginning to doubt the merit of the policy.[57]

After a year of struggling to enforce the regulations, Beijing officials managed to reduce the number of peddlers in the city only by 17 percent (from approximately 50,000 to 41,349). Shanghai's authorities, coping with three times as many vendors, actually met with better initial success, reporting a decline of more than 40 percent by year-end 1949 (from an estimated 150,000 to a count of 84,623).[58] But the numbers started to climb the following year, paralleling the influx of rural refugees. By 1952, with the disruption of the Five-Anti campaign, there were more peddlers in Shanghai than there had been in 1949.[59] Officials admitted that their approach to "managing" itinerant commerce was only a patchwork solution, and resolving the issue would have to await the systematic overhaul of the urban economy. "For the most part peddlers belong to the class of impoverished people (*qiongku renmin*). They do business with a little capital, and rely on their stalls and carts to make a living." They actually performed an important social function, bringing food (especially easily perishable items) and sundry goods to every alley and lane. "In the short term the government cannot completely solve the problem of unemployment, so the impoverished masses rely on peddling for their survival. Their stable livelihood is also related to the regulation of social order."[60]

Despite these acknowledgments, the uncontrolled mobility of peddlers challenged the imperative to demarcate the line between rightful city residents and illegitimate interlopers. Officials worried that those who did not belong in the city and enemies of the regime could easily hide among the roving vendors, whose movements were difficult to track.[61] This distrust of the peddlers' occupational mobility was born of experience. After all, during the civil war, underground CCP agents had disguised themselves as such while carrying out sabotage operations against the Nationalist regime. On the other hand, while troubling, the mobility of peddlers fundamentally differed from that of "vagrants." As officials noted above, peddlers were not "parasites"; they belonged to the laboring ranks of the "urban poor." In contrast, the nonproductive mobility of "vagrants" and "beggars" was increasingly associated with incorrigible criminals and enemies of the state. Whereas in the early transitional years officials tended to regard "vagrants" as remnants of feudal society, originating from the ranks of "laboring people" (*laodong renmin*), by 1955 *youmin* were linked to a new class of political criminals literally called "the scum of society" (*shehui zhazi*). In Shanghai, the municipal government issued a secret directive ordering a thorough search for "vagrants and scum," saying that they were "prime targets for the enemy to exploit and the hotbed of criminal activities. In fact they have become a serious threat to socialist construction and reform."[62]

The new regime's social policy thus bifurcated, with "relief for the poor" (*jiuji pinmin*) and "compulsory reform for vagrants" (*qiangpo gaizao youmin*).[63] This differentiation assumed that categories such as "the poor" and "vagrants," and attributes like "willingness" and "refusal" to work, could be clearly discerned. Yet officials conceded, time and again, that mistaken identities plagued their efforts. In Beijing, cadres sent to arrest beggars noted that because "the targets were not clearly defined, we made many errors."[64] In 1953, the Beijing authorities decided that these mistakes were the cause of turmoil at the detention centers. Beset by reports of runaways, attempted suicides, and intractable inmates refusing to work, the Civil Administration Bureau established a temporary shelter, to function as a triage center (similar to the rearrangement of GMD institutions in 1934, as discussed in chapter 3). There, cadres would have one month to conduct investigations of new detainees, according to a set of "unified and clearly understood criteria." Taking the extra time would prevent mistakes, for it was not easy to get the truth out of "cunning thieves" adept at lying and former landlords masquerading as disaster victims. After in-depth investigations, the inmates were dispatched to the permanent detention centers.[65]

In Shanghai, officials found that different agencies were conducting campaigns against "vagrants" based on contradictory criteria, creating much confusion. In 1956 there were more than fifty thousand "vagrants" in the city, plus one hundred thousand of their dependents. After six years of struggling with the issue, the problem was actually getting worse. A new decree gave local cadres two years to "make arrangements" for all of these people, using repatriation, detention, ideological work, and labor reform as necessary. The directive also warned, "We must rigorously draw the line between vagrants and the urban poor," between "vagrants and counterrevolutionaries," and between "vagrants and criminals." Cadres must make ensure that "not even one innocent person is mistaken as a vagrant."[66]

Despite these caveats, a subsequent roundup of "vagrants and scum of society" netted 13,604 people, of whom more than 1,000 turned out to be "mistakes." The source of confusion was the language defining the detention criteria: cadres found it difficult to assess to what extent a suspect presented "possible danger to social order."[67] To clarify, the municipal government deleted the "possible" qualifier and circulated a dozen examples to illustrate. In the category of those "who do not labor and habitually beg for a living," for instance, Fu Zongming was classified as a "vagrant." He was twenty-seven *sui*, a native of Chong-ming County (an island just north of Shanghai), described as "without occupation" (*wuye*) and an orphan beggar since childhood. Fu arrived in Shanghai in 1950 and sold street food for two years, and then "continued to drift about and beg for a living." By contrast, twenty-three *sui* Tang Jinfang was the counterexample, someone who was "not a vagrant." A native of Shanghai's Jiangwan district, he was one of the "urban poor" (*chengshi pinmin*) who worked as an itinerant peddler and relied primarily on government relief to survive. Although Tang had been caught begging once, his status as a city resident absolved him of the charge of vagrancy.[68] These calibrations of social danger underscore how "urban poverty" and "vagrancy" were evolving as political concepts in the early 1950s, as officials experimented with different ways of delineating the boundaries of social belonging in the city. What was at stake was the exclusion of interlopers from access to welfare benefits earmarked for urban residents, and the criminalization of "vagrants" and others who resisted the ideological project of labor reform.

Guilty of Indigence

In the early years of the People's Republic, the Communist regime thus found itself confronting an acute problem of urban transiency, just as its predecessors had throughout the twentieth century. To be sure, fundamental ideological differences underpinned the regime's vision of a new socialist state and society. Yet the tactical methods PRC officials used to address vagrancy and homelessness, and the assumptions that informed their actions, bear striking similarities not only to Nationalist institutions but also to Yuan Shikai's 1905 experimental workhouses and the International Settlement's Salvation Army Beggar Camp from 1941. One shared premise was the belief that while external circumstances reduced innumerable people to economic impoverishment, internal moral weakness caused some of them to *choose* a life of "vagrancy." The source of this character flaw was widely perceived to be rooted in the inflammatory combination of indolence and insubordination. Therefore, policing the distinction between the working and nonworking poor hinged on separating "idlers" and "vagrants" from the merely unemployed or the truly needy. In this sense, the CCP's disparagement of "social parasites" echoed sentiments first expressed by sociologists in the early 1920s, and subsequently ingrained in GMD productivism. After all, the critique that charged capitalists with subsisting on the fruits of other people's labor could also be directed at "beggars" who depended on handouts, and "vagrants" who stole or extorted alms through intimidation.

A second point of commonality between the CCP and its predecessors was the belief in the transformative power of labor. Like the administrators of the Shanghai Vagrant Workhouse in 1929 and the Beijing Municipal Relief Home in 1946, the Communist regime sought to create new citizens out of "useless" people, and in the process, transform beggars and vagrants into productive bodies for the service of the state and society. This vision of citizenship bestowed neither political nor civil nor social rights. It defined the relationship between citizens and the nation-state as one of labor extraction, and its purpose was to impose the disciplinary and coercive force of state power upon one segment of the indigent population. Viewed positively, the mantle of citizenship would return those wandering aimlessly outside of society to the embrace of the nation.

As we have seen, however, these grandiose visions proved to be elusive, if not altogether bankrupt. Aspirations for rehabilitation through labor repeatedly faltered at even the most basic level of providing adequate food and shelter to the inmates. Efforts to classify and organize the "urban poor" into discrete categories—refugees, vagrants, beggars, and so on—failed to recognize poverty as a continuum of misery. This myopia meant that time and again, by their own admission the authorities arrested the "wrong" kinds of people. Institutions aimed at enforcing labor discipline found that they could not separate their inmates into comprehensible groups and apply the proper doses of punishment and education. Caught within their own contradictions, many Republican-era workhouses were also trapped in the administrative vacuum of regime changes and political instability. Through sheer neglect, and relying on funding that evaporated with the demise of each government, institutions that sought to transform "parasites" into "producers" degenerated into prisons of disease and starvation. As we have seen, cataclysmic events—in the form of civil wars, natural disasters, invasion, and occupation—ruptured the sociological thinking about "poverty" that informed their operations. Despite incontrovertible evidence of failure, however, many of these institutions carried on, propelled by the logic of their own existence. Some were resurrected again and again, with the same bricks and mortar, at the very same locations. But however flawed, we also saw that workhouses and poorhouses concurrently served charitable functions, as asylums of last resort for those with nowhere else to turn. Given the intermingling of punitive and charitable impulses with often deplorable conditions, it is not easy to gauge the desirability of entering these institutions for those on the outside.

Lastly, throughout the first half of the twentieth century, interventions targeting the urban homeless were particularly focused on controlling the disorder they represented. Mostly young and male, "vagrants" displaced from family networks and community surveillance were prime suspects of latent criminality. Their social danger stemmed from their apparent mobility and perceived insubordination. *Bu anfen* and *bu an benfen* (literally, not content with one's place), phrases often used to describe "vagrants," suggest that the source of such insubordination was the refusal to endure fate and accept one's lot in life. They openly flouted social norms and the law, expressing their defiance and discontent through a life of itinerancy and "parasitic" dependency. But until the PRC of the late 1950s, no Chinese state was strong enough or organized enough to compel all of these "incorrigibles" to participate in the intended project of labor discipline. As we have seen, the kinds of "poor people" found at Nationalist-era workhouses were often the least able to work—the very old, the very young, the sick, the addicts—dooming the productive mission, sometimes at the very outset.

From the perspective of the urban poor and homeless, their misery and suffering were rooted in multiple displacements: physical displacement from shelter, social displacement from kinship ties so crucial in Chinese society, emotional displacement from one's native place and a place to call home. For orphans, abandoned children, demobilized soldiers, refugees from war and famine, and countless others who drifted in and out of China's cities, destitution was synonymous with being without a place. They often described themselves as "homeless drifters" (*liuli shisuo*), literally people who wander about because they have lost their "place." To cope with these dislocations, groups of refugees and straw hut dwellers banded together to claim a place and make homes for themselves, whether in makeshift shacks or in coffin repositories. These accommodations provided not only shelter for their occupants but also a place of belonging. In a time when homelessness could be a crime, and government relief entailed the deprivation of liberty and family separation, having a place to call home was crucial to self-determination. As we have seen from the letters that shantytown residents wrote, many were emboldened to fight for their homes, translating their plight into community action. In asserting that they were entitled to shelter, freedom, and a minimum standard of living, they made powerful claims for social inclusion. In their own words, the remarkable records that the urban poor left behind reveal the range of problems they confronted, their resourcefulness in coping with often desperate circumstances, and the struggle for survival in a time of profound social and political upheaval.

Guilty of Indigence has tried to bring these struggles to life, and to suggest that "the poor" were more than bit players in the drama of China's history in the early twentieth century. In tracing the shifting contours of "poverty," and well-intentioned but disastrous efforts to confine "the poor" and put them to work, I have underscored how ideologies, institutions, and practices intersected with shattering historical events to produce an extractive form of social citizenship and different forms of criminality. Throughout the decades covered in this study, "poverty" was widely perceived to be a pervasive social problem. Yet it remained constantly elusive, resistant to coherent definition and intervention.

Today, as the rising tide of prosperity in contemporary Chinese society produces sharp new patterns of inequality and homelessness, questions about public concern and indifference, entitlement and responsibility for poor relief have once again surfaced as vital social issues. The Minimum Livelihood Guarantee, a national law passed in 1999, now provides means-tested assistance to urban residents whose household income falls below a threshold determined by local living standards. But as Dorothy Solinger has argued, the implementation of the law has had the effect of creating a permanent underclass, "socially marginalised and excluded ... the effectual detritus of the country's modern, metropolitan development."[69] In 2003, the death of Sun Zhigang in a "detention and repatriation center" shocked the nation. A college graduate mistakenly identified as a "vagrant," Sun died while in the custody of Guangzhou police, beaten to death by other inmates. The ensuing controversy and public outcry led to the abolition of the detention-repatriation system. But the presence of more than one hundred million migrant workers (the "floating population") and the increasing visibility of mendicancy in China's wealthiest cities have engendered a strident discourse linking "the poor" to "social parasitism" and criminality. "McRefugees" are the new urban homeless, migrants unable to afford housing in China's glittering metropolises, who spend night after night sleeping in twenty-four-hour fast food restaurants.[70] I hope that this book has provided a historical lens for understanding these continuing contestations over the meanings of poverty and welfare in Chinese society, where enduring questions about the boundaries of social belonging are being negotiated in a different social and political context.

Notes

INTRODUCTION

1. Beijing Municipal Archive (hereafter BMA), J181-19-35442, 2, 7–8, 10–11.

2. Robert Culp, *Articulating Citizenship: Civic Education and Student Politics in Southeastern China, 1912–1940* (Cambridge, Mass.: Harvard University Asia Center, 2007). See also Henrietta Harrison, *The Making of the Republican Citizen: Political Ceremonies and Symbols in China, 1911–1929* (New York: Oxford University Press, 2000); Andrew Morris, *The Marrow of the Nation: A History of Sport and Physical Culture in Republican China* (Berkeley: University of California Press, 2004); Karl Gerth, *China Made: Consumer Culture and the Creation of the Nation* (Cambridge, Mass.: Harvard University Asia Center, 2003).

3. E.g., Ryan Dunch, *Fuzhou Protestants and the Making of a Modern China, 1857–1927* (New Haven, Conn.: Yale University Press, 2001); Michael Tsin, *Nation, Governance, and Modernity in China: Canton, 1900–1927* (Stanford: Stanford University Press, 1999); Bryna Goodman, *Native Place, City, and Nation: Regional Networks and Identities in Shanghai, 1853–1937* (Berkeley: University of California Press, 1995).

4. Merle Goldman and Elizabeth Perry, "Introduction: Political Citizenship in Modern China," in *Changing Meanings of Citizenship in Modern China*, ed. Merle Goldman and Elizabeth Perry (Cambridge, Mass.: Harvard University Press, 2002), 3.

5. Dorothy Solinger, *Contesting Citizenship in Urban China: Peasants, Migrants, the State, and the Logic of the Market* (Berkeley: University of California Press, 1999).

6. T. H. Marshall, *Citizenship and Social Class and Other Essays* (Cambridge: Cambridge University Press, 1950).

7. Bryan S. Turner, "Contemporary Problems in the Theory of Citizenship," in *Citizenship and Social Theory*, ed. Bryan S. Turner (London: Sage, 1993). On "society" as a new concept in China, see Michael Tsin, "Imagining 'Society' in Early Twentieth-Century China," in *Imagining the People: Chinese Intellectuals and the Concept of Citizenship, 1890–1920*, ed. Joshua A. Fogel and Peter G. Zarrow (Armonk, N.Y.: M.E. Sharpe, 1997), 212–31.

8. Thomas Sokoll provides a thoughtful discussion of the possibilities and limits of sources that record "the words of the poor" (*Essex Pauper Letters, 1731–1837* [Oxford: Oxford University Press, 2001], 3–9). See also Peter Brown, *Poverty and Leadership in the Later Roman Empire* (Hanover, N.H.: University Press of New England, 2002), 68–88.

9. E.g., Paul Slack, *Poverty and Policy in Tudor and Stuart England* (London: Longman, 1988); A. L. Beier, *Masterless Men: The Vagrancy Problem in England, 1560–1640* (London: Methuen, 1985); Brodwyn Fischer, *A Poverty of Rights: Citizenship and In-*

equality in Twentieth-Century Rio de Janeiro (Stanford: Stanford University Press, 2008); Michael B. Katz, *The Price of Citizenship: Redefining the American Welfare State* (Philadelphia: University of Pennsylvania Press, 2008).

10. James Boswell, *The Life of Samuel Johnson, LL.D.*, 4th ed. (London, 1804), II:129; Katz, *Price of Citizenship*, 341.

11. Liang Qizi "'Pinqiong' yu 'qiongren' guannian zai Zhongguo sushi shehui zhong de lishi yanbian" (The historical evolution of the concepts of 'poverty' and 'the poor' in Chinese popular society), in *Renguan yiyi yu shehui* (Perspectives, meanings, and society), ed. Huang Yinggui (Taibei: Institute of Ethnology, Academia Sinica, 1993), 129–57; Joanna Handlin Smith, *The Art of Doing Good: Charity in Late Ming China* (Berkeley: University of California Press, 2009).

12. Philip Kuhn, "Chinese Views of Social Classification," in *Class and Social Stratification in Post-Revolutionary China*, ed. James L. Watson (New York: Cambridge University Press, 1984), 16–28.

13. Susan Naquin, *Peking: Temples and City Life, 1400–1900* (Berkeley: University of California Press, 2000), 639.

14. The phrase comes from *The Classic of Rituals* and *The Mencius* (*Liji*, chapter 5, Wangzhi; *Mengzi*, Lianghuiwang xia).

15. *Qing shilu, Shunzhi* (Veritable records of the Qing dynasty, Shunzhi reign), 5:11–12 (repr., Beijing: Zhonghua shuju, 1985, 3:62); *Da Qing huidian shili* (Collected statutes of the Qing dynasty) (1899; repr., Beijing: Zhonghua shuju, 1991), 269:72; *Hubu zeli* (Board of Revenue regulations and precedents) (1865), 90:1–12 and 19b–52. By the eighteenth century, there was a network of shelters (temporary and permanent) and soup kitchens, supported by government funds and local contributions (Lillian Li, *Fighting Famine in North China: State, Market, and Environmental Decline, 1690s–1990s* [Stanford: Stanford University Press, 2007], 233–36).

16. Philip Kuhn, *Soulstealers: The Chinese Sorcery Scare of 1768* (Cambridge, Mass.: Harvard University Press, 1990); Matthew Sommer, *Sex, Law, and Society in Late Imperial China* (Stanford: Stanford University Press, 2000).

17. *Baojia shu jiyao* (Summary of baojia regulations), comp. Xu Dong (1868), 2:34a; David Schak, *A Chinese Beggars' Den: Poverty and Mobility in an Underclass Community* (Pittsburgh: University of Pittsburgh Press, 1988), 19–21. By all accounts, the *baojia* system's effectiveness had declined by the nineteenth century, if not earlier.

18. Pierre-Etienne Will, *Bureaucracy and Famine in Eighteenth-Century China* (Stanford: Stanford University Press, 1990), 38–49, 226–27.

19. Ibid., 258–61. The earliest references to *yigong daizhen* date to the Song dynasty (L. S. Yang, "Economic Justification for Spending—An Uncommon Idea in Traditional China," *Harvard Journal of Asiatic Studies* 20 [1957], 45–47).

20. William Rowe, *Hankow: Commerce and Society in a Chinese City, 1796–1889* (Stanford: Stanford University Press, 1984) and *Hankow: Conflict and Community in a Chinese City, 1796–1895* (Stanford: Stanford University Press, 1989); Mary Backus Rankin, *Elite Activism and Political Transformation in China: Zhejiang, 1865–1911* (Stanford: Stanford University Press, 1986).

21. E.g., Kristin Stapleton, *Civilizing Chengdu: Chinese Urban Reform, 1895–1937* (Cambridge, Mass.: Harvard University Press, 2000); Qin Shao, *Culturing Modernity: The Nantong Model, 1890–1930* (Stanford: Stanford University Press, 2004); David

Strand, *Rickshaw Beijing: City People and Politics in the 1920s* (Berkeley: University of California Press, 1989); Xiaoqun Xu, *Chinese Professionals and the Republican State: The Rise of Professional Associations in Shanghai, 1912–1937* (Cambridge: Cambridge University Press, 2000); Caroline Reeves, "The Power of Mercy: The Chinese Red Cross Society, 1900–1937" (Ph.D. diss., Harvard University, 1998); Dunch, *Fuzhou Protestants*; Goodman, *Native Place*.

22. Ian Hacking, "Making Up People," in *Reconstructing Individualism: Autonomy, Individuality, and the Self in Western Thought*, ed. Thomas Heller, et al. (Stanford: Stanford University Press, 1986), 222–36; "Making Up People," *London Review of Books* 28:16 (August 17, 2006), 23–26.

23. Notable recent works include Leo Ou-fan Lee, *Shanghai Modern: The Flowering of a New Urban Culture in China, 1930–1945* (Cambridge, Mass.: Harvard University Press, 1999); Gerth, *China Made*; Wen-hsin Yeh, *Shanghai Splendor: Economic Sentiments and the Making of Modern China, 1843–1949* (Berkeley: University of California Press, 2007).

24. Interest in the topic began in the 1990s, when the "floating population" of rural migrants first garnered attention as an increasingly disruptive presence in Chinese cities. Examples include Qu Yanbin, *Zhongguo qigai shi* (A history of Chinese beggars) (Shanghai: Shanghai wenyi, 1990); Ren Jian and Lei Fang, *Zhongguo gaibang* (Chinese beggar gangs) (Nanjing: Jiangsu guji, 1993); Wang Xuetai, *Youmin wenhua yu Zhongguo shehui* (Vagrant culture and Chinese society) (Beijing: Xueyuan, 1999).

25. Hanchao Lu, *Street Criers: A Cultural History of Chinese Beggars* (Stanford: Stanford University Press, 2005). David Schak's *A Chinese Beggars' Den* is based on anthropological fieldwork conducted in the 1970s in Taiwan.

26. Julia Strauss, *Strong Institutions in Weak Polities: State Building in Republican China, 1927–1940* (New York: Oxford University Press, 1998); Terry Bodenhorn, ed., *Defining Modernity: Guomindang Rhetorics of a New China, 1920–1970* (Ann Arbor: Center for Chinese Studies, University of Michigan, 2002); Margherita Zanasi, *Saving the Nation: Economic Modernity in Republican China* (Chicago: University of Chicago Press, 2006).

27. Lloyd Eastman, *Seeds of Destruction: Nationalist China in War and Revolution, 1937–1949* (Stanford: Stanford University Press, 1984); Morris Bian, *The Making of the State Enterprise System in Modern China: The Dynamics of Institutional Change* (Cambridge, Mass.: Harvard University Press, 2005); Stephen MacKinnon, *Wuhan, 1938: War, Refugees, and the Making of Modern China* (Berkeley: University of California Press, 2008).

28. Zwia Lipkin, *Useless to the State: "Social Problems" and Social Engineering in Nationalist Nanjing, 1927–1937* (Stanford: Stanford University Press, 2006), 11–15.

CHAPTER 1

1. The Eight Banners was the multiethnic military-administrative organization of the Qing dynasty. An imperial decree in 1644 ordered the residential segregation of the banners in the Inner City, with each occupying a defined residential zone. Nonbanners were relocated to the Outer City (Naquin, *Peking*, 290–94). On the fate of the banners

in the twentieth century, see Edward Rhoads, *Manchus & Han: Ethnic Relations and Political Power in Late Qing and Early Republican China, 1861–1928* (Seattle: University of Washington Press, 2000).

2. Today, many courtyard homes in the East City have been restored. It has become a trendy area, popular with young expatriates. Visitors seeking a taste of "old Beijing" can take pedicab tours of the neighborhoods.

3. In the 1920s, soup kitchens in Beijing fed approximately thirty to forty thousand people a day in the winter months, funded by the Capital Police, the Military Garrison, the Interior Ministry, county governments, and private charities. See Second Historical Archive, Nanjing (hereafter NJ), 1024-419, 1024-420, 1001-1792; Liu Xilian, *Beijing cishan huibian* (A collection of materials on charities in Beijing) (Beijing, 1923), 46–50.

4. "Chicken feather inns" were hostels for itinerants, so named for bedding stuffed with chicken feathers (Qi Rushan, *Gudu sanbai liushi hang* [360 trades of the old capital] [Beijing: Shumu wenxian, 1993]), 66–67.

5. "Lunpin yu yu zhi yinguo" (A discussion of the causes and effects of poverty and ignorance), *Dongfang zazhi* (Eastern Miscellany) 1:2 (April 1904), *sheshuo*, 40.

6. Feng Guifen, "Zhi yangqi yi" (On manufacturing western technology), in *Jiao-binlu kangyi* (Protests from the study of Jiaobin) (Xuehai, 1897 edition), 71a.

7. Zheng Guanying, "Yiyuan, shang" (On parliament, part I), *Shengshi weiyan* (1894 edition), in *Zheng Guanying ji*, vol. 1 (Shanghai: Renmin, 1982), 314. On the concept of commercial warfare, see Yeh, *Shanghai Splendor*, 17–24.

8. Paul Cohen, *Between Tradition and Modernity: Wang T'ao and Reform in Late Qing China* (Cambridge, Mass.: Council on East Asian Studies, Harvard University, 1974).

9. Wang Tao, "Zhong min shang" (The importance of the people, part I), in *Taoyuan wenlu waibian* (1897; repr., Zhengzhou: Zhongzhou guji, 1998), 60. Vagrants (游民) and wicked people (莠民) are rendered in the same way in *pinyin*.

10. Joan Judge, *Print and Politics: "Shibao" and the Culture of Reform in Late Qing China* (Stanford: Stanford University Press, 1996); Rebecca Karl and Peter Zarrow, eds., *Rethinking the 1898 Reform Period: Political and Cultural Change in Late Qing China* (Cambridge, Mass.: Harvard University Asia Center, 2002).

11. Yan Fu, "Yuan qiang" (On strength), in *Yan Fu wenxuan* (Selected writings of Yan Fu) (Shanghai: Shanghai yuandong, 1996), 15.

12. Yan Fu, "Yuan qiang xiuding gao" (Revised draft of "On strength"), in *Yan Fu wenxuan*, 27–28.

13. Yan Fu, "Yu Waijiaobao zhuren shu" (Letter to the editor of Diplomacy News), in *Yan Fu wenxuan*, 537.

14. Zhao Erxun, *Zhao liushou zhenglüe* (Summary of the administrative legacy of Zhao Erxun) (Ca. 1903), 7.

15. Hao Chang, *Liang Ch'i-ch'ao and Intellectual Transition in China, 1890–1907* (Cambridge, Mass.: Harvard University Press, 1971), 142–47.

16. W. Dean Kinzley, "Japan's Discovery of Poverty: Changing Views of Poverty and Social Welfare in the Nineteenth Century," *Journal of Asian History* 22:1 (1988), 1–24; James L. Huffman, *Creating a Public: People and Press in Meiji Japan* (Honolulu: University of Hawaii Press, 1997), 247–54; Hao Chang, *Liang Ch'i-ch'ao*, 132–33.

17. Liang Qichao, "Lun shengli fenli" (On production and consumption), *Xinmin congbao* (GX 28.10.1/October 31, 1902), 1–7. This essay can be found in reprints of Liang's collected works, as part of the "Xinmin shuo" series.

18. On Yan Fu's translation of *The Wealth of Nations*, see Benjamin Schwartz, *In Search of Wealth and Power: Yen Fu and the West* (Cambridge, Mass.: Belknap, 1964). A recent detailed study is Lai Jiancheng, *Yadang Shimisi yu Yan Fu: Guofu lun yu Zhongguo* (Adam Smith and Yan Fu: *The Wealth of Nations* and China) (Taibei: Sanmin, 2002).

19. Liang also elaborated on issues of political economy in "Shengjixue xueshuo yan'ge xiaoshi" (A short history of the evolution of economics), in *Yinbingshi wenji* (Taibei: Taiwan Zhonghua shuju, 1960), 5:1–61.

20. Fukuzawa Yukichi, *Fukuo jiden* (The autobiography of Fukuzawa Yukichi), *Fukuzawa Yukichi zenshu* (Tokyo: Iwanami Shoten, 1958), 7:213; "Nippon fujin ron" (On Japanese women), *Fukuzawa Yukichi zenshu*, 5:452; "Gakumon no susume" (An encouragement of learning), *Fukuzawa Yukichi zenshu*, 3:36–37.

21. Margherita Zanasi, "Fostering the People's Livelihood: Chinese Political Thought between Empire and Nation," *Twentieth-Century China* 30:1 (November 2004), 6–38.

22. Sun Wen (Sun Yat-sen), "Fakan ci" (Editorial introducing the inaugural issue), *Minbao* (People's Journal) 1 (November 26, 1905), 1–3.

23. Yun Bi (Huang Kan), "Ai pinmin" (Lamenting the poor), *Minbao* 17 (December 29, 1907), 25–32. Huang later taught at Beijing National University and universities in Wuchang and Nanjing.

24. Hygiene and disease were also salient metaphors for national deficiency, as Ruth Rogaski explains in *Hygienic Modernity: Meanings of Health and Disease in Treaty-Port China* (Berkeley: University of California Press, 2004).

25. Adam Smith, *An Inquiry into the Nature and Causes of the Wealth of Nations* (Dublin: N. Kelly, 1801), I:VIII, 72–73; Yan Fu, *Yuanfu* (*The Wealth of Nations*) (repr., Beijing: Shangwu, 1981), 1:64.

26. Paul Bailey, *Reform the People: Changing Attitudes towards Popular Education in Early Twentieth-Century China* (Vancouver: University of British Columbia Press, 1990), 110–15.

27. Angela Leung, "Relief Institutions for Children in Nineteenth-Century China," in *Chinese Views of Childhood*, ed. Anne Behnke Kinney (Honolulu: University of Hawaii Press, 1995), 251–78; Ruth Rogaski, "Beyond Benevolence: A Confucian Women's Shelter in Treaty-Port China," *Journal of Women's History* 8:4 (Winter 1997), 54–90.

28. Huang Zhonghui, "Niban Beijing shanhou gongyiju shuotie" (Proposal for establishing the Beijing Industrial Training Bureau) (1901), in *Beijing xinwen huibao* (News Magazine of Beijing) 3:1877–78; "Beijing gongyiju chuangban zhangcheng" (Beijing Industrial Training Bureau opening regulations), in Peng Zeyi, ed., *Zhongguo jindai shougong ye shi ziliao* (Source materials on the history of handicraft industries in modern China) (Beijing: Zhonghua shuju, 1984), 2:518.

29. Huang Zhonghui, "Niban Beijing," 1879–81; "Beijing gongyiju," 2:518–19. In 1904, the Training Bureau's products were included in China's vocational training exhibit at the World's Fair in St. Louis.

30. For a complete list of industrial centers established ca. 1904–11, see Peng Zeyi, *Zhongguo jindai shougong*, 2:515–76. The Qing court also created several handicrafts factories to provide job training for banner men and women (Teng Shaozhen, *Qingdai baqi zidi* [The descendents of the Eight Banners of the Qing dynasty] [Beijing: Zhongguo huaqiao, 1989], 341).

31. "Jiangxi xunfu Li Xingrui zoushe gongyi yuan yisuo" (Jiangxi Governor Li Xing-

rui memorializes on the establishment of an industrial training center) (February 1902), in Peng Zeyi, *Zhongguo jindai shougong*, 2:539.

32. Peng Zeyi, *Zhongguo jindai shougong*, 2:553–54. For other examples see *Dongfang zazhi* 1:1 (March 1904), 6 (Zhangjiakou, Zhili); *Dongfang zazhi* 2:7 (August 1905), 130 (Lianzhou, Guangdong).

33. Zhao Erxun, *Zhao liushou*, 5b–6. Zhao Erxun's brief tenure (five months) as Shanxi governor was most well known for his efforts to promote local self-government in the countryside (Roger Thompson, *China's Local Councils in the Age of Constitutional Reform, 1898–1911* [Cambridge, Mass.: Harvard University Press, 1995]).

34. Frank Dikötter, *Crime, Punishment and the Prison in Modern China* (New York: Columbia University Press, 2002), 54.

35. Zhang Zhidong, *Zhang Wenxiang gong (Zhidong) quanji zouyi* (The complete memorials of Zhang Zhidong) (Beijing, 1937), 53:13–20; Dikötter, *Crime, Punishment and the Prison*, 45.

36. Zhao Erxun memorial, *Guangxu chao donghua xulu* (Continuation of the Donghua lu, Guangxu reign) (Shanghai: Jicheng, 1909), 177:6–6b, 7b. Zhao proposed that inmates deemed "extremely stupid or wicked" be given hard labor, and the intractable ones "unwilling to submit" be flogged as punishment.

37. *Shuntian shibao* (Shuntian times), GX 28.11.28 (December 27, 1902), 1.

38. Sun Yidong, "Qingmo zuifan xiyisuo chuyi" (Initial views on late Qing criminal workhouses), in *Ming-Qing dang'an yu lishi yanjiu lunwen ji* (Beijing: Zhongguo youyi, 2000), 1300. For Yan Fu, the concept did not seem to register any specific meaning. In his translation of *The Wealth of Nations* he omitted a passing reference to "the workhouse" (*Yuanfu*, 1:64).

39. Dikötter translates *xiyisuo* as "house of hard labor," emphasizing its penal heritage. Klaus Mühlhahn renders it as "craft learning houses," underscoring its industrial training component (*Criminal Justice in China: A History* [Cambridge, Mass.: Harvard University Press, 2009], 82).

40. Zhao Erxun memorial, *Guangxu chao donghua xulu*, 177:7b.

41. "Xingbu yifu huli jinfu Zhao zouqing gesheng tongshe zuifang xiyisuo," in *Da Qing fagui daquan* (Complete laws and statutes of the Qing dynasty) (Taibei: Hongye, 1972), 10:3–4; Sun Yidong, "Qing mo zuifan," 1301; Dikötter, *Crime, Punishment and the Prison*, 46.

42. Sun Yidong, "Qing mo zuifan," 1301.

43. Yang Xinsheng, "Zhao Erxun yu Qingmo Hunan xinzheng" (Zhao Erxun and the New Policies in Hunan in the final years of the Qing dynasty), *Zhuzhou shifan gaodeng zhuanke xuexiao xuebao* 11:6 (December 2006), 71–78. Zhao remained in Hunan as governor for a little more than one year, then became Chief Minister of the Board of Revenue. Since he rapidly moved from post to post, Zhao did not have the opportunity to implement fully his proposed reforms in Shanxi or Hunan.

44. On Yuan Shikai's reforms in Zhili, see Stephen MacKinnon, *Power and Politics in Late Imperial China: Yuan Shi-kai in Beijing and Tianjin, 1901–1908* (Berkeley: University of California Press, 1980), 137–79; Thompson, *China's Local Councils*, 37–52.

45. Sun Xuemei, *Qingmo minchu Zhongguoren de Riben guan—yi Zhili sheng wei zhongxin* (Chinese views of Japan in the late Qing and early Republic—with Zhili province as the focus) (Tianjin: Renmin, 2001), 34–35.

46. Ling Fupeng, "Cheng jin jiang chaming Riben jianyu xiyi xiangxi qingxing" (Re-

port on the detailed situation of work training in Japan's prisons), in *Tianjin shi xiyisuo zhangcheng biaoce leizuan* (Compilation of regulations and documents for the Tianjin workhouse) (Tianjin, n.d. [ca. 1905]), 4–5.

47. Ibid., 6.

48. Daniel V. Botsman, *Punishment and Power in the Making of Modern Japan* (Princeton: Princeton University Press, 2005); *Penal Codes of France, Germany, Belgium and Japan* (Washington, D.C.: GPO, 1901), 146–47.

49. Sun Xuemei, *Qingmo minchu*, 51–55; Thompson, *China's Local Councils*, 44.

50. Tu Futian, *Dongying jianzhi lu* (A record of observations from Japan), 1906, 21–31, in *Riben zhengfa kaocha ji*, ed. Liu Yuzhen and Sun Xuemei (Shanghai: Shanghai guji, 2002), 135–37; Liu Xun, *Lingzhou youji* (Diary of travels to Japan), 1908, 30–31, in *Riben zhengfa kaocha ji*, 364–65; Sun Xuemei, *Qingmo minchu*, 103–7.

51. Dikötter, *Crime, Punishment and the Prison*, 34–40.

52. *Beiyang gongdu leizuan* 5:8b, 392.

53. *Dongfang zazhi* 1:1 (March 1904), 4.

54. *Beiyang gongdu leizuan* 5:8b, 392.

55. Rogaski, *Hygienic Modernity*, 175, 189.

56. *Yuan Shikai zouyi*, 3:1110. MacKinnon, *Power and Politics*, notes that construction of the proposed prison took three years, but the workhouse opened quickly (154).

57. *Tianjin shi xiyisuo zhangcheng biaoce leizuan*, 8; *Yuan Shikai zouyi*, 3:1110.

58. Mühlhahn, *Criminal Justice*, notes that many of the early criminal workhouses were housed in existing buildings and did not have specific architectural designs (82).

59. In 1670 the Kangxi Emperor issued sixteen maxims emphasizing obedience and hierarchy. His son the Yongzheng Emperor elaborated on the original points, and a vernacular version was read aloud twice a month throughout the empire (Victor Mair, "Language and Ideology in the Written Popularizations of the *Sacred Edict*," in *Popular Culture in Late Imperial China*, ed. David Johnson, Andrew J. Nathan, and Evelyn S. Rawski [Berkeley: University of California Press, 1985], 325–59).

60. "Tianjin jianyu xiyisuo banfa" (Administrative methods of the Tianjin Criminal Workhouse), *Dongfang zazhi* 3:2 (March 1906), 69–72. The methods of punishment were (in order of increasing severity) up to two months of standing in the corner for one-half the number of work hours and hard labor for the other half; one-third to one-half reduction in food for up to one month; solitary confinement in a "dark chamber" with reduced food rations for up to five nights.

61. *Yuan Shikai zouyi*, 3:1110. Yuan had hoped to establish five such institutions in Zhili. Due to insufficient funds, there was only one in Tianjin and one in Baoding (the provincial capital), with capacity for two hundred inmates in each.

62. *Beiyang gongdu leizuan* 5:27, 429.

63. Ibid., 429–33.

64. *Beiyang gongdu leizuan* 5:30, 435.

65. First Historical Archive, Beijing (hereafter FHA), 1501/8.

66. Punishment for convicts started from "hard labor" and ration reductions, and escalated to confinement in the "dark chamber" and shackles. Punishment for "poor inmates" included standing in the corner for several hours, a reduced number of holidays, ordinary solitary confinement, and expulsion (FHA 1501/8).

67. FHA 1501/8.

68. FHA 37/2 (127–28). In 1906–7 the average attendance in the workshops was 77

percent, based on a sample of daily reports. By 1909, the number of inmates had dwindled to about one hundred, but the average attendance in workshops increased to nearly 90 percent.

69. FHA 1501/8, 1906.

70. *Dongfang zazhi* 4:12 (January 1908), 559. This decree incorporated proposals from Shen Jiaben, Zhang Zhidong, and Liu Kunyi.

71. Mühlhahn, *Criminal Justice*, 28.

72. Michael Dutton, *Policing and Punishment in China: From Patriarchy to the People* (Cambridge: Cambridge University Press, 1992), 107–10.

73. Mühlhahn, *Criminal Justice*, 108–18; Timothy Brook, Jerome Bourgon, and Gregory Blue, *Death by a Thousand Cuts* (Cambridge, Mass.: Harvard University Press, 2008), 14–17, 203–21.

74. Peng Zeyi, *Zhongguo jindai shougong*, 2:533–38, 576.

75. *Dongfang zazhi* 2:11 (December 1905), 184–85.

76. *Beiyang gongdu leizuan* 5:36, 446–48.

77. Xia Dunfu memorial, *Guangxu chao donghua xulu*, 186:3b–4.

78. Board of Commerce memorial, *Guangxu chao donghua xulu*, 193:11b; BMA J181-25-8472, 31–34.

79. Wu Yinpei memorial, *Guangxu chao donghua xulu*, 193:2; Board of Commerce memorial, *Guangxu chao donghua xulu*, 193:11b; *Beijing shi zhigao* (Draft gazetteer of Beijing) (1939; repr., Beijing: Yanshan, 1998), 2:115–16, 126. On the early history of Pujitang and Gongdelin, see Naquin, *Peking*, 645–46.

80. FHA 28/1/43/13; *Beijing shi zhigao*, 2:116–18.

81. FHA 28/1/42/19, 28/1/42/31, 1501/260. A later memorial indicated that the Gongdelin Poorhouse followed the model of the Tianjin Criminal Workhouse, while the Pujitang Poorhouse was based on the Commerce Ministry's regulations for industrial training bureaus (FHA 1501/111).

82. *Dongfang zazhi* 4:10 (November 1907), 464–65; FHA 28/1 (44-37). One such venture, the Guajiatun Poorhouse (in the western suburbs), specifically modeled itself after Gongdelin. But the local gentry in charge found that they could not cobble together enough funds and turned it over to the Police Ministry (FHA 1501/10).

83. Xiliang, "Zou kaiban xiyisuo ji gexiang gongchang qingxing ze" (Memorial on establishing workhouses and the situation of various factories), (GX 33.1.19/March 3, 1907), in *Xi Qingbi zhijun zougao* (Taibei: Wenhai, 1974), 2:646–47. See also Di Wang, *Street Culture in Chengdu: Public Space, Urban Commoners, and Local Politics* (Stanford: Stanford University Press, 2003).

84. Lillian Li, *Fighting Famine*, 158–59.

85. See Rankin, *Elite Activism*; Goodman, *Native Place*.

86. In its early years, the Jiaoyangju developed a cooperative arrangement with the Tianjin Criminal Workhouse, whereby inmates sentenced to ten or more years were transferred to Tianjin's larger facility (BMA J181-25-8469, 27–31; J181-25-8470, 20–22). Under the Nationalist regime it was renamed the Ganhuasuo.

87. "Qingmo kaiban Jingshi Xiyisuo shiliao" (Historical materials on the Capital Workhouse established at the end of the Qing dynasty), *Lishi dang'an* 2 (1999), 73–74; "Waicheng Gongli Pinmin Yangjiyuan shiban zhangcheng" (Opening regulations of the Outer City Public Poorhouse), in *Qingmo Beijing chengshi guanli fagui* (Beijing's late Qing urban administration laws) (Beijing: Yanshan, 1996), 333–48.

88. *Dongfang zazhi* 4:10 (November 1907), 465; "Chuangban Jingshi Neicheng Pinmin Jiaoyangyuan zhangcheng" (Regulations for the establishment of the Capital Inner City Poorhouse) and "Neicheng Pinmin Jiaoyangyuan guanli guize" (Regulations of the Inner City Poorhouse), in *Qingmo Beijing chengshi guanli fagui*, 242, 262.

89. *Beijing shi zhigao*, 2:118–19; *Dongfang zazhi* 4:10 (November 1907), 465, 467.

90. Douglas Reynolds, *China, 1898–1912: The Xinzheng Revolution and Japan* (Cambridge, Mass.: Harvard University Press, 1993), 161–71.

91. Alison Dray-Novey, "Spatial Order and Police in Imperial Beijing," *Journal of Asian Studies* 52: 4 (November 1993), 885–922. Dray-Novey estimates that with a combined gendarmerie and banner force of 33,000 for one million residents, Beijing's ratio of one policeman for thirty inhabitants far exceeded the ratios for Paris (1:193), London (1:350), and New York (1:800) at roughly the same time (905).

92. In the eighteenth century, officials had also used travel money to disperse famine victims from the capital (Will, *Bureaucracy*, 229–35). On winter defense in the late nineteenth century, see Rowe, *Hankow: Conflict and Community*, 127–30, 229–30, 310–11.

93. MacKinnon, *Power and Politics*, 151–62; Strand, *Rickshaw Beijing*, 66–71. Strand notes conflicts between the new police and local magistrates, who resented this infringement on their authority.

94. "Weijing lü" (Police ordinances), *Da Qing fagui daquan*, 4:1–4, 1017–23.

95. FHA 28/1 (24-22); *Dongfang zazhi* 1:1 (March 1904), 4; *Dongfang zazhi* 2:10 (November 1905), 181–82.

96. Zou Yiren, *Jiu Shanghai renkou bianqian de yanjiu* (Research on population changes in old Shanghai) (Shanghai: Shanghai renmin, 1980), 90. The initial prohibition against Chinese residing in the concessions ended in 1873.

97. William Gascoyne-Cecil, *Changing China* (New York: Appleton, 1912), 104–5; Charles Dyce, *Personal Reminiscences of Thirty Years' Residence in the Model Settlement: Shanghai, 1870–1900* (London: Chapman & Hall, 1906), 48–51; Charles Ewart Darwent, *Shanghai: A Handbook for Travellers and Residents* (Shanghai: Kelly and Walsh, 1904), 103, 106, 112.

98. Gascoyne-Cecil, *Changing China*, 98–99.

99. Shanghai Municipal Council meeting minutes, December 15, 1856; January 9, 1861; July 16, 1862; December 31, 1863. Repr., *Gongbuju dongshihui huiyilu* (Shanghai: Shanghai guji, 2001), 1:87, 134, 296, 526.

100. Thomas B. Stephens, *Order and Discipline in China: The Shanghai Mixed Court, 1911–27* (Seattle: University of Washington Press, 1992). The French had a separate consular court.

101. *Land Regulations and Bye-Laws for the Foreign Settlements of Shanghai North of the Yang-King-Pang* (Shanghai, 1898), 43; *Shanhai kyodo sokai hoki zensho* (Complete laws of the Shanghai International Settlement) (Shanghai, 1926), 10; "Fazujie gongdongju zhangcheng" (Regulations of the French Concession Municipal Council), in *Shanghai zhinan* (Guide to Shanghai) (Shanghai: Shangwu, 1920), 2:28.

102. *Annual Report of the Shanghai Municipal Council, 1897*, 48. Before the establishment of the Municipal Gaol in 1897, Chinese offenders were put to work on chain gangs. At both the Municipal and French Gaols, profits from convict labor helped to subsidize the cost of maintaining the prisons (Anatol M. Kotenev, *Shanghai: Its Mixed Court and Council* [Shanghai: North-China Daily News & Herald, 1925], 45, 99;

Shanghai zujie zhi [Gazetteer of Shanghai's International Settlement] [Shanghai: Shanghai shehui kexue yuan, 2001], 306).

103. *Annual Report of the Shanghai Municipal Council, 1906*, 30–31.

104. Emily Honig, *Creating Chinese Ethnicity: Subei People in Shanghai, 1850–1980* (New Haven, Conn.: Yale University Press, 1992), 28–30; Elizabeth Perry, *Rebels and Revolutionaries in North China, 1845–1945* (Stanford: Stanford University Press, 1980), 10–47.

105. *North-China Herald*, October 5, 1906, 11.

106. Duanfang, *Duan Zhongmin gongzou gao* (Memorials of Duanfang) (repr., Taibei: Wenhai, 1967), 7:6b–7, 7:10b–11, 7:23b, 7:41b, 7:63.

107. *North-China Herald*, April 19, 1907, 148.

108. Duanfang, *Duan Zhongmin*, 7:28b–29.

109. Shanghai Municipal Council meeting minutes, November 13, 1907 (*Gongbuju dongshihui huiyilu*, 16:527); Dikötter, *Crime, Punishment and the Prison*, 103–4. After the murder of a British constable in 1907, the Consul-General appealed for an additional 250 Indians to join the municipal police (Despatch 29, FO 288/1667, March 13, 1907; in *Shanghai Political & Economic Reports, 1842–1943* [Slough, UK: Archive Editions, 2008], 381–83).

110. *The Municipal Gazette*, October 10, 1908, 257.

111. *North-China Herald*, October 17, 1908. The *North-China Herald* was the weekly digest edition of the *North-China Daily News*, Shanghai's most influential English-language publication.

112. Shanghai Municipal Council meeting minutes, May 1, 1907 (*Gongbuju dongshihui huiyilu*, 16:445).

113. Robert Bickers, *Britain in China: Community, Culture and Colonialism 1900–1949* (Manchester: Manchester University Press, 1999), 72–73, 103–4.

114. Eileen Scully, *Bargaining with the State from Afar: American Citizenship in Treaty Port China, 1844–1942* (New York: Columbia University Press, 2001), 93–95, 180–83.

115. *Annual Report of the Shanghai Municipal Council, 1909*, 43. In 1912, the Council finally acquiesced to the creation of a "casual ward for foreigners without employment."

116. Shanghai Municipal Council meeting minutes, March 15, 1905; June 14, 1905; July 22, 1908 (*Gongbuju dongshihui huiyilu*, 16:44, 98, 17:117).

117. *Dongfang zazhi* 2:10 (November 1905), 194; Mark Elvin, "The Gentry Democracy in Shanghai, 1905–1914" (Ph.D. diss., University of Cambridge, 1967), 45–46); Frederic Wakeman, Jr., *Policing Shanghai, 1927–37* (Berkeley: University of California Press, 1995), 21–22.

118. *Shanghai shi zizhi zhi* (Gazetteer of Shanghai self-government) (1915; repr., Taibei: Chengwen, 1974), 3:1030; *Shanghai xian xuzhi* (Shanghai county gazetteer, continued) (1918; repr., Taibei: Chengwen, 1970), 2:779–80.

119. *Zhengyi tongbao* 4 (March 25, 1906), 12–13; *Shanghai shi zizhi zhi*, 2:447–50. In neighboring counties (Jiading, Nanhui, Qingpu) "criminal workhouses" attached to prisons were established in 1909–10.

120. *Shanghai xian xuzhi*, 216–7; *Shanghai shi zizhi zhi*, 1:196, 2:435–38, 3:829.

121. *Shanghai Gu'eryuan baogao* (Shanghai Industrial Orphanage report) (ca. 1908), 7–8; *Shanghai Gu'eryuan baogao qingce* (Shanghai Industrial Orphanage report and ac-

counts) (1910), 1. Wang Yiting (1867–1938) was a banker and industrialist who played a prominent role (as founder or officer) in eighteen major charitable organizations in Shanghai. See Kuiyi Shen, "Wang Yiting in the Social Networks of 1910s–1930s Shanghai," in *At the Crossroads of Empires: Middlemen, Social Networks, and State-Building in Republican Shanghai*, ed. Nara Dillon and Jean Oi (Stanford: Stanford University Press, 2008), 45–64.

122. *Shanghai Gu'eryuan baogao*, 6, 18; *Shanghai Gu'eryuan baogao qingce*, 8.

123. Leung, "Relief Institutions," 251–78.

124. *Shanghai Gu'eryuan baogao*, 13; *Shanghai Gu'eryuan baogao qingce*, 6–7.

125. *Shanghai Gu'eryuan baogao*, 5, 28–30; *Shanghai Gu'eryuan baogao qingce*, 76, 78–79, 80–81.

126. *Shanghai Gu'eryuan baogao*, 30. When the orphanage's administrators discovered the truth, they made an exception and allowed the boy to stay.

127. Duanfang, *Duan Zhongmin*, 11:27–27b (repr., 3:1359–60). See also *Shibao* (Eastern times), January 11, 1910 and January 30, 1910, 1.

128. *Shanghai Pin'eryuan diyi ci baogao* (First report of the Shanghai Poor Children's Home), 1909, 1, 4, 18, 59.

129. Ibid., 15.

130. Ibid., 8, 13, 15–17, 59, 63.

131. Li Tinghan, *Pinmin jiaoyu tan* (A discussion of the education of the poor) (Shanghai: Jiaoyu zazhi she, 1911), jia:42. Li was the principal of a primary school for "poor children." Excerpts of the book were published in a major education journal.

132. In contrast, the English system of workhouses tried to discourage "pauperism" by making conditions therein as unappealing as possible, out of the conviction that those who accepted relief in the workhouse lacked the moral determination to survive outside. At the same time, those who entered did so freely, and could depart at will. In the eighteenth century there were frequent complaints that the poor would check themselves out on Sunday morning, spend the day at the pub, and check back in at night. See M. A. Crowther, *The Workhouse System, 1834–1929: The History of an English Social Institution* (Athens: University of Georgia Press, 1982).

133. The 1876 famine afflicted five provinces in north China; an estimated ten million people perished. See Kathryn Edgerton-Tarpley, *Tears from Iron: Cultural Responses to Famine in Nineteenth-Century China* (Berkeley: University of California Press, 2008).

134. "Lun pinyu yu zhi yinguo," *Dongfang zazhi* 1:2 (April 1904), 40.

CHAPTER 2

1. Shiyan (Chen Duxiu), "Pinmin de kusheng" (The laments of poor people), *Meizhou pinglun* (Weekly review) 19 (April 27, 1919), 2.

2. On sociology in China, see R. David Arkush, *Fei Xiaotong and Sociology in Revolutionary China* (Cambridge, Mass.: Harvard University Press, 1981); Yung-chen Chiang, *Social Engineering and the Social Sciences in China, 1919–1949* (New York: Cambridge University Press, 2001); Madeleine Yue Dong, *Republican Beijing: The City and Its Histories* (Berkeley: University of California Press, 2003), 211–45.

3. On the YMCA, see Shirley Garrett, *Social Reformers in Urban China: The Chinese Y.M.C.A., 1895–1926* (Cambridge, Mass.: Harvard University Press, 1970; Jun Xing,

Baptized in the Fire of Revolution: The American Social Gospel and the YMCA in China, 1919–1937 (Bethlehem, Pa.: Lehigh University Press, 1996).

4. John S. Burgess, "Beginnings of Social Investigation," *The Survey* (October 13, 1917), 41–43.

5. On the Social Service Club, see Chiang, *Social Engineering*, 28–37; Garrett, *Social Reformers*, 133–35. On the Community Service Groups, *Beijing difang ge fuwutuan baogao* (Report of each local community service group in Beijing) (Beijing, 1922).

6. Tao Menghe, "Beijing renli chefu zhi shenghuo qingxing" (The living situation of Beijing's rickshaw pullers), in *Menghe wencun* (Collected writings of Tao Menghe) (Shanghai: Yadong, 1926), 2:101–21.

7. Sidney Gamble's *Peking: A Social Survey* (New York: George H. Doran, 1921) was one of the first detailed surveys of Chinese urban life published in any language.

8. Hu Shi, "Yanjiu shehui wenti di fangfa" (Methods for studying social problems), *Dongfang zazhi* 17:13 (July 10, 1920), 113–14.

9. Qu Qiubai, "Xiandai shehuixue" (Sociology today), in *Shanghai daxue shiliao* (Historical materials on Shanghai University) (Shanghai: Fudan daxue, 1984), 326.

10. Tsin, "Imagining 'Society,'" 212–31.

11. Y. L. Tong (Tang Yueliang), "Social Conditions and Social Service Endeavor in Peking," *Chinese Social and Political Science Review* 7:3 (July 1922), 77; Tao Menghe, *Shehui wenti* (Social problem) (Shanghai: Shangwu, 1924), 175.

12. Tao Menghe, "Pinqiong yu renkou wenti" (Poverty and the problem of population), *Xin qingnian* (New youth) 7:4 (March 1920), 1.

13. Will, *Bureaucracy*, 98–99.

14. Although widely recognized as imprecise, many analysts cited the Beijing police department's figures (L. K. Tao [Tao Menghe], *Livelihood in Peking: An Analysis of the Budgets of Sixty Families* [Peking, 1928], 19; Gamble, *Peking*, 270; Y. L. Tong, "Social Conditions," 79).

15. "Benshi jipin hukou tongji" (Statistics on Shanghai's very poor households), *Shenbao*, December 26, 1928, 15.

16. Tao Menghe, *Shehui wenti*, 146–48; C. G. Dittmer, "An Estimate of the Standard of Living in China," *Quarterly Journal of Economics* 33 (November 1918), 107–28; J. B. Tayler, "The Study of Chinese Rural Economy: The Results of the Famine Commission's Investigations," Part II, *The Chinese Social and Political Science Review* 8:2 (April 1924), 252–55; Leonard Hsu, "The Problem of Poverty in China," *China Outlook* 1:3 (February 1, 1928), 2–5.

17. Gamble, *Peking*, 270. Gamble noted that these figures significantly underestimated the extent of poverty, as the police forced the destitute to leave the city. Most of them congregated in the suburbs and were not included in the data.

18. L. K. Tao, *Livelihood in Peking*, 19. The census identified 16.8 percent of families as "destitute" ("absolutely penniless"); 9.2 percent as "poor" ("incomes are insufficient even for bare subsistence"); and 47.3 percent as "the lower middle" (people with incomes "narrowly sufficient to cover their daily living expenses").

19. Tao Menghe, *Shehui wenti*, 124–25, 145–48; Qu Shiying, "Pin de yanjiu" (Research on poverty), *Xin shehui* (New Society) 6 (December 21, 1919), 2.

20. One of Tao's studies in fact demonstrated that the families receiving relief were not necessarily the ones with the lowest incomes (L. K. Tao, *Livelihood in Peking*, 20).

21. Tao Menghe, *Shehui wenti*, 125, 145; Ishii Yosaburo, "Pinkun lun" (On destitution), trans. Lu Shangtong, *Dongfang zazhi* 9:3 (September 10, 1912), 4.

22. Yu Ende, "Shehui ge'an fuwu zhi yanjiu yu Zhongguo" (Research on social casework and China), *Shehui xuejie* 1 (June 1927), 184; Tao Menghe, *Shehui wenti*, 144.

23. On the global interest in Neo-Malthusianism and population control in the 1920s, see Matthew Connelly, *Fatal Misconceptions: The Struggle to Control World Population* (Cambridge, Mass.: Belknap, 2008).

24. Gu Mengyu, "Renkou wenti, shehui wenti de suoyue" (The population problem—The key to social problems), *Xin qingnian* 7:4 (March 1920), 1. From 1906 to 1911 Gu studied at the University of Leipzig and Berlin University. He was part of the left-wing faction of the GMD and later a member of the Central Executive Committee.

25. Chen Duxiu, "Ma'ersaisi renkou lun yu Zhongguo renkou wenti" (Malthus's population theory and China's population problem), *Xin qingnian* 7:4 (March 1920), 2, 7–8.

26. Tao Menghe, "Pinqiong yu renkou wenti," 14.

27. Shortly thereafter, Shanghai's pharmacies reportedly enjoyed a brisk business importing contraceptive devices (Xie Yuanfan, *Xiandai pinglun* [Contemporary Review] 3:62 [February 13, 1926], 18). On the "Sanger effect," see Hiroko Sakamoto, "The Cult of 'Love and Eugenics' in May Fourth Movement Discourse," *positions* 12:2 (Fall 2004), 346–48.

28. Margaret Sanger, *Margaret Sanger: An Autobiography* (New York: Norton, 1938), 341–42. In 1915 Sanger's husband was arrested in New York for distributing this pamphlet, which frankly describes birth control techniques.

29. "Ying Shan Ge'er Furen" (Welcome Mrs. Sanger), *Funü zazhi* (Ladies' journal) 8:6 (June 1922), 2.

30. Sun Zhongshan (Sun Yat-sen), *Sanmin zhuyi* (Three principles of the people) (Taibei: Zhongyang wenwu gongyingshe, 1963), 18.

31. *Xiandai pinglun* 3:62 (February 13, 1926), 19–20; 3:72 (April 24, 1926), 20. This was a posthumous debate, following Sun's death in March 1925.

32. *Xiandai pinglun* 3:73 (May 1, 1926), 12–13; 3:76 (May 22, 1926), 20. In a later column Chen wrote that everyone, not just the poor, should practice birth control. Intelligence was not necessarily inherited, so intellectuals and the wealthy did not automatically produce "superior stock" (3:74 [May 8, 1926], 6–8).

33. Frank Dikötter, *Imperfect Conceptions: Medical Knowledge, Birth Defects and Eugenics in China* (London: Hurst, 1998), 105–6.

34. T. S. (Chen Duxiu), "Renkou lun de xueshuo bianqian" (A history of the development of population theories), *Xin qingnian* 7:4 (March 1920), 36.

35. Gu Mengyu, "Renkou wenti, shehui wenti de suoyue," 10, 13–14.

36. Samuel Haber, *Efficiency and Uplift: Scientific Management in the Progressive Era, 1890–1920* (Chicago: University of Chicago Press, 1964), ix–x; William Tsutsui, *Manufacturing Ideology: Scientific Management in Twentieth-Century Japan* (Princeton: Princeton University Press, 1998), 8, 10.

37. "Increasing Personal Efficiency," *Jinbu zazhi* (Progress) 3 (January 1912), 6–7; "The Efficiency Club," *Shanghai qingnian* (Shanghai young men) (February 2, 1917), 2.

38. Meng Xiancheng, "Rensheng xiaoshuai zengjia shuo" (On increasing human efficiency), *Qinghua xuebao* 3:2 (January 1918), in *Dongfang zazhi* 15:5 (May 15, 1918), 163–66.

39. Tao Menghe, "Pinqiong yu renkou wenti," *Menghe wencun*, 1:106.

40. Zhou Jianren, "Shanzhong xue de lilun yu shishi" (The principles and implemen-

tation of eugenics), *Dongfang zazhi* 18:2 (January 1921), 56, 59; "Du Zhongguo zhi yousheng wenti" (Reflections on "The question of eugenics in China") *Dongfang zazhi* 22:8 (April 25, 1925), 15–16, 20.

41. Common variations include *jiyang de ren* (paupers), *jisheng dongwu* (parasitic animals), *jisheng shenghuo* (parasitic lives).

42. Gertrude Himmelfarb, *The Idea of Poverty: England in the Early Industrial Age* (New York: Knopf, 1984); Olwen Hufton, *The Poor of Eighteenth-Century France, 1750–1789* (Oxford: Clarendon, 1974); Michael B. Katz, *In the Shadow of the Poorhouse: A Social History of Welfare in America* (New York: Basic Books, 1996).

43. Bridie Andrews, "Tuberculosis and the Assimilation of Germ Theory in China, 1895–1937," *Journal of the History of Medicine and Allied Sciences* 52 (1997), 124–26.

44. Franklin Giddings, *The Principles of Sociology* (New York: Macmillan, 1896), 127. The translation by Wu Jianchang (*Shehui xue yuanli*) is no longer extant. Wu's source was Ichikawa Genzo's *Shakaigaku teiko*.

45. Bridie Andrews, "The Making of Modern Chinese Medicine, 1895–1937" (Ph.D. diss., University of Cambridge, 1996), 223–56; Philip Cousland, *An English-Chinese Lexicon of Medical Terms* (Shanghai: Medical Missionary Association of China, 1908), 266–71; "Putong jiaoyu shang zhi shengwu xue" (The study of biology in ordinary education), *Jiaoyu zazhi* (Education journal) 2:10 (November 11, 1910), 43–50.

46. Kawakami Hajime, "Gongtong shenghuo yu jisheng shenghuo," translated in *Dongfang zazhi* 10:12 (June 1, 1914), 40–42; "Gongtong shenghuo ji jisheng shenghuo," translated in *Jiefang yu gaizao* (Emancipation and reconstruction semi-monthly) 1:1 (September 1, 1919), 68–72.

47. Charles Ellwood, *Shehuixue ji xiandai shehui wenti*, trans. Zhao Zuoxiong (Shanghai: Shangwu, 1920). Ellwood's *An Introduction to Social Psychology* appeared in a Chinese translation in 1921, followed by *The Social Problem: A Constructive Analysis* in 1922 and *Cultural Evolution* in 1933.

48. *Xin qingnian* 3:2 (April 1, 1917), 1; Zheng Zhenduo, *Xin shehui* 15 (March 21, 1920), 11–12. The Journal of the Young China Association (*Shaonian Zhongguo*) published one chapter in its entirety (1:10 [April 15, 1920], 19–36).

49. Charles Ellwood, *Sociology and Modern Social Problems* (New York: American Book Company, 1910), 283, 286, 300–308.

50. Paul B. Trescott, *Jingji Xue: The History of the Introduction of Western Economic Ideas into China, 1850–1950* (Hong Kong: Chinese University Press, 2007).

51. Jite (Charles Gide), "Shehui de jisheng wu" (Society's parasites), translated in *Dongfang zazhi* 20:19 (October 10, 1923), 62–70.

52. Charles Gide, "Shehui de jisheng" (Society's parasites), in *Xiezuo* (Cooperation), trans. Lou Tongsun (Shanghai: Shangwu, 1927), 355. Lou Tongsun was Gide's student and later assumed high-level positions in the GMD government.

53. Yu Ende, "Shehui ge'an fuwu zhi yanjiu yu Zhongguo," 184.

54. Qu Shiying, "Pin de yanjiu," 2; "Zhongguo ren de liedian" (The shortcomings of the Chinese people), *Xin shehui* 1 (November 1, 1919), 1; *Xin qingnian* 1:3 (November 15, 1915), 235.

55. Rhoads, *Manchus*, explains that in the final years of the Qing and in the early Republic, "the Manchus" became synonymous with Bannermen of all ethnic backgrounds (18–20, 67–68).

56. Ibid., 16; Y. L. Tong, "Social Conditions," 78; Gamble, *Peking*, 273.

57. Ming K. Chan and Arif Dirlik, *Schools into Fields and Factories: Anarchists, the Guomindang, and the National Labor University in Shanghai, 1927–1932* (Durham, N.C.: Duke University Press, 1991), 16–17, 33–34.

58. Rudolph Wagner, "The Concept of Work/Labor/Arbeit in the Chinese World: First Explorations," in *Die Rolle der Arbeit in verschiedenen Epochen und Kulturen*, ed. Manfred Bierwisch (Berlin: Akademie Verlag, 2003), 113–14.

59. Cai Yuanpei, "Laogong shensheng" (The sanctity of labor) and Li Dazhao, "Shumin de shengli" (The common people's triumph), both in *Xin qingnian* 5:5 (November 15, 1918); Li Dazhao, "Diji laodongzhe" (Lower class laborers), *Xin shehui* 22 (January 18, 1920), 12.

60. Ma Yinchu (1882–1982) was an outspoken advocate of population control during the era of Maoist reproductive overdrive, and paid a heavy price for those views. In recent years he has been lauded for his prescience and courage.

61. Beida cancelled classes for three days to allow faculty and students to participate in the celebrations. Other faculty also made speeches on this occasion, including Hu Shi and Tao Menghe.

62. Ma Yinchu, "Zhongguo de jingji wenti" (China's economic problems), August 1921, in *Ma Yinchu quanji* (Hangzhou: Zhejiang renmin, 1999), 1:502–7.

63. Ma Yinchu, "Zong bashi, zong bagong zhi zuyi zisha" (A general strike amounts to suicide), June 1925, in *Ma Yinchu quanji*, 2:458–59.

64. Zhixin (pseudonym), "Youfan dajia chi, yougong dajia zuo" (When there is food everyone eats, when there is work everyone works), *Meizhou pinglun*, December 22, 1918, 3.

65. Strand, *Rickshaw Beijing*, 21–23, 30–34; Jonathan Spence, *The Gate of Heavenly Peace: The Chinese and Their Revolution* (New York: Viking, 1981), 194, 265–69.

66. Li Jinghan, "Beijing wuchan jieji de shenghuo," *Shenghuo* 1:37 (July 4, 1926), 218. On Li Jinghan, see Weili Ye, *Seeking Modernity in China's Name: Chinese Students in the United States* (Stanford: Stanford University Press, 2001), 215–26.

67. Dingjie (pseudonym), "Qiongren shuo pingdeng" (Poor people talk about equality), *Shenghuo* 1:12 (December 1925), 75.

68. Li Da, "Makesi huanyuan" (Restore Marxism), *Xin qingnian* 8:5 (January 1, 1921), 1, 5; Li Da, "Laodongzhe yu shehui zhuyi" (Laborers and socialism), *Laodong jie* (Labor world) 16 (November 28, 1920), 2.

69. Mao Zedong, "Hunan nongmin yundong kaocha baogao" (Report on an investigation of the Hunan peasant movement), *Mao Zedong xuanji* (Selected works of Mao Zedong) (Shanghai: Renmin, 1991), 1:20–21. In this context, Mao is referring to a "national" revolution rather than a Communist one.

70. Mao Zedong, "Zhongguo nongmin zhong ge jieji de fenxi ji qi duiyu geming de taidu" (An analysis of the classes of the Chinese peasantry and their attitudes toward revolution), *Zhongguo nongmin* (Chinese peasantry) 1:1 (January 1926), 19–20. Mao reiterated many of these same points in "Zhongguo shehui ge jieji de fenxi" (Analysis of all the classes in Chinese society), *Zhongguo nongmin* 1:2 (February 1926), 1–13.

71. Stuart Schram, *The Thought of Mao Tse-tung* (Cambridge: Cambridge University Press, 1989), 36–38.

72. In the earliest version (January 1926) of his essay on class, Mao did characterize "poverty" as a problem, writing: "China has two problems: one is poverty (*pinfa*), the other is unemployment (*shiye*)—if we can solve the unemployment problem, then that

can be considered solving half of China's problems" ("Zhongguo nongmin," 19). Later versions of the essay omitted the passage.

73. Sun Zhongshan, *Sanmin zhuyi*, 248, 251, 264, 285–86, 305.

74. Tao Menghe, *Shehui wenti*, 9, 13.

75. "The Beggars of China," *North-China Herald*, January 9, 1926, 49. There was an element of truth to these accusations. As Hanchao Lu has described, begging was a competitive profession in Chinese cities, governed by its own organization (*Street Criers*, 108–32).

76. "The Beggars of China," 49.

77. Lu Xun, "Qiuqi zhe" (The beggar) (1924), in *Yecao* (Wild grass) (Beijing: Renmin wenxue, 1979), 6–7; "Chuangkan yan" (Preface to the inaugural issue), *Shenghuo* 1:1 (October 11, 1925), 1. See also Lu, *Street Criers*, 34–53.

78. Mingsheng (Tao Menghe), "Qigai shijie zhi Lincheng" (The beggars' world of Lincheng), *Meizhou pinglun*, March 23, 1919, 4; Song Jie, "Baohu ertong de shehui lifa" (Establish child protection social legislation), *Dongfang zazhi* 23:4 (February 25, 1926), 74.

79. Liu Xilian, *Beijing cishan huibian*, 41–46.

80. Y. L. Tong, "Social Conditions," 92; Tao Menghe, *Shehui wenti*, 167.

81. John Burgess, "Introduction," in *Beijing cishan huibian*, 2; Burgess, *The Significance of Social Work in China* (Peking: Peking Leader Press, 1925), 8; Giddings, *Principles of Sociology*, 129.

82. Lillian Li, *Fighting Famine*, 283–303; Will, *Bureaucracy*, 38–41; Naquin, *Peking*, 641–45.

83. "Weijing fafa" (Penalties for contravening police ordinances), in *Faling daquan* (Complete laws and ordinances of the Republic of China) (Shanghai: Shangwu, 1924), 498.

84. "Youmin xiyisuo zhangcheng" (Regulations of vagrant workhouses), in *Faling daquan*, 480–81.

85. BMA J181-18-21808, 6–9. Wu found European policing to be admirably strict, writing that when people found lost items on the streets, they dared not keep them but immediately turned them into the authorities.

86. Li Tong, "Ni zuzhi quanguo youmin xiyisuo qi" (Proposal to establish vagrant workhouses nationwide), *Minquan su* (Essence of people's rights) 16 (March 1916), 12–13.

87. On the broad powers of the police, see Dikötter, *Crime, Punishment and the Prison*, 62–64.

88. *Beijing shi zhigao*, 183–84.

89. BMA J181-19-9997, 9–10, 20–22; J181-18-4441, 1–2; *Beijing shi zhigao*, 183–84.

90. BMA J181-18-1310, 2–5. On kidnapping, see Gail Hershatter, *Dangerous Pleasures: Prostitution and Modernity in Twentieth-Century Shanghai* (Berkeley: University of California Press, 1997), 182–94.

91. There are a dozen other cases from 1914 in BMA J174-1-355.

92. Local gentry established the Beijing Jiliangsuo in 1907; it was incorporated into the Inner City Poorhouse two years later. On the Shanghai rescue mission, see Sue Gronewold, "Encountering Hope: The Door of Hope Mission in Shanghai and Taipei, 1900–1976" (Ph.D. diss., Columbia University, 1996).

93. BMA J181-19-1902, 3–4; J181-18-6204, 5–6; J181-19-1866, 3–14; J181-18-5820, 2–6.

94. The case is documented in BMA J181-19-6136.

95. In June 1915, after he completed his six-month term, Ding Xiang's mother posted a bond to secure his release.

96. BMA J181-18-9153, 2, 8–10.

97. BMA J181-19-29391, 2–3, 30–35; J181-19-97313, 26–27; J181-19-5656, 2–13.

98. Huang Yuansheng, "Youmin zhengzhi" (The governance of vagrants), *Shaonian Zhongguo zhoukan* (China youth weekly) (December 26, 1912), in *Minguo congshu*, second series (Shanghai: Shanghai shudian, 1990), 99:17–20.

99. Song Mingzhi, "Youmin duguo wenti ji qi jiuji zhi ce" (The problem of vagrants as national vermin and a strategy for its relief), *Zhonghua shiye jie* (Chinese industry world) 5 (May 10, 1914), 3–4, 6, 9. Song refers to unidentified sources that estimate a range of 9 to 47 percent of "unemployed people" who degenerate into "poverty." He also cites with approval B. S. Rowntree's study of poverty in York.

100. Chen Duxiu, "Zenyang dadao junfa" (How to defeat warlordism), *Xiangdao zhoubao* (The Guide Weekly) 21 (April 18, 1923), 152–53.

101. This analysis is based on a survey of approximately one hundred cases from 1914–24. The records are unevenly preserved: some precincts provided detailed notes, while others kept only brief documentation.

102. J181-18-731, 2–3; J181-19-1904, 2–4; J181-18-16387, 2–4; J181-19-1909, 2–11.

103. J181-18-2638, 2–4, 9–11.

104. J181-18-4181, 1–8 (July 1915). After each round of warlord battles for control of the capital, particularly in the volatile 1920s, groups of soldiers could be found loitering in the company of other "unemployed vagrants" (*wuye youmin*) (e.g., J181-18-16434, 5–7). Demobilized soldiers will be discussed in detail in chapter 3.

105. J181-18-4920, 2–3, 10–12; J181-18-4823, 3–21; J174-1-178, 36–40.

106. J181-18-5344, 13, 18.

107. In one case, two boys who entered the Vagrant Workhouse in 1918 remained for more than seven years (J181-19-46642, 2–3). Another boy, twelve *sui* when he arrived, "graduated" after four years in the shoemaking and music divisions. He was then "promoted" out of the "vagrant" ranks to lead the music section (J181-19-55000, 12–14).

108. NJ 1001-3864.

109. BMA J181-18-12901, 2–3, 6.

110. Arthur Waldron, *From War to Nationalism: China's Turning Point, 1924–1925* (New York: Cambridge University Press, 1995), 39–40; Bret Sheehan, *Trust in Troubled Times: Money, Banks, and State-Society Relations in Republican Tianjin* (Cambridge, Mass.: Harvard University Press, 2003), 76–89.

111. NJ 1001-1795.

112. BMA J181-18-12091; J181-18-11766; Gamble, *Peking*, 284–87, 297–300; Burgess, *Significance of Social Work*, 5. The police investigated the charges regarding misconduct at Longquan Orphanage but found no corroborating evidence (BMA J181-19-34703; J181-18-10786; J181-19-28991).

113. *Xiangshan Ciyouyuan gaikuang* (Survey of Xiangshan Children's Home) (Beiping, 1930), 100; Guan Ruiwu, "Jiefang qian de Beijing Xiangshan Ciyouyuan" (The

Fragrant Mountain Orphanage of pre-liberation Beijing), *Wenshi ziliao xuanji* 31 (1962), 158.

114. Mo Zhenliang, "Minguo shiqi de hong 卐 zihui" (The Red Swastika Society during the Republican era), in *Zhongguo mimi shehui gaiguan* (General survey of Chinese secret societies), ed. Cai Shaoqing (Nanjing: Jiangsu renmin, 1998), 115–23.

115. Hal Beckett, *Save the World Army: Adventures of Two Pioneering Salvationists in North China* (London: Salvationist, 1947), 56–59; *The War Cry*, April 1, 1922, 5. Zhao Erxun was nearly eighty years old, and spent the twilight of his life supervising the compilation of the official history of the defunct Qing dynasty.

116. William Booth, *In Darkest England, and the Way Out* (London, 1890), 90–93. The most well known of Booth's labor colonies was Hadleigh Farm in Essex.

117. *The War Cry*, March 28, 1925, 7.

118. Frederick Booth Tucker, *Muktifauj, or Forty Years with the Salvation Army in India and Ceylon* (1923; repr., London: Marshall Brothers, 1930), 196–97. On policing in colonial Ceylon, see A. C. Dep, *A History of the Ceylon Police* (Colombo, 1969), vol. 2, and John Rogers, *Crime, Justice, and Society in Colonial Sri Lanka* (London: Curzon, 1987).

119. John Burgess diary, 60, in John and Stella Fisher Burgess Papers (hereafter JSFB Papers), Manuscripts Division, Department of Rare Books and Special Collections, Princeton University Library, box 2.

120. Y. L. Tong, "Social Conditions," 91–92. Tong proposed that the Temples of Heaven and Agriculture, where the most important imperial rituals had been conducted, "now lying waste and overgrown with weeds," could be used for this purpose.

121. John Burgess diary, 89, in JSFB Papers, box 2.

122. Liu Xilian, *Jingshi laoruo linshi jiujihui baogaoshu* (Report of the Peking Dependents' Relief Society) (Beijing, 1923). Burgess suggested that in the future, "careful giving out of food and clothing, directly in the homes" would be less costly and more effective.

123. Local leaders raised a substantial fund, with a portion earmarked for the protection of women and children from marauding soldiers (*Jingshi Gongyi Lianhehui jishi* [Record of the Metropolitan Welfare Association] [Beijing, 1924], 1).

124. John Burgess, "Metropolitan Welfare Association," in *Jingshi Gongyi Lianhehui jishi* (preface, n.p.); "Some recollections of Princeton's work in China," 4–5, in JSFB Papers, box 1; David Strand, "Mediation, Representation, and Repression: Local Elites in 1920s Beijing," in *Chinese Local Elites and Patterns of Dominance*, ed. Joseph Esherick and Mary Rankin (Berkeley: University of California Press, 1990), 221–22.

125. *Jingshi Gongyi Lianhehui jishi*, 184–88; 251; Burgess, *Significance of Social Work*, 7–8.

126. John Burgess diary, 89, in JSFB Papers, box 2.

127. Burgess, "Introduction," 1–2; "To the Directors and Friends of Princeton-in-Peking" (November 1, 1921), in JSFB Papers, box 3.

128. Lillian Li, *Fighting Famine*, 295–303.

129. Walter Mallory, *China: Land of Famine* (New York: American Geographical Society, 1926), 172–74; *Report of the China Famine Relief, American Red Cross, October 1920 to September 1921* (Shanghai: Commercial Press, 1921), 8.

130. Mallory, *China*, 174.

131. Waldron, *From War to Nationalism*, 36.

132. Goodman, *Native Place*, 217–57.

133. The Federation's accounts indicate that it drew substantial income from the landholdings of existing benevolent halls incorporated therein, and received donations from trade guilds. The funds were then allocated to individual charities (*Shanghai shi dongshi hui shisan niandu yusuance* [Shanghai City Council 1924 budget], 8–9).

134. *Shanghai xian zhi* (Shanghai gazetteer) (Shanghai, 1935; repr., Taibei: Chengwen, 1975), 3:699; *Shanghai shi zizhi zhi*, 1915, 3:30; *Shanghai shi gongbao* (Gazette of Shanghai municipality) 1 (1912), 2–4, 13.

135. Zou Yiren, *Jiu Shanghai*, 90.

136. *Shenbao*, March 9, 1917, 10; January 15, 1919, 10; June 15, 1922, 14; October 13, 1922, 14; April 17, 1924, 15.

137. Bi Hui (Anonymous), "Youmin zhi zhonglei yu qi weiji" (Types of vagrants and their peril), *Qingnian jinbu* 15 (July 1918), 24.

138. *Shenbao*, July 31, 1923, 1. For similar comments, see also *Shenbao*, January 15, 1919, 10; October 13, 1922, 14; December 20, 1925, 11.

139. Lu, *Street Criers*, 93.

140. *Shanghai shi zizhi zhi*, 3:829–31. Despite this decree and other attempts to abolish the beggar tax, Lu, *Street Criers*, shows that beggar chiefs were still collecting protection money from shopkeepers in the 1920s and 1930s (125–30).

141. *Shanghai shi zizhi zhi*, 3:833–34; *Shanghai Xin Puyutang zhengxin lu* (Donation record of the New Hall for Universal Cultivation), 1917, 1–5. On the original Puyutang, see Fuma Susumu, *Chūgoku zenkai zendōshi kenkyū* (1997), trans. *Zhongguo shanhui shantang shi yanjiu* (Research on the history of China's benevolent societies) (Beijing: Shangwu, 2005), 578–82.

142. Gronewold, "Encountering Hope," 173–77; Shanghai Municipal Council meeting minutes, August 7, 1912 (18:302); June 23, 1920 (21:145–46); July 13, 1921 (21:416).

143. *The Municipal Gazette*, March 2, 1916, 56.

144. *The Municipal Gazette*, March 21, 1914, 93–94.

145. *The Municipal Gazette*, March 22, 1916, 98; March 23, 1916, 99.

146. The Committee report also quoted from the Poor Law Commission of 1905–9, to the effect that "in-door relief has bred a class of lazy parasites ... the workhouse proves to have failed in very many places, and shows the paradoxical result of rapidly increasing cost with diminished efficiency."

147. The COC reported that Portuguese applicants for aid constituted the largest contingent in 1916. In 1923, nearly half were Russians (*The Municipal Gazette*, June 15, 1916, 168–69; *Annual Report of the Shanghai Municipal Council, 1923*, 168).

148. The established Russian community in Shanghai was relatively small, numbering about four hundred in 1916, and was quickly dwarfed by refugees after the Bolshevik Revolution (*Shanghai zhinan* [Shanghai, 1916], 1:3).

149. Andrew Field, *Shanghai's Dancing World: Cabaret Culture and Urban Politics, 1919–1954* (Hong Kong: Chinese University Press, 2010), 39–42.

150. Marcia Ristaino, *Port of Last Resort: The Diaspora Communities of Shanghai* (Stanford: Stanford University Press, 2001), 39–43; *North-China Herald*, January 13, 1923, 98–100. The fleet eventually sailed for Taiwan and on to the Philippines, but the drama was repeated the following year, when three other ships bearing nearly one thousand Russian soldiers turned up.

151. By contrast, American consular officials in Shanghai had wide latitude to punish its citizens for blackening the reputation of the United States, characterized by Eileen Scully, *Bargaining*, as transients living on charity, hustlers, and sailors prone to violence (155).

152. *Shenbao*, May 22, 1922, 13; September 16, 1922, 13; October 11, 1922, 14.

153. *Shenbao*, June 29, 1922, 15; November 8, 1922, 17.

154. *Shenbao*, December 20, 1925, 11, 14.

155. *Shenbao*, June 30, 1926, 15; SMA U1-3-3357, 50–51.

156. SMA U1-3-3356, 14–15, 18, 22–23. Hardoon had been a member of both the French and International Settlement Municipal Councils.

157. Hanchao Lu, *Beyond the Neon Lights: Everyday Shanghai in the Early Twentieth Century* (Berkeley: University of California Press, 1999), chap. 3. See also *Shanghai penghu qu de bianqian* (The transformation of Shanghai's straw hut districts) (Shanghai, 1962), 9–12.

158. SMA Q201-1-12, 2–4, 12–13.

159. SMA U1-3-1372, 2. The French Concession, with a much smaller territorial footprint, had relatively fewer problems with shantytowns.

160. Ibid., 4, 7–8.

161. Ibid., 8, 11.

162. The bylaws of the International Settlement specifically prohibited straw sheds or other buildings made of flammable materials (*Land Regulations and Bye-Laws for the Foreign Settlements of Shanghai North of the Yang-King-Pang* [Shanghai, 1898], 41).

163. Honig, *Creating Chinese Ethnicity*, 47–48.

164. "Yangshupu caopeng beirao zhi canzhuang" (The pitiful sight of the Yangshupu straw huts destroyed by fire), *Shanghai Zonggonghui wurikan* (Shanghai General Labor Union gazette), 110 (March 25, 1926), 7–8. A copy of the article is filed in SMA U1-3-1370, 21.

165. "The Hand of the Agitator," *North-China Daily News*, April 6, 1926, 12.

166. SMA U1-3-1370, 53–55.

167. Ibid., 65.

168. Shanghai Municipal Council meeting minutes, September 15, 1926 (23:295); September 29, 1926 (23:300–301); December 29, 1926 (23:335–36); SMA U1-3-1370, 46.

169. NJ 1001-1798. By 1920 there were fifty-five such schools in Beijing, with 4,500 boys enrolled.

170. Tao Menghe, *Shehui wenti*, 13, 166; Gamble, *Peking*, 304–5.

CHAPTER 3

1. Hu Shi, "Foreword," in Julean Arnold, *Some Bigger Issues in China's Problems* (Shanghai, 1928), iii, emphasis in original. Arnold had also been a Mixed Court Assessor and Deputy Consul-General in Shanghai.

2. Lowe Chuan-hua (Luo Chunhua), "The Problem of Earning a Living in China," *The Chinese Nation* 1:9 (August 13, 1930), 141, 153. Luo studied at the University of Chicago, and returned to China in 1924 to work as a journalist. At the time this article

was published, he was the industrial secretary of the YMCA National Committee and a member of the Shanghai Birth Control League.

3. Lu Dongye, "Zhongguo pinqiong zhi yuanyin ji qi duice" (Reasons for China's poverty and its solutions), *Shehui banyuekan* (Society fortnightly) 1:17 (May 10, 1935), 32; Xu Shilian, *Renkou lun gangyao* (Essentials of population theory) (Beiping: Zhonghua shuju, 1933), 193–97. Based on a Japanese government analysis, the United States ranked first in per capita wealth at US$6,607, while China brought up the rear at $101. Xu estimated that China's mortality rate was between 25 and 30 per 1,000, more than twice that of Canada (10.7) and the United States (12.0).

4. Lowe Chuan-hua, "Problem of Earning," 141, 153.

5. When the GMD shifted the capital to Nanjing, Beijing (Northern Capital) was renamed Beiping (Northern Peace). To minimize confusion I retain the use of Beijing throughout.

6. Wu Zelin, "Zhongguo pinqiong wenti" (China's poverty problem), *Shenbao yuekan* 3:7 (July 1934), 31.

7. *Shenbao*, October 12, 1933, 21; Hu Shi, "Women zou na tiao lu" ("Which path should we take?"), *Zhongguo wenti* (China's problems) (Shanghai, 1932), 4.

8. Wang Kang, *Shehuixue shi* (History of sociology) (Beijing: Renmin, 1992), 278, citing a 1936 thesis by Liu Yuren, a graduate of Yanjing. Chiang, *Social Engineering*, details the rivalry between the social service and the empiricist factions in the department (46–59).

9. Arkush, *Fei Xiaotong*, 31–36.

10. Guy Alitto, *The Last Confucian: Liang Shu-ming and the Chinese Dilemma of Modernity* (Berkeley: University of California, 1979), 226–31; Chiang, *Social Engineering*, 65–70.

11. "Objectives of the Department of Sociology and Social Work (1932)," Dwight Edwards Papers, Special Collections, Yale Divinity School Library, 11/317/4846.

12. "Department of Sociology and Social Work report, 1927–1928," Dwight Edwards Papers, Dwight Edwards Papers, Special Collections, Yale Divinity School Library, 11/317/4843.

13. Zheng Jiangnan, "Jiupin zhengce de yanjiu" (Research on poor relief policies), *Guolun* (National opinion monthly) 2:2 (September 15, 1936), 276.

14. Ke Xiangfeng, *Zhongguo pinqiong wenti* (The problem of poverty in China) (Shanghai: Zhengzhong, 1935), 9–10. The Chinese terms and their English equivalents are Ke's rendering.

15. Ibid., 318–23. The Elberfeld-Hamburg model enjoyed a reputation for effectiveness in the early twentieth century (Charles Henderson, *Modern Methods of Charity* [New York: Macmillan, 1904], 5–15; F. Stuart Chapin, *An Historical Introduction to Social Economy* [New York: Century Co., 1923], 280–86).

16. Ke Xiangfeng, *Zhongguo pinqiong wenti*, 287–88, 337–39.

17. Herbert Day Lamson, *Social Pathology in China: A Source Book for the Study of Problems of Livelihood, Health, and the Family* (Shanghai: Commercial Press, 1934), xi, 3, 6–8. See also Tao Menghe, *Shehui wenti*, 160–64.

18. Jiang Jieshi (Chiang Kai-shek), "Zhongguo qingnian zhi zeren" (Responsibilities of China's youths), July 8, 1935, in *Xian Zongtong Jianggong sixiang yanlun zongji* (Complete thought and speeches of the late President Chiang) (Taibei: Zhongguo guomin dang zhongyang weiyuanhui, 1984), 13:291–92.

19. In *Saving the Nation* Zanasi provides a detailed explication of the split between different factions of the GMD and their distinct visions of productivism.

20. Frederic Wakeman, Jr. "A Revisionist View of the Nanjing Decade: Confucian Fascism," *The China Quarterly* 150 (June 1997), 395–432.

21. Li Chucai, "Shengchan jiaoyu de wojian" (My views on productive education), *Shenbao yuekan* (April 15, 1933), 71–73.

22. Wu Shangquan, *Langfei pinqiong yu jiuwang* (Waste, poverty, and salvation of national destruction) (Beiping: Dacheng, 1936), 118, 310–11.

23. "Government Provisions for Famine Relief," *The Chinese Nation* 1:18 (October 15, 1930), 352.

24. On the Communist underground, see Patricia Stranahan, *Underground: The Shanghai Communist Party and the Politics of Survival, 1927–1937* (Lanham, Md.: Rowman & Littlefield, 1998).

25. "Jiandu cishan tuanti fa" (The Law overseeing philanthropic associations), *Neizheng fagui huibian* (Collection of laws of civil administration) (Nanjing, 1931), 420–24.

26. These were the Relief Funds Committee (Zhenkuan Weiyuanhui), 1928–29; the Disaster Relief Committee (Zhenzai Weiyuanhui), 1929–30; the Relief Affairs Committee (Zhenwu Weiyuanhui), 1930–38.

27. *Jiuji shiye jihua shu* (Plan for relief work) (Nanjing, 1929), 3, 10.

28. *The Civil Code of the Republic of China* (Nanjing: Kelly & Walsh, 1931), IV:1117, 40; Susan Glosser, *Chinese Visions of Family and State, 1915–1953* (Berkeley: University of California Press, 2003), 94–97.

29. *Jiuji shiye jihua shu*, 12; "Government Provisions for Famine Relief," 351. The provinces were instructed to establish similar reserves, at the rate of Ch. $200,000 per one million people.

30. T. V. Soong, "The 1931 Floods: A Preliminary Report to the Members of the National Flood Relief Commission," *Chinese Economic Journal* 11:1 (July 1932), 67–73.

31. Chen Lingseng, "Zaihuang yu jiuji" (Famine and relief), *Shehui banyuekan* 1:2 (September 25, 1934), 10–11.

32. Ibid., 11; SMA U1-3-4139, 166. On the 1931 refugee crisis in Nanjing, see Lipkin, *Useless to the State*, 72–79.

33. Mark Swislocki, "Feast and Famine in Republican Shanghai: Urban Food Culture, Nutrition, and the State" (Ph.D. diss., Stanford University, 2001), 33–36.

34. In the early Republic, some local governments and private charities had made similar loans on a small scale.

35. "Shiban zhong zhi pinmin jieben chu," *Shehui yuekan* 1:5 (May 1929), 1, 4; Christian Henriot, *Shanghai, 1927–1937: Municipal Power, Locality, and Modernization* (Berkeley: University of California Press, 1993), 227. A loan of Ch. $20 was due to be paid back in installments within one hundred days. The interest totaled 28 cents (reduced if the principle was paid back within fifty days). Applicants were required to furnish proof of ability to conduct the intended business and provide bonded guarantors to stand surety for repayment. A similar loan program was established in 1934 in Beijing (BMA J2-7-123, 152, 169).

36. Lipkin, *Useless to the State*, 97; Alfred Lin, "Warlord, Social Welfare and Philanthropy: The Case of Guangzhou under Chen Jitang, 1929–1936," *Modern China* 30:2 (April 2004), 171–75.

37. Li Jinghan, "Beiping zuidi xiandu de shenghuo chengdu de taolun" (Discussion of the lowest standard of living in Beiping), *Shehui xuejie* 3 (1929), 1, 2–4.

38. *Beiping tebie shi shehuiju jiuji shiye xiao shi* (Brief history of Beiping Bureau of Social Affairs relief matters) (Beiping, 1929), 5–7; Niu Nai'e, "Beiping yiqian erbai pinhu zhi yanjiu" (Investigation of 1,200 poor households in Beiping), *Shehui xuejie* 7 (1933), 151. Xu Shilian reported a smaller number of "poor people" (228,354) but a higher percentage (17.6 percent) for 1930 (*Renkou lun gangyao*, 281).

39. *Beiping shi zhengfu gong'an ju yewu baogao* (Beiping Public Security Bureau work report) (Beiping, 1933), tongji.

40. Niu Nai'e, "Beiping yiqian," 151.

41. Ibid., 155, 159–61. Nearly a quarter of the men were literate; few women (less than 2 percent) could read.

42. The investigators attributed this to well-off households concealing their wealth, and the likelihood that many relied on illicit sources of income which they did not want to reveal.

43. Niu Nai'e, "Beiping yiqian," 161–65, 186.

44. Ibid., 181.

45. Ibid., 179–81. The second brother joined the army after his wife's death, and the family had no news from him. There were two other sisters who had died.

46. Ibid., 183–86.

47. On the city's decline after 1928, see Huang Ching-shu, "Peiping in Eclipse: The Move to Revive Its Former Prosperity," *The Chinese Nation* 1:35 (February 11, 1931), 884–86. Dong, *Republican Beijing*, describes a different view of Beijing's history, with nostalgia as the primary motif (246–65).

48. Niu Nai'e, "Beiping yiqian," 182–84.

49. Zhang Jingai, "Beiping zhouchang zhi yanjiu" (Research on Beiping's gruel kitchens), *Shehuixue jie* 7 (1933), 200–203. Zhang's survey included data on nineteen out of thirty soup kitchens operating in the city.

50. Ibid., 189, 205–7. For different criticisms of late imperial soup kitchens, see Lillian Li, *Fighting Famine*, 228–29.

51. *Beiping Pinmin Jiujihui zhengxinlu* (Beiping Poor Relief Society record of donations), 1933; "In War and Famine," *The War Cry*, April 14, 1928, 3; Zhang Jingai, "Beiping zhouchang," 209.

52. *Beiping tebie shi shehuiju jiuji shiye xiao shi*; BMA J2-7-401, 24–26; J2-7-160, 10.

53. *Beiping tebie shi shehuiju jiuji zhuankan* (Beiping Social Affairs Bureau special issue on relief) (Beiping, 1930), 1.

54. *Youmin xiyi yuekan* (Vagrant work training monthly) (1927), *gongdu*, 11–19; *Beiping tebie shi shehuiju jiuji shiye xiao shi*, 20.

55. *Beiping tebie shi shehuiju jiuji zhuankan*, 1, 5–7, 38–39; *Beiping tebie shi shehuiju jiuji shiye xiao shi*, 23.

56. *Beiping tebie shi shehuiju jiuji zhuankan*, 7, 42. The term at the beggar shelter was six months, but inmates could be released earlier if they could find guarantors to support the claim that they were not beggars

57. BMA J181-20-875, 2–4; J181-20-5988, 6–8. During one period of expansion, the police tried to acquire the use of a block of unused buildings belonging to the Palace Museum, located near the Forbidden City. The museum directors recoiled with horror at the prospect of "vagrants" congregating in the vicinity of the nation's foremost cultural institution (J181-20-5866, 7–14).

58. BMA J2-6-88, 26–27, 29.

59. *Beiping shi tongji lanyao* (Overview of Beiping statistics) (Beiping, 1936), 104. The death rate ranged from 13 to 20 percent per month for the year.

60. Mühlhahn, *Criminal Justice*, 88–115.

61. Xu Yamin, "Wicked Citizens and the Social Origins of China's Modern Authoritarian State, 1928–37" (Ph.D. diss., University of California, Berkeley, 2002), 471–76.

62. BMA J181-20-4375, 3–4. The same directive also targeted gambling rackets. For a detailed description of Tianqiao, see Dong, *Republican Beijing*, 172–207.

63. BMA J181-20-4072. Three others were suspects in criminal cases, two were caught stealing coal, one was a gambler, and one showed "suspicious demeanor."

64. BMA J181-20-5376, 3; *Beiping shi shizheng gongbao* 296 (April 8–15, 1935), 60–61; 297 (April 15–22, 1935), 12–13; 379 (November 9–16, 1936), 23.

65. BMA J181-20-19119, 3; *Beiping shi shizheng gongbao* 346 (March 23–30, 1936), 23–24.

66. "Beiping shi qigai tongji," *Shehui diaocha huikan* (Periodical of social investigation) (Beiping, 1930).

67. BMA J181-21-45598, 3, 6–7. In his deposition the Russian told the police that he used to work as a driver; the Estonian had been a handicraft worker in France. Neither man had a job in Beijing. The Russian intended to go to Hankou and the Estonian to Shanghai to look for work after they were deported from Beijing.

68. Diana Lary, *Warlord Soldiers: Chinese Common Soldiers, 1911–1937* (Cambridge: Cambridge University Press, 1985), 2–3, 98–99; Xu Yamin, "Wicked Citizens," 473–75.

69. BMA J181-20-7397, 2–3; J181-20-5735, 39–42; J184-2-2618, 20–21; J181-20-2933, 5–8.

70. BMA J181-21-14600; J181-21-14632; J2-6-54.

71. BMA J2-6-43, 2.

72. Frank Dikötter, Lars Laamann, and Zhou Xun, *Narcotic Culture: A History of Drugs in China* (Chicago: University of Chicago Press, 2004), 130–35; Xu Yamin, "Wicked Citizens," 103.

73. BMA J2-6-3, 3.

74. For instance, four hundred addicts were detained at a labor dormitory in the Outer Fifth District in May 1935 (BMA J2-6-63, 73). Workhouses and reformatories all around the country were regularly used as temporary shelters for addicts (Dikötter et al., *Narcotic Culture*, 130).

75. BMA J2-6-63, 41.

76. Xu Yamin, "Wicked Citizens," 103–4. In May 1935, 395 men and 63 women were detained at the center (BMA J2-6-63, 123).

77. Yuan-Huei Lin, "The Weight of Mount Tai: Patterns of Suicide in Traditional Chinese History and Culture" (Ph.D. diss., University of Wisconsin–Madison, 1990).

78. Yu-sheng Lin, "The Suicide of Liang Chi: An Ambiguous Case of Moral Conservatism," in *The Limits of Change: Essays on Conservative Alternatives in Republican China*, ed. Charlotte Furth (Cambridge, Mass.: Harvard University Press, 1976), 151–68; Bryna Goodman, "The New Woman Commits Suicide: The Press, Cultural Memory, and the New Republic," *Journal of Asian Studies* 64:1 (February 2005), 67–101; Wu Rouhua, "Zisha (2)" (Suicide), *Shehui yuekan* 1:1 (January 1929), 9–10.

79. "Zisha zhi yuanyin" (Reasons for suicide), *Shehui diaocha huikan; Beiping shi zhengfu tongji yuekan* (Beiping municipal statistics monthly) (Beiping, 1934), 55; *Shanghai tebie shi shehuiju yewu baogao* nos. 4–5 (1930), "Zisha"; Zhang Yongjin, "Zisha (1)" (Suicide), *Shehui yuekan* 1:1 (January 1929), 7–8.

80. BMA J2-6-54, 1–20, 35–40, 43–46. For numerous other cases of attempted suicides due to poverty, see BMA J2-6-56, J2-6-57, J2-6-58. Dikötter et al. describe nineteenth-century examples of people ingesting opium to commit suicide (*Narcotic Culture*, 71–72).

81. *The Criminal Code of the Republic of China* (Shanghai: Kelly & Walsh, 1935), 86, 103.

82. Qing and Republican law differentiated between "special" guarantors who promise to compensate for loss as defined in the contract, and "ordinary" guarantors who only attest to the character or identity of an individual without liability. See Andrea McElderry, "Legal Change and Guarantor Liability in the Republican Economy," in *Shijie jingji tizhi xia de Minguo shiqi jingji* (The Republican economy within the global economic framework) (Beijing: Zhongguo caizheng jingji, 2005). For the Relief Home, recognized authority figures (e.g., police or other government officials) could provide character references for applicants. Otherwise, only bonded guarantees from commercial establishments were accepted. On employment guarantors, see Emily Honig, *Sisters and Strangers: Women in the Shanghai Cotton Mills, 1919–1949* (Stanford: Stanford University Press, 1986), 90.

83. On the night of September 18, bombs exploded along the railways outside Mukden. In the confusion skirmishes broke out between the two sides, and the Japanese army seized on the incident as the pretext for invading Manchuria.

84. BMA J2-6-79, 28–29.

85. Ibid., 5–6. For many similar cases, see BMA J2-6-78 and J2-6-79.

86. BMA J2-6-58, 18–19.

87. Melissa Macauley, *Social Power and Legal Culture: Litigation Masters in Late Imperial China* (Stanford: Stanford University Press, 1998), 77–81; Xiaoqun Xu, *Trial of Modernity: Judicial Reform in Early Twentieth-Century China, 1901–1937* (Stanford: Stanford University Press, 2008), 302–28.

88. For 400 to 1,000 words, the charge was 40 cents and $1 for 1,000 to 2,000 words (the maximum length).

89. BMA J2-6-58, 20–21.

90. BMA J2-6-85, 4–5; J2-6-138, 39, 45.

91. BMA J2-6-78, 1–7.

92. BMA J2-6-56, 12–13. The request triggered a government directive to improve heating in the children's section of the Relief Home, in order to prevent exposure-related injuries.

93. BMA J2-6-55, 19–20. This is one of the few letters where the scribe was named. Chen Guiyu was probably someone like Wang Youlin (see above), who made a few coppers by writing letters on behalf of the illiterate.

94. Chen Lingseng, "Chuli jiuji shijian ganyan" (Reflections on handling relief cases), *Shehui yuekan* 1:12 (December 1929), 4. The deepest hell refers to Avici, the final place of damnation in Buddhism, where the condemned go through endless cycles of suffering, death, and rebirth.

95. SMA U1-16-1013, 7.

96. Ibid., 37–38, 42; *North-China Daily News*, May 24, 1934, 4. The logic applied even in times of crisis. In addressing the prospect that refugees would "invade" Shanghai during the 1931 summer floods, Health Commissioner J. H. Jordan recommended forming a "cordon sanitaire" around the International Settlement and setting up camps to intercept refugees. According to Jordan, "[P]rovision of unnecessary accommodation in Shanghai might in itself be a foolish procedure since it would inevitably tend to attract persons and persuade them to break the cordon" (U1-3-4139, 4–5).

97. SMA U1-3-4090, 3–4, 9–10.

98. SMA U1-16-1013, 5, 43.

99. Pan Gongzhan, "Xiandai Shanghai shehui de weiji" (The crisis in Shanghai today), *Shehui yuekan* 1:9 (September 1929), 2–3.

100. "Shanghai tebieshi zhigong shiye tongji zhi shibian" (A preliminary investigation of unemployment in Greater Shanghai), *Shehui yuekan* 1:8 (August 1929) 6.

101. Some statistics indicate that in the late 1920s, unemployment remained relatively constant at 15 to 18 percent. During the world depression of the 1930s, Shanghai's silk industry was hit hard; Japan's 1932 attack also put many out of work. The available data, however, do not show a spike in unemployment until 1935 (Wakeman, *Policing Shanghai*, 87; Henriot, *Shanghai, 1927–1937*, 96, 219).

102. Pan Gongzhan, "Xiandai Shanghai," 3, citing the population census conducted by the Public Security Bureau in June 1929.

103. "Yiqian sibai yu youmin wenhua de jieguo," 1, 4–6. A few years later, a repeat survey of 1,700 vagrants showed similar results (Chen Lingseng, "Shanghai de youmin wenti" [Shanghai's vagrancy problem], *Shehui banyuekan* [Society fortnightly] 1:4 [October 25, 1934], 10–13).

104. Chen Lingseng, "Shanghai de youmin wenti," 9; Chen Lingseng, "Shanghai qigai wenti de tantao" (Inquiry into Shanghai's beggar problem), *Shehui banyuekan* 1:6 (November 25, 1934), 13. *Biesan* has a criminal connotation and suggests shame and the complete loss of honor.

105. "Shiban zhou zhi pinmin jieben chu" (The pilot people's credit centers), *Shehui yuekan* 1:5 (May 1929), 14–16; "Zhongguo de pinqiong wenti," *Shenbao yuekan* 3:7 (July 15, 1934), 32

106. *Shanghai shi shehuiju fagui huibian* (Shanghai Social Affairs Bureau collection of laws and regulations) (Shanghai, 1930), 83–88; *Shanghai tebie shi shehuiju yewu baogao* (1929), 253–55.

107. *Shanghai tebie shi shehuiju yewu baogao* (1930), 244–48.

108. *Shehui banyuekan* 1:11–12 (February 25, 1935), 254–55.

109. *Shanghai tebie shi shehuiju yewu baogao* (1929), 240–41, 285–86; *Shanghai tebie shi shehuiju yewu baogao* (1930), 250–51.

110. *Shanghai tebie shi shehuiju yewu baogao* (1929), 251–53.

111. *Shenbao*, September 18, 1928, 14; *Shanghai tebie shi shehuiju yewu baogao* (1928), 252–54; *Shanghai tebie shi shehuiju yewu baogao* (1932), 86.

112. Donald A. Jordan, *China's Trial by Fire: The Shanghai War of 1932* (Ann Arbor: University of Michigan Press, 2001); Henriot, *Shanghai, 1927–1937*, 87–99; Nara Dillon, "The Politics of Philanthropy: Social Networks and Refugee Relief in Shanghai, 1932–1949," in *At the Crossroads of Empires*, 181–86.

113. Chan and Dirlik, *Schools into Fields*, 74–75; *Shenbao*, February 2, 1928, 14.

114. *Shenbao*, May 7, 1929, 15; May 16, 1929, 15; May 25, 1929, 20.

115. *Shenbao*, March 17, 1930, 15.

116. *Shanghai tebie shi shehuiju yewu baogao* (1929), 247–48; SMA U1-3-3357, 27. *Shanghai tebie shi shehuiju yewu baogao* (1932), 85.

117. It was also known as the Shanghai Beggars' Asylum and the Number 1 Vagrant Workhouse.

118. *Shanghai Youmin Xiqinsuo diyijie baogao* (First report of the Shanghai Vagrant Workhouse) (Shanghai, 1931), guicheng, 2–3.

119. Pan Gongzhan, "Xu" (Preface), *Shanghai Youmin Xiqinsuo diyijie baogao*, 1.

120. *Shanghai tebie shi shehuiju yewu baogao*, no. 8 (1932), 85–86.

121. *Shanghai Youmin Xiqinsuo diyijie baogao*, n.p.

122. *Shanghai tebie shi shehuiju yewu baogao* (1929), 279–80.

123. *Shanghai Youmin Xiqinsuo baogao dierbian*, 97.

124. Ibid., 29.

125. *Shanghai Youmin Xiqinsuo diyijie baogao*, zalu, 22, 25.

126. Lipkin, *Useless to the State*, 88–128. On Nanjing shantytowns, see Wu Wenhui, *Nanjing penghu jiating diaocha* (Investigation of Nanjing shantytown families), 1935, repr., *Minguo shiqi shehui diaocha congbian* (Collection of Republican-era social surveys) (Fuzhou: Fujian jiaoyu, 2004),vol. 5:2, 737–802.

127. SMA Q1-23-42, 7. Another census counted an additional 1,559 boats (Q1-23-24).

128. *Shenbao*, October 7, 1928, 15; SMA Q1-23-12, 3–5. Xu Peihuang, a graduate of MIT, later served as the Director of the Education and Public Utilities Bureaus.

129. SMA Q1-23-21, 12. These worries were largely unfounded. According to Stranahan, the CCP underground in Shanghai forged alliances with labor unions, student groups, and the Green Gang (*Underground*, 234–35). Some shantytown residents who worked as dockworkers were probably affiliated with Shanghai's gangs. But there is no direct evidence that the CCP actively recruited from the shantytown population during this period.

130. SMA Q1-23-3, 20–22; Q1-23-12, 2; Q1-23-15, 2.

131. SMA Q1-23-42, 7.

132. SMA Q1-23-2, 1–2; Q1-23-36, 6.

133. SMA Q1-23-20, 8; Q1-23-8, 1–2; Q1-23-23, 5. Private organizations also tried to build low-income housing, but the capital required was often beyond their means. For example, the Jiang-Huai Sojourner Association drafted plans to build one hundred units, for fellow provincials whose huts were destroyed by fire in April 1929. They raised two-thirds of the money, but needed government help to secure a loan for the remaining sum, a process that took nearly two years (SMA Q1-23-11, 3–4, 16–18).

134. SMA Q1-23-46, 9–10.

135. SMA Q1-23-8, 14.

136. *Shanghai shi pingmin fuli shiye yinian lai gongzuo baogao* (One year report on Shanghai commoner welfare matters) (Shanghai, 1936).

137. SMA Q1-23-9, 5–6, 10, 22, 53, 55–56, 91; *Shenbao*, June 1, 1936, 2 (supplement). Lipkin, *Useless to the State*, describes a similar situation in Nanjing, 93–94.

138. SMA Q1-23-52, 3–5, 16–20, 29, 31.

139. *Shanghai shi pingmin fuli shiye yinian lai gongzuo baogao*. Monthly household income averaged about Ch. $25. The rules limited eligibility to families with income of less than $30.

140. SMA Q5-3-3441, 7–42; Q123-1-1480, 3.

141. *Shenbao*, March 8, 1936, 14; June 20, 1936, 13; September 18, 1936, 14.

142. SMA U1-3-1370, 122–24.

143. Ibid., 84–90; U1-3-1371, 5–6.

144. SMA U1-3-1371, 110, 156–60.

145. Ibid., 161; *Shenbao*, September 15, 1932, 16.

146. T. K. Ho was the nephew of noted Chinese historian Ho Ping-ti, though T. K. was twenty-one years older.

147. SMA U1-4-3392, 120–24.

148. Ibid., 57–59. Other petitions and letters are filed throughout U1-4-3392.

149. *Shenbao*, July 16, 1936, 12; Shanghai Municipal Police Archives (hereafter SMP), 29-D7479; SMA U1-4-3390, 216.

150. *Shenbao*, August 17, 1936, 13; *Xinwenbao*, August 17, 1936.

151. SMP 29-D7479; SMA U1-4-3390, 123, 221; U1-4-3392, 78, 88–92.

152. SMA U1-4-3390, 194–95; *Shenbao*, September 3, 1936, 14; September 4, 1936, 14. Eleven were released on suspended sentences or bonds; the twelfth, "a local hooligan," was sentenced to ten months in the Municipal Gaol.

153. SMA U1-4-3390, 191; *Shenbao*, September 9, 1936, 14. Both Wang's son and the Federation demanded compensation for his wrongful death. But the son quickly retracted his claim, saying that his father had not been assaulted. Someone induced him to sign the letters; "being illiterate I know nothing about the contents of the letters" (U1-4-3390, 160).

154. SMA U1-4-3390, 110–14; 117–24; Shanghai Municipal Council meeting minutes, October 14, 1936 (27:75–76); *North-China Daily News*, October 16, 1936, 11.

155. SMA U1-4-3393, 150–54.

156. SMA U1-4-3394, 209–10; U1-4-3393, 155, 168–69.

157. *Shenbao*, April 26, 1936, 11.

158. SMA U1-4-3393, 75–76, 86–87.

159. SMA U1-4-3394, 270–71, 276–77; *Shenbao*, April 12, 1937, 1 (supplement).

160. *Shenbao*, April 27, 1937, 10; SMA U1-4-3393, 25–27.

161. SMA U1-4-3394, 283–86; Shanghai Municipal Council meeting minutes, April 28, 1937 (27:146–49).

162. Xiao Ling, "Penghu men qiandao nali qu?" (Where are the hut-dwellers to go?), *Renjian shiri* 6 (1937), 5–6. See also *Shenbao*, May 7, 1937, 1 (supplement).

163. *Fu'er mosi* (The Holmes News), May 7, 1937, 3.

164. Lu, *Beyond the Neon Lights*, 116.

CHAPTER 4

1. MacKinnon, *Wuhan;* Lu Liu, "A Whole Nation Walking: The 'Great Retreat' in the War of Resistance, 1937–1945" (Ph.D. diss., University of California, San Diego, 2002); Sun Yankui, *Kunan de renliu: Kangzhan shiqi de nanmin* (People in misery: Refugees in the War of Resistance) (Guilin: Guangxi shifan daxue, 1994).

2. Estimates for the total number of refugees range wildly, from three to ninety-five million. MacKinnon, *Wuhan* (46–47) and Liu, "Whole Nation Walking" (11–13) discuss the statistical problems of counting refugees.

3. Lu Liu, "Whole Nation Walking," chaps. 4–5; Wang Chunying, "Kangzhan shiqi nanmin shourongsuo de sheli ji qi tedian" (The establishment and special characteristics of refugee shelters during the War of Resistance), *KangRi zhanzheng yanjiu* 3 (2004), 210–11.

4. Soong May-ling, "Jinwei nantong qingming" (A plea to save refugee children), *Funü shenghuo* (Women's life) 5:11 (April 1938), repr., *Jiang Furen Song Meiling nüshi yanlun xuanji* (Selected writings and speeches of Madam Chiang Kaishek) (Taibei: Jindai Zhongguo, 1998), 65. See also M. Colette Plum, "Unlikely Heirs: War Orphans during the Second Sino-Japanese War, 1937–1945" (Ph.D. diss., Stanford University, 2006).

5. Fan Renyu, "Zenyang cong liuwang zhuandao jiuwang" (How to turn from exile to national salvation), *Nanmin zhoukan* (Refugee weekly) 5 (April 7, 1938), 2, quoted in Wang Chunying, "Kangzhan shiqi," 218–19.

6. Diana Lary, "One Province's Experience of War: Guangxi, 1937–1945," in *China at War: Regions of China, 1937–1945*, ed. Diana Lary, Stephen MacKinnon, and Ezra Vogel (Stanford: Stanford University Press, 2007), 322.

7. Li Luzi, "Chongqing neimu" (Behind the scenes in Chongqing), in *Zhanshi Chongqing fengguang* (The sights of wartime Chongqing) (1942; repr., Chongqing: Chongqing chubanshe, 1986), 204–5.

8. *Geming wenxian* (Documentary materials on the revolution) (Taibei: Zhongyang wenwu, 1983–1984), 96:455–64. Initially, private charities as well as government agencies issued such certificates, but this soon resulted in a bewildering array of formats and sizes, making it impossible to check for forgeries. In an attempt to track people's movements, the NRC mandated standardized certificates in 1939. The Commission lacked the resources, however, to enforce its own regulations (Lu Liu, "Whole Nation Walking," 219–21).

9. Kong Xiangxi, January 19, 1939, *Geming wenxian*, 96:431–32.

10. "Solving the Refugee Problem," *China at War* 2:4 (April 1939), 59. GMD-sponsored refugee factories were primarily located in Sichuan, providing employment for several thousand people. Most had more symbolic value (e.g., the "July 7th Refugee Factory" in Chongqing) than meaningful economic impact.

11. *Zhongyang ribao*, August 13, 1940, 2.

12. Liu Huiying, "Gudu lunxian qianhou zaji" (Miscellaneous records of the former capital before and after its fall), 1–3; Anonymous, "Beiping lunxian qianqian houhou" (Before and after the fall of Beiping), 4–6; Lu Yueming, "Longcheng luori ji" (Account of nightfall in a city aflame), 19–21; all in *Tieti xia de PingJin* (Beijing and Tianjin under iron hooves), ed. Aying (Hankou: Zhanshi, 1938).

13. Lincoln Li, *The Japanese Army in North China, 1937–1941: Problems of Political and Economic Control* (London: Oxford University Press, 1975), 44, 48.

14. Chapter 8 of unpublished memoir, Ida Pruitt Papers, Schlesinger Library, Radcliffe Institute, Harvard University (hereafter Ida Pruitt Papers), box 48, folder 1207.

15. Zhao Hong, "Beiping lunxian chuqi de difang weichi hui" (The Peace Preservation Committee during the initial period of the occupation of Beiping), *Beijing dang'an shiliao* 2 (1987), 46–48.

16. *Lugouqiao shibian hou Beijing zhi'an jiyao* (Summary of Beijing's public security after the Marco Polo Bridge Incident) (Beiping, 1937), 68–73, 98, 124; Zhao Hong, "Beiping lunxian," 49; George E. Taylor, *The Japanese Sponsored Regime in North China* (New York: Institute of Pacific Relations, 1939), 44.

17. *Lugouqiao shibian hou Beijing zhi'an jiyao*, 242–43, 265.

18. "Huabei zhengwu zhidao gangyao" (Outline of instructions for the north China political administration), August 12, 1937, in *KangRi zhanzheng* (The War of Resistance), ed. Zhang Bofeng and Zhuang Jianping (Chengdu: Sichuan daxue, 1997), 6:218–19.

19. BMA J2-6-138, 9–30; unpublished manuscript (untitled), Ida Pruitt Papers, box 29, folder 725.

20. "We Shall Remain Here," *The War Cry*, October 30, 1937, 7.

21. Letter to Lady Young (October 21, 1937), Ida Pruitt Papers, box 29, folder 723.

22. BMA J2-7-182, 6–12.

23. BMA J2-6-46, 79–81. By February 1940, only forty-six children remained at Longquan Orphanage.

24. Xiong Mao Yanwen, "Banian zhong Ri zhanzheng zhong de Xiangshan Ciyouyuan" (The Xiangshan Children's Home during the eight years of the war against Japan), in *Beiping Xiangshan Ciyouyuan yuanshi* (The history of the Beiping Xiangshan Children's Home) (Taibei, 1983), 101.

25. BMA J2-7-182, 24; *Shibao*, December 30, 1937, 4.

26. *Zhenji zhuankan* (Special issue on relief) (Beijing: Zhenji bu, 1939), zhuanzai, 3. Wang Yitang (1878–1948), a graduate of a Japanese military academy, had been a GMD official in Manchuria and north China. He was executed in 1948 as a traitor.

27. *Zhenji zhuankan*, gongdu, 11–12.

28. *Zhenji zhuankan*, zhuanzai, 4; jishi, 61.

29. BMA J2-1-422, 27.

30. BMA J181-22-999, 20–22; J181-22-1006, 10; *Lugouqiao shibian hou Beijing zhi'an jiyao*, 182–83.

31. BMA J181-1-295, 2.

32. Ibid., 10–13. Individual postmortem reports are filed in BMA J181-22-991.

33. BMA J181-1-295, 10–13, 17, 20–21.

34. BMA J181-22-999, 23; J181-22-10305, 4.

35. BMA J2-6-123, 20, 27–28, 30–31.

36. "Jiujiyuan gaiyao" (An outline of the Relief Home), in BMA J2-6-622, 12, 14–19.

37. BMA J2-6-142, 86–99.

38. BMA J2-6-168, 46–47; J2-6-218, 14–15; *Shehui tongji yuekan* (Social statistics monthly) 1:1 (November 1938), 41.

39. BMA J2-6-504, 27–30; J2-6-196, 7–10.

40. BMA J2-6-227, 1–13.

41. BMA J2-6-173, 12.

42. Journal entry, August 5, 1937, Ida Pruitt Papers, box 30, folder 724.

43. BMA J181-22-1229, 33–34, 57–58; BMA J181-2-2656, 6–7.

44. BMA J2-6-120, 5–7. On labor conscription, see Ju Zhifen, "Labor Conscription in North China: 1941–1945," in Lary, MacKinnon, and Vogel, *China at War*, 207–26.

45. BMA J2-6-120, 1–3, 15–17; J2-6-152, 1–2, 8–10.

46. BMA J2-6-153, 26–27. The transfers often included people who were partially or completely blind, those who were missing limbs, and many identified as "idiots."

47. BMA J181-22-10306, 3; J181-22-10307, 36–38.

48. BMA J2-6-189; J181-23-6580; J181-23-7117; J181-23-19410, 5–14; J2-1-406, 1–11.

49. "Jiujiyuan gaiyao," 3–4, 5, 7–9.

50. BMA J181-22-1007, 34–36. For instance, pressed to explain poor hygiene, Wang answered that the police provided only dilapidated uniforms. Since there were no spare sets, the clothes were never washed.

51. BMA J181-22-1004, 2–3.

52. BMA J2-1-287, 2–4, 114.

53. BMA J181-22-15536, 3; J181-23-11446, 13–19; J181-23-15564, 4–5.

54. BMA J2-1-422, 17–21.

55. Ibid., 9, 12.

56. *Shibao*, February 6, 1939. Beijing's *Shibao* 實報 was different from Shanghai's *Shibao* 時報. Editor Guan Yixian joined the collaborationist government; his newspaper was one of the few in Beijing permitted to publish without interruption through the occupation years.

57. *Shibao*, January 15, 1939; January 8, 1939.

58. *Shibao*, April 10, 1939; August 2, 1939.

59. Chi Zi'an and Wan Yongguang, "Chi 'hunhe mian' de kunan jishi" (A true record of the misery of eating 'mixed flour'), in *Riwei tongzhi xia de Beiping*, 194–98; An Bang, "Nan yi xiayan de 'hunhe mian'" (Difficult to swallow 'mixed flour'), in *Riwei tongzhi xia de Beiping*, 199–202.

60. Lincoln Li, *Japanese Army*, 13, 210–11.

61. *Xinhua ribao* (New China daily), September 7, 1943, 4.

62. SMA U1-14-405, 4; *North-China Herald*, September 1, 1937, 344; *Jiuwang ribao*, August 27, 1937; *The China Yearbook* (1939), 552. On *gudao* Shanghai, see Wen-hsin Yeh, ed., *Wartime Shanghai* (New York: Routledge, 1998) and Poshek Fu, *Passivity, Resistance, and Collaboration: Intellectual Choices in Occupied Shanghai, 1937–1945* (Stanford: Stanford University Press, 1993).

63. Marcia Ristaino, *The Jacquinot Safe Zone: Wartime Refugees in Shanghai* (Stanford: Stanford University Press, 2008); *Shanghai International Relief Committee Six Month's Report*, 1938, 1–2; *Shanghai tongshi* (General history of Shanghai) (Shanghai: Renmin, 1999), 9:89–90.

64. *North-China Herald*, December 29, 1937, 481; SMA U1-14-630, 90.

65. SMA U1-14-405, 1–4.

66. *The Chinese Recorder* 69:1 (January 1938), 18–25. For a detailed study of the early months of the refugee crisis, see Christian Henriot, "Shanghai and the Experience of War: The Fate of Refugees," *European Journal of East Asian Studies* 5:2 (2006), 215–45.

67. *Jiuwang ribao*, September 17, 1937; *North-China Herald*, September 15, 1937, 411; October 6, 1937, 24; October 20, 1937, 102, 106.

68. *Xinwenbao*, April 12, 1938, 10; *Jiuwang ribao*, September 16, 1937; "Gu chuan" (Hiring a boat), *Shanghai yiri* (One day in Shanghai) (Shanghai: Meishang, 1939), 2:40–41. Since they could not send refugees back into the war zone, organizations tried to find other outlets for their removal (e.g., arranging for passage to the interior, or emigration abroad).

69. *North-China Herald*, September 8, 1937, 364.

70. Patricia Stranahan, "Radicalization of Refugees: Communist Party Activity in Wartime Shanghai's Displaced Persons Camps," *Modern China* 26:2 (April 2000), 176–80.

71. SMP 51-8597, July 7, 1938 report. One of the confiscated pamphlets proclaimed, "Of course you are not a combatant. But who has destroyed your farm, your business and your home? You should have a close knowledge of your enemy for he is a merciless butcher of our countrymen."

72. Ibid..

73. *Shenbao* (Hankou edition), January 28, 1938, 2. Some corpses were placed in coffins and left on the streets in the hope that they would be given paupers' burials. The coffins were often stripped as well.

74. *North-China Herald*, February 2, 1938, 170; *Shenbao* (Hankou), January 20, 1938, 2; January 28, 1938, 2

75. Reprinted in *North-China Herald*, October 6, 1937, 30.

76. Goodman, *Native Place*, 6–7, 90. Advertisements in Shanghai's Chinese newspapers promoted packages ranging from "economy" to "high class." One facility in the French Concession offered rock-bottom prices (Ch. $2 a month for basic storage). Luxury packages included coffin, burial clothes, headstone, ceremony, and storage fee.

77. *Shenbao*, March 12, 1938, 11; February 8, 1939, 17; *Xinwenbao*, May 27, 1938, 11.

78. *Xinwenbao*, March 8, 1938, 9; March 12, 1938, 11; March 13, 1938, 10; May 27, 1938, 11. The ashes were stored in case families came forward to claim them later.

79. *North-China Herald*, May 25, 1938, 330. The discovery of one thousand corpses (mostly cholera victims) contributed further to the public alarm. The contractor who had been paid to bury the bodies abandoned them. They were found rotting in thirty-two small junks on Suzhou Creek (*North-China Herald*, August 10, 1938, 240).

80. *Shenbao*, January 13, 1939, 11.

81. *North-China Herald*, March 22, 1939, 498. During the last week of January 1940, more than 500 exposed corpses were found on the streets; 90 percent were children under ten. On December 28, 1941, the Public Benevolent Cemetery collected 236 bodies, a new record for the two concessions (*North-China Herald*, January 31, 1940, 163).

82. *The Chinese Recorder* 69:1 (January 1938), 20–21; *Shanghai International Relief Committee Six Month's Report*; *Shenbao*, March 6, 1939, 13. Other examples include a small refugee factory on Amoy Road, with workshops for making toothbrushes, soap, and sundry items; and a shoe repair service at one camp, where customers could dial "41806" for pick up and delivery (*Shenbao*, January 11, 1939, 11; March 25, 1939, 10; *Xinwenbao*, April 15, 1938, 12).

83. *Shenbao*, January 23, 1939, 14; *North-China Herald*, June 6, 1938, 419.

84. *North-China Herald*, March 23, 1938, 465.

85. *Shenbao*, October 17, 1938, 10; January 9, 1939, 13; February 13, 1939, 17; January 19, 1939, 13; March 1, 1939, 12; June 17, 1939, 10.

86. *Nanmin shengchanpin zhanlanhui jinian kan* (Commemorative volume of the refugee production exhibition) (Shanghai, 1939), 1.

87. *Shenbao*, February 13, 1939, 14; March 25, 1939, 10.

88. SMA U1-4-3394, 89–92.

89. Ibid., 66–68, 94.

90. SMA U1-4-3395, 97. There were frequent reports of landlords evicting their longtime legal tenants in order to profit from market conditions (*Xinwenbao*, April 15, 1938, 12; *Shenbao*, April 23, 1939, 12).

91. SMA U1-4-3394, 50–51, 95–98; SMP 29-7479; SMA R19-1-99, 89.

92. *Xinwenbao*, March 12, 1938, 9; March 15, 1938, 11; March 16, 1938, 11; March 20, 1938, 9. In another altercation two weeks later, the police evicted one thousand refugees occupying a building on Jiujiang Road. For two months the Council had tried to persuade them to leave. "In the face of stubborn resistance, especially on the part of the women," the fire department turned on high pressure water hoses to drive them out, while a riot squad surrounded the area. Confronting overwhelming force, the refugees left the building, but camped with their belongings on the sidewalks in protest (*North-China Herald*, April 4, 1938, 37).

93. SMA U1-4-3395, 139–40.

94. SMA U1-4-3394, 123–27.

95. Ibid., 112, 116–18.

96. SMA U1-4-3396, 33–34. The original letter is not in the file, only an English translation.

97. Ibid., 28.

98. Ibid., 31.

99. Ibid., 24.

100. SMA U1-4-3395, 242–43.

101. Ibid., 211–13, 242–43; "The Hut-Dwellers of Singapore Road: A Correction," *The Standard*, July 21, 1938, in SMP 28-7479.

102. A. C. Cornish wrote that Yang is "one of our No. 1 Chinese" and "although I request no special favors for Mr. Yang, may I ask that you please have some one go into this matter and if at all possible arrange that his wishes be met" (SMA U1-4-3395, 103).

103. SMA U1-4-3395, 88.

104. Ibid., 95; U1-4-3396, 6, 75. The practice of barricading shantytowns drew some criticism from foreign residents: "Better to let a few bad men escape rather than have hundreds of innocent people burned to death" (*North-China Herald*, May 24, 1939, 335).

105. SMA U1-4-3395, 92.

106. Ibid., 78, 81.

107. Ibid., 65–67, 73.

108. When Yang received the bill, he angrily contested the charges: "The barbed wire substitute did me more harm than good. If a bamboo fence was employed and a strict watch maintained, the squatters would have disappeared a year ago. However, as I did not ask for barbed wire barrier, I can see no reason why I should pay for a mistake" (SMA U1-4-3395, 41).

109. *North-China Herald*, March 16, 1938, 432; March 23, 1938, 475; May 25, 1938, 311, 345.

110. SMA U1-4-3394, 2–7, 9–10. By year-end 1938, the number of huts had increased to 10,044.

111. Ibid., 34–35.

112. Ibid., 29–31; *North-China Daily News*, May 27, 1938, 6.

113. Reprinted in *North-China Herald*, June 1, 1938, 378.

114. SMA U1-4-3395, 224, 226, 230, 232, emphasis in original.

115. Ibid., 203–4, 206–7.

116. *Shenbao*, October 16, 1938, 10.

117. SMA U1-14-617, 5, 33–38. The Council emphasized again that it did not want to "create a precedent for the upkeep of refugees generally" (SMA U1-14-616, 39).

118. SMA U1-14-630, 97, 119; U1-14-617, 5.

119. SMA U1-14-617, 87–88; U1-14-630, 2.

120. SMA U1-14-617, 80; *North-China Herald*, January 3, 1940, 12; *The China Yearbook* (1939), 555; *Shenbao*, November 4, 1939, 9.

121. SMA U38-2-2213, 13, 17–22, 48; *Shenbao*, April 11, 1939, 11; May 25, 1939, 18; *North-China Herald*, February 15, 1939, 284; *Shanghai Evening Post*, October 23, 1939; February 21, 1940.

122. SMA U1-16-1016, 28; U1-16-1017, 9.

123. SMA U1-16-4863, n.p.; *North-China Herald*, May 1, 1940, 175; July 2, 1941, 11

124. *Shenbao*, March 20, 1939, 10.

125. *North-China Daily News*, May 25, 1940, 2. For other complaints, see *North-China Herald*, March 23, 1938, 475; January 11, 1939, 70; October 18, 1939, 113; September 4, 1941, 504.

126. *North-China Herald*, January 25, 1939, 139. See also October 27, 1937, 141; December 14, 1938, 451.

127. These editorials and letters were clipped and circulated to the police and other departments for action or comment.

128. *Xinwenbao*, March 10, 1939, 11; *Shenbao*, February 1, 1939, 15; April 11, 1939, 11.

129. SMA U1-16-1013, 74, 78.

130. *North-China Herald*, January 3, 1940, 12; January 31, 1940, 182.

131. SMA U1-16-1016, 23–27.

132. *North-China Herald*, July 3, 1940, 14.

133. SMA U1-16-1013, 69, 71–72.

134. Chief Health Inspector P. S. Page's phrase, SMA U1-16-1013, 72.

135. SMA U1-16-1017, 3–5, 9; *North-China Herald*, March 6, 1940, 363.

136. SMA U1-16-1017, 9. *The Municipal Gazette*, March 29, 1940, 18. See verbatim sentiments in *North-China Herald*, November 27, 1940, 334 and *The Municipal Gazette*, November 29, 1940, 201.

137. SMA U1-16-1017, 19.

138. SMA U1-16-1017, 9, 22, 24–25, 27.

139. Ibid., 27–28.

140. Three weeks later Hayashi Yukichi, the seventy-year-old chairman of the Japanese Ratepayers Association, shot Keswick at the annual meeting. He survived to become the head of Britain's secret service after Pearl Harbor. See Frederic Wakeman, Jr., *Shanghai Badlands: Wartime Terrorism and Urban Crime, 1937–1941* (New York: Cambridge University Press, 1996), 100–103.

141. *Shenbao*, December 19, 1940, 9; *North-China Herald*, December 25, 1940, 492; January 8, 1941, 55.

142. SMA U1-16-1017, 57.

143. *Shenbao*, January 8, 1941, 9; *North-China Herald*, January 29, 1941, 174.

144. *Shenbao*, March 24, 1941, 7; *North-China Herald*, March 26, 1941, 488.

145. "Annual Report for 1941," Salvation Army International Heritage Centre, William Booth College, London, CHI/2/1, folder 2, 12–13.

146. SMA U1-16-1017, 62; *North-China Herald*, October 1, 1941, 18; Jun Ke, "Qigai shourongsuo fangwenji" (Record of a visit to the beggar camp), May 15, 1941, repr., *Jiu Shanghai fengqing lu* (Record of customs of old Shanghai) (Shanghai: Wenhui, 1998), 2:316–18.

147. SMA U1-16-1013, 85–89; *Shenbao*, October 10, 1941, 12.

148. This option was chosen because it could be immediately occupied and could be expanded to accommodate ten thousand people (SMA U1-16-1013, 85–89; *Shenbao*, November 1, 1941, 10).

149. SMA U1-16-1013, 85–89; *Xinwenbao*, November 9, 1941, 9; *Shenbao*, October 17, 1941, 11; *China Press*, November 5, 1941; November 26, 1941.

150. *Shenbao*, December 6, 1941, 7; January 9, 1942, 3; *Xinwenbao*, January 9, 1942, 4.

151. Okazaki was Japan's former consul-general in Shanghai. The Japanese did not intervene in the French Concession, where the Vichy government had taken control in 1940 (*Shanghai zujie zhi*, 109, 678–79). On the transition to Japanese authority, see Robert Bickers, "Settlers and Diplomats: The End of British Hegemony in the International Settlement, 1937–1945," in *In the Shadow of the Rising Sun: Shanghai under Japanese Occupation*, ed. Christian Henriot and Wen-hsin Yeh (New York: Cambridge University Press, 2004), 247–49.

152. Christian Henriot, "Rice, Power and People: The Politics of Food Supply in Wartime Shanghai (1937–1945)," *Twentieth-Century China* 26:1 (November 2000), 54–58.

153. *Xinwenbao*, February 8, 1942, 4; *Shenbao*, March 18, 1942, 3; July 16, 1942, 5. In March 1943 there were approximately three to four thousand refugee children left in Shanghai (*Shenbao*, March 5, 1943, 5).

154. *Shenbao*, February 14, 1942, 5; March 20, 1942, 4; March 25, 1942, 4; June 12, 1942, 4.

155. SMA U1-16-1017, 28, 58, 74, 78–80, 83; *Shenbao*, March 26, 1942, 5.

156. SMA U1-14-628, 58.

157. Timothy Brook, "The Great Way Government of Shanghai," in *In the Shadow of the Rising Sun*, 158.

158. Parks Coble, *Chinese Capitalism in Japan's New Order: The Occupied Lower Yangzi, 1937–1945* (Berkeley: University of California Press, 2003), 68–69.

159. "Shi jingcha ju guanyu baogao Hu bei fenju niju xiaomi daofei banfa cheng ji shifu zhiling" (Police report and government order on Shanghai North precinct proposed plan to eliminate robber-bandits), in *Riwei Shanghai shi zhengfu* (Shanghai puppet municipal government) (Shanghai: Dang'an, 1987), 197–98; "Shi jingcha ju guanyu baogao dongfang jiebei banfa cheng ji shifu zhiling" (Police report and government order on winter defense preparations), in *Riwei Shanghai shi zhengfu*, 209.

160. After Wang Jingwei's death in 1944, Chen Gongbo succeeded him as the head of state. He was executed in 1946 for treason.

161. SMA R52-1-125, 1–4; R50-1-114, 3, 13–14, 20–22.

162. SMA U38-5-1669, 234–35; U1-16-1019, 33.

163. *Shijie Hong卍 Zihui jingban Shanghai liumin xiqin suo gongzuo gaikuang* (Report of the Shanghai Indigent Training Institute run by the World Red Swastika Society) (Shanghai, 1943), 6; SMA Q120-3-65, 21.

164. SMA R15-2-56, 7–9.

165. Ibid., 7–11.

166. SMA R15-2-48, 2, 20. Six of the eighteen were partially blind and were allowed to remain at the Relief Home.

167. Ibid., 22–23, 26.

168. SMA R15-2-49 (2), 93–95.

169. Ibid., 98.

170. Ibid., 59–60; R15-2-49 (3), 107; R15-2-44, 24; R15-2-45, 12–15. In July 1944, seventy-two children were sent to Nanjing.

171. SMA R15-2-54, 3–4, 12; R36-11, 259. In 1944 the Social Welfare Ministry in Nanjing ordered all municipalities and provinces to establish labor camps for the detention of "hooligans, local ruffians, beggars and vagrants." The Shanghai labor camp was located at the former Number Two Model Prison, which had been used as a refugee shelter (SMA R18-1-308, 2–3).

172. Arch Carey, *The War Years at Shanghai* (New York: Vantage, 1967), 95. Ash Camp had served as temporary barracks for British troops in years past.

173. *Shenbao*, December 22, 1944, 2; SMA R15-2-68, 153; R15-2-14, 24–25, 47–48. Successive military garrisons occupied Zhongshan Village, which suffered the least damage. When they vacated and left an unpaid bill of Ch. $90,000, the utility company cut off the power, leaving the residents without water or electricity.

174. *Shenbao*, August 15, 1940, 13; November 23, 1940, 13; Zhou Xianwen, "Shuo pin" (Speaking of poverty), *Dongfang zazhi* 40:12 (June 30, 1944), 23–26.

CHAPTER 5

1. *Shenbao*, August 10, 1946, 10; articles from *Xinwenbao* and *Xinyebao*, reprinted in *Shehui yuekan* 1:3 (September 1946), 73–75.

2. *UNRRA in China, 1945–1947* (Washington, D.C., 1948), 119.

3. SMA Q6-9-881, 92, 99; *Shehui yuekan* 2:3 (March 5, 1947), 22.

4. BMA J2-6-584, 5.

5. Gu Zhenggang, "Sanshi qi nian xiaban niandu shehui xingzheng shizheng fangzhen" (Guiding principles for the implementation of social administration in the second half of 1948), *Shehui jianshe* (Social construction) 1:4 (August 1948), 1–3; Zhang Hongxun, *Shehui gongzuo tongxun yuekan*, 4:11 (November 15, 1947), in *Geming wenxian*, 100:18–21.

6. "Shehui jiuji fa" (Social relief law), *Geming wenxian*, 97:351–57.

7. Suzanne Pepper, *Civil War in China: The Political Struggle, 1945–1949* (Berkeley: University of California Press, 1978), 58–72, 99, 110, 126; *Renmin ribao*, December 14, 1947, 1.

8. Pepper, *Civil War*, 42–93; Jeffrey Wasserstrom, *Student Protests in Twentieth-Century China: The View from Shanghai* (Stanford: Stanford University Press, 1991), 225–27.

9. "Zheli bu shi tiantang!" (This is no paradise!), *Qunzhong* (The Masses) 11:10 (July 7, 1946), 20–21.

10. *Guancha* 1:9 (October 26, 1946), 14.

11. *Zhongyang ribao*, November 30, 1946, 4.

12. *UNRRA in China*, 2, 144; *CNRRA: Its Purpose, Functions and Organization* (Shanghai, 1946), 20.

13. "Wanquan chumai" (Complete sell-out), *Qunzhong* 13:6 (November 25, 1946), 10:177; "Lianzong yunwang jiefangqu jiuji wuzi" (CNRRA relief supplies sent to liberated areas), *Qunzhong* 14:8 (February 23, 1947), 10:599.

14. On Yan'an Way, its myths, and complicated realities see Mark Selden, *The Yenan Way in Revolutionary China* (Cambridge, Mass.: Harvard University Press, 1971); Dai Qing, *Wang Shiwei and "Wild Lilies": Rectification and Purges in the Chinese Communist Party, 1942–1944*, trans. Nancy Liu and Lawrence Sullivan (Armonk, N.Y.: M.E. Sharpe, 1993).

15. *Xinhua ribao*, March 18, 1945, 2; July 26, 1945, 3.

16. Sigrid Schmalzer, *The People's Peking Man: Popular Science and Human Identity in Twentieth-Century China* (Chicago: University of Chicago Press, 2008), 60–62.

17. *Xinhua ribao*, October 3, 1943, 2; *Jiefang ribao*, May 1, 1944, 4.

18. Steven Levine, *Anvil of Victory: The Communist Revolution in Manchuria, 1945–1948* (New York: Columbia University Press, 1987), 24, 144–48.

19. Zhang Zhiyi, "Zai diren de xinzang li" (In the heart of the enemy), in *Zhonggong dixia dang xianxing ji*, ed. Xiong Xianghui (repr., Taibei: Chuanji, 1991), 133, 152–53, 156–57; Joseph K. S. Yick, *Making Urban Revolution in China: The CCP-GMD Struggle for Beiping-Tianjin, 1945–1949* (Armonk, N.Y.: M.E. Sharpe, 1995), esp. 65–75.

20. *Jiefang zhanzheng shiqi Zhonggong Beiping dixiadang douzheng shiliao* (Historical materials on struggles of the Communist underground in Beiping during the War of Liberation) (Beijing: Zhonggong Beijing shiwei dangshi yanjiushi, 1996), 9–44; *Shanghai shi Huxi diqu chengshi pinmin geming douzheng shi ziliao* (Historical materials on the revolutionary struggles of the urban poor in Shanghai's Western District) (Shanghai, 1988), 10–18.

21. BMA J2-6-298, 24–25; J2-6-325, 29–30. Police precincts and *baojia* leaders provided the data on "poor" households, categorized as "destitute" (*chipin*) and "less poor" (*cipin*).

22. BMA J2-6-358, 1; J2-6-422, 1–4; J2-6-616, 40–44.

23. BMA J2-6-616, 56–57.

24. BMA J2-6-401, 150–51; J2-6-420, 27, 31.

25. BMA J2-6-420, 2–21. A similar incident occurred in October 1948, involving over two thousand students from Shanxi (J2-6-420, 52–55). In 1948, there were twenty to thirty thousand student refugees in Beijing, and as many in Nanjing (Pepper, *Civil War*, 174–75).

26. BMA J2-6-359, 1–3; J2-6-361, 8–9; J2-6-358, 7–8.

27. BMA J2-6-348, 13–14. Officials instructed Su to obtain a reference from his native place association and register at the refugee shelter.

28. BMA J2-6-371, 24–26. Sun was referred to the Number 1 Refugee Station.

29. Many examples are in BMA J2-6-347, J2-6-351, J2-6-353.

30. BMA J2-6-351, 1–2.

31. BMA J2-6-361, 12–14. The Hebei association forwarded Song's letter to the Social Affairs Bureau, which responded that the government had already granted refugees at the Ditan Shelter a one-month extension.

32. BMA J2-6-300, 16.

33. BMA J2-6-373, 11–13. Xiao assumed that upon departure the residents would go/return to the countryside to become "the backbone of the nation's new villages."

34. BMA J2-6-435, 59–63; J2-6-279, 29.

35. BMA J2-6-449, 1–2.

36. Many examples are in BMA J2-6-272, J2-6-274, J2-6-279, and J2-6-340.

37. BMA J2-6-274; J2-6-290.

38. BMA J2-6-346, 10–19. For other examples, see letters in J2-6-347 and J2-6-349.

39. BMA J2-6-335; J2-6-339.

40. BMA J2-6-320, 8–12.

41. BMA J2-6-280; J2-6-281.

42. Wedding photographs filed in BMA J2-6-281, J2-6-283, and J2-6-315, which I was allowed to see in 2002, have been removed from the open-access records at the Beijing Municipal Archive.

43. It was easy to conceal a previous marriage, e.g., by claiming that the first wife had died in one's hometown.

44. Several cases of former prostitutes who married from the Relief Home are in BMA J2-6-315.

45. Rogaski, "Beyond Benevolence," 77–80.

46. BMA J2-6-283, 34–36.

47. BMA J2-7-1131, 12–22; J1-3-188, 3–8.

48. BMA J184-2-1836, 3–4; J185-2-10042, 4.

49. BMA J181-16-251, 14–15; J184-2-1836, 11.

50. BMA J181-2-38921, 16.

51. BMA J2-1-422, 4–5; J2-1-416, 36–37, 75–76.

52. BMA J2-7-1150, 37; J183-2-37743, 1.

53. BMA J2-6-312, 17–19.

54. BMA J2-6-448, 5–8.

55. BMA J2-1-581, 2–16; J2-6-363, 3–6, 9–11.

56. Pepper, *Civil War*, 210–11; Zou Yiren, *Jiu Shanghai*, 90–91.

57. Pan Tao, "Minguo shiqi Subei shuizai zaikuang jianshu" (Brief description of floods in Subei during the Republican period), *Minguo dang'an* 4 (1998), 108–10; David Faure, *The Rural Economy of Pre-Liberation China: Trade Expansion and Peasant Livelihood in Jiangsu and Guangdong, 1870 to 1937* (New York: Oxford University Press, 1989), 47.

58. Honig, *Creating Chinese Ethnicity*, 2–3, 30–31.

59. Chen Yung-fa, *Making Revolution: The Communist Movement in Eastern and Central China, 1937–1945* (Berkeley: University of California Press, 1986). The Communists withdrew after the New Fourth Army incident of January 1941, but returned shortly thereafter.

60. Liu Jiping, "Lun muqian Huazhong jiefangqu jiaoyu gongzuo" (Discussion of current educational work in Central China's liberated areas), in *Jiefang zhanzheng chuqi Su Wan bianqu jiaoyu* (1946; repr., Beijing: Renmin jiaoyu, 1983), 6.

61. Pepper, *Civil War*, 298–99; Jiang Zhiliang, "Jiefang zhanzheng zhong de Jiangsu" (Jiangsu during the War of Liberation), *Jiangsu difang zhi* 2 (1999), 19.

62. Wang Maogong, "Subei shuizai baogao" (Report on the Subei floods), in *Subei shuizai baogao shu* (1947), 2. The epidemics included outbreaks of black fever, blood flukes, and other parasitic diseases.

63. Yang Jianhua, "Jiuzai fanghuang" (Relieve disaster, prevent famine), *Qunzhong* 11:6 (June 10, 1946), 12. On the famine of 1877, see Edgerton-Tarpley, *Tears from Iron*; He Hanwei, *Guangxu chunian Huabei de da hanzai* (The great drought in the Huabei region during the early Guangxu years) (Hong Kong: Zhongwen daxue, 1980).

64. "Subei nanmin huixiang" (Subei refugees return home), *Dagong bao* (L'Impartial) (June 4, 1946), 1.

65. Transcript of Marshall–Chiang meeting, June 30, 1946, in *Xian Zongtong Jianggong sixiang yanlun zongji*, 38:202.

66. "Subei wenti da kewen" (Answers to visitors' questions about Subei), *Qunzhong* 12:1 (July 28, 1946), 12.

67. "Subei shuizai zhenxiang" (The truth about the Subei floods), *Qunzhong* 12:8 (September 14, 1946), 12.

68. For most of its publishing life *Shenbao* had been an independent paper based in the International Settlement. In 1945, the GMD allowed *Shenbao* to resume publication under government supervision. Although not an official Party publication, its editorial line became much more pro-GMD (Ma Guangren, ed. *Shanghai xinwen shi, 1850–1949* [History of Shanghai newspapers, 1850–1949] [Shanghai: Fudan daxue, 1996], 999–1002).

69. *Shenbao*, October 6, 1946, 3; October 8, 1946, 10; October 12, 1946, 2; October 16, 1946, 9; November 6, 1946, 9.

70. Wang Maogong, "Subei shuizai," 1.

71. Zhang Yiping, "Ziran zaihai, zhengzhi douzheng yu Subei minsheng" (Natural calamity, political struggle, and Subei people's life) (M.A. thesis, Nanjing Normal University, 2004), 10.

72. *Shenbao*, October 3, 1946, 2; December 2, 1946, 3; *Shanhou jiuji zongshu Su Ning fenshu yewu baogao* (Report of Su-Ning branch relief association) (1946), 1–6.

73. Honig, *Creating Chinese Ethnicity*, 37–41.

74. *Shenbao*, July 24, 1946, 8; July 26, 1946, 4; August 20, 1946, 4.

75. *Shanghai Subei nanmin jiuji baogao* (Report on relief of Subei refugees in Shanghai) (Shanghai, 1947), 89–91, 95–96.

76. Honig, *Creating Chinese Ethnicity*, 72.

77. *Shenbao*, September 1, 1946, 12; September 28, 1946, 4; November 21, 1946, 6. The rickshaw ban was scheduled to be phased in over three years.

78. *Shanghai Subei nanmin jiuji baogao*, 96; *Shenbao*, December 4, 1946, 6.

79. A similar ban in Tianjin in 1946 was not enforced (Yick, *Making Urban Revolution*, 144).

80. "Tanfan saodong kuoda" (Street vendor disturbances expand), *Xinmin wanbao* (New citizens evening news) (December 1, 1946), 1; *North-China Daily News*, December 1, 1946, 1–2; "Lun Shanghai minluan" (On the popular disturbances in Shanghai), *Guancha* 1:16 (December 24, 1946), 3–5. Reports differ as to who fired the first shots.

81. *North-China Daily News*, December 3, 1946, 2. These tins were probably

UNRRA supplies. The report suggests that the peddlers pilfered them from cargo at the port. But some UNRRA supplies were sold on the open market to pay work relief wages, while other shipments, stolen by staff members, were sold on the black market.

82. *Shenbao*, December 3, 1946, 5.

83. *Shenbao*, December 2, 1946, 12; "Weekend Riots," *North-China Daily News*, December 4, 1946, 5.

84. "Lun Shanghai tanfan fengchao" (Discussion of the Shanghai street vendors' unrest), *Qunzhong* 13:8 (December 9, 1946), 10:212.

85. Wu Kaixian, "Shehui jiuji shiye zhi zhongyao" (The importance of social relief work), *Shehui yuekan* 1:5 (November 1946), 3. Wu Kaixian had been in charge of the GMD underground movement in Shanghai during the Sino-Japanese War. On Wu's connections to gang boss Du Yuesheng, see Brian G. Martin, "Resistance and Cooperation: Du Yuesheng and the Politics of the Shanghai United Committee, 1940–1945," in *In the Shadow of the Rising Sun*, 187–208.

86. SMA Q1-12-1689, 11; Q109-1-261, 12.

87. SMA Q6-9-867, 21.

88. Rae Levine, "Memorandum on the Problem of Caring for 182 Homeless Children at the Chaohoching Camp," in SMA Q6-9-868, 46. Levine was one of several hundred UNRRA staff on loan to CNRRA.

89. SMA Q1-12-1689, 11–13; Q6-9-985, 34; Q6-9-896, 65.

90. SMA Q6-9-988, 27; Q6-9-890, 7–14.

91. SMA Q6-9-909, 3–4, 37; Q6-9-937, 14–16; Q6-9-943, 2; Q6-9-959, 2; Q149-3-314, 13, 22. Statistics on inmates for December 1947–March 1949 can be found in Q6-9-923, Q6-9-924, and Q6-9-929.

92. Some examples include a fish peddler who got into an altercation with other vendors; a deaf teenager selling popsicles on the street, who got into a fight with local hooligans; and numerous runaway apprentices (SMA Q6-9-915, 26, 36).

93. SMA Q145-4-84, 18; Q6-9-959, 14, 22; Q6-9-918, 18–19, 66; Q6-9-915, 10.

94. SMA Q6-9-985, 36; Q6-9-963, 10–11. The division for the disabled and infirm also moved several times, from one ramshackle facility to another, before settling into a livestock market and sharing the premises with animals (Q6-9-984, 64–66, 88–89).

95. SMA Q6-9-969, 51–52; Q6-9-963, 11. The majority had attended some primary school; a few had middle school education.

96. SMA Q6-9-933, 11, 15; Q6-9-952, 9; Q153-4-31, 19.

97. Details on the Relief Home's numerous problems are in SMA Q6-9-890, Q6-9-913, and Q6-9-935.

98. SMA Q6-9-959, 23–24. In October 1947, three former prostitutes at the women's center intentionally started a fire, intending to run away during the panic (SMA Q6-9-972, 37–39).

99. SMA Q6-9-969, 39–40; Q6-9-943, 11–12, 33, 35, 44.

100. SMA Q6-9-973, 85–92; Q1-12-1495, 55–56.

101. Summarized from SMA Q6-9-964, which contains all of the documents related to this case.

102. SMA Q6-9-964, 32–36.

103. Ibid., 8. This is a transcription of the letter. The original is not in the file.

104. Ibid., 11–12.

105. Ibid., 26–27, 37–50.

106. Although Mrs. Huang lived for more than a month after the incident, there is no record of any attempt to question her. She remained at the hospital the entire time, and could have been unconscious.

107. SMA Q6-9-964, 15.

108. SMA Q6-9-966, 6–7. The other accusations about Director Sha included allegations that she locked new inmates in a cage, sold off the inmates' personal property, and embezzled food rations to support her drug habit (Q6-9-964, 55–56).

109. SMA Q6-9-942, 35; Q6-9-890, 7–14.

110. See SMA Q6-9-913 and Q6-9-953. The Relief Home received a commission for each successful recruit.

111. SMA Q139-4-80, 6.

112. SMA Q153-4-31 57.

113. SMA Q109-1-261, 12; Q139-4-80, 22; Q131-4-96, 4–5.

114. SMA Q6-9-959, 11.

115. In July 1946, He Dekui faced accusations of treason for his work for the International Settlement during the Sino-Japanese War. After a storm of controversy, an investigation concluded that the charges were unfounded.

116. SMA Q106-1-96, 26; Q109-1-261, 9; Q106-1-153, 28; Q106-1-211, 22.

117. SMA Q106-1-151, 8–9.

118. Zhang Shude, "Dongling bihansuo gongzuo de huigu" (A review of the work of the winter shelters), *Shehui yuekan* 2:3 (March 5, 1947), 22, 26–27.

119. SMA Q106-1-26, 15.

120. Ibid., 16–17.

121. SMA Q106-1-90, 24–25.

122. Ibid., 22–23. For other complaints about the separation of families at the winter shelters, see SMA Q106-1-26, 2; Q6-9-855, 17.

123. Q106-1-91, 38; Q145-2-760, 41; Q106-1-96, 4, 29. Wrongful detentions were an equally serious issue at the Relief Home. Hundreds of release petitions are in SMA Q6-9-914, 915, 916, 917, 918, 919, 920, 921, and 922.

124. SMA Q153-4-31, 56–57. The police chief later instructed his officers that native Shanghai "beggar vagrants" should not be classified as "refugees" and should be sent the workhouse (SMA Q139-4-80, 57).

125. SMA Q106-1-17, 16, 34. Many of the runaways took the blankets, clothing, toothbrushes, and other items issued to them, depleting the shelters' limited supplies.

126. Ibid., 16; Zhang Shude, "Dongling bihansuo," 26.

127. SMA Q143-4-59, 7–8; Q106-1-64, 20.

128. SMA Q106-1-15, 13; Q106-1-27, 7, 47; Q106-1-94, 8.

129. SMA Q106-1-142, 12–26, 28, 42–49, 52–54; Q106-1-183, 22–27, 36, 40, 48; Q106-1-162, 1–2.

130. SMA Q106-1-183, 2–3, 8–11, 14–17. Eleven refugees were sent to the workhouse for punishment; several others were expelled.

131. *Shanghai penghu qu de bianqian*, 7.

132. SMA Q6-15-109, 23–24, 47. The regulations included detailed rules on location, size, and building materials. The initial exemption was one year, extended to two years in December 1945.

133. "Qudi penghu yougan" (Thoughts on the ban on straw huts), *Qunzhong* 13:9 (December 16, 1946), 10:263.

134. SMA Q109-1-650, 8–10. Examples of applications are filed in SMA Q6-9-739 and Q1-11-80.

135. SMA Q1-11-177, 2–3.

136. Ibid., 10–11. Conflicts between factory owners and hut dwellers were especially numerous, since the premises usually included spacious grounds that could accommodate many huts.

137. SMA Q109-1-650, 8–10; Q1-11-70, 3–5. Zhao Zukang (1900–1995) was a Cornell-trained engineer, best known for being the last GMD mayor of Shanghai, a post he held for four days before surrendering to the CCP.

138. SMA Q6-9-746, 20–28.

139. SMA Q6-9-739, 28–29.

140. SMA Q6-9-745, 87–89.

141. Ibid., 105–7.

142. Pingjiang Gongsuo was an association of sojourners from Pingjiang County, Hunan. Goodman, *Native Place* (38–45) discusses the different terms for organizations that represented people from the same native place (*huiguan, gongsuo, tongxianghui*, and so on). To minimize confusion, I use "native place association" throughout.

143. SMA Q106-1-111, 5–6.

144. SMA Q1-10-190, 3.

145. "Burn all, kill all, loot all" was actually the Japanese scorched-earth campaign during WWII.

146. SMA Q6-9-652, 5. The 300,000 figure is certainly an exaggeration. Most estimates for the number of Subei refugees in Shanghai claim 100,000.

147. Ibid., 7–8, 23, 52; Q1-10-190, 21, 23.

148. The Chao-Hui association represented the natives of Chaoyang and Huilai counties in Guangdong.

149. SMA Q1-10-190, 12, 18, 37, 45; Q6-9-652, 18.

150. Shao Yong, *Minguo banghui* (Gangs in the Republican period) (Fuzhou: Fujian renmin, 2002), 378. Zheng Ziliang was executed in 1951 as a "counter-revolutionary." Du Yuesheng died in Hong Kong in 1949.

151. SMA Q1-10-190, 69.

152. Ibid., 82.

153. Ibid., 28, 42, 43.

154. Ibid., 75–78, 81, 90.

155. Ibid., 86–87.

156. SMA Q6-9-652, 184–90; Q1-10-190, 119–20, 129.

157. SMA Q106-1-29, 37; Q106-1-115, 63; Q1-10-190, 177.

158. SMA Q1-10-190, 112, 177, 207, 225; Q106-1-187, 20.

159. SMA Q1-10-190, 155. More than seventy other huts at the Chao-Hui cemetery were not demolished, since 350 people occupied them and refused to leave.

160. Ibid., 104, 112, 201; Q106-1-193, 3–4; Q6-9-652, 71. The Yanxu, Xijin, and Yangzhou Associations' coffin repositories were all located in Zhabei. Jingjiang's were in Nanshi.

161. SMA Q1-10-190, 102.

162. See Pepper, *Civil War*, 95–96 for a summary of this view.

163. Ibid., 121–26.

164. Jiang Jingguo, "Shanghai wang hechu qu?" (Where is Shanghai headed?) in

Jiang Jingguo zai Shanghai (Jiang Jingguo in Shanghai), ed. Cai Zhenyun (Nanjing: Zhonghua, 1948), 45–46, 49.

Epilogue

1. "Shanghai's Millions Quickly Swing into Line behind the Communists," *New York Times*, May 27, 1949, 4; *Renmin ribao*, May 27, 1949, 1; Odd Arne Westad, *Decisive Encounters: The Chinese Civil War, 1946–1950* (Stanford: Stanford University Press, 2003), 246–52.

2. December 13, 1948, directive, in *Beijing dangshi yanjiu* (Beijing Party history research) 6 (1989), 3–4; Levine, *Anvil of Victory*, 144–50; Kenneth Lieberthal, *Revolution and Tradition in Tientsin, 1949–1952* (Stanford: Stanford University Press, 1980), 28–40.

3. Shi Hongxi, *Jieguan Shanghai qinliji* (Personal experiences of the Shanghai takeover) (Shanghai, 1997), 235; Elizabeth Perry, "Masters of the Country? Shanghai Workers in the Early People's Republic," in *Dilemmas of Victory*, ed. Jeremy Brown and Paul Pickowicz (Cambridge, Mass.: Harvard University Press, 2007), 59–71.

4. SMA B168-1-494, 1; B168-1-500, 4.

5. Lieberthal, *Revolution and Tradition*, 32.

6. *Renmin ribao*, April 19, 1949, 2; BMA 2-1-55, 48.

7. Of the more than thirty thousand ex-soldiers found in the spring of 1949, the majority claimed to be long-time Beijing residents without homes or native place ties. More than half were eventually persuaded and/or coerced into leaving the city. "Beiping shi chuli Guomindang liusan guanbin de gongzuo zongjie" (Summary report regarding the disposition of Nationalist *liusan* officials and soldiers in Beiping), *Beiping jiefang* (The liberation of Beiping) (Beijing: Zhongguo dang'an, 2009), 2:640–44; BMA 40-1-38, 3–6.

8. BMA 1-6-237, 25.

9. Ibid., 1–2, 10–12, 14–15.

10. SMA B168-1-494, 3; B168-1-498, 16; *Jiefang ribao*, December 15, 1949, 2.

11. SMA B168-1-494, 7–10.

12. *Jiefang ribao*, September 13, 1949, 1; SMA B168-1-494, 9, 14.

13. BMA 2-1-13, 11; SMA B168-1-494, 14–17.

14. "Ba jishengzhe biancheng shengchanzhe!" (Convert parasites into producers!) *Renmin ribao*, May 9, 1949, 2; April 19, 1949, 2.

15. BMA 2-1-55, 3–4.

16. SMA B168-1-924, 5–7; *Renmin ribao*, April 19, 1949, 2.

17. "Shourong qigai gongzuo zongdian" (Summary points regarding the work of detaining beggars), *Beiping jiefang*, 2:750, 755.

18. SMA 168-1-496, 4. Qi Shoukang, the head of the Disabled Asylum, was the only director who remained.

19. Of the monks, one Communist official observed, "No matter no young or old, regardless of their religious persuasion, they all retain a strong parasitic ideology" (BMA 2-1-55, 48).

20. "Zhonggong Beiping Shiwei guanyu shourong qigai gongzuo zongjie" (CCP Beiping Municipal Committee summary report regarding the work of detaining beg-

gars), *Beijing shi zhongyao wenxian xuanbian 1948.12–1949* (Beijing: Zhongguo dang'an, 2001), 598.

21. Ibid., 598, 602–5. Aminda Smith describes the techniques of "speaking bitterness" ("Reeducating the People: The Chinese Communists and the 'Thought Reform' of Beggars, Prostitutes, and Other 'Parasites'" [Ph.D. diss., Princeton University, 2006], 105–8).

22. BMA 2-1-55, 43; Smith, "Reeducating the People," 116–18.

23. SMA B168-1-931, 3.

24. SMA B168-1-500, 2–6; *Jiefang ribao*, December 20, 1949, 4.

25. SMA B168-1-931, 8.

26. SMA B168-1-924, 7–8.

27. SMA B168-1-931, 8–11.

28. Ruan Qinghua, *Shanghai youmin gaizao yanjiu* (Research on the reform of vagrants in Shanghai) (Shanghai: Cishu, 2009), 131–32.

29. SMA B168-1-925, 1–4, 76–81. Cadres worried constantly about their marital prospects. Many received letters from parents badgering them to return to get married. One cadre was so desperate that he tried to marry one of the "vagrants"; the few unmarried women among the detainees were highly sought after (79).

30. SMA B168-1-925, 16–20.

31. SMA B1-1-39, 1–5.

32. Ibid., 3.

33. Ibid., 2–4; B168-1-925, 45–46.

34. SMA B1-1-39, 16–19.

35. SMA B169-1-501, 69–70. By year-end 1951, when transfers were suspended, more than twelve thousand "vagrants" had been sent to Subei.

36. Ibid., 45–46. The successive tides of rural refugees would continue until the strict enforcement of the *hukou* system in the late 1950s.

37. Ibid., 5.

38. Peng Zhen, "Zhangwo dang de jiben zhengce zuohao ruchenghou de gongzuo" (Firmly grasp the Party's fundamental policies to do a good job after entering the city), in *Beijing shi zhongyao wenxian xuanbian 1948.12–1949*, 74. Peng Zhen became the Mayor of Beijing in 1951, a post he held until he was purged at the beginning of the Cultural Revolution in 1966.

39. SMA B168-1-505, 18; Li Xiaowei, "Xin Zhongguo chengli chuqi chengshi pinmin de shenghuo jiuzhu yanjiu," *Jiaoxue yu yanjiu* 8 (2009), 63; BMA 9-2-96, 3, 129–30. On the treatment of soldiers and military dependents, see Neil Diamant, *Embattled Glory: Veterans, Military Families, and the Politics of Patriotism in China, 1949–2007* (Lanham, Md.: Rowman & Littlefield, 2009).

40. BMA 2-8-51, 3–6. The policy came to fruition in the late 1950s, with the establishment and enforcement of the urban *hukou* system (see Solinger, *Contesting Citizenship in Urban China*).

41. Peng Zhen, "Zai shi zhi'an gongzuo huiyi shang de jianghua" (Speech delivered at municipal security meeting), February 19, 1949, in *Beijing shi zhongyao wenxian xuanbian 1948.12–1949*, 164; SMA B168-1-498, 3–4, 16; B168-1-686, 19; *Renmin ribao*, September 13, 1950, 1.

42. BMA 2-3-57, 14, 26.

43. SMA B168-1-686, 9–13, 19–21.

44. There were an estimated two hundred thousand households, with nearly one million people, living in straw huts (*Shanghai penghu qu de bianqian*, 7).

45. *Shanghai penghu qu de bianqian*, 53–60; SMA A60-1-25, 1–11.

46. Perry, "Masters of the Country?"; *Beijing shizheng bao* no. 9 (1951), 70–74; BMA 2-8-51, 5.

47. Peng Zhen, "Zai quanshi zhigong jiji fenzi dahui shang de baogao" (Report at the all-city meeting of workers and activists), March 20, 1949, in *Beijing shi zhongyao wenxian xuanbian 1948.12–1949*, 251.

48. Eddy U, "The Making of *Zhishifenzi*: The Critical Impacts of the Registration of Unemployed Intellectuals in the Early PRC," *The China Quarterly* 173 (2003), 104–7. According to U's analysis, the official figures understated the extent of unemployment. The "Five-Anti" campaign targeted bribery, tax evasion, theft of state property, cheating on government contracts, and stealing state economic information.

49. BMA 110-1-265, 20–25, 35.

50. "Jiefang chuqi Shanghai tanfan guanli gongzuo gaikuang baogao" (Report on the work of managing Shanghai's peddlers in the early Liberation period), April 1953, repr., *Shanghai dang'an shiliao yanjiu* 6 (2009), 332.

51. "Ye Jianying tongzhi zai tanfan zuotanhui shang de jianghua" (Comrade Ye Jianying's speech at the peddlers meeting), May 23, 1949, in BMA 2-1-94, 1–3.

52. Ibid., 3–10.

53. BMA 2-1-94, 11–14; Zhang Shifei, "Beijing jiefang chuqi de zhengli tanfan gongzuo" (The work of organizing peddlers during Beijing's early liberation period), *Beijing dangshi* 2 (2004), 45–46.

54. "Zhonggong Beiping shiwei guanyu zhengli tanfan gongzuo de zongjie" (The CCP Beiping Municipal Committee summary report on organizing peddlers), August 1949, *Beiping jiefang*, 2:768–70. A committee for "organizing the city's appearance" was announced in early May 1949, but soon disbanded (*Renmin ribao*, May 14, 1949, 1).

55. BMA 4-9-51, 12–14, 20–22; 2-1-94, 27. In 1950, a nineteen-tier tax system based on capitalization value was adopted, aimed at constraining the growth of large vendors and protecting small peddlers.

56. BMA 22-10-159, 5, 12. Commerce Bureau officials asked the Public Security Bureau for help, but were told that they too were short-handed.

57. BMA 22-10-125, 10–11.

58. Ibid., 14–16; "Jiefang chuqi Shanghai tanfan guanli gongzuo gaikuang baogao," 323. The initial campaign to reorganize peddlers in Shanghai was a joint effort among several municipal agencies. The participation of the Public Security Bureau, which Beijing's effort did not have, may account for its greater success (BMA 22-10-159, 5).

59. Enforcement was particularly lax during the Five-Anti campaign, with cadres distracted by the turmoil. In addition, growing unemployment meant more people took to making their living on the streets.

60. "Jiefang chuqi Shanghai tanfan guanli gongzuo gaikuang baogao," 327.

61. BMA 22-10-159, 12, 51; SMA B168-1-14, 31.

62. SMA B2-1-21, 2–3; Ruan Qinghua, *Shanghai youmin*, 232. The term *shehui zhazi* has a strong criminal connotation. For instance, in the aftermath of the 1989 Tian'anmen student protests, the government news agency frequently identified the ringleaders as *shehui zhazi*.

63. BMA 2-3-79, 8–9; SMA 168-1-505, 18–19; Wu Yunfu, "Zhongguo renmin jiuji

zonghui gongzuo baogao" (All-China People's Relief Association report), November 25, 1952, *Minzheng gongzuo shouce* 5 (1953), 166, 170; Ji Gang, "Guanyu chengshi fuli gongzuo de baogao" (Report on urban relief and welfare work), November 27, 1952, *Minzheng gongzuo shouce* 5 (1953), 179–80.

64. BMA 2-3-57, 14.

65. BMA 14-2-88, 18–20.

66. SMA B168-1-49, 14–16.

67. Ibid., 10

68. Ibid., 18.

69. Dorothy Solinger, "The *Dibao* Recipients: Mollified Anti-Emblem of Urban Modernization," *China Perspectives* 4 (2008), 37.

70. In March 2010, a McDonald's clerk in Shanghai was stabbed to death when he tried to evict one such McRefugee.

Glossary

anfen — 安分
baojia — 保甲
beiruo — 卑弱
biesan — 癟三
bihansuo — 避寒所
bu anfen / benfen — 不安分 / 本分
chengshi pinmin — 城市貧民
chipin — 赤貧
chong — 蟲
chulu — 出路
cipin — 次貧
Cishantuan — 慈善團
daishu fei — 代書費
daoliu — 倒流
dongfang — 冬防
du — 蠹
duli shengcun — 獨立生存
duomin — 惰民
e'gai — 惡丐
erliuzi — 二流子
feimin, wu — 廢民, 物
fenpei bujun — 分配不均
Funü Jiaoyangsuo — 婦女教養所
fuqiang — 富強
ganhua jiaoyu — 感化教育
ganhuasuo — 感化所
gong — 工
gongde — 公德
Gongdelin — 功德林
gongmin — 公民
gongyichang, ju, suo — 工藝場, 局, 所
gongzhensuo — 工賑所
guandu shangban — 官督商辦
guangua dugu — 鰥寡獨孤
guomin — 國民
gudao — 孤島
guorong — 國容

huiguan—會館
hunhe mian—混合面
Jiangbei—江北
jiaoyangyuan—教養院
jiji shengchan—積極生產
jijiu—急救
jimin—饑民
Jingshi Youmin Xiyisuo—京師游民習藝所
jipin—極貧
jisheng chong—寄生蟲
jiujiyuan—救濟院
jiyang—寄養
jusong—拘送
lanmin—懶民
laochong—痨蟲
laodong renmin—勞動人民
laodong shensheng—勞動神聖
laoyu—牢獄
liuli shisuo—流離失所
liumin—流民
Liumin Xiqinsuo—流民習勤所
lunluo funü—淪落婦女
mao—蟊
maozei—蟊賊
mianzi—面子
minsheng—民生
nanmin—難民
Nanmin Nantong Shourongsuo—難民難童收容所
nanmin zijisuo—難民自給所
neirong—內容
nuanchang—暖廠
penghu—棚戶
pin—貧
pingdeng—平等
pingmin—平民
pinkun—貧困
pinmin—貧民
pinnong—貧農
pinqiong—貧窮
pinshi—貧士
Pujitang—普濟堂
qiang—強
qiangpo gaizao—強迫改造
qianshansuo—遷善所
qigai—乞丐
qiliusuo—棲流所

Qinshengyuan — 勤生院
qiongku renmin — 窮苦人民
qiufan — 囚犯
queshi wufa shengchan — 確實無法生產
renzha — 人渣
ruo — 弱
shehui diaocha — 社會調查
shehui geming — 社會革命
shehui jisheng chong — 社會寄生蟲
shehui jiuji — 社會救濟
shehui xue — 社會學
shehui zhazi — 社會渣子
Shehuiju — 社會局
shengchan zijiu — 生產自救
shirong — 市容
shisuo — 失所
shiye — 失業
shouliu — 收留
shourong — 收容
shusan weiyuanhui — 疏散委員會
Songhu Jiaoyangyuan — 淞滬教養院
Subei — 蘇北
Tianjin Zuifan Xiyisuo — 天津罪犯習藝所
tongxianghui — 同鄉會
wufa jixu shenghuo — 無法繼續生活
wuye — 無業
xiaoji shiyu — 消極施與
Xin Puyutang — 新普育堂
Xinmincun — 新民村
xiyisuo, chang — 習藝所, 廠
xunyu — 訓育
yangjiyuan — 養濟院
yangmin — 養民
yao chifan yao shengchan — 要吃飯 要生產
yigong daizhen — 以工代賑
yilai — 依賴
youduo wulai — 游惰無賴
youmin — 游民
Youmin Laodongying — 游民勞動營
youmin wuchan jieji — 游民無產階級
Youmin Xiqinsuo — 游民習勤所
youmin — 莠民
yu — 愚
ziben — 資本
zili — 自力
zili — 自立

zishi qili — 自食其力
zitou — 自投
zixinsuo — 自新所
ziyou — 自由
ziyuan — 自願
zuifan xiyisuo — 罪犯習藝所
zuo'er daishi — 坐而待食

Bibliography

Beijing Municipal Archive 北京市檔案館 (BMA).

Dwight Edwards Papers, Special Collections, Yale Divinity School Library.

First Historical Archive, Beijing 第一歷史檔案館 (FHA).

John and Stella Fisher Burgess Papers, Manuscripts Division, Department of Rare Books and Special Collections, Princeton University Library (JSFB Papers).

Ida Pruitt Papers, Schlesinger Library, Radcliffe Institute, Harvard University (Ida Pruitt Papers).

Second Historical Archive, Nanjing 第二歷史檔案館 (NJ).

Shanghai Municipal Archive 上海市檔案館 (SMA).

Shanghai Municipal Police Archives, National Archives and Records Administration, microfilm edition (SMP).

Alitto, Guy. *The Last Confucian: Liang Shu-ming and the Chinese Dilemma of Modernity.* Berkeley: University of California Press, 1979.

Andrews, Bridie. "The Making of Modern Chinese Medicine, 1895–1937." Ph.D. dissertation, University of Cambridge, 1996.

———. "Tuberculosis and the Assimilation of Germ Theory in China, 1895–1937." *Journal of the History of Medicine and Allied Sciences* 52 (1997), 114–51.

Annual Report of the Shanghai Municipal Council. Shanghai.

Arkush, R. David. *Fei Xiaotong and Sociology in Revolutionary China.* Cambridge, Mass.: Harvard University Press, 1981.

Arnold, Julean. *Some Bigger Issues in China's Problems.* Shanghai, 1928.

Bailey, Paul J. *Reform the People: Changing Attitudes towards Popular Education in Early Twentieth-Century China.* Vancouver: University of British Columbia Press, 1990.

Baojia shu jiyao 保甲書輯要 (Summary of *baojia* regulations). Comp. Xu Dong 徐棟. 1868.

Beckett, Hal. *Save the World Army: Adventures of Two Pioneering Salvationists in North China.* London: Salvationist, 1947.

Beier, A. L. *Masterless Men: The Vagrancy Problem in England, 1560–1640.* London: Methuen, 1985.

Beijing difang ge fuwutuan baogao 北京地方各服務團報告 (Report of each local community service group in Beijing). Beijing, 1922.

Beijing shi zhigao 北京市志稿 (Draft gazetteer of Beijing). Ed. Wang Tingxie 王廷燮. 1939. Reprint, Beijing: Yanshan, 1998.

Beijing shi zhongyao wenxian xuanbian 北京市重要文獻選編 (Selected important documents of Beijing). Ed. Beijing shi dang'an guan 北京市檔案館 (Beijing Municipal Archive). Beijing: Zhongguo dang'an, 2001.

Beijing xinwen huibao 北京新聞滙報 (News magazine of Beijing). Beijing.

Beiping jiefang 北平解放 (The liberation of Beiping). Ed. Beijing shi dang'an guan 北京市檔案館 (Beijing Municipal Archive). Beijing: Zhongguo dang'an, 2009.

Beiping Pinmin Jiujihui zhengxinlu 北平貧民救濟會徵信錄 (Beiping Poor Relief Society record of donations). Beiping, 1933.

Beiping shi shizheng gongbao 北平市市政公報 (Official bulletin of the Beiping municipal government). Beiping, 1928–37.

Beiping shi tongji lanyao 北平市統計覽要 (Overview of Beiping statistics). Beiping, 1936.

Beiping shi zhengfu gong'an ju yewu baogao 北平市政府公安局業務報告 (Beiping Public Security Bureau work report). Beiping, 1933.

Beiping shi zhengfu tongji yuekan 北平市政府統計月刊 (Beiping municipal statistics monthly). Beiping, 1934.

Beiping tebie shi shehuiju jiuji shiye xiao shi 北平特別市社會局救濟事業小史 (Brief history of Beiping Bureau of Social Affairs relief matters). Beiping, 1929.

Beiping tebie shi shehuiju jiuji zhuankan 北平特別市社會局救濟專刊 (Beiping Bureau of Social Affairs special issue on relief). Beiping, 1930.

Beiyang gongdu leizuan 北洋公牘類纂 (Classified collection of public documents of the Northern Ports Commissioner of Trade). 1907. Reprint, Taibei: Wenhai, 1966.

Bi Hui 皕誨 (Anonymous). "Youmin zhi zhonglei yu qi weiji" 游民之種類與其危機 (Types of vagrants and their peril). *Qingnian jinbu* 青年進步 15 (July 1918), 24.

Bian, Morris. *The Making of the State Enterprise System in Modern China: The Dynamics of Institutional Change.* Cambridge, Mass.: Harvard University Press, 2005.

Bickers, Robert. *Britain in China: Community, Culture and Colonialism 1900–1949.* Manchester: Manchester University Press, 1999.

———. "Settlers and Diplomats: The End of British Hegemony in the International Settlement, 1937–1945." In *In the Shadow of the Rising Sun: Shanghai under Japanese Occupation*, ed. Christian Henriot and Wen-hsin Yeh. New York: Cambridge University Press, 2004, 229–56.

Bodenhorn, Terry, ed. *Defining Modernity: Guomindang Rhetorics of a New China, 1920–1970.* Ann Arbor: Center for Chinese Studies, University of Michigan, 2002.

Booth, William. *In Darkest England, and the Way Out.* London, 1890.

Boswell, James. *The Life of Samuel Johnson, LL.D.* 4th ed. London, 1804.

Botsman, Daniel. *Punishment and Power in the Making of Modern Japan.* Princeton: Princeton University Press, 2005.

Brokaw, Cynthia. *The Ledgers of Merit and Demerit: Social Change and Moral Order in Late Imperial China.* Princeton: Princeton University Press, 1991.

Brook, Timothy. "The Great Way Government of Shanghai." In *In the Shadow of the Rising Sun: Shanghai under Japanese Occupation*, ed. Christian Henriot and Wen-hsin Yeh. New York: Cambridge University Press, 2004, 157–86.

Brook, Timothy, Jerome Bourgon, and Gregory Blue. *Death by a Thousand Cuts.* Cambridge, Mass.: Harvard University Press, 2008.

Brown, Peter. *Poverty and Leadership in the Later Roman Empire.* Hanover, N.H.: University Press of New England, 2002.

Burgess, John S. "Beginnings of Social Investigation." *The Survey* (October 13, 1917), 41–43.

———. *The Significance of Social Work in China.* Peking: Peking Leader Press, 1925.

Carey, Arch. *The War Years at Shanghai*. New York: Vantage, 1967.

Chan, Ming K., and Arif Dirlik. *Schools into Fields and Factories: Anarchists, the Guomindang, and the National Labor University in Shanghai, 1927–1932*. Durham, N.C.: Duke University Press, 1991.

Chang, Hao. *Liang Ch'i-ch'ao and Intellectual Transition in China, 1890–1907*. Cambridge, Mass.: Harvard University Press, 1971.

Chapin, F. Stuart. *An Historical Introduction to Social Economy*. New York: Century Co., 1923.

Chen Yung-fa. *Making Revolution: The Communist Movement in Eastern and Central China, 1937–1945*. Berkeley: University of California Press, 1986.

Chiang, Yung-chen. *Social Engineering and the Social Sciences in China, 1919–1949*. New York: Cambridge University Press, 2001.

The China Yearbook. Shanghai: The North-China Daily News & Herald, 1939.

The Chinese Nation. Shanghai.

The Chinese Recorder. Shanghai.

The Civil Code of the Republic of China. Nanjing: Kelly & Walsh, 1931.

CNRRA: Its Purpose, Functions and Organization. Shanghai, 1946.

Coble, Parks. *Chinese Capitalism in Japan's New Order: The Occupied Lower Yangzi, 1937–1945*. Berkeley: University of California Press, 2003.

Cohen, Paul. *Between Tradition and Modernity: Wang T'ao and Reform in Late Qing China*. Cambridge, Mass.: Council on East Asian Studies, Harvard University, 1974.

Connelly, Matthew. *Fatal Misconceptions: The Struggle to Control World Population*. Cambridge, Mass.: Belknap, 2008.

Cousland, Philip. *An English-Chinese Lexicon of Medical Terms*. Shanghai: Medical Missionary Association of China, 1908.

The Criminal Code of the Republic of China. Shanghai: Kelly & Walsh, 1935.

Crowther, M. A. *The Workhouse System: 1834–1929: The History of an English Social Institution*. Athens: University of Georgia Press, 1982.

Culp, Robert. *Articulating Citizenship: Civic Education and Student Politics in Southeastern China, 1912–1940*. Cambridge, Mass.: Harvard University Asia Center, 2007.

Da Qing fagui daquan 大清法規大全 (Complete laws and statutes of the Qing dynasty). Taibei: Hongye, 1972.

Da Qing Huidian Shili 大清會典事例 (Collected statutes of the Qing dynasty, with substatutes based on precedent). 1899 ed. Reprint, Beijing: Zhonghua shuju, 1991.

Dagong bao 大公報 (L'Impartial). Tianjin.

Dai Qing. *Wang Shiwei and "Wild Lilies": Rectification and Purges in the Chinese Communist Party, 1942–1944*. Trans. Nancy Liu and Lawrence Sullivan. Armonk, N.Y.: M.E. Sharpe, 1993.

Darwent, Charles Ewart. *Shanghai: A Handbook for Travellers and Residents*. Shanghai: Kelly and Walsh, 1904.

Dep, A. C. *A History of the Ceylon Police*. Colombo, 1969.

Diamant, Neil. *Embattled Glory: Veterans, Military Families, and the Politics of Patriotism in China, 1949–2007*. Lanham, Md.: Rowman & Littlefield, 2009.

Dikötter, Frank. *Crime, Punishment and the Prison in Modern China*. New York: Columbia University Press, 2002.

———. *Imperfect Conceptions: Medical Knowledge, Birth Defects and Eugenics in China*. London: Hurst, 1998.

Dikötter, Frank, Lars Laamann, and Zhou Xun. *Narcotic Culture: A History of Drugs in China*. Chicago: University of Chicago Press, 2004.

Dillon, Nara. "The Politics of Philanthropy: Social Networks and Refugee Relief in Shanghai, 1932–1949." In *At the Crossroads of Empires: Middlemen, Social Networks, and State-Building in Republican Shanghai*, ed. Nara Dillon and Jean Oi. Stanford: Stanford University Press, 2008, 179–205.

Dittmer, C. G. "An Estimate of the Standard of Living in China." *Quarterly Journal of Economics* 33 (November 1918), 107–28.

Dong, Madeleine Yue. *Republican Beijing: The City and Its Histories*. Berkeley: University of California Press, 2003.

Dongfang zazhi 東方雜誌 (Eastern Miscellany). Shanghai.

Dray-Novey, Alison. "Spatial Order and Police in Imperial Beijing." *Journal of Asian Studies* 52:4 (November 1993), 885–922.

Duanfang 端方. *Duan Zhongmin gong zougao* 端忠敏公奏稿 (Memorials of Duanfang). Reprint, Taibei: Wenhai, 1967.

Dunch, Ryan. *Fuzhou Protestants and the Making of a Modern China, 1857–1927*. New Haven, Conn.: Yale University Press, 2001.

Dutton, Michael. *Policing and Punishment in China: From Patriarchy to the People*. Cambridge: Cambridge University Press, 1992.

Dyce, Charles. *Personal Reminiscences of Thirty Years' Residence in the Model Settlement: Shanghai, 1870–1900*. London: Chapman & Hall, 1906.

Eastman, Lloyd. *Seeds of Destruction: Nationalist China in War and Revolution, 1937–1949*. Stanford: Stanford University Press, 1984.

Edgerton-Tarpley, Kathryn. *Tears from Iron: Cultural Responses to Famine in Nineteenth-Century China*. Berkeley: University of California Press, 2008.

Ellwood, Charles. *Shehui xue ji xiandai shehui wenti* 社會學及現代社會問題 (Sociology and modern social problems). Trans. Zhao Zuoxiong 趙作雄. Shanghai: Shangwu, 1920.

———. *Sociology and Modern Social Problems*. New York: American Book Company, 1910.

Elvin, Mark. "The Gentry Democracy in Shanghai, 1905–1914." Ph.D. dissertation, University of Cambridge, 1967.

Faling daquan 法令大全 (Complete laws and ordinances of the Republic of China). Shanghai: Shangwu, 1924.

Faure, David. *The Rural Economy of Pre-Liberation China: Trade Expansion and Peasant Livelihood in Jiangsu and Guangdong, 1870 to 1937*. New York: Oxford University Press, 1989.

Feng Guifen 馮桂芬. *Jiaobinlu kangyi* 校邠盧抗議 (Protests from the study of Jiaobin). Xuehai, 1897.

Field, Andrew. *Shanghai's Dancing World: Cabaret Culture and Urban Politics, 1919–1954*. Hong Kong: Chinese University Press, 2010.

Fischer, Brodwyn. *A Poverty of Rights: Citizenship and Inequality in Twentieth-Century Rio de Janeiro*. Stanford: Stanford University Press, 2008.

Fu, Poshek. *Passivity, Resistance, and Collaboration: Intellectual Choices in Occupied Shanghai, 1937–1945*. Stanford: Stanford University Press, 1993.

Fu'er mosi 福爾摩斯 (The Holmes News). Shanghai.

Fukuzawa Yukichi 福澤諭吉. *Fukuzawa Yukichi zenshu* 福澤諭吉全集 (Complete works of Fukuzawa Yukichi). Tokyo: Iwanami Shoten, 1958.

Fuma Susumu 夫馬進. *Chūgoku zenkai zendōshi kenkyū* (Research on the history of China's benevolent societies). Trans. *Zhongguo shanhui shantang shi yanjiu* 中國善會善堂史研究. 1997. Beijing: Shangwu, 2005.

Funü zazhi 婦女雜誌 (Ladies' journal). Shanghai.

Gamble, Sidney. *Peking: A Social Survey*. New York: George H. Doran, 1921.

Garrett, Shirley. *Social Reformers in Urban China: The Chinese Y.M.C.A., 1895–1926.* Cambridge, Mass.: Harvard University Press, 1970.

Gascoyne-Cecil, William. *Changing China*. New York: Appleton, 1912.

Geming wenxian 革命文獻 (Documentary materials on the revolution). Taibei: Zhongyang wenwu, 1983–1984.

Gerth, Karl. *China Made: Consumer Culture and the Creation of the Nation*. Cambridge, Mass.: Harvard University Asia Center, 2003.

Giddings, Franklin. *The Principles of Sociology*. New York: Macmillan, 1896.

Gide, Charles. "Shehui de jisheng" 社會的寄生 (Society's parasites). In *Xiezuo* 協作 (Cooperation), trans. Lou Tongsun 樓桐孫. Shanghai: Shangwu, 1927, 329–61.

Glosser, Susan. *Chinese Visions of Family and State, 1915–1953*. Berkeley: University of California Press, 2003.

Goldman, Merle, and Elizabeth Perry. "Introduction: Political Citizenship in Modern China." In *Changing Meanings of Citizenship in Modern China*, ed. Merle Goldman and Elizabeth Perry. Cambridge, Mass.: Harvard University Press, 2002, 1–19.

Gongbuju dongshihui huiyilu 公部局董事會會議錄 (Meeting minutes of the Municipal Council). Reprint, Shanghai: Shanghai guji, 2001.

Goodman, Bryna. *Native Place, City, and Nation: Regional Networks and Identities in Shanghai, 1853–1937*. Berkeley: University of California Press, 1995.

———. "The New Woman Commits Suicide: The Press, Cultural Memory, and the New Republic." *Journal of Asian Studies* 64:1 (February 2005), 67–101.

Gronewold, Sue. "Encountering Hope: The Door of Hope Mission in Shanghai and Taipei, 1900–1976." Ph.D. dissertation, Columbia University, 1996.

Guan Ruiwu 關瑞梧. "Jiefang qian de Beijing Xiangshan Ciyouyuan" 解放前的北京香山慈幼院 (The Fragrant Mountain Orphanage of pre-Liberation Beijing). In *Wenshi ziliao xuanji* 文史資料選輯 31 (1962), 155–66.

Guancha 觀察 (The Observer). Shanghai.

Guangxu chao donghua xulu 光緒朝東華續錄 (Continuation of the Donghua lu, Guangxu reign). Shanghai: Jicheng, 1909.

Guolun 國論 (National opinion monthly). Shanghai.

Haber, Samuel. *Efficiency and Uplift: Scientific Management in the Progressive Era, 1890–1920*. Chicago: University of Chicago Press, 1964.

Hacking, Ian. "Making Up People." In *Reconstructing Individualism: Autonomy, Individuality, and the Self in Western Thought*, ed. Thomas Heller, et al. Stanford: Stanford University Press, 1986, 222–36.

———. "Making Up People." *London Review of Books* 28:16 (August 17, 2006), 23–26.

Harrison, Henrietta. *The Making of the Republican Citizen: Political Ceremonies and Symbols in China, 1911–1929*. New York: Oxford University Press, 2000.

He Hanwei 何漢威. *Guangxu chunian Huabei de da hanzai* 光緒出年華北的大旱災 (The great drought in the Huabei region during the early Guangxu years). Hong Kong: Zhongwen daxue, 1980.

Henderson, Charles. *Modern Methods of Charity*. New York: Macmillan, 1904.

Henriot, Christian. "Rice, Power and People: The Politics of Food Supply in Wartime Shanghai (1937–1945)." *Twentieth-Century China* 26:1 (November 2000), 41–84.

———. *Shanghai, 1927–1937: Municipal Power, Locality, and Modernization*. Berkeley: University of California Press, 1993.

———. "Shanghai and the Experience of War: The Fate of Refugees." *European Journal of East Asian Studies* 5:2 (2006), 215–45.

Hershatter, Gail. *Dangerous Pleasures: Prostitution and Modernity in Twentieth-Century Shanghai*. Berkeley: University of California Press, 1997.

Himmelfarb, Gertrude. *The Idea of Poverty: England in the Early Industrial Age*. New York: Knopf, 1984.

Honig, Emily. *Creating Chinese Ethnicity: Subei People in Shanghai, 1850–1980*. New Haven, Conn.: Yale University Press, 1992.

———. *Sisters and Strangers: Women in the Shanghai Cotton Mills, 1919–1949*. Stanford: Stanford University Press, 1986.

Hsu, Leonard (Xu Shilian). "The Problem of Poverty in China." *China Outlook* 1:3 (February 1, 1928), 2–5.

Hu Shi 胡適. *Zhongguo wenti* 中國問題 (China's problems). Shanghai, 1932.

Huang Yuansheng 黃遠生. "Youmin zhengzhi" 游民政治 (The governance of vagrants). *Shaonian Zhongguo zhoukan* 少年中國週刊 (China youth weekly), December 26, 1912. Reprint, *Minguo congshu* 民國叢書, second series. Shanghai: Shanghai shu-dian, 1990, 99:17–20.

Hubu zeli 戶部則例 (Board of Revenue regulations and precedents). 1865 ed.

Huffman, James L. *Creating a Public: People and Press in Meiji Japan*. Honolulu: University of Hawaii Press, 1997.

Hufton, Olwen. *The Poor of Eighteenth-Century France, 1750–1789*. Oxford: Clarendon, 1974.

Ji Gang 紀綱. "Guanyu chengshi fuli gongzuo de baogao" 關於城市福利工作的報告 (Report on urban relief and welfare work), November 27, 1952. *Minzheng gongzuo shouce* 民政工作手冊 5 (1953), 174–82.

Jiang Jieshi (Chiang Kai-shek) 蔣介石. *Xian Zongtong Jianggong sixiang yanlun zongji* 先總統蔣公思想言論總集 (Complete works of the late President Chiang). Taibei: Zhongguo guomin dang zhongyang weiyuanhui, 1984.

Jiang Jingguo 蔣經國. "Shanghai wang hechu qu?" 上海往何處去 (Where is Shanghai headed?). In *Jiang Jingguo zai Shanghai* 蔣經國在上海 (Jiang Jingguo in Shanghai), ed. Cai Zhenyun 蔡真雲. Nanjing: Zhonghua, 1948, 45–56.

Jiang Zhiliang 姜志良. "Jiefang zhanzheng zhong de Jiangsu" 解放戰爭中的江蘇 (Jiangsu during the War of Liberation). *Jiangsu difang zhi* 江蘇地方志 2 (1999), 18–20.

Jiaoyu zazhi 教育雜誌 (Education journal). Shanghai.

"Jiefang chuqi Shanghai tanfan guanli gongzuo gaikuang baogao" (Report on the work of managing Shanghai's peddlers in the early Liberation period) 解放初期上海攤販管理工作概況報告, April 1953. Reprint, *Shanghai dang'an shiliao yanjiu* 上海檔案史料研究 6 (2009), 322–36.

Jiefang ribao 解放日報 (Liberation daily). Shanghai.

Jiefang yu gaizao 解放與改造 (Emancipation and reconstruction semi-monthly). Shanghai.

Jiefang zhanzheng shiqi Zhonggong Beiping dixiadang douzheng shiliao 解放戰爭時期中共北平地下黨鬥爭史料 (Historical materials on struggles of the Communist underground in Beiping during the War of Liberation). Beijing: Zhonggong Beijing shiwei dangshi yanjiushi, 1996.

Jinbu 進步 (Progress). Shanghai.

Jingshi Gongyi Lianhehui jishi 京師公益聯合會紀事 (Record of the Metropolitan Welfare Association). Beijing, 1924.

Jite (Charles Gide). "Shehui de jisheng wu" 社會的寄生物 (Society's parasites). Trans. Cang Yuan 蒼園. *Dongfang zazhi* 20:19 (October 10, 1923), 62–70.

Jiuji shiye jihua shu 救濟事業計畫書 (Plan for relief work). Nanjing, 1929.

Jiuwang ribao 救亡日報 (National salvation daily). Shanghai.

Jordan, Donald A. *China's Trial by Fire: The Shanghai War of 1932*. Ann Arbor: University of Michigan Press, 2001.

Ju Zhifen. "Labor Conscription in North China: 1941–1945." In *China at War: Regions of China, 1937–1945*, ed. Diana Lary, Stephen MacKinnon, and Ezra Vogel. Stanford: Stanford University Press, 2007, 207–26.

Judge, Joan. *Print and Politics: "Shibao" and the Culture of Reform in Late Qing China*. Stanford: Stanford University Press, 1996.

Jun Ke 鈞客. "Qigai shourongsuo fangwenji" 乞丐收容所訪問記 (Record of a visit to the beggar camp), May 15, 1941. Reprint, *Jiu Shanghai fengqing lu* 舊上海風情錄 (Record of customs of old Shanghai). Shanghai: Wenhui, 1998, 2:316–18.

KangRi zhanzheng 抗日戰爭 (The War of Resistance), ed. Zhang Bofeng 章伯鋒 and Zhuang Jianping 庄建平. Chengdu: Sichuan daxue, 1997.

Karl, Rebecca, and Peter Zarrow, eds. *Rethinking the 1898 Reform Period: Political and Cultural Change in Late Qing China*. Cambridge, Mass.: Harvard University Asia Center, 2002.

Katz, Michael B. *The Price of Citizenship: Redefining the American Welfare State*. Philadelphia: University of Pennsylvania Press, 2008.

———. *In the Shadow of the Poorhouse: A Social History of Welfare in America*. New York: Basic Books, 1996.

Ke Xiangfeng 柯象峰. *Zhongguo pinqiong wenti* 中國貧窮問題 (The problem of poverty in China). Shanghai: Zhengzhong, 1935.

Kinzley, W. Dean. "Japan's Discovery of Poverty: Changing Views of Poverty and Social Welfare in the Nineteenth Century." *Journal of Asian History* 22:1 (1988), 1–24.

Kotenev, Anatol. *Shanghai: Its Mixed Court and Council*. Shanghai: North-China Daily News & Herald, 1925.

Kuhn, Philip. "Chinese Views of Social Classification." In *Class and Social Stratification in Post-Revolutionary China*, ed. James L. Watson. New York: Cambridge University Press, 1984, 16–28.

———. *Soulstealers: The Chinese Sorcery Scare of 1768*. Cambridge, Mass.: Harvard University Press, 1990.

Lai Jiancheng 賴建誠. *Yadang Shimisi yu Yan Fu: Guofu lun yu Zhongguo* 亞當史密斯與嚴復: 國富論與中國 (Adam Smith and Yan Fu: *The Wealth of Nations* and China). Taibei: Sanmin, 2002.

Lamson, Herbert Day. *Social Pathology in China: A Source Book for the Study of Problems of Livelihood, Health, and the Family*. Shanghai: Commercial Press, 1934.

Land Regulations and Bye-Laws for the Foreign Settlements of Shanghai North of the Yang-King-Pang. Shanghai, 1898.

Lary, Diana. "One Province's Experience of War: Guangxi, 1937–1945." In *China at War: Regions of China, 1937–1945*, ed. Diana Lary, Stephen MacKinnon, and Ezra Vogel. Stanford: Stanford University Press, 2007, 314–34.

———. *Warlord Soldiers: Chinese Common Soldiers, 1911–1937*. Cambridge: Cambridge University Press, 1985.

Lee, Leo Ou-fan. *Shanghai Modern: The Flowering of a New Urban Culture in China, 1930–1945*. Cambridge, Mass.: Harvard University Press, 1999.

Leung, Angela Ki Che (Liang Qizi). "Relief Institutions for Children in Nineteenth-Century China." In *Chinese Views of Childhood*, ed. Anne Behnke Kinney. Honolulu: University of Hawaii Press, 1995, 251–78.

Levine, Steven. *Anvil of Victory: The Communist Revolution in Manchuria, 1945–1948*. New York: Columbia University Press, 1987.

Li Da 李達. "Laodongzhe yu shehui zhuyi" 勞動著與社會主義 (Laborers and socialism). *Laodong jie* 勞動界 (Labor world) 16 (November 28, 1920), 1–3.

Li Dazhao 李大釗. "Diji laodongzhe" 低級勞動著 (Lower class laborers). *Xin shehui* 新社會 (New Society) 22 (January 18, 1920), 12.

———. "Makesi huanyuan" 馬克思還原 (Restore Marxism). *Xin Qingnian* 新青年 (New youth) 8:5 (January 1, 1921), 1–8.

Li Jinghan 李景漢. "Beiping zuidi xiandu de shenghuo chengdu de taolun" 北平最低限度的生活程度的討論 (Discussion of the lowest standard of living in Beiping). *Shehui xuejie* 社會學界 (Sociological world) 3 (1929), 1–16.

Li, Lillian. *Fighting Famine in North China: State, Market, and Environmental Decline, 1690s–1990s*. Stanford: Stanford University Press, 2007.

Li, Lincoln. *The Japanese Army in North China, 1937–1941: Problems of Political and Economic Control*. London: Oxford University Press, 1975.

Li Luzi 李魯子. "Chongqing neimu" 重慶內幕 (Behind the scenes in Chongqing). In *Zhanshi Chongqing fengguang* 戰時重慶風光 (The sights of wartime Chongqing). 1942. Reprint, Chongqing: Chongqing chubanshe, 1986.

Li Tinghan 李廷翰. *Pinmin jiaoyu tan* 貧民教育譚 (A discussion of the education of the poor). Shanghai: Jiaoyu zazhi she, 1911.

Li Tong 李彤. "Ni zuzhi quanguo youmin xiyisuo qi" 擬組織全國游民習藝所啟 (Proposal to establish vagrant workhouses nationwide). *Minquan su* 民權素 (Essence of people's rights) 16 (March 1916), 12–13.

Li Xiaowei 李小尉. "Xin Zhongguo chengli chuqi chengshi pinmin de shenghuo jiuzhu yanjiu" 新中國成立初期城市貧民的生活救助研究 (Research on relief and assistance to the urban poor in the early years of New China). *Jiaoxue yu yanjiu* 教學與研究 8 (2009), 61–67.

Liang Jinhan 梁錦漢. *Jingshi dier jianyu baogao shu* 京師第二監獄報告書 (Report of the Capital Number Two Prison). Beijing, 1919.

Liang Qichao 梁啟超. "Lun shengli fenli" 論生利分利 (On production and consumption). *Xinmin congbao* 新民叢報 (New citizen journal) (GX 28.10.1/October 31, 1902), 1–7.

———. *Yinbingshi wenji* 飲冰室文集. Taibei: Taiwan Zhonghua shuju, 1960.

Liang Qizi 梁其姿. "'Pinqiong' yu 'qiongren' guannian zai Zhongguo sushi shehui zhong de lishi yanbian" '貧窮'與 '窮人'觀念在中國俗世社會中的歷史演變 (The historical evolution of the concepts of "poverty" and "the poor" in Chinese popular society). In *Renguan yiyi yu shehui* 人觀意義與社會 (Perspectives, meanings, and society), ed. Huang Yinggui 黃應貴. Taibei: Institute of Ethnology, Academia Sinica, 1993, 129–62.

———. *Shishan yu jiaohua: Ming Qing de cishan zuzhi* 施善與教化: 明清的慈善組織 (Charity and edification:—Philanthropic organizations of the Ming and Qing dynasties). Taibei: Lianjing chuban, 1997.

Lieberthal, Kenneth. *Revolution and Tradition in Tientsin, 1949–1952*. Stanford: Stanford University Press, 1980.

Lin, Alfred. "Warlord, Social Welfare and Philanthropy: The Case of Guangzhou under Chen Jitang, 1929–1936." *Modern China* 30:2 (April 2004), 151–98.

Lin, Yuan-Huei. "The Weight of Mount Tai: Patterns of Suicide in Traditional Chinese History and Culture." Ph.D. dissertation, University of Wisconsin–Madison, 1990.

Lin, Yu-sheng. "The Suicide of Liang Chi: An Ambiguous Case of Moral Conservatism." In *The Limits of Change: Essays on Conservative Alternatives in Republican China*, ed. Charlotte Furth. Cambridge, Mass.: Harvard University Press, 1976, 151–68.

Lipkin, Zwia. *Useless to the State: "Social Problems" and Social Engineering in Nationalist Nanjing, 1927–1937*. Stanford: Stanford University Press, 2006.

Lishi dang'an 歷史檔案 (Historical Archives). Beijing.

Liu Jiping 劉季平. "Lun muqian Huazhong jiefangqu jiaoyu gongzuo" 論目前華中解放區教育工作 (Discussion of current educational work in Central China's liberated areas). In *Jiefang zhanzheng chuqi Su Wan bianqu jiaoyu* 解放戰爭初期蘇皖邊區教育. 1946. Reprint, Beijing: Renmin jiaoyu, 1983, 5–37.

Liu, Lu. "A Whole Nation Walking: The 'Great Retreat' in the War of Resistance, 1937–1945." Ph.D. dissertation, University of California, San Diego, 2002.

Liu Xilian 劉錫廉. *Beijing cishan huibian* 北京慈善彙編 (A collection of materials on charities in Beijing). Beijing, 1923.

———. *Jingshi laoruo linshi jiujihui baogaoshu* 京師老弱臨時救濟會報告書 (Report of the Peking Dependents' Relief Society). Beijing, 1923.

Liu Yuzhen 劉雨珍 and Sun Xuemei 孫雪梅, eds. *Riben zhengfa kaocha ji* 日本政法考察記. Shanghai: Shanghai guji, 2002.

Lowe Chuan-hua (Luo Chunhua). "The Problem of Earning a Living in China." *The Chinese Nation* 1:9 (August 13, 1930), 141–53.

Lu, Hanchao. *Beyond the Neon Lights: Everyday Shanghai in the Early Twentieth Century*. Berkeley: University of California Press, 1999.

———. *Street Criers: A Cultural History of Chinese Beggars*. Stanford: Stanford University Press, 2005.

Lu Xun 魯迅. "Qiuqi zhe" 求乞者 (The beggar). 1924. Reprint, *Yecao* 野草 (Wild grass). Beijing: Renmin wenxue, 1979.

Lugouqiao shibian hou Beijing zhi'an jiyao 盧溝橋事變後北京治安紀要 (Summary of Beijing's public security after the Marco Polo Bridge Incident). Beiping, 1937.

Ma Guangren 馬光仁, ed. *Shanghai xinwen shi, 1850–1949* 上海新聞史, 1850–1949 (History of Shanghai newspapers, 1850–1949). Shanghai: Fudan daxue, 1996.

Ma Yinchu 馬寅初. *Ma Yinchu quanji* 馬寅初全集 (Complete works of Ma Yinchu). Hangzhou: Zhejiang renmin, 1999.

Macauley, Melissa. *Social Power and Legal Culture: Litigation Masters in Late Imperial China*. Stanford: Stanford University Press, 1998.

MacKinnon, Stephen. *Power and Politics in Late Imperial China: Yuan Shi-kai in Beijing and Tianjin, 1901–1908*. Berkeley: University of California Press, 1980.

———. *Wuhan, 1938: War, Refugees, and the Making of Modern China*. Berkeley: University of California Press, 2008.

Mair, Victor. "Language and Ideology in the Written Popularizations of the *Sacred Edict*." In *Popular Culture in Late Imperial China*, ed. David Johnson, Andrew J. Nathan, and Evelyn S. Rawski. Berkeley: University of California Press, 1985, 325–59.

Mallory, Walter H. *China: Land of Famine*. New York: American Geographical Society, 1926.

Mao Zedong 毛澤東. "Hunan nongmin yundong kaocha baogao" 湖南農民運動考察報告 (Report on an investigation of the Hunan peasant movement). In *Mao Zedong xuanji* 毛澤東選集 (Selected works of Mao Zedong). Shanghai: Renmin, 1991, 1:12–44.

———. "Zhongguo nongmin zhong ge jieji de fenxi ji qi duiyu geming de taidu" 中國農民中各階級的分析及其對於革命的態度 (An analysis of the classes of the Chinese peasantry and their attitudes toward revolution." *Zhongguo nongmin* 中國農民 (Chinese peasantry) 1:1 (January 1926), 13–20.

———. "Zhongguo shehui ge jieji de fenxi" 中國社會各階級的分析 (Analysis of all the classes in Chinese society). *Zhongguo nongmin* 中國農民 (Chinese peasantry) 1:2 (February 1926), 1–13.

Marshall, T. H. *Citizenship and Social Class and Other Essays*. Cambridge: Cambridge University Press, 1950.

Martin, Brian G. "Resistance and Cooperation: Du Yuesheng and the Politics of the Shanghai United Committee, 1940–1945." In *In the Shadow of the Rising Sun: Shanghai under Japanese Occupation*, ed. Christian Henriot and Wen-hsin Yeh. New York: Cambridge University Press, 2004, 187–208.

———. *The Shanghai Green Gang: Politics and Organized Crime, 1919–1937*. Berkeley: University of California Press, 1996.

McElderry, Andrea. "Legal Change and Guarantor Liability in the Republican Economy." In *Shijie jingji tizhi xia de Minguo shiqi jingji* 世界經濟體制下的民國時期經濟 (The Republican economy within the global economic framework). Beijing: Zhongguo caizheng jingji, 2005, 330–42.

Meijer, Marinus. *The Introduction of Modern Criminal Law in China*. Hong Kong: Lung Men, 1967.

Meizhou pinglun 每週評論 (Weekly review). Shanghai.

Minbao 民報 (People's journal). Tokyo.

Mo Zhenliang 莫振良. "Minguo shiqi de hong 卐 zihui" 民國時期的紅字會 (The Red Swastika Society during the Republican era). In *Zhongguo mimi shehui gaiguan* 中國秘密社會概觀 (General survey of Chinese secret societies), ed. Cai Shaoqing 蔡少卿. Nanjing: Jiangsu renmin, 1998, 115–23.

Morris, Andrew. *The Marrow of the Nation: A History of Sport and Physical Culture in Republican China*. Berkeley: University of California Press, 2004.

Mühlhahn, Klaus. *Criminal Justice in China: A History*. Cambridge, Mass.: Harvard University Press, 2009.

The Municipal Gazette. Shanghai, 1908–21.

Nanmin shengchanpin zhanlan hui jinian kan 難民生產品展覽會紀念刊 (Commemorative volume of the refugee production exhibition). Shanghai, 1939.

Naquin, Susan. *Peking: Temples and City Life, 1400–1900*. Berkeley: University of California Press, 2000.

Neizheng fagui huibian 內政法規彙編 (Collection of laws of civil administration). Nanjing, 1931.

Niu Nai'e 牛鼐鄂. "Beiping yiqian erbai pinhu zhi yanjiu" 北平一千二百貧戶之研究 (Research of 1,200 poor households in Beiping). *Shehui xuejie* 社會學界 (Sociological world) 7 (1933), 147–87.

The North-China Daily News and *North-China Herald*. Shanghai.

Pan Gongzhan 潘公展. "Xiandai Shanghai shehui de weiji" 現代上海社會的危機 (The crisis in Shanghai today). *Shehui yuekan* 社會月刊 1:9 (September 1929), 2–3.

Pan Tao 潘濤. "Minguo shiqi Subei shuizai zaikuang jianshu" 民國時期蘇北水災災況簡述 (Brief description of floods in Subei during the Republican period). *Minguo dang'an* 民國檔案 4 (1998), 108–10.

Penal Codes of France, Germany, Belgium and Japan. Washington, D.C.: GPO, 1901.

Peng Zeyi 鵬澤益, ed. *Zhongguo jindai shougong ye shi ziliao* 中國近代手工業史資料 (Source materials on the history of handicraft industries in modern China). Beijing: Zhonghua shuju, 1984.

Peng Zhen 彭真. "Zai quanshi zhigong jiji fenzi dahui shang de baogao" 在全市職工積極份子大會上的報告 (Report at the all-city meeting of workers and activists). In *Beijing shi zhongyao wenxian xuanbian* 北京市重要文獻選編, *1948.12–1949*. Beijing: Zhongguo dang'an, 2001, 251–58.

———. "Zhangwo dang de jiben zhengce zuohao ruchenghou de gongzuo" 掌握黨的基本政策做好入城後的工作 (Firmly grasp the Party's fundamental policies to do a good job after entering the city). In *Beijing shi zhongyao wenxian xuanbian* 北京市重要文獻選編, *1948.12–1949*. Beijing: Zhongguo dang'an, 2001, 69–76.

Pepper, Suzanne. *Civil War in China: The Political Struggle, 1945–1949*. Berkeley: University of California Press, 1978.

Perry, Elizabeth. "Masters of the Country? Shanghai Workers in the Early People's Republic." In *Dilemmas of Victory*, ed. Jeremy Brown and Paul Pickowicz Cambridge, Mass.: Harvard University Press, 2007, 59–79.

———. *Rebels and Revolutionaries in North China, 1845–1945*. Stanford: Stanford University Press, 1980.

Plum, M. Colette. "Unlikely Heirs: War Orphans during the Second Sino-Japanese War, 1937–1945." Ph.D. dissertation, Stanford University, 2006.

Qi Rushan 齊如山. *Gudu sanbai liushi hang* 故都三百六十行 (360 trades of the old capital). Beijing: Shumu wenxian, 1993.

Qing shilu, Shunzhi 清實錄, 順治 (Veritable records of the Qing dynasty, Shunzhi reign), 5:11–12. Reprint, Beijing: Zhonghua shuju, 1985, 3:62.

Qingmo Beijing chengshi guanli fagui 清末北京城市管理法規 (Beijing's late Qing urban administration laws). Ed. Tian Tao 田濤 and Guo Chengwei 郭成偉. Beijing: Yan-shan, 1996.

Qu Yanbin 曲彥斌. *Zhongguo qigai shi* 中國乞丐史 (A history of Chinese beggars). Shanghai: Shanghai wenyi, 1990.

Qunzhong 群眾 (The Masses). Shanghai.

Rankin, Mary Backus. *Elite Activism and Political Transformation in China: Zhejiang, 1865–1911*. Stanford: Stanford University Press, 1986.

Reeves, Caroline. "The Power of Mercy: The Chinese Red Cross Society, 1900–1937." Ph.D. dissertation, Harvard University, 1998.

Ren Jian 任建 and Lei Fang 雷方. *Zhongguo gaibang* 中國丐幫 (Chinese beggar gangs). Nanjing: Jiangsu guji, 1993.

Renmin ribao 人民日報 (People's daily). Beijing.

Report of the China Famine Relief, American Red Cross, October 1920 to September 1921. Shanghai: Commercial Press, 1921.

Reynolds, Douglas. *China, 1898–1912: The Xinzheng Revolution and Japan*. Cambridge, Mass.: Harvard University Press, 1993.

Rhoads, Edward J. M. *Manchus & Han: Ethnic Relations and Political Power in Late Qing and Early Republican China, 1861–1928*. Seattle: University of Washington Press, 2000.

Ristaino, Marcia. *The Jacquinot Safe Zone: Wartime Refugees in Shanghai*. Stanford: Stanford University Press, 2008.

———. *Port of Last Resort: The Diaspora Communities of Shanghai*. Stanford: Stanford University Press, 2001.

Riwei Shanghai shi zhengfu 日偽上海市政府 (Shanghai puppet municipal government). Shanghai: Dang'an, 1987.

Riwei tongzhi xia de Beiping 日偽統治下的北平 (Beiping under Japanese occupation). Ed. Wenshi ziliao weiyuanhui. Beijing: Beijing chubanshe, 1987.

Rogaski, Ruth. "Beyond Benevolence: A Confucian Women's Shelter in Treaty-Port China." *Journal of Women's History* 8:4 (Winter 1997), 54–90.

———. *Hygienic Modernity: Meanings of Health and Disease in Treaty-Port China*. Berkeley: University of California Press, 2004.

Rogers, John D. *Crime, Justice, and Society in Colonial Sri Lanka*. London: Curzon, 1987.

Rowe, William. *Hankow: Commerce and Society in a Chinese City, 1796–1889*. Stanford: Stanford University Press, 1984.

———. *Hankow: Conflict and Community in a Chinese City, 1796–1895*. Stanford: Stanford University Press, 1989.

Ruan Qinghua 阮清華. *Shanghai youmin gaizao yanjiu* 上海游民改造研究 (Research on the reform of vagrants in Shanghai). Shanghai: Cishu, 2009.

Sakamoto, Hiroko. "The Cult of 'Love and Eugenics' in May Fourth Movement Discourse." *positions* 12:2 (Fall 2004), 329–76.

Sanger, Margaret. *Margaret Sanger: An Autobiography*. New York: Norton, 1938.

Schak, David. *A Chinese Beggars' Den: Poverty and Mobility in an Underclass Community*. Pittsburgh: University of Pittsburgh Press, 1988.

Schmalzer, Sigrid. *The People's Peking Man: Popular Science and Human Identity in Twentieth-Century China*. Chicago: University of Chicago Press, 2008.

Schram, Stuart. *The Thought of Mao Tse-tung*. Cambridge: Cambridge University Press, 1989.

Schwartz, Benjamin. *In Search of Wealth and Power: Yen Fu and the West*. Cambridge, Mass.: Belknap, 1964.

Scully, Eileen. *Bargaining with the State from Afar: American Citizenship in Treaty Port China, 1844–1942*. New York: Columbia University Press, 2001.

Selden, Mark. *The Yenan Way in Revolutionary China*. Cambridge, Mass.: Harvard University Press, 1971.

Shanghai Daxue shiliao 上海大學史料 (Historical materials on Shanghai University). Ed. Huang Meizhen 黄美真. Shanghai: Fudan, 1984.

Shanghai Gu'eryuan baogao 上海孤兒院報告 (Shanghai Industrial Orphanage report). Ca. 1908.

Shanghai Gu'eryuan baogao qingce 上海孤兒院報告清冊 (Shanghai Industrial Orphanage report and accounts). 1910.

Shanghai International Relief Committee Six Month's Report. Shanghai, 1938.

Shanghai penghu qu de bianqian 上海棚戶的變遷 (The transformation of Shanghai's straw hut districts). Shanghai, 1962.

Shanghai Pin'eryuan diyi ci baogao 上海貧兒院第一次報告 (First report of the Shanghai Children's Poorhouse). 1909.

Shanghai Political & Economic Reports, 1842–1943. Ed. Robert Jarman. Slough, UK: Archive Editions, 2008.

Shanghai qingnian 上海青年 (Shanghai young men). Shanghai.

Shanghai shi gongbao 上海市公報 (Gazette of Shanghai municipality). Shanghai.

Shanghai shi Huxi diqu chengshi pinmin geming douzheng shi ziliao 上海市滬西城市貧民革命鬥爭史資料 (Historical materials on the revolutionary struggles of the urban poor in Shanghai's Western District). Shanghai, 1988.

Shanghai shi pingmin fuli shiye yinian lai gongzuo baogao 上海市平民福利事業一年來工作報告 (One year report on Shanghai commoner welfare matters). Shanghai, 1936.

Shanghai shi shehuiju fagui huibian 上海市社會局法規彙編 (Shanghai Social Affairs Bureau collection of laws and regulations). Shanghai, 1930.

Shanghai shi shehuiju gongzuo baogao (Shanghai Social Affairs Bureau report) 上海市社會局工作報告. Shanghai, 1946.

Shanghai shi zizhi zhi 上海市自治志 (Gazetteer of Shanghai self-government). 1915. Reprint, Taibei: Chengwen, 1974.

Shanghai Subei nanmin jiuji baogao 上海蘇北難民救濟報告 (Report on relief of Subei refugees in Shanghai). Shanghai, 1947.

Shanghai tebie shi shehuiju yewu baogao 上海特別市社會局業務報告 (Shanghai Special Municipality Social Affairs Bureau report). 1928–32.

Shanghai tongshi 上海通史 (General history of Shanghai). Shanghai: Renmin, 1999.

Shanghai xian xuzhi 上海縣續志 (Shanghai county gazetteer, continued). 1918. Reprint, Taibei: Chengwen, 1970.

Shanghai xian zhi 上海縣志 (Shanghai gazetteer). Shanghai, 1935. Reprint, Taibei: Chengwen, 1975.

Shanghai Xin Puyutang zhengxin lu 上海新普育堂徵信錄 (Donation record of the New Hall for Universal Cultivation). 1917.

Shanghai yiri 上海一日 (One day in Shanghai). Shanghai: Meishang, 1939.

Shanghai Youmin Xiqinsuo baogao dierbian 上海游民習勤所報告第二編 (Shanghai Vagrant Workhouse report, second edition). Shanghai, 1936.

Shanghai Youmin Xiqinsuo diyijie baogao 上海游民習勤所第一屆報告 (First report of the Shanghai Vagrant Workhouse). Shanghai, 1931.

Shanghai zhinan 上海指南 (Guide to Shanghai). Shanghai: Shangwu, 1920.

Shanghai zujie zhi 上海租界志 (Gazetteer of Shanghai's International Settlement). Shanghai: Shanghai shehui kexue yuan, 2001.

Shanhai kyodo sokai hoki zensho 上海共同租界法規全書 (Complete laws of the Shanghai International Settlement). Shanghai, 1926.

Shanhou jiuji zongshu Su Ning fenshu yewu baogao 善後救濟總署蘇寧分署業務報告 (Report of Su-Ning branch relief association). 1946.

Shao, Qin. *Culturing Modernity: The Nantong Model, 1890–1930*. Stanford: Stanford University Press, 2004.

Shao Yong 邵雍. *Minguo banghui* 民國幫會 (Gangs in the Republican period). Fuzhou: Fujian renmin, 2002.

Shaonian Zhongguo 少年中國 (Journal of the Young China Association). Shanghai.

Sheehan, Bret. *Trust in Troubled Times: Money, Banks, and State-Society Relations in Republican Tianjin*. Cambridge, Mass.: Harvard University Press, 2003.

Shehui banyuekan 社會半月刊 (Society fortnightly). Shanghai.

Shehui diaocha huikan 社會調查彙刊 (Periodical of social investigation). Beiping, 1930.

Shehui jianshe 社會建設 (Social construction). Nanjing.

Shehui tongji yuekan 社會統計月刊 (Social statistics monthly). Beijing.

Shehui xuejie 社會學界 (Sociological world). Beijing.

Shehui yuekan 社會月刊 (Society monthly). Shanghai.

Shen, Kuiyi. "Wang Yiting in the Social Networks of 1910s–1930s Shanghai." In *At the Crossroads of Empires: Middlemen, Social Networks, and State-Building in Republican Shanghai*, ed. Nara Dillon and Jean Oi. Stanford: Stanford University Press, 2008, 45–64.

Shenbao 申報 (Shanghai times). Shanghai and Hankou.

Shenbao yuekan 申報月刊 (Shanghai times monthly). Shanghai.

Shenghuo 生活 (Life). Shanghai.

Shi Hongxi 石鴻熙. *Jieguan Shanghai qinliji* 接管上海親歷記 (Personal experiences of the Shanghai takeover). Shanghai: Shanghai shi zhengxie wenshi ziliao jibu, 1997.

Shibao 時報 (Eastern times). Shanghai.

Shibao 實報 (Truth post). Beijing.

Shijie Hong卐 Zihui jingban Shanghai liumin xiqin suo gongzuo gaikuang 世界紅卐字會經辦上海流民習勤所工作概況 (Report of the Shanghai Indigent Training Institute run by the World Red Swastika Society). Shanghai, 1943.

Shuntian shibao 順天時報 (Shuntian times). Beijing.

Slack, Paul. *The English Poor Law, 1531–1782*. Basingstoke, UK: Macmillan, 1990.

———. *Poverty and Policy in Tudor and Stuart England*. London: Longman, 1988.

Smith, Adam. *An Inquiry into the Nature and Causes of the Wealth of Nations*. Dublin: N. Kelly, 1801.

Smith, Aminda. "Reeducating the People: The Chinese Communists and the 'Thought Reform' of Beggars, Prostitutes, and Other 'Parasites.'" Ph.D. dissertation, Princeton University, 2006.

Smith, Joanna Handlin. *The Art of Doing Good: Charity in Late Ming China*. Berkeley: University of California Press, 2009.

Sokoll, Thomas, ed. *Essex Pauper Letters, 1731–1837*. Oxford: Oxford University Press, 2001.

Solinger, Dorothy. *Contesting Citizenship in Urban China: Peasants, Migrants, the State, and the Logic of the Market*. Berkeley: University of California Press, 1999.

———. "The *Dibao* Recipients: Mollified Anti-Emblem of Urban Modernization." *China Perspectives* 4 (2008), 36–46.

Sommer, Matthew. *Sex, Law, and Society in Late Imperial China*. Stanford: Stanford University Press, 2000.

Song Mingzhi 宋銘之. "Youmin duguo wenti ji qi jiuji zhi ce" 游民蠹國問題及其救濟之策 (The problem of vagrants as national vermin and a strategy for its relief). *Zhonghua shiye jie* 中華實業界 (Chinese industry world) 5 (May 10, 1914), 1–9.

Soong May-ling (Song Meiling) 宋美齡. "Jinwei nantong qingming" 謹為難童請命 (A plea to save refugee children), *Funü shenghuo* 婦女生活 5:11 (April 1938). Reprint, *Jiang Furen Song Meiling nüshi yanlun xuanji* 蔣夫人宋美齡女士言論選集 (Selected writings and speeches of Madam Chiang Kaishek). Taibei: Jindai Zhongguo, 1998, 64–66.

Soong, T. V. "The 1931 Floods: A Preliminary Report to the Members of the National Flood Relief Commission." *Chinese Economic Journal* 11:1 (July 1932), 67–73.

Spence, Jonathan. *The Gate of Heavenly Peace: The Chinese and Their Revolution*. New York: Viking, 1981.

Stapleton, Kristin. *Civilizing Chengdu: Chinese Urban Reform, 1895–1937*. Cambridge, Mass.: Harvard University Press, 2000.

Stephens, Thomas B. *Order and Discipline in China: The Shanghai Mixed Court, 1911–27*. Seattle: University of Washington Press, 1992.

Stranahan, Patricia. "Radicalization of Refugees: Communist Party Activity in Wartime Shanghai's Displaced Persons Camps." *Modern China* 26:2 (April 2000), 166–93.

———. *Underground: The Shanghai Communist Party and the Politics of Survival, 1927–1937*. Lanham, Md.: Rowman & Littlefield, 1998.

Strand, David. "Mediation, Representation, and Repression: Local Elites in 1920s Beijing." In *Chinese Local Elites and Patterns of Dominance*, ed. Joseph Esherick and Mary Rankin. Berkeley: University of California Press, 1990.

———. *Rickshaw Beijing: City People and Politics in the 1920s*. Berkeley: University of California Press, 1989.

Strauss, Julia. *Strong Institutions in Weak Polities: State Building in Republican China, 1927–1940*. New York: Oxford University Press, 1998.

Sun Wen 孫文 (Sun Yat-sen). "Fakan ci" 發刊詞 (Editorial introducing the inaugural issue). *Minbao* 民報 (People's journal) 1 (November 26, 1905), 1–3.

Sun Xuemei 孫雪梅. *Qingmo Minchu Zhongguoren de Riben guan—yi Zhili sheng wei zhongxin* 清末民初中國人的日本觀—以直隸省為中心 (Chinese views of Japan in the late Qing and early Republic—with Zhili province as the focus). Tianjin: Renmin, 2001.

Sun Yankui 孫艷魁. *Kunan de renliu: Kangzhan shiqi de nanmin* 苦難的人流: 抗戰時期的難民 (People in misery: Refugees in the War of Resistance). Guilin: Guangxi shifan daxue, 1994.

Sun Yidong 孫以東. "Qingmo zuifan xiyisuo chuyi" 清末罪犯習藝所初議 (Initial views on late Qing criminal workhouses). In *Ming-Qing dang'an yu lishi yanjiu lun-wen ji* 明清檔案與歷史研究論文集. Beijing: Zhongguo youyi, 2000, 1296–1311.

Sun Zhongshan 孫中山 (Sun Yat-sen). *Sanmin zhuyi* 三民主義 (Three Principles of the People). Taibei: Zhongyang wenwu gongyingshe, 1963.

The Survey. New York.

Swislocki, Mark. "Feast and Famine in Republican Shanghai: Urban Food Culture, Nutrition, and the State." Ph.D. dissertation, Stanford University, 2001.

Tao, L. K. (Tao Menghe). *Livelihood in Peking: An Analysis of the Budgets of Sixty Families.* Peking, 1928.

Tao Menghe 陶孟和. *Menghe wencun* 孟和文存 (Collected writings of Tao Menghe). Shanghai: Yadong, 1926.

———. *Shehui wenti* 社會問題 (Social problem). Shanghai: Shangwu, 1924.

Tayler, J. B. "The Study of Chinese Rural Economy: The Results of the Famine Commission's Investigations," Part II. *The Chinese Social and Political Science Review* 8:2 (April 1924), 252–55.

Taylor, George E. *The Japanese Sponsored Regime in North China.* New York: Institute of Pacific Relations, 1939.

Teng Shaozhen 滕紹箴. *Qingdai baqi zidi* 清代八旗子弟 (The descendents of the Eight Banners of the Qing dynasty). Beijing: Zhongguo huaqiao, 1989.

Thompson, Roger. *China's Local Councils in the Age of Constitutional Reform, 1898–1911.* Cambridge, Mass.: Harvard University Press, 1995.

Tianjin shi xiyisuo zhangcheng biaoce leizuan 天津市習藝所章程表冊類纂 (Compilation of regulations and documents for the Tianjin Workhouse). Tianjin, n.d. (ca. 1905).

Tieti xia de PingJin 鐵蹄下的平津 (Beijing and Tianjin under iron hooves). Ed. Aying 阿英. Hankou: Zhanshi, 1938.

Tong, Y. L. (Tang Yueliang). "Social Conditions and Social Service Endeavor in Peking." *Chinese Social and Political Science Review* 7:3 (July 1922), 75–93.

Trescott, Paul B. *Jingji Xue: The History of the Introduction of Western Economic Ideas into China, 1850–1950.* Hong Kong: Chinese University Press, 2007.

Tsin, Michael. "Imagining 'Society' in Early Twentieth-Century China." In *Imagining the People: Chinese Intellectuals and the Concept of Citizenship, 1890–1920*, ed. Joshua Fogel and Peter Zarrow. Armonk, N.Y.: M.E. Sharpe, 1997, 212–31.

———. *Nation, Governance, and Modernity in China: Canton, 1900–1927.* Stanford: Stanford University Press, 1999.

Tsutsui, William. *Manufacturing Ideology: Scientific Management in Twentieth-Century Japan.* Princeton: Princeton University Press, 1998.

Tucker, Frederick Booth. *Muktifauj, or Forty Years with the Salvation Army in India and Ceylon.* 1923. Reprint, London: Marshall Brothers, 1930.

Turner, Bryan S. "Contemporary Problems in the Theory of Citizenship." In *Citizenship and Social Theory*, ed. Bryan S. Turner. London: Sage, 1993, 1–18.

U, Eddy. "The Making of *Zhishifenzi*: The Critical Impacts of the Registration of Unemployed Intellectuals in the Early PRC." *The China Quarterly* 173 (2003), 100–121.

UNRRA in China, 1945–1947. Washington, D.C., 1948.

Wagner, Rudolph. "The Concept of Work/Labor/Arbeit in the Chinese World: First

Explorations." In *Die Rolle der Arbeit in verschiedenen Epochen und Kulturen*, ed. Manfred Bierwisch. Berlin: Akademie Verlag, 2003, 103–36.

Wakeman, Frederic, Jr. *Policing Shanghai, 1927–37*. Berkeley: University of California Press, 1995.

———. "A Revisionist View of the Nanjing Decade: Confucian Fascism." *The China Quarterly* 150 (June 1997), 395–432.

———. *Shanghai Badlands: Wartime Terrorism and Urban Crime, 1937–1941*. New York: Cambridge University Press, 1996.

Waldron, Arthur. *From War to Nationalism: China's Turning Point, 1924–1925*. New York: Cambridge University Press, 1995.

Wang Chunying 王春英. "Kangzhan shiqi nanmin shourongsuo de sheli ji qi tedian" 抗戰時期難民收容所的設立及其特點 (The establishment and special characteristics of refugee shelters during the War of Resistance). *KangRi zhanzheng yanjiu* 抗日戰爭研究 3 (2004), 201–20.

Wang, Di. *Street Culture in Chengdu: Public Space, Urban Commoners, and Local Politics, 1870–1930*. Stanford: Stanford University Press, 2003.

Wang Kang 王康. *Shehuixue shi* 社會學史 (History of sociology). Beijing: Renmin, 1992.

Wang Maogong 王懋功. "Subei shuizai baogao" 蘇北水災報告 (Report on the Subei floods). *Subei shuizai baogao shu* 蘇北水災報告書 (1947), 1–3.

Wang Tao 王韜. *Taoyuan wenlu waibian* 弢園文錄外編 (Sequel to the collected works of Taoyuan). 1897. Reprint, Zhengzhou: Zhongzhou guji, 1998.

Wang Xuetai 王學太. *Youmin wenhua yu Zhongguo shehui* 游民文化與中國社會 (Vagrant culture and Chinese society). Beijing: Xueyuan, 1999.

The War Cry. New York.

Wasserstrom, Jeffrey. *Student Protests in Twentieth-Century China: The View from Shanghai*. Stanford: Stanford University Press, 1991.

Westad, Odd Arne. *Decisive Encounters: The Chinese Civil War, 1946–1950*. Stanford: Stanford University Press, 2003.

Will, Pierre-Etienne. *Bureaucracy and Famine in Eighteenth-Century China*. Stanford: Stanford University Press, 1990.

Wu Shangquan 吳尚權. *Langfei pinqiong yu jiuwang* 浪費貧窮與救亡 (Waste, poverty, and salvation of national destruction). Beiping: Dacheng, 1936.

Wu Wenhui 吳文暉. *Nanjing penghu jiating diaocha* 南京棚戶家庭調查 (Investigation of Nanjing shantytown families). 1935. Reprint, *Minguo shiqi shehui diaocha congbian* 民國時期社會調查叢編 (Collection of Republican-era social surveys). Fuzhou: Fujian jiaoyu, 2004, Vol. 5:2, 737–802.

Wu Yunfu 伍雲甫. "Zhongguo renmin jiuji zonghui gongzuo baogao" 中國人民救濟總會工作報告 (All-China People's Relief Association report). *Minzheng gongzuo shouce* 民政工作手冊 5 (1953), 165–73.

Xiandai pinglun 現代評論 (Contemporary review). Beijing.

Xiangdao zhoubao 響導週報 (The guide weekly). Shanghai.

Xiangshan Ciyouyuan gaikuang 香山慈幼院概況 (Survey of Xiangshan Children's Home). Beiping, 1930.

Xiao Ling 蕭苓. "Penghu men qiandao nali qu?" 棚戶們遷到那裡去? (Where are the hut-dwellers to go?), *Renjian shiri* 人間十日 6 (1937), 5–6.

Xiliang 錫良. *Xi Qingbi zhijun zougao* 錫清弼制軍奏稿 (Military administration memorials of Xiliang). Taibei: Wenhai, 1974.

Xin Qingnian 新青年 (New youth). Shanghai.

Xin shehui 新社會 (New society). Beijing.

Xing, Jun. *Baptized in the Fire of Revolution: The American Social Gospel and the YMCA in China, 1919–1937*. Bethlehem, Pa.: Lehigh University Press, 1996.

Xinhua ribao 新華日報 (New China daily). Chongqing.

Xinmin wanbao 新民晚報 (New citizens evening news). Shanghai.

Xinwenbao 新聞報 (Daily news). Shanghai.

Xiong Mao Yanwen 熊毛彥文. "Banian zhong Ri zhanzheng zhong de Xiangshan Ciyouyuan" 八年中日戰爭中的香山慈幼院 (The Xiangshan Children's Home during the eight years of the war against Japan). In *Beiping Xiangshan Ciyouyuan yuanshi* 北平香山慈幼院院史 (The history of the Beiping Xiangshan Children's Homes). Taibei, 1983, 101–6.

Xiong Xianghui 熊向暉, ed. *Zhonggong dixia dang xianxing ji* 中共地下黨現形記 (The current situation of the Communist underground). Reprint, Taibei: Chuanji, 1991.

Xu Shilian 徐仕廉. *Renkou lun gangyao* 人口論綱要 (Essentials of population theory). Beiping: Zhonghua shuju, 1933.

Xu, Xiaoqun. *Chinese Professionals and the Republican State: The Rise of Professional Associations in Shanghai, 1912–1937*. Cambridge: Cambridge University Press, 2000.

———. *Trial of Modernity: Judicial Reform in Early Twentieth-Century China, 1901–1937*. Stanford: Stanford University Press, 2008.

Xu, Yamin. "Wicked Citizens and the Social Origins of China's Modern Authoritarian State, 1928–37." Ph.D. dissertation, University of California, Berkeley, 2002.

Yan Fu 嚴復. *Yan Fu wenxuan* 嚴復文選 (Selected writings of Yan Fu). Shanghai: Shanghai yuandong, 1996.

———. *Yuanfu* 原富 (*The Wealth of Nations*). Reprint, Beijing: Shangwu, 1981.

Yang Jianhua 楊健華. "Jiuzai fanghuang" 救災防荒 (Relieve disaster, prevent famine). *Qunzhong* 11:6 (June 10, 1946), 12.

Yang, L. S. "Economic Justification for Spending—An Uncommon Idea in Traditional China." *Harvard Journal of Asiatic Studies* 20 (1957), 36–52.

Yang Xinsheng 楊信生. "Zhao Erxun yu Qingmo Hunan xinzheng" 趙爾巽與清末湖南新政 (Zhao Erxun and the New Policies in Hunan in the final years of the Qing dynasty). *Zhuzhou shifan gaodeng zhuanke xuexiao xuebao* 株洲師範高等專科學校學報 11:6 (December 2006), 71–78.

Ye, Weili. *Seeking Modernity in China's Name: Chinese Students in the United States*. Stanford: Stanford University Press, 2001.

Yeh, Wen-hsin. *Shanghai Splendor: Economic Sentiments and the Making of Modern China, 1843–1949*. Berkeley: University of California Press, 2007.

———, ed. *Wartime Shanghai*. New York: Routledge, 1998.

Yick, Joseph K. S. *Making Urban Revolution in China: The CCP-GMD Struggle for Beiping-Tianjin, 1945–1949*. Armonk, N.Y.: M.E. Sharpe, 1995.

Youmin xiyi yuekan 游民習藝月刊 (Vagrant work training monthly). Beijing.

Yuan Shikai zouyi 元世凱奏議 (Memorials of Yuan Shikai). 3 vols. Tianjin: Tianjin guji, 1987.

Yun Bi 運鐅 (Huang Kan 黃侃). "Ai pinmin" 哀貧民 (Lamenting the poor). *Minbao* 民報 17 (December 29, 1907), 32–35.

Zanasi, Margherita. "Fostering the People's Livelihood: Chinese Political Thought between Empire and Nation." *Twentieth-Century China* 30:1 (November 2004), 6–38.

———. *Saving the Nation: Economic Modernity in Republican China*. Chicago: University of Chicago Press, 2006.

Zhang Jingai 張金陔. "Beiping zhouchang zhi yanjiu" 北平粥廠之研究 (Research on Beiping's gruel kitchens). *Shehuixue jie* 社會學界 (Sociological world) 7 (1933), 189–222.

Zhang Shifei 張世飛. "Beijing jiefang chuqi de zhengli tanfan gongzuo" 北京解放初期的整理攤販工作 (The work of organizing peddlers during Beijing's early liberation period). *Beijing dangshi* 北京黨史 (Beijing Party History) 2 (2004), 45–46.

Zhang Yiping 張一平. "Ziran zaihai, zhengzhi douzheng yu Subei minsheng" 自然災害政治鬥爭與蘇北民生 (Natural calamity, political struggle, and Subei people's life). M.A. thesis, Nanjing Normal University, 2004.

Zhang Zhidong 張之洞. *Zhang Wenxiang gong (Zhidong) quanji zouyi* 張文襄(之洞)全集奏議 (The complete memorials of Zhang Zhidong). Beijing, 1937.

Zhang Zhiyi 張執一. "Zai diren de xinzang li" 在敵人的心臟裡 (In the heart of the enemy). In *Zhonggong dixia dang xianxing ji* 中共地下黨現形記, ed. Xiong Xianghui 熊向暉. Taibei: Chuanji, 1991, 127–61.

Zhao Erxun 趙爾巽. *Zhao liushou zhenglüe* 趙留手政略 (Summary of the administrative legacy of Zhao Erxun). Ca. 1903.

Zhao Hong 趙紅. "Beiping lunxian chuqi de difang weichi hui" 北平淪陷初期的地方維持會 (The Peace Preservation Committee during the initial period of the occupation of Beiping). *Beijing dang'an shiliao* 北京檔案史料 2 (1987), 46–48.

Zheng Guanying 鄭官應. *Shengshi weiyan* 盛世危言 (Warnings for a prosperous age) (1894 edition). In *Zheng Guanying ji* 鄭官應集, vol. 1. Shanghai: Renmin, 1982.

Zhengfu gongbao 政府公報 (Official bulletin of the municipal government). Beijing.

Zhengyi tongbao 政藝通報 (Journal of politics and arts). Shanghai.

Zhenji zhuankan 賑濟專刊 (Special issue on relief). Beijing: Zhenji bu, 1939.

"Zhonggong Beiping shiwei guanyu shourong qigai gongzuo zongjie" 中共北平市委關於收容乞丐工作總結 (CCP Beiping Municipal Committee summary report regarding the work of detaining beggars). In *Beijing shi zhongyao wenxian xuanbian* 北京市重要文獻選編, *1948.12–1949*. Beijing: Zhongguo dang'an, 2001, 598–613.

Zhonghua Minguo shi dang'an ziliao huibian 中華民國史檔案資料彙編 (Collection of archival materials on the history of the Republic of China). Nanjing: Jiangsu guji, 1994.

Zhongyang ribao 中央日報 (Central daily). Nanjing and Chongqing.

Zhou Jianren 周建人 and Chen Changheng 陳長蘅. *Jinhualun shanzhongxue* 進化論善種學 (Evolution and eugenics). Shanghai: Shangwu, 1923.

Zhou Xianwen 周憲文. "Shuo pin" 說貧 (Speaking of poverty). *Dongfang zazhi* 東方雜誌 40:12 (June 30, 1944), 23–26.

Zou Yiren 鄒依仁. *Jiu Shanghai renkou bianqian de yanjiu* 舊上海人口變遷的研究 (Research on population changes in old Shanghai). Shanghai: Shanghai renmin, 1980.

Index